The Toyota Way

The Toyota Way

14 Management Principles from the World's Greatest Manufacturer

Jeffrey K. Liker

McGraw-Hill

New York Chicago San Francisco Lisbon
London Madrid Mexico City Milan New Delhi
San Juan Seoul Singapore Sydney Toronto

18 19 20 FGR/FGR 0 9 8

ISBN 0-07-139231-9

Editorial and production services provided by CWL Publishing Enterprises, Inc., Madison, WI, www.cwlpub.com.

This publication is designed to provide accurate and authoritative information in regard to the subject matter covered. It is sold with the understanding that neither the author nor the publisher is engaged in rendering legal, accounting, or other professional service. If legal advice or other expert assistance is required, the services of a competent professional person should be sought.

> —*From a Declaration of Principles jointly adopted by a Committee of the American Bar Association and a Committee of Publishers*

McGraw-Hill books are available at special quantity discounts to use as premiums and sales promotions, or for use in corporate training programs. For more information, please write to the Director of Special Sales, McGraw-Hill, Two Penn Plaza, New York, NY 10121-2298. Or contact your local bookstore.

 This book is printed on recycled, acid-free paper containing a minimum of 50% recycled de-inked fiber.

Contents

v

Dedication

To Deb, Emma, and Jesse
and Our Amazing Life Journey

Foreword

When I joined Toyota after 18 years in the U.S. automobile business, I didn't know exactly what to expect. But I was hopeful. I knew that I wasn't comfortable with the direction that American automobile manufacturing was taking, and I felt Toyota might be different. In no time at all I noticed a fundamental difference between Toyota and my previous employers. At a Toyota/GM joint venture plant in Fremont, California, called NUMMI (New United Motor Manufacturing), I witnessed the transformation of a workforce from one of the worst in the General Motors system to one of the best in any manufacturing facility in the United States. The difference was the "Toyota Way." In this book, Dr. Liker explains the management systems, thinking, and philosophy that form the foundation of Toyota's success, providing the reader with valuable insights that can be applied to any business or situation. While there are many books that provide insight into the tools and methods of Toyota's Production System (TPS), Professor Liker's book is unique in its explanation of the broader principles at work in the Toyota culture.

The Toyota Way is not the Japanese Way or the American Way or even the Gary Convis Way of managing. It is the fundamental way that Toyota views its world and does business. The Toyota Way, along with the Toyota Production System, make up Toyota's "DNA." This DNA was born with the founders of our company and continues to be developed and nurtured in our current and future leaders.

The Toyota Way can be briefly summarized through the two pillars that support it: "Continuous Improvement" and "Respect for People." Continuous improvement, often called *kaizen*, defines Toyota's basic approach to doing business. Challenge everything. More important than the actual improvements that individuals contribute, the true value of continuous improvement is in creating an atmosphere of continuous *learning* and an environment that not only accepts, but actually *embraces* change. Such an environment can only be created where there is respect for people—hence the second pillar of the Toyota Way. Toyota demonstrates this respect by providing employment security and seeking to engage team members through active participation in improving their jobs. As managers, we must take the responsibility for developing and nurturing mutual trust and understanding among all team members. I believe management has no more critical role than to motivate and engage large numbers of people to work together toward a common goal. Defining and explaining what the goal is, sharing a path to achieving it, motivating people to take the journey with you, and assisting them by removing obstacles—those are management's reasons for being. We must engage the minds of people to support and contribute their ideas to the organization. In my experience, the Toyota Way is the best method for fulfilling this role.

However, readers of this book should understand that each organization must develop its own way of doing business. The Toyota Way is the special product of the people who created Toyota and its unique history. Toyota is one of the most successful companies in the world. I hope this book will give you an understanding of what has made Toyota successful, and some practical ideas that you can use to develop your own approach to business.

—Gary Convis
Managing Officer of Toyota and President,
Toyota Motor Manufacturing, Kentucky

Preface

I n 1982 when I first arrived as a new assistant professor at the University of Michigan, Ann Arbor, the automotive industry was in serious turmoil in the midst of a national recession. The situation seemed dire. The Ford Motor company was seriously flirting with bankruptcy. The Big 3 were losing market share fast.

There was a lot of debate at the time over the root cause. The party line among Detroit auto executives was that the cause was the "Japanese invasion." Japan, Inc. had banded together with industry and government colluding to set up trade barriers to prevent American cars from being sold in Japan and artificially lowering prices of Japanese cars in the United States. Of course, in the minds of U.S. companies, as long as the root cause was unfair business practices, there was no need to seriously change the way they built cars. Instead, political channels would right the wrongs.

Around this time I was fortunate to be invited by David Cole and Robert Cole (two University of Michigan professors who were leading the study of the Japanese quality movement) to work on a U.S.-Japan automotive study. This research was an effort to help U.S. companies learn from the Japanese automakers. My project focused on how automakers worked with their suppliers on new product development in the U.S. and Japan. The numerous studies that made up the overall U.S.-Japan auto study covered many aspects of the industry, and all the studies collectively pointed to a single conclusion. Whatever was going on with Japan's government and the value of the yen and other macro-economic factors, Japanese auto companies were very good at engineering and building cars. They were not necessarily financial or marketing whizzes. They were not the leaders in advanced manufacturing technology, at least not in complex automation. They "designed in quality" and built in quality at every step of the process, and they did it with remarkably few labor hours. Not only were Japan's automakers good, their top suppliers were also world class in engineering and manufacturing, and they worked together as a team.

But even in these early stages of my introduction to the auto industry in Japan, there were indications that Toyota was different from the other Japanese automakers. While the basic product development process seemed similar across the three automakers, and the top tier suppliers were all integrally part of the product development process, there was a sense of partnership between Toyota and its suppliers that we did not see as strongly in the *keiretsu* of Mazda and Nissan.

Later, in 1991 John Campbell and I received a grant to create the Japan Technology Management Program at the University of Michigan, Ann Arbor, which I am still directing. The goals of this program are to learn about the practices that have helped the best Japanese companies become strong globally, teach what we learn to our students and industry, and encourage technically oriented students to learn about Japanese language and culture through courses and internships in Japan. This research program allowed me to continue my studies of the Japanese auto industry, and I chose to focus more intensively on Toyota, in particular its product development process and the Toyota Production System. The U.S. government grant focused on transfer of learning so I began studying Toyota's efforts to transfer its practices to its U.S.-based subsidiaries and American companies' efforts to learn from Toyota.

By the early 1990s all of the Big 3 auto producers had woken up to the reality of Japanese quality and concluded that Toyota was the company to beat. They were all actively studying Toyota and creating their own versions of Toyota's systems. They benchmarked the company on its production system, product development system, and supplier relationship management. Their great interest in Toyota's systems has given me an opportunity to teach about Toyota's production system and product development process, and get my hands dirty consulting to implement these systems. I have had opportunities to work in America, the United Kingdom, and Mexico in industries including automotive, paint manufacturing, nuclear fuel rod assembly, ship building, ship repair, an engineering professional organization, and lawncare equipment. I have taught lean change agents from over one thousand companies worldwide, and my participation in lean transformation has given me a deeper understanding of what is involved in transforming a culture and learning from Toyota.

My studies of U.S. companies working to implement versions of the Toyota Production System led to a book I edited called *Becoming Lean: Experiences of U.S. Manufacturers* (Liker, 1997), winner of a Shingo Prize (in honor of Shigeo Shingo who helped create the TPS) in 1998. Articles I co-authored on Toyota's product development system and supplier management in *Sloan Management Review* and

Harvard Business Review also won Shingo Prizes. But it was not until I was invited to write *The Toyota Way* that I had an opportunity to pull together in one volume 20 years of observations of Toyota and companies learning from Toyota.

Reading this book might give you the impression that I am a strong advocate for Toyota. As a professor and social scientist, I work at being objective, but I will admit I am a fan of the Toyota Way. I believe Toyota has raised continuous improvement and employee involvement to a unique level, creating one of the few examples of a genuine learning enterprise in human history—not a small accomplishment.

Much of the research behind this book has come from 20 years of visits to Japan and interviews in Toyota facilities there and in the United States. When I was asked to write this book, I immediately asked Toyota for support through additional interviews specifically focused on the Toyota Way. They graciously agreed. As it turned out, they had just launched their own internal version of the Toyota Way to keep the "Toyota DNA" strong as they globalize and entrust international team members to run subsidiaries. This was the pet project of Fujio Cho, President of Toyota Motor Company, who learned the Toyota Way from one of its inventors, Taiichi Ohno, and he agreed to a rare, personal interview. I asked him what was unique about Toyota's remarkable success. His answer was quite simple.

> *The key to the Toyota Way and what makes Toyota stand out is not any of the individual elements.... But what is important is having all the elements together as a system. It must be practiced every day in a very consistent manner—not in spurts.*

Over a one-year period I was able to interview over 40 Toyota managers and executives from manufacturing, sales, product development, logistics, service parts, and production engineering. I gathered over 120 hours of interviews, all transcribed. Included in these interviews were several former Toyota managers who left to apply what they learned to U.S. Companies and several suppliers to Toyota. I visited many Toyota plants, supplier plants, Toyota's sales offices, a parts distribution center, a supplied parts cross-dock, the Arizona proving ground, and the Toyota Technical Center.

I have thought about what impact I would like to make on readers of *The Toyota Way*. First, I have had a special opportunity to get inside the culture of a unique and high performing company and wish to share my insights. Second, Toyota is a model to many companies throughout the world so I wish to provide a different look at what makes Toyota so successful. The fundamental insight I have from my studies of Toyota is that its success derives from balancing the role of people in an organizational culture that expects and values their continuous improvements, with a technical system focused on high-value-added "flow." This leads to my third and more challenging goal: to help other companies learn from Toyota and themselves so they can continuously improve on what they do.

To capture the complexity of the Toyota Way and the Toyota Production System (TPS), I divided the book into three parts. Part One introduces you to the present success and history of Toyota. It describes how TPS evolved as a new paradigm of manufacturing, transforming businesses across industries. As a way of showing the Toyota Way in action, you will see how the Toyota Way was applied to the development of the Lexus and the Prius. In Part Two I cover the 14 principles of the Toyota Way that I identified through my research. These key principles drive the techniques and tools of the Toyota Production System and the management of Toyota in general. The 14 principles are divided into four sections:

- *Long-Term **Philosophy***. Toyota is serious about long-term thinking. The focus from the very top of the company is to add value to customers and society. This drives a long-term approach to building a learning organization, one that can adapt to changes in the environment and survive as a productive organization. Without this foundation, none of the investments Toyota makes in continuous improvement and learning would be possible.

- *The Right **Process** Will Produce the Right Results*. Toyota is a process-oriented company. They have learned through experience what processes work, beginning with the ideal of one-piece flow, (see Chapter 8 for details). Flow is the key to achieving best quality at the lowest cost with high safety and morale. At Toyota this process focus is built into the company's DNA, and managers believe in their hearts that using the right process will lead to the results they desire.

- *Add Value to the Organization by Developing Your **People and Partners***. The Toyota Way includes a set of tools that are designed to support people continuously improving and continuously developing. For example, one-piece flow is a very demanding process that quickly surfaces problems that demand fast solutions—or production will stop. This suits Toyota's employee development goals perfectly because it gives people the sense of urgency needed to confront business problems. The view of management at Toyota is that they build people, not just cars.

- *Continuously Solving Root **Problems** Drives Organizational Learning*. The highest level of the Toyota Way is organizational learning. Identifying root causes of problems and preventing them from occurring is the focus of Toyota's continuous learning system. Tough analysis, reflection, and communication of lessons learned are central to improvement as is the discipline to standardize the best-known practices.

Part Three of the book discusses how organizations can apply the Toyota Way and what actions they can take to become a lean, learning organization. One chapter focuses specifically on applying Toyota Way principles to service organizations that do not manufacture products.

Understanding Toyota's success and quality improvement systems does not automatically mean you can transform a company with a different culture and circumstances. Toyota can provide inspiration, demonstrate the importance of stability in leadership and values that go beyond short-term profit, and suggest how the right combination of philosophy, process, people, and problem solving can create a learning enterprise. I believe all manufacturing and service companies that want to be successful in the long term must become learning enterprises. Toyota is one of the best models in the world. Though every company must find its own way and learn for itself, understanding the Toyota Way can be one giant step on that journey.

—Jeffrey K. Liker, Ph.D.
University of Michigan, Ann Arbor

Acknowledgments

This book is the product of 20 years of study of Toyota. Much of that work was done under the auspices of the Japan Technology Management Program at University of Michigan, Ann Arbor, where I am currently Director. This program was started in 1991 with generous funding through the U.S. Air Force Office of Scientific Research (AFOSR), but it really began with the vision of Senator Jeff Bingaman of New Mexico. Senator Bingaman worked behind the scenes to get the funding to support university programs like mine to learn from Japan, send technically oriented students to Japan on internships, and share what we learned with others in the United States. At that time in the late '80s and early '90s, the "learning trade imbalance" was huge—with most of the learning going from the U.S. to Japan and little coming back. There were many reasons for this, but one was that the U.S. did not want to listen. The phenomenal success of companies like Toyota woke us up, and Toyota has contributed greatly to bringing more balance into the exchange of learning.

Toyota has been remarkably open in sharing its source of competitive advantage with the rest of the world. A milestone was Eiji Toyoda's decision in 1982 when, as chairman, he, along with Shoichiro Toyoda, President, approved the agreement with GM to create NUMMI, a joint auto manufacturing venture specifically intended to teach the "Toyota Way" to GM. That meant sharing Toyota's crown jewel, the famous Toyota Production System, with its principal global competitor. Another milestone in opening up TPS to the world was the decision to create the Toyota Supplier Support Center in 1992 for the purpose of teaching the Toyota Production System to U.S. companies by setting up working models in plants across industries. I personally benefited from this remarkable openness.

Unfortunately, I cannot acknowledge all of the individuals at Toyota who graciously agreed to lengthy interviews and reviewed parts of this book for accuracy.

But several were particularly influential in my learning about the Toyota Way. These included (job titles are from the time of the interviews):

- Bruce Brownlee, General Manager, Corporate Planning and External Affairs of the Toyota Technical Center—my key liaison for the book.
- Jim Olson, Senior Vice President, Toyota Motor Manufacturing North America—carefully considered the Toyota Way book and then supported Toyota's full participation to get it right.
- Jim Wiseman, Vice President, Toyota Motor Manufacturing, North America—opened the doors to the Toyota Production System in manfacturing.
- Irv Miller, Group Vice President, Toyota Motor Sales—opened the door to the world of sales and distribution at Toyota.
- Fujio Cho, President of Toyota Motor Company—shared his passion for the Toyota Way.
- Gary Convis, President of Toyota Motor Manufacturing, Kentucky and Managing Officer of Toyota— helped me understand the process of an American learning the depths of the Toyota Way.
- Toshiaki (Tag) Taguchi, President and CEO of Toyota Motor North America—provided insights into the Toyota Way in Sales.
- Jim Press, Executive Vice President and Chief Operating Officer of Toyota Motor Sales, USA—gave me deep insights into the philosophy of the Toyota Way.
- Al Cabito, Group Vice President, Sales Administration, Toyota Motor Sales, USA—provided great insights into Toyota's emerging build-to-order strategy.
- Tadashi (George) Yamashina, President, Toyota Technical Center, USA— introduced me to *hourensou* and a deeper appreciation of *genchi genbutsu*.
- Kunihiko (Mike) Masaki, former President, Toyota Technical Center— took every opportunity to get me in the door at Toyota to study the Toyota Way.
- Dave Baxter, Vice President, Toyota Technical Center—shared more hours than I had a right to ask for explaining Toyota's product development system and its underlying philosophy.
- Ed Mantey, Vice President, Toyota Technical Center—Ed is a real engineer who is living proof Toyota can train American engineers who deeply understand the Toyota Way.
- Dennis Cuneo, Senior Vice President, Toyota Motor North America— drew on his wealth of experience at NUMMI and beyond and helped me understand Toyota's commitment to social responsibility.
- Dick Mallery, Partner, Snell and Wilmer—passionately described how as a

lawyer for Toyota he has been transformed by the Toyota Way.

- Don Jackson, Vice President, Manufacturing, Toyota Motor Manufacturing, Kentucky—explained and demonstrated what it means to respect and involve workers on the shop floor.
- Glenn Uminger, Assistant General Manager, Business Management & Logistics Production Control, Toyota Motor Manufacturing, North America, Inc—explained how an accountant at Toyota could develop a TPS support office and then lead logistics for North America—having fun at every step.
- Teruyuki Minoura, former President, Toyota Motor Manufacturing, North America—chilled me with real life stories of learning TPS at the feet of the master Taiichi Ohno.
- Steve Hesselbrock, Vice President Operations, Trim Masters—shared generously of his years of learning to be one of the best Toyota seat suppliers in the world through trial by fire.
- Kiyoshi Imaizumi, President Trim Masters—gave me the real story on what it took to be a Toyota supplier in Japan.
- Ichiro Suzuki, former Chief Engineer, Lexus and Executive Advisory Engineer—showed me what a real super engineer can be.
- Takeshi Uchiyamada, Senior Managing Director and former Chief Engineer, Prius—taught me what it means to lead a revolutionary project (Prius) by working through people.
- Jane Beseda, GM and VP North American Parts Operations—articulated for me the Toyota Way view of information technology and automation in a way that made the light bulbs come on.
- Ken Elliott, Service Parts Center National Manager—shared his story of building the Toyota Way culture in a new parts distribution center.
- Andy Lund, Program Manager, Sienna, Toyota Technical Center—shared insights into the translation of Toyota's culture in Japan into U.S. operations from the perspective of an American who grew up in Japan.
- Jim Griffith, Vice President, Toyota Technical Center—always with humor corrected misconceptions and challenged my understanding of the Toyota Way.
- Chuck Gulash, Vice President, Toyota Technical Center—on a test-track drive taught me "attention to detail" in vehicle evaluation.
- Ray Tanguay, President, Toyota Motor Manufacturing, Canada—taught me that technological innovation and TPS can go hand in hand.

I owe a special debt to John Shook, the former Toyota manager who helped start up NUMMI, the Toyota Technical Center, and the Toyota Supplier Support Center. John has dedicated his career to understanding the Toyota Way. He brought this passion to the University of Michigan where he joined us for several years as Director of our Japan Technology Management Program and continues to be a leader in the Lean community. John was my mentor on TPS, teaching me first the basics and then, as I developed my understanding, the ever more sophisticated lessons in the philosophy of the Toyota Way.

Most of this book was written in 2003 when I was privileged to spend a very cold East Coast winter in sunny and warm Phoenix visiting my former student and now Professor Tom Choi of Arizona State University. With a nice, private office without windows in the mornings and afternoons of golf, it was the perfect climate for writing. The four-month adventure with my loving wife Deborah and my children Jesse and Emma is a once-in-a-lifetime memory.

This book looks beyond Toyota's Production System across the company, including parts logistics and supply chain management. My understanding of "lean logistics" has been greatly enhanced by research funded by the Sloan Foundation's Trucking Industry Program, led by my close friend and colleague Chelsea (Chip) White at Georgia Institute of Technology.

Finally, I had a lot of editing and writing help. When informed by my publisher that my book was twice as long as allowable, in a panic I called my former developmental editor, Gary Peurasaari, to bail me out. He worked his magic on every page in this book, reorganizing content where necessary, but more importantly, and in the true Toyota Way fashion, he eliminated wasted words, bringing value-added words to life. He was more of a partner in writing than an editor. Then Richard Narramore, the editor at McGraw-Hill who asked me to write the book, lead me through a second major rewrite bringing the book to a new level. It is a testimony to the Toyota Way that these two individuals got so engrossed in the book they spent night and day painstakingly helping to craft the right words to describe this precious philosophy of management.

Part One

The World-Class Power of the Toyota Way

Chapter 1

The Toyota Way: Using Operational Excellence as a Strategic Weapon

We place the highest value on actual implementation and taking action. There are many things one doesn't understand and therefore, we ask them why don't you just go ahead and take action; try to do something? You realize how little you know and you face your own failures and you simply can correct those failures and redo it again and at the second trial you realize another mistake or another thing you didn't like so you can redo it once again. So by constant improvement, or, should I say, the improvement based upon action, one can rise to the higher level of practice and knowledge.

—Fujio Cho, President, Toyota Motor Corporation, 2002

Toyota first caught the world's attention in the 1980s, when it became clear that there was something special about Japanese quality and efficiency. Japanese cars were lasting longer than American cars and required much less repair. And by the 1990s it became apparent that there was something even more special about Toyota compared to other automakers in Japan (Womack, Jones, and Roos, 1991). It was not eye-popping car designs or performance—though the ride was smooth and the designs often very refined. It was the way Toyota engineered and manufactured the autos that led to unbelievable consistency in the process and product. Toyota designed autos faster, with more reliability, yet at a competitive cost, even when paying the relatively high wages of Japanese workers. Equally impressive was that every time Toyota showed an apparent weakness and seemed vulnerable to the competition, Toyota miraculously fixed the problem and came back even stronger. Today Toyota is the third-largest auto manufacturer in the world, behind General Motors and Ford, with global vehicle sales of over six million per year in 170 countries. However, Toyota is far more profitable than any other auto manufacturer. Auto industry analysts estimate that Toyota will pass Ford in global vehicles sold in 2005, and if current trends continue, it will eventually pass GM to become the largest automaker in the world.

Every automotive industry insider and many consumers are familiar with Toyota's dramatic business success and world-leading quality:

- Toyota's annual profit at the end of its fiscal year in March 2003, was $8.13 billion—larger than the combined earnings of GM, Chrysler, and Ford, and the biggest annual profit for any auto maker in at least a decade. Its net profit margin is 8.3 times higher than the industry average.
- While stock prices of the Big 3 were falling in 2003, Toyota's shares had increased 24% over 2002. Toyota's market capitalization (the total value of the company's stock) was $105 billion as of 2003—higher than the combined market capitalization of Ford, General Motors, and Chrysler. This is an amazing statistic. Its return on assets is 8 times higher than the industry average. The company has made a profit every year over the last 25 years and has $20-$30 billion in its cash war chest on a consistent basis.
- Toyota has for decades been the number one automaker in Japan and a distant fourth behind the "Big 3" automakers in North America. But in August of 2003, for the first time, Toyota sold more vehicles in North America than one of the "Big 3" automakers (Chrysler). It seems that Toyota could eventually become a permanent member of the "Big 3" U.S. automakers. (Of 1.8 million Toyota/Lexus vehicles sold in North America in 2002, 1.2 million were made in North America. Toyota is rapidly building new production capacity in the U.S., at a time when U.S. manufacturers are looking for opportunities to close plants, reduce capacity and move production abroad.)
- In 2003 the Toyota nameplate was on track to sell more vehicles in the U.S. than either of the two brandnames that have led U.S. sales for the past 100 years—Ford and Chevrolet. Camry was the top-selling U.S. passenger car in 2003 and five of the years prior. Corolla was the top selling small car in the world.
- Toyota not long ago was known for making small, basic transportation vehicles, yet in ten years leaped out to become the leader in luxury vehicles. Lexus was introduced in 1989 and in 2002 outsold BMW, Cadillac, and Mercedes-Benz in the U.S. for the third year in a row.
- Toyota invented "lean production" (also known as "the Toyota Production System" or "TPS"), which has triggered a global transformation in virtually every industry to Toyota's manufacturing and supply chain philosophy and methods over the last decade. The Toyota Production

System is the foundation of dozens of books on "lean" including two best-sellers: *The Machine That Changed the World: The Story of Lean Production* (Womack, Jones, Roos, 1991) and *Lean Thinking* (Womack, Jones, 1996). Toyota employees are sought out by companies in almost every industry throughout the world for their expertise.

■ Toyota has the fastest product development process in the world. New cars and trucks take 12 months or less to design, while competitors typically require two to three years.

■ Toyota is benchmarked as the best in class by all of its peers and competitors throughout the world for high quality, high productivity, manufacturing speed, and flexibility. Toyota automobiles have consistently been at the top of quality rankings by J.D. Powers and Associates, *Consumer Reports*, and others for many years.

Much of Toyota's success comes from its astounding quality reputation. Consumers know that they can count on their Toyota vehicle to work right the first time and keep on working, while most U.S. and European automotive companies produce vehicles that may work when new but almost certainly will spend time in the shop in a year or so. In 2003 Toyota recalled 79% fewer vehicles in the U.S. than Ford and 92% fewer than Chrysler. According to a 2003 study in *Consumer Reports*, one of the most widely read magazines for auto-buying customers, 15 of the top 38 most reliable models from any manufacturer over the last seven years were made by Toyota/Lexus. No other manufacturer comes close. GM, Mercedes, and BMW have no cars on this list. Not a single Toyota is on the dreaded "vehicles to avoid" list, while a handful of Fords, almost 50 percent of the GMs, and more than 50 percent of the Chryslers are to be avoided, according to *Consumer Reports*.

Here are some other statistics from *Consumer Reports'* 2003 annual auto issue:

■ In the small car category (Toyota Corolla, Ford Focus/Escort, GM Cavalier, and Chrysler Neon), Toyota won each of the last three years for overall reliability, as well as the prior three years, and predicted reliability for the 2003 model year.

■ For family sedans, the Toyota Camry beat out the Ford Taurus, the GM Malibu, and Dodge Intrepid, winning in the last three years, the three prior years, and predicted reliability for the 2003 model year.

■ More than half of all Toyota used cars are singled out as "recommended for purchase," compared with less than 10 percent of the Fords, 5 percent of the GMs, and none of the Chryslers.

■ Toyota/Lexus has also dominated the J.D. Powers "initial quality" and long-term durability rankings for years. Toyota's Lexus was again the #1 most reliable car, according to the J.D. Powers 2003 quality survey, followed by Porsche, BMW, and Honda.

What is the secret of Toyota's success? The incredible consistency of Toyota's performance is a direct result of operational excellence. Toyota has turned operational excellence into a strategic weapon. This operational excellence is based in part on tools and quality improvement methods made famous by Toyota in the manufacturing world, such as just-in-time, kaizen, one-piece flow, jidoka, and heijunka. These techniques helped spawn the "lean manufacturing" revolution. But tools and techniques are no secret weapon for transforming a business. Toyota's continued success at implementing these tools stems from a deeper business philosophy based on its understanding of people and human motivation. Its success is ultimately based on its ability to cultivate leadership, teams, and culture, to devise strategy, to build supplier relationships, and to maintain a learning organization.

This book describes 14 principles which, based on my 20 years of studying the company, constitute the "Toyota Way." These 14 principles are also the foundation of the Toyota Production System (TPS) practiced at Toyota manufacturing plants around the world. For ease of understanding, I have divided the principles into four categories, all starting with "P"—Philosophy, Process, People/Partners, and Problem Solving (see Figure 1-1). (For an executive summary of the 14 principles of the Toyota Way, see chapter 4.)

About the same time that I started writing this book, Toyota was unveiling its own internal "Toyota Way" document for training purposes. This document greatly influenced my thinking about the 14 principles and consequently I have incorporated the four high-level principles from that document (*Genchi Genbutsu*, *Kaizen*, Respect and Teamwork, and Challenge) and correlated them to my four principle categories of Philosophy, Process, People/Partners, and Problem Solving (see Figure 1-1).

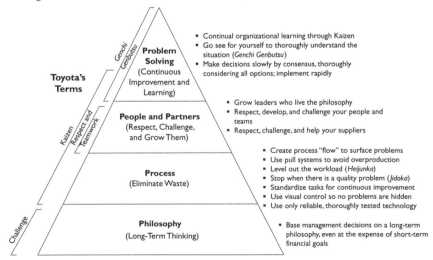

Figure 1-1. A "4 P" model of the Toyota Way

The Toyota Way and the Toyota Production System (Toyota's manufacturing method) are the double helix of Toyota's DNA; they define its management style and what is unique about the company. In this book I hope to explain and show how the Toyota model of success can be applied in any organization, to improve any business process, from sales to product development, marketing, logistics, and management. To assist you in this journey, I offer numerous examples of what Toyota does to maintain such a high level of achievement as well as explore companies from a variety of industries and service operations that have effectively applied Toyota's principles.

The Toyota Production System (TPS) and Lean Production

The Toyota Production System is Toyota's unique approach to manufacturing. It is the basis for much of the "lean production" movement that has dominated manufacturing trends (along with Six Sigma) for the last 10 years or so. Despite the huge influence of the lean movement, I hope to show in this book that most attempts to implement lean have been fairly superficial. The reason is that most companies have focused too heavily on tools such as 5S and just-in-time, without understanding lean as an entire system that must permeate an organization's culture. In most companies where lean is implemented, senior management is not involved in the day-to-day operations and continuous improvement that are part of lean. Toyota's approach is very different.

What exactly is a lean enterprise? You could say it's the end result of applying the Toyota Production System to all areas of your business. In their excellent book, *Lean Thinking*, James Womack and Daniel Jones define lean manufacturing as a five-step process: defining customer value, defining the value stream, making it "flow," "pulling" from the customer back, and striving for excellence. To be a lean manufacturer requires a way of thinking that focuses on making the product flow through value-adding processes without interruption (one-piece flow), a "pull" system that cascades back from customer demand by replenishing only what the next operation takes away at short intervals, and a culture in which everyone is striving continuously to improve.

Taiichi Ohno, founder of TPS, said it even more succinctly:

All we are doing is looking at the time line from the moment the customer gives us an order to the point when we collect the cash. And we are reducing that time line by removing the non-value-added wastes. (Ohno, 1988)

As we will see in more detail in Chapter 2, Toyota developed the Toyota Production System after World War II at a time when it faced very different business conditions than Ford and GM. While Ford and GM used mass production, economies of scale, and big equipment to produce as many parts as possible, as cheaply as possible, Toyota's market in post-war Japan was small. Toyota also had to make a variety of vehicles on the same assembly line to satisfy its customers. Thus, the key to their operations was flexibility. This helped Toyota make a critical discovery: when you make lead times short and focus on keeping production lines flexible, you actually get higher quality, better customer responsiveness, better productivity, and better utilization of equipment and space. While Ford's traditional mass production looks good when you measure the cost per piece on an individual machine, what customers want is a much greater variety of choices than traditional manufacturing can offer cost-effectively. Toyota's focus in the 1940s and '50s on eliminating wasted time and material from every step of the production process—from raw material to finished goods—was designed to address the same conditions most companies face today: *the need for fast, flexible processes that give customers what they want, when they want it, at the highest quality and affordable cost.*

A focus on "flow" has continued to be a foundation for Toyota's success globally in the 21st century. Companies like Dell have also become famous for using short lead times, high inventory turns, and getting paid fast to rapidly develop a fast growing company. But even Dell is just beginning on the road to becoming the sophisticated "lean enterprise" that Toyota has developed through decades of learning and hard work.

Unfortunately, most companies are still using the mass production techniques that worked so well for Henry Ford in the 1920s, when flexibility and customer choice were not important. The mass production focus on efficiency of individual processes goes back to Frederick Taylor and his "scientific management" at the beginning of the 20th century. Like the creators of the Toyota Production System, Taylor tried to eliminate waste from production processes. He observed workers and tried to eliminate every second of inefficient motion. Mass production thinkers have long understood that machine downtime is another obvious non-value-added waste—a machine shut down for repair is not making parts that could make money. But consider the following counter-intuitive truths about non-value-added waste within the philosophy of TPS.

- *Often the best thing you can do is to idle a machine and stop producing parts.* You do this to avoid over production, the fundamental waste in TPS.
- *Often it is best to build up an inventory of finished goods in order to level out the production schedule, rather than produce according to the actual fluctuating demand of customer orders.* Leveling out the schedule (*heijunka*) is a foundation for flow and pull systems and for minimizing inventory in the supply chain. (Leveling production means smoothing out the volume and mix of items produced so there is little variation in production from day to day.)

- *Often it is best to selectively add and substitute overhead for direct labor.* When waste is stripped away from your value-adding workers, you need to provide high-quality support for them as you would support a surgeon performing a critical operation.

- *It may not be a top priority to keep your workers busy making parts as fast as possible.* You should produce parts at the rate of customer demand. Working faster just for the sake of getting the most out of your workers is another form of over production and actually leads to employing more labor overall.

- *It is best to selectively use information technology and often better to use manual processes even when automation is available and would seem to justify its cost in reducing your headcount.* People are the most flexible resource you have. If you have not efficiently worked out the manual process, it will not be clear where you need automation to support the process.

In other words, Toyota's solutions to particular problems often seem to add waste rather than eliminate it. The reason for these seemingly paradoxical solutions is that Ohno had learned from his experiences walking the shop floor a very particular meaning of non-valued-added waste: it had little to do with running labor and equipment as hard as possible, and everything to do with the manner in which raw material is transformed into a saleable commodity. For Ohno, the purpose of his journey through the shop floor was to identify activities that added value to raw material, and get rid of everything else. He learned to map the value stream of the raw material moving to a finished product that the customer was willing to pay for. This was a radically different approach from the mass production thinking of merely identifying, enumerating, and eliminating the wasted time and effort in the existing production processes.

As you make Ohno's journey for yourself, and look at your own organization's processes, you will see materials, invoicing, service calls, and prototype parts in R&D (you fill in the blank for your business process) being transformed into something the customer wants. But on closer inspection, they are often being diverted into a pile, someplace where they sit and wait for long periods of time, until they can be moved to the next process or transformation. Certainly, people do not like to be diverted from their journeys and to wait on long lines. Ohno viewed material as having the same degree of impatience. Why? If any large batches of material are produced and then sit and wait to be processed, if service calls are backed up, if R&D is receiving prototype parts they don't have time to test, then this sitting and waiting to move to the next operation becomes waste. This results in both your internal and external customers becoming impatient. This is why TPS starts with the customer, by asking, "What value are we adding from the customer's perspective?" *Because the only thing that adds value in any type of process— be it in manufac-*

turing, marketing, or a development process—is the physical or information transforma-
tion of that product, service, or activity into something the customer wants.

Why Companies Often Think They Are Lean—But Aren't

When I first began learning about TPS, I was enamored of the power of one-piece flow. The more I learned about the benefits of flowing and pulling parts as they were needed, rather than pushing and creating inventory, the more I wanted to experience the transformation of mass production processes into lean processes first hand. I learned that all the supporting tools of lean such as quick equipment changeovers, standardized work, pull systems, and error proofing, were all essential to creating flow. But along the way, experienced leaders within Toyota kept telling me that these tools and techniques were not the key to TPS. Rather the power behind TPS is a company's management commitment to continuously invest in its people and promote a culture of continuous improvement. I nodded like I knew what they were talking about and continued to study how to calculate kanban quantities and set up one-piece flow cells. After studying Toyota for almost 20 years and observing the struggles companies have had applying lean manufacturing, what these Toyota teachers (called *sensei*) told me is finally sinking in. As this book attempts to show, the Toyota Way consists of far more than just a set of lean tools like "just-in-time."

Let's say you bought a book on creating one-piece flow cells or perhaps went to a training class or maybe even hired a lean consultant. You pick a process and do a lean improvement project. A review of the process reveals lots of "muda" or "waste," Toyota's term for anything that takes time but does not add value for your customer. Your process is disorganized and the place is a mess. So you clean it up and straighten out the flow in the process. Everything starts to flow faster. You get better control over the process. Quality even goes up. This is exciting stuff so you keep doing it on other parts of the operation. What's so hard about this?

I have visited hundreds of organizations that claim to be advanced practitioners of lean methods. They proudly show off their pet lean project. And they have done good work, no doubt. But having studied Toyota for twenty years it is clear to me that in comparison they are rank amateurs. It took Toyota decades of creating a lean culture to get to where they are and they still believe they are just learning to understand "the Toyota Way." What percent of companies outside of Toyota and their close knit group of suppliers get an A or even a B+ on lean? I cannot say precisely but it is far less than 1%.

The problem is that companies have mistaken a particular set of lean tools for deep "lean thinking." Lean thinking based on the Toyota Way involves a far deeper and more pervasive cultural transformation than most companies can begin to imagine. Starting with a project or two to generate some enthusiasm is the right thing to do. The purpose of this book is to explain the Toyota culture and the principles it is based on.

Here is one example of what I find disturbing in the lean movement in the U.S. The Toyota Supplier Support Center (TSSC) was established by Toyota in the U.S. to work with U.S. companies to teach them TPS. Its leader, Mr. Hajime Ohba, (a disciple of Taiichi Ohno who founded TPS) fashioned the center after a similar Toyota consulting organization in Japan. They have worked with many U.S. companies in different industries, in each case doing a "lean project" which consists of transforming one production line of a company using TPS tools and methods—typically in a 6-9 month period. Usually companies come to TSSC and apply for these services; however, in 1996 TSSC took the unusual step of approaching an industrial sensor manufacturing company that I will call "Lean Company X." It was strange that Toyota would offer to help this company because Lean Company X was already widely regarded as a best-practice example of lean manufacturing. It had become a common tour site for companies wishing to see world-class manufacturing in the U.S. Lean Company X even won the Shingo Prize for Manufacturing, an American—based award in honor of Shigeo Shingo, who contributed to the creation of the Toyota Production System. At the time they agreed to work with TSSC, the plant's world-class manufacturing work included:

■ Established production cells
■ Problem-solving groups of workers
■ Company work time and incentives for worker problem solving
■ A learning resource center for employees

The Shingo Prize at the time was based largely on showing major improvements in key measures of productivity and quality. The reason TSSC wanted to work with Lean Company X was for mutual learning, because it was known as a best-practice example. TSSC agreed to take one product line in this "world-class" plant and use the methods of TPS to transform it. At the end of the nine-month project, the production line was barely recognizable compared with its original "world-class" state and had attained a level of "leanness" the plant could not have thought possible. This production line had leapfrogged the rest of the plant on all key performance measures, including:

■ 93% reduction in lead-time to produce the product (from 12 days to 6.5 hours)
■ 83% reduction in work-in-process inventory (from 9 to 1.5 hours)
■ 91% reduction in finished-goods inventory (from 30,500 to 2,890 units)
■ 50% reduction in overtime (from 10 hours to 5 hours/person-week)
■ 83% improvement in productivity (from 2.4 to 4.5 pieces/labor hour)

When I lecture at companies on the Toyota Way, I describe this case and ask, "What does this tell you?" The answer is always the same: "There is always room for continuous improvement." But were these improvements small, incremental continuous improvements?" I ask. No. These were radical improvements. If you look at the original state of the production line at the beginning of the nine-month project, it is clear from the results that the company was in fact far from being world-class—12 days of lead-time to make a sensor, 9 hours of work-in-process, 10 hours overtime per person-week. The implications of this case (and cases I've seen even in 2003) are clear and disturbing:

- This "lean plant" was not even close to being lean based on Toyota's standards, despite being nationally recognized as a lean facility.
- The actual changes implemented by the company before TSSC showed up barely scratched the surface.
- Visitors were coming to the plant convinced they were seeing world-class manufacturing—suggesting they did not have a clue what world-class manufacturing is.
- The award examiners who chose to honor this plant in the name of Shigeo Shingo did not understand any more than the visitors what the Toyota Production System really is. (They have improved a great deal since then.)
- Companies are hopelessly behind Toyota in their understanding of TPS and lean.

I have visited hundreds of companies and taught employees from over one thousand companies. I have compared notes with many of those I have taught. I have also visited a number of the U.S. plants that were fortunate to have received assistance from TSSC, which has consistently helped companies achieve a level of improvement like "Lean Company X." Unfortunately, I see a persistent trend in the inability of these companies to implement TPS and lean. Over time, the lean production line TSSC sets up degrades rather than improves. Little of what Toyota has taught ultimately is spread to other, less efficient production lines and other parts of the plant. There is a "lean production cell" here and a pull system there and the time it takes to changeover a press to a new product has been reduced, but that is where the resemblance to an actual Toyota lean model ends. What is going on?

The U.S. has been exposed to TPS for at least two decades. The basic concepts and tools are not new. (TPS has been operating in some form in Toyota for well over 40 years.) The problem, I believe, is that U.S. companies have embraced lean tools but do not understand what makes them work together in a system. Typically management adopts a few of these technical tools and even struggles to go beyond the amateurish application of them to create a technical system. But they do not understand the power behind true TPS: the continuous improvement culture needed to sustain the principles of the Toyota Way. Within the 4P model

I mentioned earlier, most companies are dabbling at one level—the "Process" level (see Figure 1-2). Without adopting the other 3Ps, they will do little more than dabble because the improvements they make will not have the heart and intelligence behind them to make them sustainable throughout the company. Their performance will continue to lag behind those companies that adopt a true culture of continuous improvement.

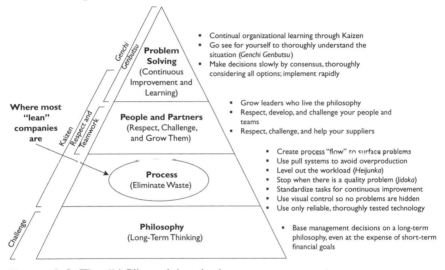

Figure 1-2. The "4 P" model and where most companies are

The quote at the beginning of this chapter from Mr. Fujio Cho, President of Toyota, is not just rhetoric. From the executives "up to" the shop floor workers performing the value-added work, Toyota challenges people to use their initiative and creativity to experiment and learn. It is interesting that labor advocates and humanists for years have criticized assembly line work as being oppressive and menial labor, robbing workers of their mental faculties. Yet when Toyota sets up assembly lines, it selects only the best and brightest workers, and challenges them to grow in their jobs by constantly solving problems. Similarly, Toyota staffs sales, engineering, service parts, accounting, human resources, and every aspect of the business with carefully selected individuals and gives them the directive to improve their processes and find innovative ways to satisfy their customers. Toyota is a true learning organization that has been evolving and learning for most of a century. This investment in its employees should frighten those traditional mass production companies that merely focus on making parts and counting quarterly dollars while changing leaders and organizational structures every few years.

Using the Toyota Way for Long-Term Success

Critics often describe Toyota as a "boring company." This is the kind of boring I like. Top quality year in and year out. Steadily growing sales. Consistent profitability. Huge cash reserves. Of course, operational efficiency by itself can be dangerous. Think of the Swiss companies that were so efficient in making mechanical watches yet are now out of business. Along with operational efficiency you need to be constantly improving and innovating to stay ahead of the competition and avoid obsolescence. Given its track record, Toyota has accomplished this in spades.

But despite Toyota's worldwide reputation as the best manufacturer in the world, no business book (in English) has explained for the general business reader the unique business principles and philosophy that has made the Toyota/Lexus brand synonymous with quality and reliability. *The Toyota Way* is the first book to introduce this thinking outside of Japan. It explains to the managers in any environment—blue-collar, white-collar, manufacturing, or service industry—how managers can dramatically improve their business processes by:

- Eliminating wasted time and resources
- Building quality into workplace systems
- Finding low-cost but reliable alternatives to expensive new technology
- Perfecting business processes
- Building a learning culture for continuous improvement

The Toyota Way includes profiles of a diverse group of organizations that have had great success in using Toyota's principles to improve quality, efficiency, and speed. While many people feel it is difficult to apply Toyota's way of thinking outside of Japan, Toyota is in fact doing just that—building learning organizations in many countries throughout the world to teach the Toyota Way. In fact, I did much of the research for this book in the United States, where Toyota is on the way to building an autonomous branch of the company led and operated by Americans.

This book is a blueprint of Toyota's management philosophy. It provides the specific tools and methods that can help you become the best in your industry on cost, quality, and service. The Toyota Way is a lesson, vision, and inspiration for any organization that wants to be successful in the long-term.

Chapter 2

How Toyota Became the World's Best Manufacturer:
The Story of the Toyoda Family and the Toyota Production System

I plan to cut down on the slack time within work processes and in the shipping of parts and materials as much as possible. As the basic principle in realizing this plan, I will uphold the "just in time" approach. The guiding rule is not to have goods shipped too early or too late."[1]
—Kiichiro Toyoda, founder of Toyota Motor Company, 1938

The most visible product of Toyota's quest for excellence is its manufacturing philosophy, called the Toyota Production System (TPS). TPS is the next major evolution in efficient business processes after the mass production system invented by Henry Ford, and it has been documented, analyzed, and exported to companies across industries throughout the world. Outside of Toyota, TPS is often known as "lean" or "lean production," since these were the terms made popular in two best-selling books, *The Machine That Changed the World* (Womack, Jones, Roos, 1991) and *Lean Thinking* (Womack, Jones, 1996). The authors make it clear, however, that the foundation of their research on lean is TPS and Toyota's development of it.

Although Toyota now has over 240,000 employees around the world, in many ways it is still a large "family business" with considerable influence still exercised by the founding Toyoda family. In order to understand TPS and the Toyota Way, and how the company became the world's best manufacturer, it is helpful to first understand the history and personalities of the founding family members, who left an indelible mark on the Toyota culture. What is most important about this is not the fact that one family has control, (Ford is similar in this respect), but the remarkable consistency of leadership and philosophy throughout the history of Toyota. The roots of all of the Toyota Way principles can be traced back to the very beginnings of the company. And the "DNA" of the Toyota Way is encoded in each and every Toyota leader whether a Toyoda family member or not.

The Toyoda Family: Generations of Consistent Leadership

The story begins with Sakichi Toyoda, a tinkerer and inventor, not unlike Henry Ford, who grew up in the late 1800s in a remote farming community outside of Nagoya. At that time, weaving was a major industry and the Japanese government, wishing to promote the development of small businesses, encouraged the creation of cottage industries spread across Japan. Small shops and mills employing a handful of people was the norm. Housewives made a little spending money by working in these shops or at home. As a boy, Toyoda learned carpentry from his father and eventually applied that skill to designing and building wooden spinning machines. In 1894 he began to make manual looms that were cheaper but worked better than existing looms.

Toyoda was pleased with his looms, but disturbed that his mother, grandmother, and their friends still had to work so hard spinning and weaving. He wanted to find a way to relieve them of this punishing labor, so he set out to develop power-driven wooden looms.

This was an age when inventors had to do everything themselves. There were no large R&D departments to delegate work to. When Toyoda first developed the power loom, there was no available power to run the loom, so he turned his attention to the problem of generating power. Steam engines were the most common source of power, so he bought a used steam engine and experimented with running the looms from this source. He figured out how to make this work by trial and error and getting his hands dirty—an approach that would become part of the foundation of the Toyota Way, *genchi genbutsu*. In 1926, He started Toyoda Automatic Loom Works, the parent firm of the Toyota Group and still a central player in the Toyota conglomerate (or *keiretsu*) today.

Toyoda's endless tinkering and inventing eventually resulted in sophisticated automatic power looms that became "as famous as Mikimoto pearls and Suzuki violins" (Toyoda, 1987). Among his inventions was a special mechanism to automatically stop a loom whenever a thread broke—an invention that evolved into a broader system that became one of the two pillars of the Toyota Production System, called *jidoka* (automation with a human touch). Essentially, jidoka means building in quality as you produce the material or "mistake proofing." It also refers to designing operations and equipment so your workers are not tied to machines and are free to perform value-added work.

Throughout his life, Sakichi Toyoda was a great engineer and later referred to as Japan's "King of Inventors." However, his broader contribution to the development of Toyota was his philosophy and approach to his work, based on a zeal for continuous improvement. Interestingly, this philosophy, and ultimately the Toyota Way, was significantly influenced by his reading of a book first published in England in 1859 by Samuel Smiles entitled *Self-Help* (Smiles, 2002). It preaches the virtues of industry, thrift, and self-improvement, illustrated with stories of great inventors like James Watt, who helped develop the steam engine. The book so inspired Sakichi Toyoda that a copy of it is on display under glass in a museum set up at his birth site.

As I read Samuel Smiles' book, I could see how it influenced Toyoda. First of all, Smiles' inspiration for writing the book was philanthropic. It grew out of his efforts to help young men in difficult economic circumstances who were focused on improving themselves—Smiles' goal was not to make money. Second, the book chronicles inventors whose natural drive and inquisitiveness led to great inventions that changed the course of humanity. For example, Smiles concludes that the success and impact of James Watt did not come from natural endowment but rather through hard work, perseverance, and discipline. These are exactly the traits displayed by Sakichi Toyoda in making his power looms work with steam engines. There are many examples throughout Smiles' book of "management by facts" and the importance of getting people to pay attention actively—a hallmark of Toyota's approach to problem solving based on *genchi genbutsu*.

The Toyota Automotive Company

His "mistake-proof" loom became Toyoda's most popular model, and in 1929 he sent his son, Kiichiro, to England to negotiate the sale of the patent rights to Platt Brothers, the premier maker of spinning and weaving equipment. His son negotiated a price of 100,000 English pounds, and in 1930 he used that capital to start building the Toyota Motor Corporation (Fujimoto, 1999).

It is perhaps ironic that the founder of Toyota Motor Company, Kiichiro Toyoda, was a frail and sickly boy, who many felt did not have the physical capacity to become a leader. But his father disagreed and Kiichiro Toyoda persevered. When Sakichi Toyoda tasked his son with building the car business, it was not to increase the family fortune. He could just as well have handed over to him the family loom business. Sakichi Toyoda was undoubtedly aware that the world was changing and power looms would become yesterday's technology while automobiles were tomorrow's technology. But more than this, he had put his mark on the industrial world through loom making and wanted his son to have his opportunity to contribute to the world. He explained to Kiichiro:

Everyone should tackle some great project at least once in their life. I devoted most of my life to inventing new kinds of looms. Now it is your turn. You should make an effort to complete something that will benefit society. (Reingold, 1999)

Kiichiro's father sent him to the prestigious Tokyo Imperial University to study mechanical engineering; he focused on engine technology. He was able to draw on the wealth of knowledge within Toyoda Automatic Loom Works on casting and machining metal parts. Despite his formal engineering education, he followed in his father's footsteps of learning by doing. Shoichiro Toyoda, his son, described Kiichiro Toyoda as a "genuine engineer" who:

... gave genuine thought to an issue rather than rely on intuition. He always liked to accumulate facts. Before he made the decision to make an automobile engine he made a small engine. The cylinder block was the most difficult thing to cast, so he gained a lot of experience in that area and, based on the confidence he then had, he went ahead. (Reingold, 1999)

His approach to learning and creating mirrored that of his father. After World War II, Kiichiro Toyoda wrote, "I would have grave reservations about our ability to rebuild Japan's industry if our engineers were the type who could sit down to take their meals without ever having to wash their hands."

He built Toyota Automotive Company on his father's philosophy and management approach, but added his own innovations. For example, while Sakichi Toyoda was the father of what would become the *jidoka* pillar of the Toyota Production System, Just-In-Time was Kiichiro Toyoda's contribution. His ideas were influenced by a study trip to Ford's plants in Michigan to see the automobile industry as well as seeing the U.S. supermarket system of replacing products on the shelves just in time as customers purchased them. As discussed in Chapter 11, his vision was at the root of the *kanban* system, which is modeled after the supermarket system. Notwithstanding these achievements, it was his actions as a leader, like his father, that left the largest imprint on Toyota.

Along the way to building a car company World War II happened, Japan lost, and the American victors could have halted car production. Kiichiro Toyoda was very concerned that the post-war occupation would shut down his company. On the contrary, the Americans realized the need for trucks in order to rebuild Japan and even helped Toyota to start building trucks again.

As the economy revitalized under the occupation, Toyota had little difficulty getting orders for automobiles, but rampant inflation made money worthless and getting paid by customers was very difficult. Cash flow became so horrendous that at one point in 1948 Toyota's debt was eight times its total capital value (Reingold, 1999). To avoid bankruptcy, Toyota adopted strict cost-cutting policies, including voluntary pay cuts by managers and a 10 percent cut in pay for all employees. This was part of a negotiation with employees in lieu of layoffs, to maintain Kiichiro Toyoda's policy against firing employees. Finally, even the pay cuts were not enough. This forced him to ask for 1,600 workers to "retire" voluntarily. This led to work stoppages and public demonstrations by workers, which at the time were becoming commonplace across Japan.

Companies go out of business every day. The usual story we hear these days is of the CEO hanging on and fighting to salvage his or her sweetheart option packages or perhaps selling off the company to be broken up for any valuable assets. It is always some other person's fault that the company has failed. Kiichiro Toyoda took a different approach. He accepted responsibility for the failing of the automobile company and resigned as president, even though in reality the problems were well beyond his or anyone else's control. His personal sacrifice helped to quell worker dissatisfaction. More workers voluntarily left the company and labor peace was restored. However, his tremendous personal sacrifice had a more profound impact on the history of Toyota. Everyone in Toyota knew what he did and why. The philosophy of Toyota to this day is to think beyond individual concerns to the long-term good of the company, as well as to take responsibility for problems. Kiichiro Toyoda was leading by example in a way that is unfathomable to most of us.

Toyoda family members grew up with similar philosophies. They all learned to get their hands dirty, learned the spirit of innovation, and understood the values of the company in contributing to society. Moreover, they all had the vision of creating a special company with a long-term future. After Kiichiro Toyoda, one of the Toyoda family leaders who shaped the company was Eiji Toyoda, the nephew of Sakichi and younger cousin of Kiichiro. Eiji Toyoda also studied mechanical engineering, entering Tokyo Imperial University in 1933. When he graduated, his cousin Kiichiro gave him the assignment of setting up, all by himself, a research lab in a "car hotel" in Shibaura (Toyoda, 1987).

By "car hotel," Kiichiro was referring to the equivalent of a large parking garage. These were jointly owned by Toyota and other firms, and were necessary to encourage car ownership among the small number of wealthy individuals who could afford cars. Eiji Toyoda started by cleaning a room in one corner of the building himself and getting some basic furniture and drafting boards. He worked alone for a while and it took one year to finally build a group of about 10 people. His first task was to research machine tools, which he knew nothing about. He also checked defective cars, as one role of the car hotel was to service Toyota products. In his spare time, he would check out companies that could make auto parts for Toyota. He also had to find reliable parts suppliers in the Tokyo area in time for the completion of a Toyota plant.

So Eiji Toyoda, like his cousin and uncle, grew up believing that the only way to get things done was to do it yourself and get your hands dirty. When a challenge arose, the answer was to try things—to learn by doing. With this system of beliefs and values, it would be unimaginable to hand over the company to a son, cousin, or nephew who did not get his hands dirty and truly love the automobile business. The company values shaped the development and selection of each generation of leaders.

Eventually Eiji Toyoda became the president and then chairman of Toyota Motor Manufacturing. He helped lead and then presided over the company during its most vital years of growth after the war and through its growth into a global powerhouse. Eiji Toyoda played a key role in selecting and empowering the leaders who shaped sales, manufacturing, and product development, and, most importantly, the Toyota Production System.

Now the Toyota Way has been spread beyond the leaders in Japan to Toyota associates around the world. But since today's leaders did not go through the growing pains of starting a company from scratch, Toyota is always thinking about how to teach and reinforce the value system that drove the company founders to get their hands dirty, to truly innovate and think deeply about problems based on actual facts. This is the legacy of the Toyoda family.

The Development of the Toyota Production System (TPS)[2]

Toyota Motor Corporation struggled through the 1930s, primarily making simple trucks. In the early years, the company produced poor-quality vehicles with primitive technology (e.g., hammering body panels over logs) and had little success. In the 1930s, Toyota's leaders visited Ford and GM to study their assembly lines and carefully read Henry Ford's book, *Today and Tomorrow* (1926). They tested the conveyor system, precision machine tools, and the economies of scale idea in their loom production. Even before WWII, Toyota realized that the Japanese market was too small and demand too fragmented to support the high production volumes in the U.S. (A U.S. auto line might produce 9,000 units per month, while Toyota would produce only about 900 units per month, and Ford was about 10 times as productive.) Toyota managers knew that if they were to survive in the long run they would have to adapt the mass production approach for the Japanese market. But how?

Now jump ahead to Toyota's situation after World War II, in 1950. It had a budding automotive business. The country had been decimated by two atom bombs, most industries had been destroyed, the supply base was nil, and consumers had little money. Imagine being the plant manager, Taiichi Ohno. Your boss, Eiji Toyoda, has returned from another tour of U.S. plants, including the

Ford's River Rouge complex, and he calls you into his office. He calmly hands you a new assignment. (Don't all bosses come back from trips with assignments?) The assignment is to improve Toyota's manufacturing process so that it equals the productivity of Ford. It makes you wonder what Toyoda could have been thinking. Based on the mass production paradigm of the day, economies of scale alone should have made this an impossible feat for tiny Toyota. This was David trying to take on Goliath.

Ford's mass production system was designed to make huge quantities of a limited number of models. This is why all Model T's were originally black. In contrast, Toyota needed to churn out low volumes of different models using the same assembly line, because consumer demand in their auto market was too low to support dedicated assembly lines for one vehicle. Ford had tons of cash and a large U.S. and international market. Toyota had no cash and operated in a small country. With few resources and capital, Toyota needed to turn cash around quickly (from receiving the order to getting paid). Ford had a complete supply system, Toyota did not. Toyota didn't have the luxury of taking cover under high volume and economies of scale afforded by Ford's mass production system. It needed to adapt Ford's manufacturing process to achieve simultaneously high quality, low cost, short lead times, and flexibility.

One-Piece Flow, a Core Principle

When Eiji Toyoda and his managers took their 12-week study tour of U.S plants in 1950, they were expecting to be dazzled by their manufacturing progress. Instead they were surprised that the development of mass production techniques hadn't changed much since the 1930s. In fact, the production system had many inherent flaws. What they saw was lots of equipment making large amounts of products that were stored in inventory, only to be later moved to another department where big equipment processed the product, and so on to the next step. They saw how these discrete process steps were based on large volumes, with interruptions between these steps causing large amounts of material to sit in inventory and wait. They saw the high cost of the equipment and its so-called efficiency in reducing the cost per piece, with workers keeping busy by keeping the equipment busy. They looked at traditional accounting measures that rewarded managers who cranked out lots of parts and kept machines and workers busy, resulting in a lot of overproduction and a very uneven flow, with defects hidden in these large batches that could go undiscovered for weeks. Entire workplaces were disorganized and out of control. With big forklift trucks moving mountains of materials everywhere, the factories often looked more like warehouses. To say the least, they were not impressed. In fact, they saw an opportunity to catch up.

Fortunately for Ohno, his assignment from Eiji Toyoda to "catch up with Ford's productivity" didn't mean competing head-on with Ford. He just had to focus on improving Toyota's manufacturing within the protected Japanese market—a daunting assignment nonetheless. So Ohno did what any good manager would have done in his situation: he benchmarked the competition through further visits to the U.S. He also studied Ford's book, *Today and Tomorrow*. After all, one of the major components that Ohno believed Toyota needed to master was continuous flow and the best example of that at the time was Ford's moving assembly line. Henry Ford had broken the tradition of craft production by devising a new mass production paradigm to fill the needs of the early 20th century. A key enabler of mass production's success was the development of precision machine tools and interchangeable parts (Womack, Jones, Roos, 1991). Using principles from the scientific management movement pioneered by Frederick Taylor, Ford also relied heavily on time studies, very specialized tasks for workers, and a separation between the planning done by engineers and the work performed by workers.

In his book Ford also preached the importance of creating continuous material flow throughout the manufacturing process, standardizing processes, and eliminating waste. But while he preached it, his company didn't always practice it. His company turned out millions of black Model T's and later Model A's using wasteful batch production methods that built up huge banks of work-in-process inventory throughout the value chain, pushing product onto the next stage of production (Womack, Jones, Roos, 1991). Toyota saw this as an inherent flaw in Ford's mass production system. Toyota did not have the luxury of creating waste, it lacked warehouse and factory space and money, and it didn't produce large volumes of just one type of vehicle. But it determined it could use Ford's original idea of continuous material flow (as illustrated by the assembly line) to develop a system of one-piece flow that flexibly changed according to customer demand and was efficient at the same time. Flexibility required marshaling the ingenuity of the workers to continually improve processes.

Creating the Manufacturing System That Changed the World

In the 1950s, Ohno returned to the place he understood best, the shop floor, and went to work to change the rules of the game. He did not have a big consulting firm, Post-it® notes, or PowerPoint to reinvent his business processes. He could not install an ERP system or use the Internet to make information move at the speed of light. But he was armed with his shop-floor knowledge, dedicated engineers, managers, and workers who would give their all to help the company succeed. With this he began his many "hands-on" journeys through Toyota's few factories, applying the principles of jidoka and one-piece flow. Over years and then decades of practice, he had come up with the new Toyota Production System.[3] Of course, Ohno and his team did not do this alone.

Along with the lessons of Henry Ford, TPS borrowed many of its ideas from the U.S. One very important idea was the concept of the "pull system," which was inspired by American supermarkets. In any well-run supermarket, individual items are replenished as each item begins to run low on the shelf. That is, material replenishment is initiated by consumption. Applied to a shop floor, it means that Step 1 in a process shouldn't make (replenish) its parts until the next process after it (Step 2) uses up its original supply of parts from Step 1 (that is down to a small amount of "safety stock"). In TPS, when Step 2 is down to a small amount of safety stock, this triggers a signal to Step 1 asking it for more parts.

This is similar to what happens when you fill the gas tank in your car. As in "Step 2," your car signals a need for more fuel when the gauge tells you that fuel is low. Then you go to the gas station, Step 1, to refill. It would be foolish to fill your gas tank when you're not low on gas, but the equivalent of this—overproduction—happens all the time in mass production.   At Toyota every step of every manufacturing process has the equivalent of a "gas gauge" built in, (called *kanban*), to signal to the previous step when its parts need to be replenished. This creates "pull" which continues cascading backwards to the beginning of the manufacturing cycle. In contrast, most businesses use processes that are filled with waste, because work in Step 1 is performed in large batches before it is needed by Step 2. This "work in process" must then be stored and tracked and maintained until needed by step 2—a waste of many resources. Without this pull system, just-in-time (JIT), one of the two pillars of TPS (the other is *jidoka,* built-in quality), would never have evolved.

JIT is a set of principles, tools, and techniques that allows a company to produce and deliver products in small quantities, with short lead times, to meet specific customer needs. Simply put, JIT delivers the right items at the right time in the right amounts. The power of JIT is that it allows you to be responsive to the day-by-day shifts in customer demand, which was exactly what Toyota needed all along.

Toyota also took to heart the teachings of the American quality pioneer, W. Edwards Deming. He gave U.S. quality and productivity seminars in Japan and taught that, in a typical business system, meeting and exceeding the customers' requirements is the task of everyone within an organization. And he dramatically broadened the definition of "customer" to include both internal and external customers. Each person or step in a production line or business process was to be treated as a "customer" and to be supplied with exactly what was needed, at the exact time needed. This was the origin of Deming's principle, "the next process is the customer." The Japanese phrase for this, *atokotei wa o-kyakusama,* became one of the most significant expressions in JIT, because in a pull system it means *the preceding process must always do what the subsequent process says*. Otherwise JIT won't work.

Deming also encouraged the Japanese to adopt a systematic approach to problem solving, which later became known as the Deming Cycle or Plan-Do-Check-Act (PDCA) Cycle, a cornerstone of continuous improvement. The Japanese term for continuous improvement is *kaizen* and is the process of making incremental improvements, no matter how small, and achieving the lean goal of eliminating all waste that adds cost without adding to value.[4] *Kaizen* teaches individuals skills for working effectively in small groups, solving problems, documenting and improving processes, collecting and analyzing data, and self-managing within a peer group. It pushes the decision making (or proposal making) down to the workers and requires open discussion and a group consensus before implementing any decisions. *Kaizen* is a total philosophy that strives for perfection and sustains TPS on a daily basis.

When Ohno and his team emerged from the shop floor with a new manufacturing system, it wasn't just for one company in a particular market and culture. What they had created was a new paradigm in manufacturing or service delivery—a new way of seeing, understanding, and interpreting what is happening in a production process, that could propel them beyond the mass production system.

By the 1960s, TPS was a powerful philosophy that all types of businesses and processes could learn to use, but this would take a while. Toyota did take the first steps to spread "lean" by diligently teaching the principles of TPS to their key suppliers. This moved its isolated lean manufacturing plants toward a total lean extended enterprise—when everyone in the supply chain is practicing the same TPS principles. A powerful business model indeed! Still, the power of TPS was mostly unknown outside of Toyota and its affiliated suppliers until the first oil shock of 1973 that sent the world into a global recession, with Japan among the hardest hit. Japanese industry went into a tailspin and the name of the game was survival. But the Japanese government began to notice when Toyota went into the red for less time than other companies and came back to profitability faster. The Japanese government took the initiative to launch seminars on TPS, even though it understood only a fraction of what made Toyota tick.

In the early '80s when I visited Japan, it was my experience that as you moved out of Toyota City and Toyota's group of affiliates to other Japanese companies, the application of TPS principles quickly became watered down and weakened. It would still be a while before the world would understand the Toyota Way and the new paradigm of manufacturing.

Part of the problem was that mass production after World War II focused on cost, cost, cost. "Make bigger machines and through economies of scale drive down cost." "Automate to replace people if it can be cost justified." This kind of thinking ruled the manufacturing world until the 1980s. Then the business world got the quality religion from Deming, Joseph Juran, Kaoru Ishikawa, and other quality gurus. It learned that focusing on quality actually reduced cost more than focusing only on cost. Finally, in the 1990s, through the work of MIT's Auto Industry Program and the bestseller based on its research, *The Machine That Changed the World* (Womack, Jones, Roos, 1991), the world manufacturing community discovered "lean production"—the authors' term for what Toyota had learned decades earlier through focusing on speed in the supply chain: *shortening lead time by eliminating waste in each step of a process leads to best quality and lowest cost, while improving safety and morale.*

Conclusion

Toyota started with the values and ideals of the Toyoda family. To understand the Toyota Way, we must start with the Toyoda family. They were innovators, they were pragmatic idealists, they learned by doing, and they always believed in the mission of contributing to society. They were relentless in achieving their goals. Most importantly, they were leaders who led by example.

TPS evolved to meet the particular challenges Toyota faced as it grew as a company. It evolved as Taiichi Ohno and his contemporaries put these principles to work on the shop floor through years of trial and error. When we take a snapshot of this at a point in time, we can describe the technical features and accomplishments of TPS. But the way that Toyota developed TPS and the challenges it faced and the approach it took to solving these problems is really a reflection of the Toyota Way. Toyota's own internal Toyota Way document talks about the "spirit of challenge" and the acceptance of responsibility to meet that challenge. The document states:

> We accept challenges with a creative spirit and the courage to realize our own dreams without losing drive or energy. We approach our work vigorously, with optimism and a sincere belief in the value of our contribution.

And further:

> We strive to decide our own fate. We act with self-reliance, trusting in our own abilities. We accept responsibility for our conduct and for maintaining and improving the skills that enable us to produce added value.

These powerful words describe well what Ohno and the team accomplished. Out of the rubble of WWII they accepted a seemingly impossible challenge—match Ford's productivity. Ohno accepted the challenge and, "with a creative spirit and courage," solved problem after problem and evolved a new production system. He and the team did it themselves and did not look to be bailed out by the Japanese government or any third party. This same process has been played out time and time again throughout the history of Toyota.

Notes

1. From a speech given at the completion of the Toyota Koromo plant.
2. A succinct and informative discussion of the history of the Toyota Production System is provided in Takahiro Fujimoto's book, *The Evolution of a Manufacturing System at Toyota* (New York: Oxford University Press, 1999). Some of the facts in this section are based on that book.
3. Still one of the best and surprisingly readable overviews of the Toyota Production System is Taiichi Ohno's own book, *Toyota Production System: Beyond Large-Scale Production* (Portland, OR: Productivity Press, 1988). Ohno gives a very personalized account of the system in a story fashion.
4. Actually kaizen means "change for the better" and can refer to very large changes or small, incremental changes. Because Western firms tend to focus on breakthrough innovation and are weak at continuously improving in small amounts, this has been the focus of teaching *kaizen* to Western firms. Sometimes *kaikaiku* is used to refer to major, revolutionary changes.

Chapter 3

The Heart of the Toyota Production System: Eliminating Waste

Many good American companies have respect for individuals, and practice kaizen and other TPS tools. But what is important is having all the elements together as a system. It must be practiced every day in a very consistent manner—not in spurts—in a concrete way on the shop floor.
—Fujio Cho, President, Toyota Motor Corporation

We touched on the philosophy of eliminating waste, or *muda*, as they say in Japan, in Chapter 2, with Ohno's journey through the shop floor. He spent a great deal of time there, learning to map the activities that added value to the product and getting rid of non-value-adding activity. It's important to take a closer look at this, because many of the tools of TPS and principles of the Toyota Way derive from this focused behavior.

I want to be clear that the Toyota Production System is not the Toyota Way. TPS is the most systematic and highly developed example of what the principles of the Toyota Way can accomplish. The Toyota Way consists of the foundational principles of the Toyota culture, which allow TPS to function so effectively. Though they are different, the development of TPS and its stunning success are intimately connected with the evolution and development of the Toyota Way.

When applying TPS, you start with examining the manufacturing process from the customer's perspective. The first question in TPS is always "*What does the customer want from this process?*" (Both the internal customer at the next steps in the production line and the final, external customer.) This defines value. Through the customer's eyes, you can observe a process and separate the value-added steps from the non-value-added steps. You can apply this to any process—manufacturing, information, or service.

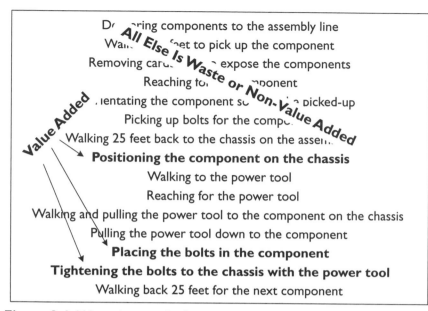

Delivering components to the assembly line
Walking X feet to pick up the component
Removing cardboard to expose the components
Reaching for the component
Orientating the component so it can be picked-up
Picking up bolts for the component
Walking 25 feet back to the chassis on the assembly line
Positioning the component on the chassis
Walking to the power tool
Reaching for the power tool
Walking and pulling the power tool to the component on the chassis
Pulling the power tool down to the component
Placing the bolts in the component
Tightening the bolts to the chassis with the power tool
Walking back 25 feet for the next component

All Else Is Waste or Non-Value Added

Value Added

Figure 3-1. Waste in a truck chassis assembly line

Take the example of a manual assembly operation on a truck chassis assembly line (see Figure 3-1). The operator takes many individual steps, but generally only a small number of the steps add value to the product, as far as the customer is concerned. In this case, only the three steps identified add value. Some of the non-value-added steps are necessary; for example, the operator has to reach to get the power tool. The point is to minimize the time spent on non-value-added operations by positioning the tools and material as close as possible to the point of assembly.

Toyota has identified seven major types of non-value-adding waste in business or manufacturing processes, which are described below. You can apply these to product development, order taking, and the office, not just a production line. There is an eighth waste, which I have included.

1. *Overproduction.* Producing items for which there are no orders, which generates such wastes as overstaffing and storage and transportation costs because of excess inventory.
2. *Waiting (time on hand).* Workers merely serving to watch an automated machine or having to stand around waiting for the next processing step, tool, supply, part, etc., or just plain having no work because of stockouts, lot processing delays, equipment downtime, and capacity bottlenecks.
3. *Unnecessary transport or conveyance.* Carrying work in process (WIP) long distances, creating inefficient transport, or moving materials, parts, or finished goods into or out of storage or between processes.

4. *Overprocessing or incorrect processing.* Taking unneeded steps to process the parts. Inefficiently processing due to poor tool and product design, causing unnecessary motion and producing defects. Waste is generated when providing higher-quality products than is necessary.
5. *Excess inventory.* Excess raw material, WIP, or finished goods causing longer lead times, obsolescence, damaged goods, transportation and storage costs, and delay. Also, extra inventory hides problems such as production imbalances, late deliveries from suppliers, defects, equipment downtime, and long setup times.
6. *Unnecessary movement.* Any wasted motion employees have to perform during the course of their work, such as looking for, reaching for, or stacking parts, tools, etc. Also, walking is waste.
7. *Defects.* Production of defective parts or correction. Repair or rework, scrap, replacement production, and inspection mean wasteful handling, time, and effort.
8. *Unused employee creativity.* Losing time, ideas, skills, improvements, and learning opportunities by not engaging or listening to your employees.

Ohno considered the fundamental waste to be overproduction, since it causes most of the other wastes. Producing more than the customer wants by any operation in the manufacturing process necessarily leads to a build-up of inventory somewhere downstream: the material is just sitting around waiting to be processed in the next operation. Mass or larger-batch manufacturers might ask, "What's the problem with this, as long as people and equipment are producing parts?" The problem is that big buffers (inventory between processes) lead to other suboptimal behavior, like reducing your motivation to continuously improve your operations. Why worry about preventive maintenance on equipment when shutdowns do not immediately affect final assembly anyway? Why get overly concerned about a few quality errors when you can just toss out defective parts? Because by the time a defective piece works its way to the later operation where an operator tries to assemble that piece, there may be weeks of bad parts in process and sitting in buffers.[1]

Figure 3-2 shows this waste through a simple time line for the process of casting, machining, and assembling. As in most traditionally managed operations, most of the time spent on material is actually wasted. Anyone who has been through a lean manufacturing or TPS seminar will recognize this figure, so I will not belabor the point. From a lean perspective, the first thing you should do in approaching any process is to map the value stream following the circuitous path of material (or paper or information) through your process. It is best to walk the actual path to get the full experience. You can draw this path on a layout and calculate the time and distance traveled and then give it the highly technical name of

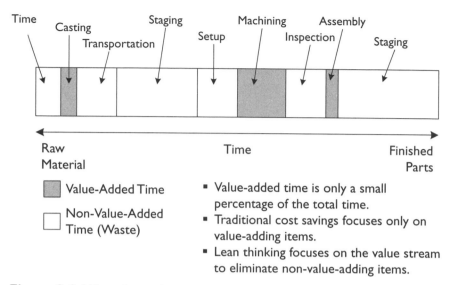

Figure 3-2. Waste in a value system

"spaghetti diagram." Even people who have worked inside a factory for most of their adult lives will be amazed at the results of this exercise. The point of Figure 3-2 is that we have taken very simple transformation processes and stretched them to the point that the value added is barely recognizable.

I discovered an astonishing example of this while consulting for a manufacturer of steel nuts. The engineers and managers in my seminar assured me that their process could not benefit from lean manufacturing because it was so simple. Rolls of steel coil came in and were cut, tapped, heat-treated, and put into boxes. Material flew through the automated machines at the rate of hundreds of nuts a minute. When we followed the value (and non-value) stream, their claim became comical. We started at the receiving dock, and every time I thought the process must be finished, we walked across the factory one more time to another step. The nuts at some point left the factory for a few weeks to be heat-treated, because management had calculated that contracting out heat-treating was more economical. When all was said and done, the nut-making process that took seconds for most operations, with the exception of heat-treating, which could take a few hours, typically took weeks and sometimes months. We calculated percent value added for different product lines and got numbers ranging from .008 percent to 2 or 3 percent. Eyes opened! To make matters worse, equipment downtime was a common problem, idling machines and allowing for large buildups of material around them. Some clever manager had figured out that contracting outside skill trades was cheaper than hiring full-time people. So there was often nobody around to fix a machine when it went down, let alone do a good job on preventive maintenance.

Local efficiencies were emphasized at the cost of slowing down the value stream by creating large amounts of in-process and finished-goods inventory and taking a long time to identify problems (defects) that reduced quality. As a result, the plant was not flexible to changes in customer demand.

Traditional Process Improvement vs. Lean Improvement

The traditional approach to process improvement focuses on identifying local efficiencies—"Go to the equipment, the value-added processes, and improve uptime, or make it cycle faster, or replace the person with automated equipment." The result might be a significant percent improvement for that individual process, but have little impact on the overall value stream. This is especially true because in most processes there are relatively few value-added steps, so improving those value-added steps will not amount to much. Without lean thinking, most people can't see the huge opportunities for reducing waste by getting rid of or shrinking non-value-added steps.

In a lean improvement initiative, most of the progress comes because a large number of non-value-added steps are squeezed out. In the process, the value-added time is also reduced. We can see this most vividly by taking a process like the nut-making example and creating a one-piece-flow cell.

In lean manufacturing, a *cell* consists of a close arrangement of the people, machines, or workstations in a processing sequence. You create cells to facilitate *one-piece flow* of a product or service, through various operations, for example, welding, assembly, packing, one unit at a time, at a rate determined by the needs of the customer and with the least amount of delay and waiting.

Take the case of the nut. If you line up the processes needed to create it in a cell and then pass the nut or very small lots of nuts from one operation to another in a one-piece flow, what once took weeks to complete can now be done in hours. And this case is not unusual. The magic of making huge gains in productivity and quality and big reductions in inventory, space, and lead time through one-piece flow has been demonstrated over and over in companies throughout the world. It always seems miraculous and the results are always the same. This is why the one-piece-flow cell is the ultimate in lean production. It has eliminated most of Toyota's eight kinds of waste.

In fact, the ultimate goal of lean manufacturing is to apply the ideal of one-piece flow to all business operations, from product design to launch, order taking, and physical production. Anyone I know who has experienced the power of lean thinking becomes a zealot and wants to rid the world of waste, applying it to every process, from administrative to engineering. But I caution that, as with every other tool or process, the answer is not to blindly apply it by putting cells everywhere. For example, the nut plant had created a cell for cutting and tapping.

Unfortunately, they also bought very expensive and complex computerized equipment. The equipment was broken a lot of the time, creating delays. And the nuts still had to leave the cell for heat-treating—taking weeks before they came back. Inventory still piled up. The "lean cell" became a joke to the shop-floor workers who could see the waste—a serious setback to the lean improvement process.

The "TPS House" Diagram: A System Based on a Structure, Not Just a Set of Techniques

For decades Toyota was doing just fine in applying and improving TPS on the shop floor day in and day out without documenting TPS theory. Workers and managers were constantly learning new methods and variations on old methods through actual practice on the shop floor. Communication was strong in what was a relatively small company, so "best practices" developed within Toyota spread to other Toyota plants and ultimately to suppliers. But as the practices matured within Toyota, it became clear that the task of teaching TPS to the supply base was never ending. So Taiichi Ohno disciple Fujio Cho developed a simple representation—a house.

The "TPS house" diagram (see Figure 3-3) has become one of the most recognizable symbols in modern manufacturing. Why a house? Because a house is a structural system. The house is strong only if the roof, the pillars, and the foundation are strong. A weak link weakens the whole system. There are different versions of the house, but the core principles remain the same. It starts with the goals of best quality, lowest cost, and shortest lead time—the roof. There are then two outer pillars—just-in-time, probably the most visible and highly publicized characteristic of TPS, and *jidoka,* which in essence means never letting a defect pass into the next station and freeing people from machines—automation with a human touch. In the center of the system are people. Finally there are various foundational elements, which include the need for standardized, stable, reliable processes, and also *heijunka,* which means leveling out the production schedule in both volume and variety. A leveled schedule or *heijunka* is necessary to keep the system stable and to allow for minimum inventory. Big spikes in the production of certain products to the exclusion of others will create part shortages unless lots of inventory are added into the system.

Each element of the house by itself is critical, but more important is the way the elements reinforce each other. JIT means removing, as much as possible, the inventory used to buffer operations against problems that may arise in production. The ideal of one-piece flow is to make one unit at a time at the rate of customer demand or takt (German word for meter). Using smaller buffers (removing the "safety net") means that problems like quality defects become immediately visible. This reinforces *jidoka,* which halts the production process. This means workers must resolve the problems immediately and urgently to resume production. At the

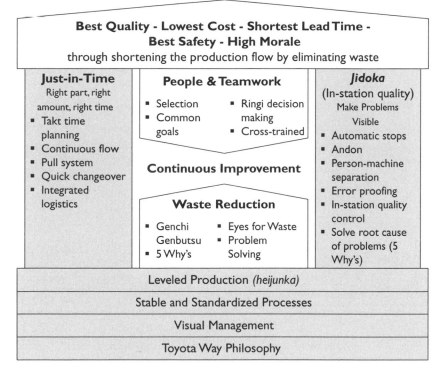

Figure 3-3. The Toyota Production System

foundation of the house is stability. Ironically, the requirement for working with little inventory and stopping production when there is a problem causes instability and a sense of urgency among workers. In mass production, when a machine goes down, there is no sense of urgency: the maintenance department is scheduled to fix it while inventory keeps the operations running. By contrast, in lean production, when an operator shuts down equipment to fix a problem, other operations will soon stop producing, creating a crisis. So there is always a sense of urgency for everyone in production to fix problems together to get the equipment up and running. If the same problem happens repeatedly, management will quickly conclude that this is a critical situation and it may be time to invest in Total Productive Maintenance (TPM), where everyone learns how to clean, inspect, and maintain equipment. A high degree of stability is needed so that the system is not constantly stopped. People are at the center of the house because only through continuous improvement can the operation ever attain this needed stability. People must be trained to see waste and solve problems at the root cause by repeatedly asking why the problem really occurs. Problem solving is at the actual place to see what is really going on (*genchi genbutsu*).

In some versions of the "house" model, several of the Toyota Way philosophies are added into the foundation, such as "respect for humanity." While Toyota often presents this house with the goals of cost, quality, and timely delivery, in actuality their plants follow a common practice in Japan of focusing on QCDSM (quality, cost, delivery, safety, and morale) or some variation. Toyota will never sacrifice the safety of their workers for production. And they do not need to, as eliminating waste does not imply creating stressful, unsafe work practices. As Ohno wrote:[2]

> *Every method available for man-hour reduction to reduce cost must, of course, be pursued vigorously; but we must never forget that safety is the foundation of all our activities. There are times when improvement activities do not proceed in the name of safety. In such instances, return to the starting point and take another look at the purpose of that operation. Never be satisfied with inaction. Question and redefine your purpose to attain progress.*

Conclusion

TPS is not a toolkit. It is not just a set of lean tools like just-in-time, cells, 5S (sort, stabilize, shine, standardize, sustain, discussed in Chapter 13), *kanban*, etc. It is a sophisticated system of production in which all of the parts contribute to a whole. The whole at its roots focuses on supporting and encouraging people to continually improve the processes they work on. Unfortunately, many books about lean manufacturing reinforce the misunderstanding that TPS is a collection of tools that lead to more efficient operations. The purpose of these tools is lost and the centrality of people is missed. When looked at more broadly, TPS is about applying the principles of the Toyota Way. The initial focus was on the shop floor, but the principles are broad and, in fact, apply just as well to engineering and business service operations.

In the next chapter, we will review the 14 principles of the Toyota Way, which are the basis of the culture behind TPS and the focus of this book. In Chapters 5 and 6 we will see the 14 principles in action—with the story of the challenges Toyota overcame to develop the Lexus and the Prius.

Notes

1. The concept of value-added and non-value-added work is eloquently explained by James P. Womack and Daniel T. Jones in *Lean Thinking* (1996). They introduce the value stream perspective that is the essence of lean thinking, based on the Toyota Production System.
2. From the unpublished, internal Toyota document, "High Quality with Safety: Kanban and Just-in-Time," by Taiichi Ohno.

Chapter 4

The 14 Principles of the Toyota Way:
An Executive Summary of the Culture Behind TPS

Since Toyota's founding we have adhered to the core principle of contributing to society through the practice of manufacturing high-quality products and services. Our business practices and activities based on this core principle created values, beliefs and business methods that over the years have become a source of competitive advantage. These are the managerial values and business methods that are known collectively as the Toyota Way.

—Fujio Cho, President Toyota
(from the Toyota Way document, 2001)

The Toyota Way Is More than Tools and Techniques

So you set up your kanban system. (*Kanban* is the Japanese word for "card," "ticket," or "sign" and is a tool for managing the flow and production of materials in a Toyota-style "pull" production system.) You plug in the andon, which is a visual control device in a production area that alerts workers to defects, equipment abnormalities, or other problems using signals such as lights, audible alarms, etc. Finally, with these devices your workplace looks like a Toyota plant. Yet, over time your workplace reverts to operating like it did before. You call in a Toyota Production System (TPS) expert who shakes her head disapprovingly. What is wrong?

The real work of implementing Lean has just begun. Your workers do not understand the culture behind TPS. They are not contributing to the continuous improvement of the system or improving themselves. In the Toyota Way, it's the people who bring the system to life: working, communicating, resolving issues, and growing together. From the first look at excellent companies in Japan practicing lean manufacturing, it was clear that the workers were active in making improvement suggestions. But the Toyota Way goes well beyond this; it encourages, supports, and in fact demands employee involvement.

The more I have studied TPS and the Toyota Way, the more I understand that it is a system designed to provide the tools for people to continually improve their work. The Toyota Way means more dependence on people, not less. It is a culture, even more than a set of efficiency and improvement techniques. You depend upon the workers to reduce inventory, identify hidden problems, and fix them. The workers have a sense of urgency, purpose, and teamwork because if they don't fix it there will be an inventory outage. On a daily basis, engineers, skilled workers, quality specialists, vendors, team leaders, and—most importantly—operators are all involved in continuous problem solving and improvement, which over time trains everyone to become better problem solvers.

One lean tool that facilitates this teamwork is called 5S (sort, stabilize, shine, standardize, sustain, discussed in Chapter 13), which is a series of activities for eliminating wastes that contribute to errors, defects, and injuries. In this improvement method, the fifth S, sustain, is arguably the hardest. It's the one that keeps the first four S's going by emphasizing the necessary education, training, and rewards needed to encourage workers to properly maintain and continuously improve operating procedures and the workplace environment. This effort requires a combination of committed management, proper training, and a culture that makes sustaining improvement a habitual behavior from the shop floor to management.

This chapter provides a synopsis of the 14 principles that constitute the Toyota Way. The principles are organized in four broad categories: 1) Long-Term Philosophy, 2) The Right Process Will Produce the Right Results (this utilizes many of the TPS tools), 3) Add Value to the Organization by Developing Your People, and 4) Continuously Solving Root Problems Drives Organizational Learning. Note that Part II of this book is also organized into these same four categories—the four "P's" of the Toyota Way model in Chapter 1. In the following two chapters, I will demonstrate some of these 14 principles at work in the development of Lexus and Prius. If you would like to jump ahead to begin the detailed discussion of these 14 principles, you can skip to Chapter 7 now. However, I do advise that you peruse the principles below.

Executive Summary of the 14 Toyota Way Principles

Section I: Long-Term Philosophy

Principle 1. Base your management decisions on a long-term philosophy, even at the expense of short-term financial goals.

- Have a philosophical sense of purpose that supersedes any short-term decision making. Work, grow, and align the whole organization toward a common purpose that is bigger than making money. Understand your place in the history of the company and work to bring the company to the next level. Your philosophical mission is the foundation for all the other principles.
- Generate value for the customer, society, and the economy—it is your starting point. Evaluate every function in the company in terms of its ability to achieve this.
- Be responsible. Strive to decide your own fate. Act with self-reliance and trust in your own abilities. Accept responsibility for your conduct and maintain and improve the skills that enable you to produce added value.

Section II: The Right Process Will Produce the Right Results

Principle 2. Create continuous process flow to bring problems to the surface.

- Redesign work processes to achieve high value-added, continuous flow. Strive to cut back to zero the amount of time that any work project is sitting idle or waiting for someone to work on it.
- Create flow to move material and information fast as well as to link processes and people together so that problems surface right away.
- Make flow evident throughout your organizational culture. It is the key to a true continuous improvement process and to developing people.

Principle 3. Use "pull" systems to avoid overproduction.

- Provide your downline customers in the production process with what they want, when they want it, and in the amount they want. Material replenishment initiated by consumption is the basic principle of just-in-time.
- Minimize your work in process and warehousing of inventory by stocking small amounts of each product and frequently restocking based on what the customer actually takes away.
- Be responsive to the day-by-day shifts in customer demand rather than relying on computer schedules and systems to track wasteful inventory.

Principle 4. Level out the workload (*heijunka*). (Work like the tortoise, not the hare.)

- Eliminating waste is just one-third of the equation for making lean successful. Eliminating overburden to people and equipment and eliminating unevenness in the production schedule are just as important—yet generally not understood at companies attempting to implement lean principles.
- Work to level out the workload of all manufacturing and service processes as an alternative to the stop/start approach of working on projects in batches that is typical at most companies.

Principle 5. Build a culture of stopping to fix problems, to get quality right the first time.

- Quality for the customer drives your value proposition.
- Use all the modern quality assurance methods available.
- Build into your equipment the capability of detecting problems and stopping itself. Develop a visual system to alert team or project leaders that a machine or process needs assistance. *Jidoka* (machines with human intelligence) is the foundation for "building in" quality.
- Build into your organization support systems to quickly solve problems and put in place countermeasures.
- Build into your culture the philosophy of stopping or slowing down to get quality right the first time to enhance productivity in the long run.

Principle 6. Standardized tasks are the foundation for continuous improvement and employee empowerment.

- Use stable, repeatable methods everywhere to maintain the predictability, regular timing, and regular output of your processes. It is the foundation for flow and pull.
- Capture the accumulated learning about a process up to a point in time by standardizing today's best practices. Allow creative and individual expression to improve upon the standard; then incorporate it into the new standard so that when a person moves on you can hand off the learning to the next person.

Principle 7. Use visual control so no problems are hidden.

- Use simple visual indicators to help people determine immediately whether they are in a standard condition or deviating from it.
- Avoid using a computer screen when it moves the worker's focus away from the workplace.
- Design simple visual systems at the place where the work is done, to support flow and pull.
- Reduce your reports to one piece of paper whenever possible, even for your most important financial decisions.

Principle 8. Use only reliable, thoroughly tested technology that serves your people and processes.

- Use technology to support people, not to replace people. Often it is best to work out a process manually before adding technology to support the process.

- New technology is often unreliable and difficult to standardize and therefore endangers "flow." A proven process that works generally takes precedence over new and untested technology.

- Conduct actual tests before adopting new technology in business processes, manufacturing systems, or products.

- Reject or modify technologies that conflict with your culture or that might disrupt stability, reliability, and predictability.

- Nevertheless, encourage your people to consider new technologies when looking into new approaches to work. Quickly implement a thoroughly considered technology if it has been proven in trials and it can improve flow in your processes.

Section III: Add Value to the Organization by Developing Your People and Partners

Principle 9. Grow leaders who thoroughly understand the work, live the philosophy, and teach it to others.

- Grow leaders from within, rather than buying them from outside the organization.

- Do not view the leader's job as simply accomplishing tasks and having good people skills. Leaders must be role models of the company's philosophy and way of doing business.

- A good leader must understand the daily work in great detail so he or she can be the best teacher of your company's philosophy.

Principle 10. Develop exceptional people and teams who follow your company's philosophy.

- Create a strong, stable culture in which company values and beliefs are widely shared and lived out over a period of many years.

- Train exceptional individuals and teams to work within the corporate philosophy to achieve exceptional results. Work very hard to reinforce the culture continually.

- Use cross-functional teams to improve quality and productivity and enhance flow by solving difficult technical problems. Empowerment occurs when people use the company's tools to improve the company.

- Make an ongoing effort to teach individuals how to work together as teams toward common goals. Teamwork is something that has to be learned.

Principle 11. Respect your extended network of partners and suppliers by challenging them and helping them improve.

- Have respect for your partners and suppliers and treat them as an extension of your business.
- Challenge your outside business partners to grow and develop. It shows that you value them. Set challenging targets and assist your partners in achieving them.

Section IV: Continuously Solving Root Problems Drives Organizational Learning

Principle 12. Go and see for yourself to thoroughly understand the situation (*genchi genbutsu*).

- Solve problems and improve processes by going to the source and personally observing and verifying data rather than theorizing on the basis of what other people or the computer screen tell you.
- Think and speak based on personally verified data.
- Even high-level managers and executives should go and see things for themselves, so they will have more than a superficial understanding of the situation.

Principle 13. Make decisions slowly by consensus, thoroughly considering all options; implement decisions rapidly.

- Do not pick a single direction and go down that one path until you have thoroughly considered alternatives. When you have picked, move quickly but cautiously down the path.
- *Nemawashi* is the process of discussing problems and potential solutions with all of those affected, to collect their ideas and get agreement on a path forward. This consensus process, though time-consuming, helps broaden the search for solutions, and once a decision is made, the stage is set for rapid implementation.

Principle 14. Become a learning organization through relentless reflection (*hansei*) and continuous improvement (*kaizen*).

- Once you have established a stable process, use continuous improvement tools to determine the root cause of inefficiencies and apply effective countermeasures.
- Design processes that require almost no inventory. This will make wasted time and resources visible for all to see. Once waste is exposed, have employees use a continuous improvement process (*kaizen*) to eliminate it.
- Protect the organizational knowledge base by developing stable personnel, slow promotion, and very careful succession systems.

- Use *hansei* (reflection) at key milestones and after you finish a project to openly identify all the shortcomings of the project. Develop counter-measures to avoid the same mistakes again.
- Learn by standardizing the best practices, rather than reinventing the wheel with each new project and each new manager.

It is quite possible to use a variety of TPS tools and still be following only a select few of the Toyota Way principles. The result will be short-term jumps on performance measures that are not sustainable. On the other hand, an organization that truly practices the full set of Toyota Way principles will be following TPS and on its way to a sustainable competitive advantage.

In courses I have taught on lean manufacturing, a common question is "How does TPS apply to my business? We do not make high-volume cars; we make low-volume, specialized products" or "We are a professional service organization, so TPS does not apply to us." This line of thinking tells me they are missing the point. Lean is not about imitating the tools used by Toyota in a particular manu-facturing process. Lean is about developing principles that are right for your organization and diligently practicing them to achieve high performance that con-tinues to add value to customers and society. This, of course, means being com-petitive and profitable. Toyota's principles are a great starting point. And Toyota practices these principles far beyond its high-volume assembly lines. For example, we will see in the next chapter how some of these principles are applied in the pro-fessional service organizations that design Toyota's products.

Chapter 5

The Toyota Way in Action:
The "No Compromises"
Development of Lexus

Even if the target seems so high as to be unachievable at first glance, if you explain the necessity to all the people involved and insist upon it, everyone will become enthusiastic in the spirit of challenge, will work together, and achieve it.
— Ichiro Suzuki, chief engineer of the first Lexus

Toyota is known as a very conservative company. When I first heard of this reputation in Japan in 1983, I was surprised. I had thought of Toyota as a very innovative company and that's why I was there—to learn about the innovative practices of Toyota that were dominating the auto industry. But informed Japanese just laughed and said Toyota is "very conservative, even by Japanese standards." "What does 'conservative' mean in this case?" I asked. A typical response was "conservative politically, conservative styling, conservative financially, conservative in changing their ways ... you name it." Certainly much of this "conservatism" derives from the Toyota Way culture, which gives continuity to its excellence.

Yet central to the Toyota Way is innovation—never getting complacent and always staying a step ahead of trends in the market. There are many levels of innovation—from the small workplace changes made by plant workers on the shop floor to fundamental breakthroughs in production technology and vehicle engineering. It's also true that most of what goes on in Toyota's vehicle centers is routine product development making incremental change from one model to the next. But the beauty of the Toyota Way is that it allows Toyota to periodically break from this "conservative" mold and innovatively develop a new vehicle with a new developmental approach. These are defining moments for Toyota.

All of the engineers I interviewed for this book agreed that two of the best examples of the Toyota Way in action were the Lexus and the Prius—two break-through vehicles that reshaped Toyota as a company. The next two chapters tell these stories, in order to flesh out the principles of the Toyota Way.

Lexus: A New Car, a New Division by the Michael Jordan of Chief Engineers

Yukiyasu Togo was a successful Toyota executive in charge of Toyota Motor Sales, USA, in Southern California. His friends and associates were also well-to-do executives. But few would consider buying a Toyota. Mercedes and BMW were more their style. This bothered Togo. He was a fighter and not willing to accept being second-class. Making high-quality, fuel-efficient, and economical cars was fine, but he saw no reason why Toyota could not also make luxury vehicles competing with the best in the world. "Maybe what we need is a luxurious car that would create a new image, a car of high quality, perhaps even up-market of the Mercedes-Benz" (as quoted in Reingold, 1999).

To do this, Togo realized Toyota would need a new sales channel and name. He took his idea to management. At first he faced resistance. At Toyota this was not unusual. Much of Toyota's success derives from incremental improvements year in and year out—part of that conservative mindset. Building a luxury car meant breaking the mold from sturdy and reliable but basic Japanese built cars to competing with the kings of luxury in Europe. Also the development of a luxury car would mean simultaneously developing a vehicle and a brand: a car company within a car company. But after some debate it was clear that Toyota was not living up to its challenge of staying a step ahead of trends in the market and the concept for the Lexus was born.

Such an effort could not be entrusted to just anybody. In this case, the task was given to one of the best and most revered chief engineers in Toyota's history, Ichiro Suzuki, who was introduced to me as the "Michael Jordan" of chief engineers and a "legend" within Toyota. His comments in this chapter are from an interview I had with him at the Toyota Technical Center in Ann Arbor, Michigan, in April 2002, just a few months away from "real" retirement. Toyota had called him out of retirement to act as an "Executive Advisory Engineer." Basically, he was making one last tour of duty to teach the younger generation what it took to be an excellent engineer at Toyota. (Principle 9, *Grow leaders who thoroughly understand the work, live the philosophy, and teach it to others.*)

Listening to the Customer and Benchmarking the Competition

Developing a good concept, with its associated targets, will make or break any vehicle development program. If the concept is not well thought through and does not properly identify the market and how the vehicle will hit the market just right, then even excellent execution of the program will not matter. Efficiency does not equal effectiveness when it comes to developing a new product. Effectiveness starts with what is popularly being called the "fuzzy front end," when judgment and qualitative data often play a greater role than precise scientific and engineering analysis. In Toyota Way terms, thorough consideration in decision making (Principle 13: *Make decisions slowly by consensus, thoroughly considering all options, implement rapidly*) means carefully thinking through the pros and cons of all the possible solutions, based on the facts, before charging ahead down a given path. The Lexus began with a thorough evaluation of the goals of the vehicle led by insightful and experienced engineers. To set his targets, Suzuki carefully considered the competition.

Suzuki started with focus group interviews in the U.S. at a Marriott Hotel on Long Island—a fairly affluent area. This was not a huge survey, but rather just two groups of about a dozen people each. Individuals within groups were assigned to focus on particular vehicles they owned. For example, in Group A four people were Audi 5000 owners, one was a BMW 528e owner, two people owned a Benz 190E, and three people owned a Volvo 740/760. Group B almost directly paralleled this makeup. Suzuki classified what he heard into reasons for purchase, reasons for rejection of other competitive vehicles, and the image they had of different cars. He simplified the results into a number of tables, qualitatively summarizing the results using terms that evoke emotion more than scientific precision (see Figures 5-1 and 5-2).

	Reason for Purchase	Reasons for Rejection of Competitors
Benz	Quality, investment value, sturdy	Too small, weaker style appeal (vs. BMW)
BMW	Style, handling, functional	Too many on road
Audi	Style, space, affordability	Poor quality, poor service
Volvo	Safety, reliability, quality, sturdy	Boxy styling
Jaguar	Most attractive styling	Poor quality, small interior

Figure 5-1. Reasons for purchase and rejection of competitive luxury vehicles (1980s)

European	Quality, investment value, sturdy
American (Cadillac)	Gadgets and gimmics, poor quality, big, overstated, sofa on wheels (too soft ride), rattle after 6 months
Japanese (Nissan Maxima)	Too small, no status, busy, no successful image (Acura = well made Honda, stretched Accord)

Figure 5-2. Image of European, American, and Japanese luxury cars (1980s)

Figure 5-1 shows the reasons for purchase and rejection. There are no surprises here, but it is worth noting how succinctly the table summarizes what many of us have thought and even felt about these various vehicles back in the mid-1980s. So much is captured with so few words. This is a part of Toyota's visual management; reflected in Principle 7, *Use visual control so no problems are hidden.* In these summary grids, Suzuki strives to communicate on one piece of paper so the reader sees at a glance the most important points for decision making.

Figure 5-2 similarly summarizes a broader set of images associated with European, U.S., and Japanese luxury cars. The first thing the groups focused on was status and prestige—image. Mercedes-Benz was most associated with status and success; Japanese models were not. Clearly a major hurdle for Suzuki was to overcome the rooted stereotype of Japanese cars being practical, efficient, reliable vehicles, but never luxurious. A rank ordering of what was important to buyers of Mercedes in particular was as follows (1=most important):

1. Status and prestige of image
2. High quality
3. Resale value
4. Performance (e.g., handling, ride, power)
5. Safety

More than any of the other information gathered, this rank ordering struck an emotional nerve because Suzuki viewed a car essentially as a vehicle of transportation, not "an ornament." When he listened to people talk about Mercedes-Benz, status and prestige were number one, while performance, the actual basic function of the car, was only number four. Perhaps because of his engineering bias, Suzuki could not accept people choosing Mercedes-Benz's status appeal over performance. It was a car, after all, not an "ornament." According to Suzuki:

The car is not something that sits around, it's something that needs to move around. So I thought. I want to build a car that beats Mercedes-Benz in the most basic function a car has, its driving performance.

Suzuki asked himself, what does it mean to have a high-quality product? What does it mean to have a high-quality luxury vehicle? What can you put into a car that makes people owning it feel like "they're wealthy, ... they have a lot, spiritually speaking?" And, what can you put into a car that, as the years go on, you become more and more attached to that car? So the two characteristics he felt were most important were, in the order of importance, exceptional functional performance and an elegant appearance, not traditionally a Toyota strength. "Mercedes-Benz was kind of a cold vehicle in terms of styling. It's changed since then, but I decided that the vehicle should have human warmth, beauty, elegance, refinement." He felt if Toyota could make a car that performed not slightly better than Benz, but considerably better than Benz, with improved styling, then Toyota might be able to change its image and compete.

But having exceptional functional performance and human warmth are somewhat contradictory to one another, because when you build in performance you're going to lose some of the warmth and human characteristics. It's not enough to try to make these qualities exist at the same time, because that implies a trade-off. What Suzuki wanted was to fuse these two characteristics, so they become one and the same thing. But this would take some high-level engineering and design decisions. So he developed quantitative targets for the vehicle with that in mind.

Figure 5-3 summarizes the targets that Suzuki set for the Lexus as compared with BMW and Mercedes—the main competition. They were based on the assumption that the Lexus could do it all. "So when I showed this to the engineers at Toyota they all laughed at me. They said it was impossible," explained Suzuki.

So he thought about this some more. He picked apart the different elements.

If you want to make a car that goes very fast, it's very well-suited to also reducing the aerodynamic resistance. So these two elements are harmonious. When you get up to speeds of 250 km/h your air resistance reaches levels of about 95 percent or over. So the more you're able to reduce this aerodynamic coefficient, the more speed you're going to be able to achieve. So these things suit each other well, these two targets. Similarly, improving the fuel economy is very harmonious with the goal of reducing the vehicle mass. However, we didn't know what to do with the quietness factor because to reduce the quietness to an extreme level, that leads to higher mass. So we needed to start acting on a new operating principle. And the new principle we adopted was not to dampen the noise that exists but to reduce the amount of noise at its source, by making quieter engines.

Suzuki explained that adding structure (mass) to reduce noise was only dealing with the surface problem. The root cause of the noise and vibration that customers experience was the engine. One technique that is part of *kaizen* (con-

	Celsior (LS400)	Mercedes 420 SE/ 560 SE	BMW 735i
Top Speed	250 km/h (European)	222 km/h (European)	220 km/h (European)
Fuel Consumption (local-highway)	23.5 mpg or more (USA) 7.0 km/l or more (Japan)	19 mpg (USA) 5.4 km/l (Japan)	18.8 mpg (USA)
Noise Characteristics	Extremely quiet up to top speed (58 db @ 100 km/h) (73 db @ 200 km/	61 db (100 km/h) 76 db (200 km/h)	63 db (100 km/h) 78 db (200 km/h)
Aerodynamics (C_D)**	.28~.29	.32	.37
Vehicle Weight	1,710 kg (USA)	1,760 kg (USA)	1,760 kg (USA)

*Shown are Lexus targets compared with the two target vehicles based on 4.2L engines. **Coefficient of drag.

Figure 5-3. Targets for Lexus

tinuous improvement—Principle 14) is to ask why a problem exists five times, going to a deeper level with each "Why?" to get to the root cause of the problem. So, by understanding the root cause of the problem and identifying countermeasures to dampen the noise, Suzuki reasoned he could eliminate the problem of engine noise, without resorting to a surface solution—adding mass. He then developed a list of performance trade-offs, where he wanted to have A yet also B, and C yet also D. For example, he wanted to have very good handling and stability at high speeds, yet at the same time have good ride comfort. These are summarized in Figure 5-4 as a set of "no-compromise" goals. This led to the two guiding goals for the Lexus program.

1. Cut noise, vibration, and harshness at the source (rather than with after-the-fact measures).
2. Maintain the "yet" concepts, balancing without compromising on traditional auto design trade-offs.

The first one, at the source, turned out to be largely driven by the accuracy of the parts—the precision with which the parts are manufactured.

Achieving No-Compromise Objectives

Since so much of the success of Lexus depended on achieving these breakthrough performance objectives for the engine, and since this depended so heavily on pro-

1. Great high-speed handling/stability	YET	A pleasant ride
2. Fast and smooth ride	YET	Low fuel consumption
3. Super quiet	YET	Light weight
4. Elegant styling	YET	Great aerodynamics
5. Warm	YET	Functional interior
6. Great stability at high speed	YET	Great C_D value (low friction)

Figure 5-4. "No-compromise" goals

duction engineering, Suzuki presented a number of strict requirements to the engine production engineers, whose response was largely discouraging. Their first reaction was that you cannot make parts that are more precise than the tolerances of the precision instruments you're using to make them. At the time, Toyota had the most precise instruments in the world for machining engine parts (e.g., high-precision machine tools for machining castings into crankshafts, pistons, etc.). And so Suzuki said, "Oh, OK, I see your point." But backing away from these breakthrough performance objects would mean the end of his "dream car." So he turned to his superiors for help and was able to get them formed into a Flagship Quality Committee (The "FQ Committee").

This committee was composed of head executives representing three divisions in Toyota—R&D, production engineering, and the manufacturing plant. The person who at that time was in charge of production engineering was Akira Takahashi. He told Suzuki, "Look, Toyota's already making products that are exceptionally high quality and to bring in more precise equipment to meet the accuracy and precision demands you're asking is out of control, it's ridiculous. You're asking too much." Not willing to give up, Suzuki said, "OK, I'll tell you what. Try to make one of these high-precision products, an engine or transmission, and if we can't do that, if that doesn't work out, I'll quit. I will give up on my request."

Takahashi agreed he could make one of anything as long as it didn't have to be in mass production. So he put together a team of his best engine engineers and they developed one high-precision engine that met Suzuki's tight specifications. It was a hand-built engine and, when it was tested in an existing vehicle, there was remarkably little vibration with extremely good fuel economy. The team of engineers and Takahashi got very excited and they immediately began discussing how they could replicate this with mass production equipment. By working with Takahashi and going to his superiors and creating the FQ Committee, Suzuki was in a very clever way practicing Principle 13: *Make decisions slowly by consensus, thor-*

oughly considering all options; implement rapidly (nemawashi). The *nemawashi* part of this principle is to take the time to build consensus across and up and down the organization. By asking the engineers to build an actual engine, he was using the Toyota propensity for *genchi genbutsu* (Principle 12: *Go and see for yourself to thoroughly understand the situation*). In this case, he chose to work on an actual engine instead of speculating about its viability based on theoretical arguments.

As Suzuki explained:

> *The people at each one of these different departments, R&D, production engineering, and so on and so forth are looking toward the policy of their superiors to see how to act, and naturally once I was able to bring Mr. Takahashi from production engineering over to my side, things became much easier to do. So there were various troubles and problems along the way, however, every time that happened I would say thousands of times, tens of thousands of times, "counter measures at the source, follow the concept of 'this yet that.'" The end result was not just my effort alone, but all the people along the way who originally opposed what I was doing, and who all came around and were able to achieve all these targets that I had set in the first place.*

Another key engineering feat was to cut down on wind noises. The engineers would attach many tiny microphones to the window at the clay model stage, and then check to see if they had achieved a quiet noise level. The "yet" challenge was trying to balance aerodynamics with styling. If you try to adopt elegant styling, you tend to bring down the aerodynamic efficiency. On the other hand, if you have good aerodynamic efficiency, styling will suffer. Styling developed a bunch of clay models to achieve the distinctive and refined appearance Suzuki was after and the stylists were obviously very proud of them. Unfortunately, none of them passed the stringent aerodynamics test. So what do you do?

Suzuki's approach, as with the engine, was to find the most talented engineers, challenge them with the goal, and ask them to try real things rather than just analyze and theorize. So he found an exceptional aerodynamics engineer and, choosing a clay model from the styling studio, challenged him to modify the design until it achieved the correct aerodynamic results. The aerodynamics engineer said, "I will take that clay model and reach the goals that you want—0.28 on the coefficient of drag." The aerodynamics engineer decided to physically cut and modify the clay model himself, a job normally done by the modeler, requiring several iterations with a lot of verbal discussion between the modeler and the engineer. He cut here and there and finally ended up with a vehicle that was aerodynamically matched to the target. It looked terrible. He had lost all the fine styling features of the designers. But through this process he was able to understand the aerodynamic characteristics much more quickly and deeply than if he had been giving verbal instructions to the clay modelers and waiting for the revised models.

Through this hands-on experience, he uncovered reference points that he could feed to the stylists to simultaneously improve aerodynamic performance while achieving excellent styling. By deciding to personally cut the clay, which Suzuki encouraged, the aerodynamics engineer sped up the development of Lexus *and* got a deeper understanding of the aerodynamics. This was another example of Principle 12 *(genchi genbutsu)*.

As a result of Suzuki's engineering approach of achieving no-compromise objectives, the Lexus program took off and accomplished exactly what he wanted—a smart design and a very smooth ride. The feel of the ride at 100 kph and 160 kph was practically the same, despite the fact that you were traveling 1.6 times faster. To say the least, the consumer was impressed, and it showed in the numbers sold. At the time of the Lexus launch, Mercedes-Benz's three models (300E, 420SE, 560SEL) had no rival in the U.S. market. But Lexus, with only one model, was able to sell, in one year, 2.7 times the number of all three of those well-established Mercedes combined. As of 2002, the Lexus was the best-selling luxury car in the United States.

The creation of the Lexus spawned an entirely new luxury division of Toyota and placed their image in the elite of the luxury market—the original goal of visionary Togo. It also gave rise to a new spirit of innovation in Toyota's engineering. When Toyota started out in the automobile business, the engineers had no choice but to be innovative. As Toyota became a global powerhouse with clearly delineated product families, its thousands of engineers became specialists tweaking the next Crown and the next Camry.[1]

Lexus broke the behavioral mold and engineers who had known only the conservative, risk-averse Toyota suddenly were working on a bold, new, challenging project. This renewed spirit would carry over into an entirely new project, with new objectives and challenges. Toyota was about to reinvent its vehicle development process with the Prius.

Note

1. In fact, the innovative enthusiasm was almost too contagious. At some point, the vehicle content of the Camry and other cars rose to the point that costs got out of control. Toyota chief engineers had to be reined in and design appropriate levels of content while relying more on standardized parts to cut costs. This was one benefit of the later reorganization of Toyota into vehicle centers with vehicle center heads, as discussed in the next chapter. It is also an example of how Toyota is a learning organization.

Chapter 6

The Toyota Way in Action: New Century, New Fuel, New Design Process—Prius[1]

Creativity, Challenge and Courage: the Three C's
—Shoichiro Toyoda, former President, 1980s

Toyota executives considered the early 1990s to be a very dangerous business climate for Toyota. The problem was that Toyota was too successful. It was the peak of the Japanese bubble economy and prosperity seemed like it would never end in Japan. Toyota's business was booming. This is exactly the environment that leads many companies into complacency. But the biggest crisis, from the perspective of Toyota leaders, is when associates do not believe there is a crisis or do not feel the urgency to continuously improve the way they work.

At that time Toyota had a very strong product development system for creating routine variations of existing vehicle models, but the company had not changed its basic product development system for decades. Toyota Chairman Eiji Toyoda was concerned and took every opportunity he could to preach crisis. At one Toyota board meeting, he asked, "Should we continue building cars as we have been doing? Can we survive in the 21st century with the type of R&D that we are doing? ... There is no way that this [booming] situation will last much longer."

Much like Toyota deciding it should produce a luxury car even though they were doing just fine, Toyoda was practicing Principle 1: *Base your management decisions on a long-term philosophy, even at the expense of short-term financial goals.* Though Toyota's short-term financial situation was exceptional at the time of both the Lexus and the Prius conceptions, it challenged itself because of long-term future considerations. In fact, Toyota still had a crisis mentality, and Toyota leaders regularly stir the pot even creating a crisis when necessary.

It was Yoshiro Kimbara, then Executive VP of R&D, following Toyoda's lead, who founded Global 21 (G21)—the car that became the Prius. Kimbara led a project committee tasked with researching new cars for the 21st century. In its humble beginnings, the only real guidance was to develop a fuel-efficient, small-sized car—exactly the opposite of the bigger and bigger gas guzzlers that were selling at the time. In addition to the small size, a distinguishing feature of the original vision was a large, spacious cabin. Thus, it had to be small and efficient but feel big inside—a major design challenge from the start.

The Prius Blueprint

Risuke Kubochi, General Manager of General Engineering, stepped forward and agreed to lead the effort. He was formerly the chief engineer of Celica. He had a reputation for being aggressive and not terribly friendly, but strongly determined to accomplish any task he undertook. Kubochi personally selected 10 middle managers to work on his team. This working-level committee reported directly to a high-level committee of Toyota board members, informally known as *kenjinkai* ("committee of wise men"), that met weekly. The project had the highest-level executive sponsors from the very beginning.

At first the G21 project was not defined as a hybrid vehicle project. There were two goals:

1. Develop a new method for manufacturing cars for the 21st century.
2. Develop a new method of developing cars for the 21st century.

The committee's job was simply to identify the general concept, and it saw the first task as mainly a packaging issue—how to minimize vehicle size, yet maximize interior space. It also set a target for fuel economy. The then current engine in a basic Corolla got 30.8 mpg and the target was set at 50 percent more, 47.5 mpg. This was thought to be a groundbreaking target. Although the committee was aware of a hybrid engine project, they assumed it would not be ready in time for the G21. The committee members all had full-time jobs apart from the G21 and at first met weekly.

The committee began meeting in September 1993 and had just three months to present their concept to a high-level executive committee. About 30 people, including Executive VP Kimbara and member of the board Masumi Konishi, attended the meeting. Obviously three months was too short to build an actual prototype. But the committee was not satisfied simply presenting ideas, so they developed a half-scale blueprint for the vehicle that took up a good part of a wall.

One of the working-level members that Kubochi had selected was Sateshi Ogiso, who would be the only person who stayed with the Prius until its actual launch years later. The G21 as a clean sheet was a dream project for a young engineer. Ogiso had been charged with organizing the committee meetings and thus was given a kind of leadership role. At the design review session, Ogiso was about to prompt Kubochi to begin the presentation, but was stunned when Kubochi preempted him with "Ogiso, I would like you to make the report." Ogiso was just a 32-year-old youngster who had only recently made "engineer-in-charge." He quickly recognized that he had been tricked, which wasn't the first time that Kubochi had put him on the spot in order to cultivate his leadership ability. But he did an excellent job of giving the report, which was very favorably received by the executive committee. The requirements for the vehicle were identified as:

1. Roomy cabin space, achieved through maximizing the length of the wheelbase.
2. A relatively high seat position, to facilitate getting in and out of the car.
3. An aerodynamic exterior, with a 1500 mm height, a little less than a minivan.
4. A fuel economy of 20 kilometers per liter (47.5 mpg).
5. A small horizontally placed engine with a continuously variable automatic transmission (which improves fuel efficiency).

Phase I of this project illustrates three Toyota Way principles.

1. *Principle 9. Grow leaders who thoroughly understand the work, live the philosophy, and teach it to others.* We see how involved high-level executives are in a very abstract and future-oriented project that is seen as central to the future of the company—with active sponsorship, including weekly meetings with the study group.
2. *Principle 10. Develop exceptional people and teams who follow your company's philosophy.* We see how some of the best people step up to a challenging project that is seen as important to the company and then work extremely hard after hours to meet aggressive deadlines. They had three months as an extracurricular activity to do extensive research and develop a vision for the project. We also get a glimpse of how leaders at Toyota develop young people. Kubochi could have taken credit for leading this effort, but it was more important to provide a life lesson to Ogiso, who later reflected that "by being placed in the critical situation to give the presentation, I learned to organize issues in my head as I spoke, and acquired a sense of self-confidence" (Itazaki, 1999).
3. *Principle 12. Go and see for yourself to thoroughly understand the situation (genchi genbutsu).* The team felt uncomfortable presenting only abstract concepts so short of building an actual model, they did the next best thing—they developed a half-size blueprint so the executives could picture the actual vehicle.

An Unlikely Chief Engineer Invents a New Approach to Car Development

The next step was to develop a more detailed blueprint for the vehicle. High-level executives pondered who should lead the effort and settled on the unlikely choice of Takeshi Uchiyamada as the chief engineer. Uchiyamada hadn't been groomed to be a chief engineer and never even aspired to this role. His technical background was in test engineering and he had never worked in vehicle design. He had been assigned to "technical administration" and in fact led the reorganization of Toyota's product development organization into "vehicle development centers," the largest reorganization in its history. His intention after working in technical administration was to go back to research. Yet, here he was tagged by high-level executives to lead this program blessed by the chairman of the company.

While on the surface Toyota's decision to appoint Uchiyamada as chief engineer might at first glance seem hasty and illogical, in fact it followed Principle 13: *Make decisions slowly by consensus, thoroughly considering all options; implement rapidly (nemawashi).* In fact, Uchiyamada was uniquely qualified for the task for several reasons. First, this was the first project in decades that involved truly breakthrough technology and would need a level of research support uncharacteristic of most development projects. Uchiyamada came from research. While he was not a design engineer, he did love cars, had a very deep technical engineering background, and his father had been the chief engineer for the Crown—a flagship Toyota vehicle—so it was in his blood. Second, the project was not housed in one vehicle center and would require someone who had an excellent understanding of the new organization to marshal resources, which Uchiyamada possessed, having been one of the chief architects of the new, recently implemented organization structure. Third, a central purpose of the project was to develop a new approach to vehicle development. Someone who had been raised under the old system to be a chief engineer could be blinded by the current system. Someone with proven organizational design skills was needed to take a fresh look.

No one was more surprised by this decision than Uchiyamada. As he explained to me:

> As a chief engineer, if there are supplier problems it is the responsibility to visit the supplier and check the line and solve the problems. I did not even know what I was looking for to know what to do in many cases.... One of the personifications of the chief engineer is that they know everything, so even when developing different parts of the vehicle you know where the bolts can go together as well as what the customer wants.

So what could Uchiyamada do, since he did not "know everything"? He surrounded himself with a cross-functional team of experts and relied on the team.

One of the most important results of the Prius project from an organizational design perspective was the creation of the *obeya* system of vehicle development, which is now the new standard for Toyota. *Obeya* means "big room." It is like the control room. In the old vehicle development system, the chief engineer traveled about, meeting with people as needed to coordinate the program. For the Prius, Uchiyamada gathered a group of experts in the "big room" to review the progress of the program and discuss key decisions. The project team found a room outside the fray of normal day-to-day affairs, which became known for housing a weird, top-secret group (G21 project) endorsed by top management. During the development process, Uchiyamada documented in real time the experience of designing a new breakthrough design from scratch. This led to a very confidential 200-page document that can be reviewed only with special high-level permission. Toyota executives achieved their goal of reinventing the company's design process by intentionally selecting a non-expert chief engineer.

The 21st-Century Car: Environmentally Friendly, Conserving Natural Resources

Uchiyamada proved to be a creative leader, yet very focused on achieving aggressive timing targets. In fact, the more detailed conceptual blueprint was completed in just six months. Normally the first step in this phase would have been to develop a physical prototype. But Uchiyamada decided that if they quickly made a prototype they would get mired in the details of improving it. He wanted to thoroughly discuss multiple alternatives before narrowing in on a decision. My associates and I have termed this "set-based concurrent engineering" (discussed further in Chapter 19), in which sets of alternatives are broadly considered rather then focusing in on a single solution.[2] There were many examples of this set-based thinking throughout the Prius development.

In the early stages, the team was quickly bogged down in discussing technical details of power-train technology. Uchiyamada saw this as a problem. He called the team together and said, "Let's stop this. Let's stop focusing on hardware. We engineers tend to focus on hardware. However, what we need to do with this car is to focus on the 'soft' aspects, not the hardware. Let's forget everything about hardware and review from the beginning the concept of the car that we are trying to build from the ground up" (Itazaki, 1999). Uchiyamada then lead a brainstorming session of key concepts to describe characteristics of the 21st-century car. Several days later, after many keywords had been generated and discussed, they reduced the list to two key words that ended up driving all subsequent development: "natural resources" and "environment."

Automobiles account for about 20 percent of the carbon dioxide from all human sources, yet about one fourth of the world's population enjoys their benefits. The goal for the G21 was stated as a "small, fuel-efficient car." Ultimately, a hybrid engine was the key to the solution. An electric vehicle certainly would have been fuel-efficient and would have produced almost zero emissions, but it was not considered practical or convenient. You need a separate infrastructure to recharge the batteries, the distance between charges is short with the known technology, and the batteries that have the needed power are huge. The car would be a "battery carrier." Fuel cell technology, on the other hand, had great promise, but the technology was not nearly developed to the point of being viable and was possibly decades off.

Hybrid technology had a nice blend of fuel economy, low emissions, and practicality. The basic idea is to let the gas engine do what it does well and the battery-driven motor do what it does well, thus recapturing as much as possible the energy generated during driving and braking. Internal combustion engines are not very efficient at acceleration but are very efficient once a certain rpm level is reached. Electric motors are much more efficient at rapid acceleration. When gas engines are running, they can then recharge the batteries, so there is a harmony between the gas engine and the electric motor. In the most sophisticated hybrids, computers determine which of the two engines is most efficient, based on speed, road grade, number of passengers, and other variables. Even the energy used in braking can be recovered as electrical energy.

The Hybrid Gets a Push from the Top

At this point in 1994, the team still had rejected the notion of a hybrid engine. It was considered too new and risky technology. In September 1994, the team met with Executive VP Akihiro Wada and Managing Director Masanao Shiomi and the hybrid technology came up, but no conclusion was reached. The G21 group was given an additional task besides the continued development of the G21. They were asked to present the G21 as Toyota's concept vehicle for the Tokyo auto show in October 1995. This meant they had just a year to develop what would become the showcase product of the auto show.

When they met with Wada in November 1994, he casually said, "By the way, your group is also working on the new concept car for the Motor Show, right? We recently have decided to develop that concept as a hybrid vehicle. That way, it would be easy to explain its fuel economy" (Itazaki, 1999). Shortly after this, in another meeting with Wada and Shiomi near the end of 1994, the bar was set even higher. It seems they concluded a 50 percent fuel economy improvement was not enough for a 21st-century car. They wanted double the current fuel economy. Uchiyamada protested that this would be impossible with current engine technology, to which they replied, "Since you are already developing a hybrid vehicle for the Motor Show, there is no reason not to use a hybrid for the production model" (Itazaki, 1999).

It then became apparent to the team what these two executives were trying to do. They did not want to come out and order the team to make a hybrid. Instead, they warmed them up by requesting a hybrid that did not have to be a production model for the auto show. They then led them to the natural conclusion that a true 21st-century car had to have breakthrough fuel economy and thus a hybrid seemed the only practical alternative. Though this approach appears to go against the general spirit of Principle 8, *Use only reliable, thoroughly tested technology that serves your people and processes*, Toyota always wants to consider every new technology "thoroughly" and adapt it when it is appropriate. And the 21st-century car was about developing a breakthrough. At the time, the hybrid system already was a thoroughly considered technology. What was different for Toyota was that this technology hadn't yet been proven on a mass production basis. So, when Uchiyamada took up the challenge, he got one important concession from management: that he could select the finest engineers available within the company to work on the hybrid system.

Phase III: Accelerating the Development Project

From the time Uchiyamada agreed to develop a hybrid concept vehicle in November 1994 until the deadline for the auto show in October 1995, there was less than a year to develop at least a workable hybrid engine and the vehicle itself. With extreme time pressure, the temptation would be to make a very fast decision on the hybrid technology and get to work on it immediately. Instead the team reexamined all its options with painstaking thoroughness (illustrating Principle 13). They used a "set-based" approach, considering 80 hybrid types and systematically eliminating engines that did not meet the requirement, narrowing it down to 10 types. The team carefully considered the merits of each of these and then selected the best four. Each of these four types was then evaluated carefully through computer simulation. Based on these results, they were confident enough to propose one alternative to the G21 team in May 1995, just six months later.

Up to this point, the focus was on concept development and research into alternative technologies. Now there was a clear direction for the program and technology to build the first mass-production hybrid vehicle. Toyota's board could approve an actual budget, human resources, and a rough timeline. In June 1995, the Prius became an official development project. Since there was a great deal of new product technology as well as the task of developing a new manufacturing system, they developed a three-year plan. The first year would focus on developing a complete prototype. The second year would focus on working out the details through thorough research. The third year would focus on finalizing the production version and production preparation. Based on their best analysis, a stretch target of starting actual production the end of 1998 was forecast, with some cushion if needed to delay this until early 1999. They were very proud of their aggressive schedule.

A New President with a New Mission—Prius Leads the Way

But something important happened in August 1995. Toyota named a new president, Hiroshi Okuda, the first non-Toyoda family member to be the president in the history of the company. From the outside, he was viewed as unusual for the Toyota culture. Okuda was more overtly aggressive in his business dealings, including globalization. He also had a business background, rather than an engineering or manufacturing background, and seemed to call things as he saw them, in contrast to past presidents, who were more indirect and cautious in what they said. Such a big move obviously had a reason. It was clear that there were new challenges ahead to globalize and prepare for the 21st century.

While one might expect a non-engineer and a new executive who wants to put his imprint on the company to significantly change the direction and priorities of the company, Okuda stayed with Toyota's overall game plan. He just pursued it faster and more aggressively. In the case of the G21, he might have neglected it as the pet project of a former executive. Instead, he embraced it even more aggressively. When he asked Wada when the hybrid vehicle would be ready, Wada explained that they were aiming for December 1998, "if all goes well." Okuda said, "That is too late; no good. Can you get it done a year earlier? There will be great significance in launching the car early. This car may change the course of Toyota's future and even that of the auto industry" (Itazaki, 1999).

Wada and his team felt a great deal of pressure, but also renewed excitement, given Okuda's belief in the seminal importance of the project. The target was moved to December 1997.

At last the prototype Prius was publicly unveiled at the October 1995 Toyota auto show, and it was a hit. The team was energized. But they would need that energy to develop a true production hybrid vehicle, with a new target date less than two years away. Here they were, responsible for a highly advertised vehicle breaking new ground and there was no clay model and no styling design and they still needed to engineer all the major (and mostly new) systems of the vehicle.

The timing pressure was immense, but it did not push project leaders to cut corners. Uchiyamada refused to compromise even on a lower-risk approach. For example, there was a suggestion he use a hybrid-driven Camry for the first hybrid vehicle, since it was larger and could easily house the more complex engine and electric motor. The other advantage was that the difference in fuel economy between the existing model and the hybrid vehicle would be dramatic.

Uchiyamada rejected this suggestion, saying:

> *We are trying to build a car for the 21st century, and our work isn't about applying the hybrid system on existing models. If we take the conventional method of first trying out the system in a large car, we would end up making too many compromises in terms of cost and size. There would be less waste if we worked with a smaller car from the beginning.*

The Clay Model Freeze—15 Months to Go

Over the next few months, Uchiyamada worked closely with the styling studios, the artists of the industry, to design the Prius. Finally, in July 1996, Uchiyamada had a car to develop. Once a car style development process reaches this point, it is called a clay model freeze—though auto executives are notorious for making significant changes in the basic styling well after the so-called "freeze." Not so at Toyota. Toyota stands out in sticking to its decision on the vehicle styling at clay model freeze. It goes through an unusual degree of "thoroughness in decision making" (*nemawashi*) to make a good decision at this point.

Uchiyamada, who had never led a new car development program, had just 17 months from the July decision date to produce the Prius. The actual design review and formal approval by the board was in September, so from that point there was really only 15 months. In addition to developing the technology, Toyota had to develop and prepare a new manufacturing process, create a new sales plan to sell the Prius, and even prepare the service organization to service the vehicle. In 1996 the auto industry standard for developing vehicles, particularly in the U.S., was five to six years. But as early as 1982, Japanese auto companies were developing vehicles in 48 months. So when U.S. auto companies heard that Toyota was on an 18-month development cycle—from clay model to start of production—they were in awe. But the 18-month cycle in Toyota was typical for a variation of an existing model—and the breakthrough Prius had only 15 months.

Toyota engineers worked slavishly, canceling all vacations, to engineer the body based on the clay model selected in July. In September they made a formal presentation to the board, which approved it. From then on, the development of the vehicle was a marathon race to reach Okuda's target date of December 1997. In the mindset of Principle 10, *Develop exceptional people and teams who follow your company's philosophy*, everyone understood they had to make personal sacrifices to work on this project that was so visibly important to the company and had such aggressive goals and timing targets. As an example, Takehisa Yaegashi was a senior manager who had supervised many engine development projects and was personally recruited by a board member to lead the hybrid engine team. When he agreed, he immediately went home, explained the situation to his wife, and moved into the company dormitory to get away from all distractions.

The development process did not always go smoothly. Itazaki (1999) provides an engaging blow-by-blow description of the process, the numerous problems encountered, and the creative and even courageous resolution of these problems. For example, the battery driving the motor portion of the hybrid was a continual problem. A key requirement was to make the battery as small as possible so that the Prius would not be viewed as a "battery carrier," yet still have the power needed to meet the target of doubling the fuel efficiency of the car. In fact they needed to make the battery one-tenth the size of an electric vehicle battery. It turned out the battery was very sensitive to heat conditions and would shut down on hot days. It also shut down if the weather was too cold. Executives, including the president, were coming through on test drives, but the vehicle would shut down. A key part of the solution was to put the battery in the trunk, which was the most protected from heat and the easiest to keep cool. After struggling to resolve these and other battery-related problems, Toyota decided to start a joint venture company with Matsushita Electric called Panasonic EV Energy, with the idea of eventually selling the battery to other auto producers. Though Toyota felt a bit pushed into this partnership, it does not take partnerships lightly and took on the challenge characteristic of Principle 11: *Respect your extended network of partners and suppliers by challenging them and helping them improve.* Together, two corporate cultures managed to overcome their differences and blend into a viable, working company.

In 1997, one thousand Toyota engineers were feverishly working to make the December target for the start of mass production. But incredibly, Toyota still did not have a workable prototype. Normally, just before mass production, prototypes have been tested and work almost perfectly. In the case of the Prius, however, since R&D was being done simultaneously with product development, practically every new technical breakthrough required a new prototype car. And the new prototypes almost never ran properly the first time. This was very disturbing, as the young test engineers and production engineers had never seen a vehicle in such bad condition so close to launch. Senior engineers were feeling a sense of déjà vu from their early years at Toyota, when every vehicle launch program was like this.

Toyota president Okuda was not an engineer, but he was an exceptional manager and leader who understood how to motivate people. As December was approaching, he wanted to give the team a little push. The launch date for the Prius had been kept confidential and was known only inside the company. Conferring with Wada, they decided to make a public announcement in March. They knew that a public announcement would make it a matter of pride and social responsibility for Toyota's engineers to deliver on time. Okuda, in his speech to the press, stated:

> *Toyota has developed a hybrid system that is an answer to the environmental problems of the 21st century. It achieves a fuel economy that is twice that of*

conventional cars of the same class, emitting half as much CO_2. We would like to launch this car within this year.

Uchiyamada described to me his reaction:

In August 1995 I asked for more than three years for development. Mr. Okuda said we should launch at the end of 1997 and do your best. If it is impossible you can delay the launching time. So I said OK. But in the beginning of 1997 it was already publicly announced by Mr. Okuda that Toyota would come up with a hybrid. We had climbed the ladder and the ladder was taken out from under us. We actually worked 24 hours a day (two shifts), changing the people.

The Prius did launch on time. In fact, it launched in October 1997, two months ahead of the December target date, and the world's first mass production hybrid car was offered to the Japanese market, soon to be followed by a U.S. launch. The price was subsidized by Toyota, at an amazingly low two million yen in Japan, not much more than a Corolla, but Okuda knew that, as volumes increased and cost reduction opportunities were identified, they could make money at that price. At launch the Prius took first place in the two most prestigious automotive competitions in Japan, winning both the coveted "Japan Car of the Year" and "RJC New Car of the Year." Toyota was bombarded with inquires from potential customers and, the month after launch, orders for 3500 units had been received—over three times the monthly sales target. This was very unusual for a car costing two million yen and being sold at no discount. Worldwide sales since then have continued to grow, to over 120,000 units by early 2003. Toyota has 80 percent of the world hybrid market and has many hybrid vehicles in development.

Critics of Toyota's heavy investment in Prius, estimated to be in the hundreds of millions to $1 billion, have questioned the return on investment. Koji Endo, an equity analyst of Credit Suisse First Boston in Tokyo estimates Toyota must sell 300,000 hybrids annually to pay off the investment. Toyota is not there yet.[3] The second generation Prius came out in 2003 as a substantial improvement over the first in styling and fuel economy going from 48 mpg to 55 mpg. Advanced sales greatly exceeded expectations. And a hybrid version of the Lexus RX330 will only add to the sales and payback on investment.

But the goals of the Prius were farther-reaching than short-term profitability. One benefit for society was the opening of a mass market for more environment-friendly cars. A J.D. Power study late in 2002 found 60 percent of those surveyed in the U.S. would "definitely" or "strongly" consider buying a hybrid. J.D. Power forecasts demand to reach 500,000 per year by 2006 and to keep rising. For Toyota, a benefit was the development of young engineers who now understand what it takes to develop new technology (Principle 10: *Develop exceptional people and teams who follow your company's philosophy*"). Toyota also developed new technical capabilities in hybrid engines through the Prius and is now selling key components to other manufacturers. Finally, it made fundamental innovations in its product development process that are being used for all vehicle development. By this measure, the returns on the Prius project are priceless and the investment is almost trivial. The importance of the Prius was the learning. Toyota employees knocked themselves out to do it their way, in house, and develop knowledge and new capabilities along the way.

Toyota's New Product Development Process

The seemingly impossible deadlines set by top leadership for the Prius project and the numerous technical challenges faced by the Prius engineers dramatically improved Toyota's already excellent product development process in two key ways:

1. *The cross-functional team and chief engineer work together almost daily in the same room* (obeya). In Toyota's traditional approach, in the planning phase the chief engineer comes up with a concept, discusses it with the design groups and planning groups, and formulates a concrete plan as a result of joint discussion with those groups. With the Prius, a team of specialists from the various design, evaluation, and manufacturing functional groups sat in a big room with the chief engineer and made decisions in real time. Joining that group were not only the design engineers, but the production engineers as well so they could have discussions together. To assist these discussions, computer-assisted design (CAD) terminals were put into the room and it became known as "*obeya*" (big room). The *obeya* serves two purposes—information management and on-the-spot decision making. The *nemawashi* process can take a great deal of time to make decisions, but in *obeya* the right players are there to make decisions on the spot. There are many visual management tools (Principle 7) in the *obeya*—drawings of vehicles and schedules with checkpoints, so team members can quickly see where they are in every aspect of the program.

How often are people in the room? "It varies," according to Uchiyamada, "but usually once every two days at least the whole team assembles there. One day for the *obeya* and the other day the chief engineer is in his own separate office. *Obeya* is the war room." Before the Prius project, the chief engineer as an individual controlled everything, but with *obeya* a cross-functional team now controls the program. Since the Prius, the *obeya* system has evolved and is now a standard part of Toyota's development process.

2. *Simultaneous engineering.* Manufacturing and production engineers are now involved very early in the design process—working with design engineers at the concept development stage, to give input on manufacturing issues. This level of cooperation at such an early stage is unusual in the auto industry. Toyota had been

incorporating simultaneous engineering for several years before the Prius. But Uchiyamada intensified it. Because so much was new and because of the intense time pressures, there was unparalleled cooperation across divisions and between design and manufacturing for the Prius.

As a result of these innovations, along with innovations in the use of computer technology, Toyota's product development process is now routinely down to 12 months or less for derivative vehicles in Japan, an impressive feat, considering that most competitors require twice this long. But the cornerstone of Toyota's product development system is not computers or organizational changes. The cornerstone is still the chief engineer and the Toyota Way principles he and Toyota's engineers live out in their work. According to Uchiyamada:

> *The role of the chief engineer has not changed too much. The personality of the CE and getting people to cooperate continues to be very important. The personality and perseverance and the ability of the CE really determine the success of the car.*

Other Toyota Way Principles from the Prius Story

Notably missing from my recounting of this story are Principles 2-6 of the Toyota Way (under the category, *The Right Process Will Produce the Right Results*). These deal more with the processes used at Toyota to do the detailed work. These principles (creating flow, leveling the work load, stopping the process to ensure high quality, standardization) are central to product development and to the development of these breakthrough vehicles. They were the details of the day-to-day process that allowed the Prius to be completed in record time once the G21 group had settled on the technical concept.

Other key Toyota Way principles that can be seen in the stories of the Lexus and the Prius include the following.

Principle 1. Base your management decisions on a long-term philosophy, even at the expense of short-term financial goals. Both the Lexus and the Prius projects were long-term investments in the future of the company. At the time the Prius project was initiated, nobody knew whether hybrid vehicles would go anywhere. But Toyota decided to be the first and bet that hybrids would be an investment in the future. The best people with active support from the very top of the company were assigned to the Prius and they all felt like they were working on a project that was critical to the future of the company. Similarly, who knew whether the Lexus could successfully penetrate the luxury market dominated by European prestige? Investing in the future, not short-term profits, was the focus of these projects.

Principle 9. Grow leaders who thoroughly understand the work, live the philosophy, and teach it to others. Both of these programs were driven by leaders who were absolutely committed to the success of the programs. In general, chief engineers epitomize the leadership philosophy of Toyota. They grow up in the system, starting with the most basic engineering work and only gradually, after 15-20 years of engineering practice, getting project management responsibility. They are selected because of their combination of technical skills and leadership abilities developed through these years of experience. They seem to fit the "this yet that" philosophy of Suzuki at work in the development of Lexus. They are leaders, yet they are also exceptional engineers. They are visionaries with a broad perspective, yet they understand the development of the vehicle down to the tiniest detail. They are independent thinkers doing what they believe is best for the customer and the product, yet they are experts at working the Toyota network and can garner all the resources and approvals needed. They do a lot of work as individuals that other managers might delegate, yet they are able to motivate all those who touch the project to do exceptional engineering work that at first seems impossible.

Principle 13. Make decisions slowly by consensus, thoroughly considering all options; implement rapidly (nemawashi). It's clear that the chief engineers are target-driven and timing-driven, yet always willing to step back and reflect on the range of options that are available. One thing remarkable about both the Lexus and the Prius is the "no-compromise" attitude of the chief engineers. At some point, with the intense time pressure to do a seemingly impossible job, one would expect the leader to say, "OK, let's pick a direction and just get on with it." But repeatedly throughout the Prius development, Uchiyamada would step back and say, "Let's stop and reflect" (*hansei*). "Let's rethink what this project is about." "Let's test every possible design for a hybrid engine in the world." "Let's have a design competition and get all the styling studios to generate competitive designs" (as discussed in Chapter 19). Suzuki decided to do what had never been done in engine technology, aerodynamics, and fuel economy through experimenting and trying new ideas. These do not seem to be the things a rational person does to get a job done quickly. But central to the Toyota Way is thorough consideration in decision making. It is not acceptable to quickly choose a direction and go racing off in that direction. Exploring all possible alternatives and considering pros and cons of each while consulting all partners who have something to offer allows Toyota to execute fast, once a decision is finally made, without backtracking to remake decisions.

Is Toyota a conservative company? Yes. Does it seem to be very plodding and slow to make changes? Yes, certain types of changes. Is it innovative? Remarkably so. In this regard, Toyota itself is another of Suzuki's "yets." Go slow, build on the past, and thoroughly consider all implications of decisions, yet move aggressively to beat the competition to market with exceptional products that break the mold. This is the Toyota Way.

Notes

1. The Prius case is based on an interview with Takeshi Uchiyamada, Chief Engineer of the original Prius, and a book on Prius written by a Japanese journalist, *The Prius That Shook the World: How Toyota Developed the World's First Mass-Production Hybrid Vehicle*, by Hideshi Itazaki, translated by A. Yamada and M. Ishidawa (Tokyo: The Kikkan Kogyo Shimbun, Ltd., 1999).

2. Allen C. Ward, Jeffrey K. Liker, John J. Cristiano, and Durward K. Sobek II, "The Second Toyota Paradox: How Delaying Decisions Can Make Better Cars Faster," *Sloan Management Review,* Vol. 36, No. 3, Spring 1995, pp. 43-61.

2. John L. Bloomberg, electronic newsletter, September 29, 2003.

Part Two

The Business Principles of the Toyota Way

Section I

Long-Term Philosophy

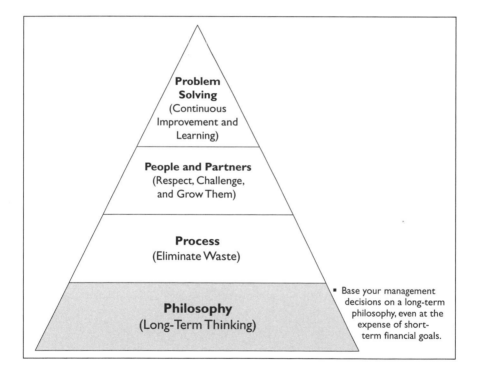

Chapter 7

Principle 1:
Base Your Management Decisions on a Long-Term Philosophy, Even at the Expense of Short-Term Financial Goals

The most important factors for success are patience, a focus on long-term rather than short-term results, reinvestment in people, product, and plant, and an unforgiving commitment to quality.
—Robert B. McCurry, former Executive V.P., Toyota Motor Sales

In the last few decades, the world has been moving in the direction of capitalism as the dominant socio-economic system. The prevailing belief is that if individuals and companies pursue their self-interests, supply and demand will magically lead to innovation, economic growth, and overall economic well-being for humanity. While it is comforting to think we can all simply do what is best for our short-term economic interests and all will be well in the world, there is a dark side to the pursuit of self-interest as the engine for economic growth. We see it with Enron and other scandals and the aftermath of extreme distrust of large corporations and the morality of corporate executives. We see it when there is an economic downturn and millions of people are thrown out of their jobs to fend for themselves.

A Mission Greater than Earning a Paycheck

Can a modern corporation thrive in a capitalistic world and be profitable while doing the right thing, even if it means that short-term profits are not always the first goal? I believe that Toyota's biggest contribution to the corporate world is that of providing a real-life example that this is possible.

Throughout my visits to Toyota in Japan and the United States, in engineering, purchasing, and manufacturing, one theme stands out. Every person I have talked with has a sense of purpose greater than earning a paycheck. They feel a greater sense of mission for the company and can distinguish right from wrong with regard to that mission. They have learned the Toyota Way from their Japanese *sensei* (mentors) and the message is consistent: *Do the right thing for the company, its employees, the customer, and society as a whole.* Toyota's strong sense of mission and commitment to its customers, employees, and society *is the foundation for all the other principles* and the missing ingredient in most companies trying to emulate Toyota.

When I interviewed Toyota executives and managers for this book, I asked them why Toyota existed as a business. The responses were remarkably consistent. For example, Jim Press, Executive Vice President and C.O.O. of Toyota Motor Sales in North America and one of two American Managing Directors of Toyota, explained:

> *The purpose of the money we make is not for us as a company to gain, and it's not for us as associates to see our stock portfolio grow or anything like that. The purpose is so we can reinvest in the future, so we can continue to do this. That's the purpose of our investment. And to help society and to help the community, and to contribute back to the community that we're fortunate enough to do business in. I've got a trillion examples of that.*

This is not to say that Toyota does not care about cutting costs. Shortly after World War II, Toyota nearly went bankrupt, which led to the resignation of the company founder—Kiichiro Toyoda. Toyota pledged to become debt-free. Cost reduction has been a passion since Taiichi Ohno began eliminating wasted motions on the shop floor. Often this led to removing a worker from a line or cell, to be placed in another job so one less worker had to be hired in the future. Toyota now has a rigorous "Total Budget Control System" in which monthly data is used to monitor the budgets of all the divisions down to the tiniest expenditure.

I asked many of the Toyota managers I interviewed if cost reduction is a priority and they just laughed. Their answers amounted to "You haven't seen anything until you've experienced the cost-consciousness of Toyota—down to pennies." Yet cost reduction is not the underlying principle that drives Toyota. For example, Toyota would no sooner fire its employees because of a temporary downturn in sales than most of us would put our sons and daughters out on the street because our stock investments went bad. Toyota executives understand their place in the history of the company. They are working within a long-term philosophical mission to bring the company to the next level. The company is like an organism nurturing itself, constantly protecting and growing its offspring, so that it can continue to grow and stay strong. In this day and age of cynicism about the ethics of corporate officers and the place of large capitalistic corporations in civilized society, the Toyota Way provides an alternative model of what happens when you align almost 250,000 people to a common purpose that is bigger than making money. Toyota's starting point in business is to generate value for the customer, society, and the economy.

Doing the Right Thing for the Customer

I asked Jim Press how he learned the Toyota Way. He explained that the reason he joined the company was partly to move on from an environment at Ford where there was constant tension between doing business the way it should be done and the way it actually was done. When he went to a social event, he avoided telling people he worked for Ford. He explained:

> *People told me all the problems with their Ford cars and I had seen the end result when working in a service department of a Ford dealership. One job I had was driving a Thunderbird before it was shipped, and I could tell how badly the customers were going to complain. Intuitively I knew that was not right.*
>
> *In contrast, Toyota is aligned around satisfying the customer. It felt like I finally had found a home. The learning process was from the people I worked with from Japan. The executive coordinators from Japan really were here not only to guide the company's development but the development of the people. The environment allowed you to do business the way you knew it should be done. Toyota was a company that did not say it, they did it. We saw it firsthand.*

Press described an early example of Toyota's commitment to doing the right thing for the customer during the "Nixon shock" of 1971. President Nixon had imposed an import surcharge and also the yen was starting to float.

> *We had in dealerships at any one given time three different prices for the same car—three dealer costs, three different MSRPs. You went into three dealerships and there were three 1971 Coronas, the same color, same specs, with three different prices. The dealers had paid three different dealer costs. It was a mess. We were a very young company then. Finally, Nixon's import surcharge was reversed, but the government did not pay us back. We still went back and paid every customer and dealer for all that extra tax they had paid on cars they purchased from us. We lost money. But we did it to satisfy the customer and to gain their long-term interest in us .... We were the only company that did it. We got approval from Japan and it was not a time when we were real rich, either. We struggled to make payroll.*

Jim Press then fast-forwards to Lexus in 1996-1997:

> *We wanted to have a distinctive Lexus-like ride and wanted to break new ground in ride quality. To get that, our tire compounds were fairly soft. And*

so even though the customers experienced a good ride and the tires were well within our specs, they did not last as long initially as many customers wished. I think 5-7 percent of the customers actually complained about tire life. To us that is a big deal, as we are used to dealing in complaint levels of far less than 1 percent. So we sent the owners of every Lexus where these tires were specified a coupon they could redeem for $500 and apologized if they had any inconvenience with their tires and felt that they wore out early. Many of these were customers who had already sold their cars. The way you treat the customer when you do not owe them anything, like how you treat somebody who cannot fight back—that is the ultimate test of character.

The NUMMI Story: Building Trust with Employees

In the early 1980s, Toyota formed a joint venture with GM. It was Toyota's first overseas plant and they did not want to go it alone. They agreed to teach GM the principles of the Toyota Production System (TPS). Toyota proposed to take over a light truck factory in Fremont, California that had been closed by GM in 1982 and run it according to the principles of the Toyota Way. Dennis Cuneo, now Senior VP of Toyota Motor Manufacturing North America, was an attorney for Toyota at the time. He explains:

The perception that everybody had at that time was that the Toyota Production System just worked people to death. It was just basically "Speed up!" In fact, I remember the first meeting we had in the union hall with union leadership and there was this gentleman by the name of Gus Billy. He was sitting at the end of the table and we were talking about the Toyota Production System and kaizen, etc. He said, "It sounds like a production speed-up to me. It's the whole concept of making all these suggestions, trying to suggest your way out of a job."

This was not an isolated hostile attitude. Even when the plant had been run by GM, the union local had the reputation of being militant, to the point of calling illegal wildcat strikes. Nevertheless, when Toyota took over management of the plant, against the advice of GM, Toyota decided to bring back the UAW local—and bring back the specific individuals who represented this UAW local in the plant. Cuneo says:

I think it surprised GM. Some of the labor relations staff advised us not to. We took a calculated risk. We knew that the former GM workforce needed leadership—and the Shop Committee comprised the natural leaders of that workforce. We had to change their attitudes and opinions. So we sent the shop committee to Japan for three weeks. They saw firsthand what the TPS was all about. And they came back "converted" and convinced a skeptical rank and file that this Toyota Production System wasn't so bad.

In fact, under Toyota's new management, when the old factory reopened in 1984, it surpassed all of GM's plants in North America in productivity, quality, space, and inventory turns. It is often used as an example of how TPS can be successfully applied in a unionized U.S. plant with workers who had grown up learning the traditional culture of General Motors and the traditional adversarial relationships between union and management. Cuneo says the key was building trust with the workers:

> *We built trust early on with our team members. GM had problems selling the Nova in 1987 to '88, and they substantially cut the orders to our plant. We had to reduce production and were running at about 75 percent capacity, but we didn't lay anybody off. We put people on kaizen teams and found other useful tasks for them. Of all the things we did at NUMMI, that did the most to establish trust.*

According to Cuneo, GM's initial motivation for entering the venture was to outsource production of a small car. As GM learned more about the TPS, they became more interested in using NUMMI as a learning laboratory. Hundreds of General Motors executives, managers, and engineers have come through the doors of NUMMI, only to be transformed by the teachings of TPS by the time they returned to GM. I have visited GM plants in the U.S. and China and the bible for manufacturing is a version of the Toyota Production System first written by Mike Brewer, an early "alum" of NUMMI sent by GM to learn TPS. GM's "Global Manufacturing System" is a direct copy of the Toyota Production System.

Unfortunately, it took about 15 years for GM to take the lessons of NUMMI seriously. When they began to take it seriously, it took GM about five years before they really began to see improved productivity and quality, corporate wide (as seen in the auto industry's *Harbour Reports* and customer surveys by J.D. Powers and *Consumer Reports*).

You may be asking, "Why would Toyota teach their coveted lean manufacturing system to a major competitor, GM?" There were lots of different motivations for starting the joint venture. But at least one consideration was that Toyota realized GM was the world's largest carmaker and was struggling in its manufacturing operations. By helping to raise the level of manufacturing at GM, they were helping society and the community, as well as creating high-paying manufacturing jobs for Americans. The senior executives at Toyota speak of giving back something to the U.S. for the help they provided Japan to rebuild its industry after World War II. This is not mere lip service or pie-in-the-sky idealism. They really believe it.

Don't Let Business Decisions Undermine Trust and Mutual Respect

Toyota understands that maintaining the jobs of associates is part of its obligation to the community and society. A great example of this is the case of Toyota's longest-running manufacturing operation in the United States—a truck bed plant called TABC.

In the 1960s the U.S. imposed a 30 percent surcharge on trucks that were imported, called the "chicken tax." It was in retaliation for Europeans refusing to import poultry. To get around this duty tax, most foreign companies imported trucks without the truck beds and the truck was then considered a part rather than a truck. They imported the bed separately, which was also a part, and bolted the truck and bed together at the port. Toyota also wanted to avoid the duty, but decided to build the truck beds in the U.S., partly because it would also contribute to local employment. They chose Long Beach, California, because it was near the port where Toyota trucks entered the U.S.

TABC was actually the first U.S. company to seriously and successfully apply TPS and today it has 600 employees. In June 2002 TABC celebrated its 30th anniversary in Long Beach. But the celebration could have been a dismal affair, because in 2001 Toyota decided to move the truck bed business to a new factory in Mexico. This sounds like a familiar corporate scenario of chasing low-wage Mexican labor. However, this story ends differently, because Toyota was following the Toyota Way principles. Toyota had a variety of reasons for wanting a Mexican truck bed plant, including building vehicles where they were being sold and avoiding tougher environmental laws for paint in California that required major new investments to their U.S. facility. I'll let Cuneo explain what Toyota did and why they didn't lay anyone off.

> That Long Beach plant's 30 years old; it's landlocked. Who's keeping California manufacturing facilities open, right? Many companies are looking for an excuse to shut down their California facilities. But we and our top management in Japan recognized that the TABC workforce has performed well. With limited resources, they've really implemented TPS. It would be unfair and send the wrong message to the team members at our other plants to penalize a workforce that has done everything we've asked of them. So we're finding additional work for TABC. During my stay at NUMMI back in the late '80s, GM closed its Norwood plant here in Cincinnati, which was a pretty productive plant. They were building Firebirds and Camaros and they shipped all that production to their Van Nuys plant because it made short-term economic sense. I remember some of the GM guys at NUMMI who later lamented, "Here we had this Norwood plant that had really improved pro-

ductivity, etc., and what did we do? We shut them down." And so, when you're asking team members on the line to give you a hundred percent, to find ways to add more content to the job to improve productivity, what do they get in return? And if what they get in return is a weekly wage but a pink slip as soon as we have a downturn, it's hard to engender that trust and mutual respect that you need. So you can't just say human resources are our most important asset; you have to walk the talk every day. And people really watch what you do, rather than listen to what you say. That's the Toyota System. It goes back to this whole concept of stakeholders. If the financial analysts on Wall Street were the primary stakeholders for Toyota, we couldn't do something like that. It's just a big difference in philosophy. It's always been that way with Toyota.

My interview with Cuneo was in February 2002, when it was not clear how Toyota was going to keep the TABC plant open, though Toyota was committed to finding new work. By June the plant was celebrating its 30th anniversary and its new business venture with Hino Motors, an affiliated company partly owned by Toyota. Instead of closing it down, Toyota has helped TABC expand its operations to build new trucks, making it the first new vehicle assembly operation to build trucks in California since NUMMI opened in 1984. An article reporting on the celebration noted, "At today's anniversary celebration, TABC also presented checks for $2,000 each to ten area organizations as a way to thank the community for its part in the company's 30-year success. In addition, the company recognized ten TABC team members who have been with the company since its start-up in 1972."[1]

So instead of 600 laid-off workers collecting unemployment, the company was celebrating and giving money away to community organizations. Toyota has since given TABC additional responsibility for manufacturing 68,000 four-cylinder engines per year for the Tacoma truck—to a plant in California with its high cost of doing business. For most companies, this makes absolutely no sense, based on short-term economic logic. But Toyota was practicing Principle 1: *Base your management decisions on a long-term philosophy, even at the expense of short-term financial goals.* Toyota wasn't measuring this investment in terms of quarterly budgets; it was measuring it in the ongoing respect the customer and its employees have for their company and products. And, of course, through TPS Toyota knew this sophisticated and committed workforce could build in quality and continue to eliminate waste. Toyota believes this is what drives profits in the long run.

Here's another example of Toyota's deep sense of responsibility to the community, from a conversation I had with Cuneo:

Dennis: "I just got a note two days ago from one of our Senior Managing Directors in Japan about odor complaints from a couple of homeowners who lived close to our Georgetown [Kentucky] plant. These houses were close to the plant and should have been purchased when we originally built the plant. Recently we set aside some money to buy those houses. The homeowners were using the odor complaints as negotiating leverage. Once the news of odor complaints reached Japan, we received a note from a Senior Managing Director asking us what we planned to do about the complaints. Our policy is zero violations—this was simply a complaint to gain negotiating leverage. So I had to explain the difference between a complaint and a violation."

Jeff: "That's a couple of houses?"

Dennis: "Yeah, two houses."

Jeff: "Two houses and the Managing Directors write a letter?"

Dennis: "Two guys are really complaining 'cause they want to get a higher price for their property. So I have a senior managing director writing us a note saying, 'Here's our policy: zero violations.' I mean, what's that tell you?"

Jeff: "I can throw out a number of hypotheses. One is that to some degree that is Japanese. The Japanese are very concerned about harmony, disharmony. To some degree there's almost a paranoia about any problem in the United States because of potential tensions with the government. On the other hand, I could attribute it to more of a value system. Where do you think it falls out there?"

Dennis: "Value system. Of course, you want to avoid regulatory and legal issues, but this goes more to the value system. We, Toyota, have made this commitment to the environment. Our policy is zero violations. That's one of our eight global performance indicators, along with quality, productivity, etc."

You may question the purity of Toyota's motives. Surely a Japanese company that has penetrated such a major part of the U.S. market had to be concerned about political repercussions of any negative publicity. But Toyota's zero violations policy goes beyond purely political motives. Toyota executives really try to do the right thing.

Use Self-Reliance and Responsibility to Decide Your Own Fate

One of my favorite discussions of the history of the development of the Japanese automobile industry is a book by Michael Cusumano, *The Japanese Automobile Industry* (Cusumano, 1985), that contrasts in detail the evolution of Nissan and the evolution of Toyota. In his book, Cusumano clearly illustrates the different trajectories of the two companies.

One of the key differences is that Toyota always chose a path of self-reliance and "let's do it ourselves," rather than relying on outside business partners. For example, when Toyota wanted to get into the luxury car business, it didn't buy BMW. Instead it created its own luxury division, Lexus, from scratch, in order to learn and understand for itself the essence of a luxury car (in the *genchi genbutsu* spirit).

Like the small farmers of old who had to build their own houses, repair their own equipment, and creatively solve all their own problems, Toyota Motor Company started small with few resources. Everyone had to chip in on every activity and do what was necessary to engineer and build a car. In fact, in the 1930s the president of Toyoda Automatic Loom, Kodama Risaburo, thought the automotive business was risky and was reluctant to invest all but minimal capital in the new venture (Cusumano, 1985). So the Toyota automobile company had to learn to make everything for itself.

While many companies can claim to value self-reliance, Toyota actually lives this philosophy on a corporate institutional level. Toyota Motor Company founder, Kiichiro Toyoda, said:

> My father was not educated. The only strength he had was to believe in one thing all the way: that the Japanese have latent capabilities. The automatic loom was the product of this conviction.

Kiichiro, son of Sakichi and the first president of Toyota Motor Company, carried on the tradition of his father's self-reliant philosophy. In the 1920s he was an engineering student, but not just an engineering student going to class and passing tests. Like his father, he actually invented things, and by 1926-1928 he was inventing processes to build a car. Jim Press, a Toyota history buff, explains how this "do-it-yourself" philosophy played out in the new car company led by Kiichiro:

> Toyota's orientation from the very beginning was anybody could go hire a mechanic and hire an engineer and hire this and buy that. Toyota's view was that before they could build a car, they needed to perfect new revolutionary processes to build a mold, to build an engine, to go back to that level. And that's what makes the company different. Going back to the essence.

Later, when other Japanese automakers were willing to buy kits from U.S. car-makers and assemble knockoffs of their vehicles, Toyota chose to design and build its own cars, drawing on pieces of designs from a variety of U.S. vehicles. In fact, Toyota was the first automobile company in Japan to develop vehicles without technical assistance agreements with the more advanced automobile companies in Europe and the U.S. It didn't want to be dependent on outside assistance.

In both a physical and psychological sense, Toyota is somewhat isolated from the rest of Japan. Toyota City is almost in the middle of nowhere. To get there requires going to Nagoya, a major though not central city in Japan. Then a long train ride and finally a taxi will get you to Toyota headquarters. Even now, with Toyota and its suppliers populating the landscape, there is a rural flavor. And Toyota executives proudly proclaim themselves unsophisticated country bump-kins. Mikio Kitano, formerly President of Toyota Motor Manufacturing Kentucky and a director of the company at the time I visited his office, had a huge stuffed animal gorilla in his office. He described himself to me as an ape—not like the sophisticates of Tokyo.

At Toyota the companion to self-reliance is responsibility for its own successes and failures. In *Toyota Way 2001* it states: "We strive to decide our own fate. We act with self-reliance, trusting in our own abilities. We accept responsibility for our conduct and for maintaining and improving the skills that enable us to produce added value."

Toyota's Mission Statement and Guiding Principles

We get a flavor of what distinguishes Toyota from excerpts of its mission statement for its North American operations compared with that of Ford (Figure 7-1). Ford's mission statement seems reasonable. The company is concerned about being a leader in its products and services and wants to continually improve these to pros-per as a business and provide a "reasonable return" to its stockholders—"the own-ers" of the business.

In contrast, Toyota does not mention stockholders, even though at this time it was listed on the New York Stock Exchange. It does not even mention the qual-ity of its products even though we know that is a passion within Toyota. The pur-

Toyota Motor Manufacturing North America MISSION	Ford Motor Company MISSION
1. As an American company, contribute to the economic growth of the *community* and the United States.	1. Ford is a worldwide leader in automotive and automotive-related products and services as well as in newer industries such as aerospace, communications, and financial services.
2. As an independent company, *contribute to the stability* and *well-being of team members*.	2. Our mission is to *improve continually* our products and services to meet our customer's needs, allowing us to prosper as a business and to *provide a reasonable return* to our stockholders, the owners of our business.
3. As a Toyota group company, contribute to the *overall growth of Toyota* by adding value to our customers.	

Figure 7-1. Toyota's mission versus Ford's

pose of Toyota is *not* to make a quality product that will sell well and make money for owners. That is a requirement in order to achieve the mission. The true mission, according to this statement, has three parts:

1. Contribute to the economic growth of the country in which it is located (external stakeholders).
2. Contribute to the stability and well being of team members (internal stakeholders).
3. Contribute to the overall growth of Toyota.

The poignant message is that the company must enhance the growth of society or it cannot contribute to its external or internal stakeholders. This is its *reason* for making excellent products. Toyota challenges its workers to contribute to Toyota and make a place in its history. Toyota genuinely wants its associates to grow and learn, to invest in long-term technologies, and create lasting customer satisfaction with the goal of getting repeat business for life.

Another look at Toyota's guiding principles comes from the following internal document (see Figure 7-2). It was revised after Toyota's global expansion, to emphasize the company's responsibility as a global citizen. The principles here accurately express Toyota's feeling of responsibility to its business partners for stable, long-term growth, and *mutual* benefits.

---

1. **Honor** the language and spirit of the law of every nation and undertake open and fair corporate activities to be a good corporate citizen of the world.
2. **Respect** the culture and customs of every nation and contribute to economic and social development through corporate activities in the communities.
3. **Dedicate** ourselves to providing clean and safe products and to enhancing the quality of life everywhere through all our activities.
4. **Create** and develop advanced technologies and provide outstanding products and services that fulfill the needs of customers worldwide.
5. **Foster** a corporate culture that enhances individual creativity and teamwork value, while honoring mutual trust and respect between labor and management.
6. **Pursue** growth in harmony with the global community through innovative management.
7. **Work** with business partners in research and creation to achieve stable, long-term growth and mutual benefits, while keeping ourselves open to new partnerships.

Figure 7-2. Guiding principles at Toyoto Motor Corporation

Unfortunately most companies still suffer from short-term myopia. I give presentations about Toyota throughout the world, and I often get questions that make perfect sense for companies whose only goal is today's profits. Examples include:

- Will Toyota still use JIT if there is a major disaster that shuts down the supply chain?
- Doesn't Toyota lay off employees when business is bad for a particular product in a plant?
- If Toyota does not lay off employees, what do they do with them?
- Now that Toyota is listed on the New York Stock Exchange, aren't they more concerned about quarterly earnings?
- How does Toyota cost justify investments in technology for "quick changeover" and "right-sized equipment" to create one-piece flow?

The answer to all these shortsighted questions is simply that Toyota's business decisions are driven by its philosophies. It will not abandon them at the drop of a hat. The only way it will change its philosophies of manufacturing, investment, and managing people is if there is a fundamental shift in the world that threatens its long-term survival … after very thorough analysis. The philosophies discussed in this chapter did not grow up overnight and Toyota will not drop them overnight. John Shook, reflecting back on what he learned as a manager at Toyota, explains this well:

> Toyota intuited many years ago that it must focus on survival and the integration of all corporate functions toward ensuring that survival. TPS, then, is the result of efforts to direct all activities to support the goal of firm survival. This is vastly different from the narrow goal of "making money," though in most micro-instances of actual work performance, they may appear to be virtually the same thing …. I posit here that Toyota has evolved the most effective form of industrial organization ever devised. At the heart of that organization is a focus on its own survival. It is this focus that enables Toyota to behave as a natural organism, enabling it to evolve as a truly emergent system. (Shook, 2002)

Create a Constancy of Purpose and Place in History

When I think about Toyota and how it operates, I keep on coming back to quality guru W. Edwards Deming's famous edict: "Constancy of purpose." Constancy of purpose explains why, in any given year, if you bet Toyota will make a profit, you will probably win. If you bet that its sales will grow over the year before, you will probably win. You will not see huge growth spurts from one year to the next or major shifts in strategy. You will not see boardroom coups where a new regime takes over and remakes the company. Rather, you will see a slow and steady movement forward year in and year out. This is "constancy of purpose," as I believe Deming envisioned it, that goes beyond short-term profits and enriching a few executives. The Toyota Way is about adding value to customers, employees, and society. It provides a framework for Toyota to make short-term and long-term decisions, and it rallies employees around a shared purpose that is bigger than any of them.

The Gutting of Chrysler's Culture: A Cautionary Tale

Anyone who witnessed the rebirth of Chrysler under Lee Iacocca knows that one of the best product decisions he made was to invest in the K-Car, the basis for all the new passenger cars introduced in the 1980s. It saved the company from ruin. Then, in the 1990s, he was willing to step back and allow some remarkable leaders like Bob Eaton and Tom Stallkamp and Bob Lutz and François Castaing to reshape the company. A major focus was in product development, where vehicle centers (modeled after Honda) were created to realign the old functional organization into a product-driven organization. Engineers responsible for electrical components, body engineering, chassis engineering, and manufacturing engineering were all put together under one general manager, who took a role something like the Toyota chief engineer. These groups had a single focus—produce excellent vehicles that customers will want to buy at a low cost so Chrysler could make a profit. This led to the LH series of vehicles (Chrysler Concorde, Dodge Intrepid, etc.), a modernized minivan, the Neon, an award-winning new Jeep Grand Cherokee, and even the quirky but popular PT Cruiser. Each general manager was learning from the last one and the organization, at least in product development, was getting stronger and stronger. In the meantime, Tom Stallkamp was revolutionizing purchasing and creating what a *Harvard Business Review* article called an "American *keiretsu*" (Dyer, 1996). Chrysler soon became the world's most profitable car company in terms of profit per vehicle—not the biggest, but the most profitable per vehicle.

Toyota was actually concerned by these developments. Up to that point, no U.S. company had shown signs of getting it right and developing a culture that could compete with Toyota. But Chrysler was beginning to get it right.

Fortunately for Toyota, Chrysler was bought by Daimler. Chrysler's renaissance proved to be just another flash-in-the-pan threat that would vanish as quickly as it appeared. By 2000, Chrysler was again on the verge of bankruptcy and scrambling to simply break even. What happened?

The merger of Daimler and Chrysler was initially portrayed as a cooperative venture of equals that would learn the best of the best from each other. Soon it became obvious this was an out-and-out takeover. Of course, in any takeover there is a cleansing of the old guard who resist change—so out the door went all of these fine leaders who were starting to truly build something. And out the door went what they were trying to build, until all that mattered was short-term cost cutting to regain profitability. And out the door went the "partnership" with suppliers that Stallkamp had carefully built ... and the trust ... and the sharing of technology that was taking place in developing new vehicles ....

It is not clear what Daimler's long-term purpose was in buying Chrysler. In the short term, it seemed logical to expand from a European luxury carmaker to enter the U.S. market in full force making lower-tier vehicles. But did Daimler really think through the implications of integrating a very different company with a culture completely different from their own? Did they think through the implications for public opinion in the U.S.? Did they think through what effect their purchasing and management style would have on the existing culture of Chrysler?

By gutting the leadership of Chrysler, Daimler gutted the culture that Chrysler was proudly building—a culture that made companies like Toyota nervous. Instead of building on this proud culture and protecting it, Daimler tore it down through radical cost cutting, eviscerating Chrysler's strengths. From Toyota's perspective, the appropriate response might be "Thank you, Daimler, for doing what we could not and would not do to a competitor. You destroyed its culture."

Note

1. *Automotive Intelligence News*, www.autointell.com, June 12, 2002.

Section II

The Right Process Will Produce the Right Results

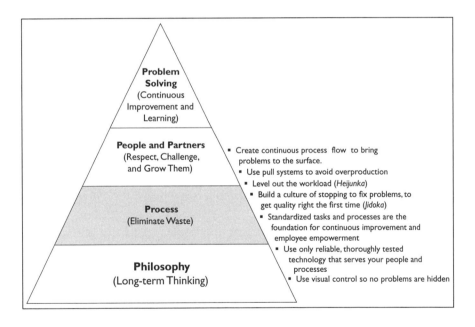

Problem Solving
(Continuous Improvement and Learning)

People and Partners
(Respect, Challenge, and Grow Them)

Process
(Eliminate Waste)

Philosophy
(Long-term Thinking)

- Create continuous process flow to bring problems to the surface.
- Use pull systems to avoid overproduction
- Level out the workload (*Heijunka*)
- Build a culture of stopping to fix problems, to get quality right the first time (*Jidoka*)
- Standardized tasks and processes are the foundation for continuous improvement and employee empowerment
- Use only reliable, thoroughly tested technology that serves your people and processes
- Use visual control so no problems are hidden

Chapter 8

Principle 2:
Create Continuous Process Flow to Bring Problems to the Surface

If some problem occurs in one-piece flow manufacturing then the whole production line stops. In this sense it is a very bad system of manufacturing. But when production stops everyone is forced to solve the problem immediately. So team members have to think, and through thinking team members grow and become better team members and people.
> —Teruyuki Minoura, former President,
> Toyota Motor Manufacturing, North America

Toyota leaders truly believe that if they create the right process the results will follow. In this chapter we begin looking at the first of seven of the 14 Toyota Way principles that are part of the second broad category, *The Right Process Will Produce the Right Results*. Within these seven principles are most of the TPS tools for improving manufacturing processes as well as the more routine processes for product development and service organizations—what many companies mistakenly believe is "lean thinking." Important and powerful as these tools and processes are, they are only the "tactical" or "operations" aspect of the Toyota Way and becoming lean. As you learned in Chapter 7, these tools are far more effective when they are supported by a company-wide, long-term management philosophy.

Most Business Processes Are 90% Waste and 10% Value-Added Work

A good place for any company to begin the journey to lean is to create continuous flow wherever applicable in its core manufacturing and service processes. Flow is at the heart of the lean message that shortening the elapsed time from raw materials to finished goods (or services) will lead to the best quality, lowest cost, and shortest delivery time. Flow also tends to force the implementation of a lot of the other lean tools and philosophies such as preventative maintenance and built-in quality (*jidoka*). A lean expression is that lowering the "water level" of inventory exposes problems (like rocks in the water) and you have to deal with the problems or sink. Creating flow, whether of materials or of information, lowers the water level and exposes inefficiencies that demand immediate solutions. Everyone concerned is motivated to fix the problems and inefficiencies because the process will shut down if they don't. Traditional business processes, in contrast, have the capacity to hide vast inefficiencies without anyone noticing—people just assume that a typical process takes days or weeks to complete. They don't realize that a lean process might accomplish the same thing in a matter of hours or even minutes.

To illustrate the fact that most business processes are full of waste, let's say you have been promoted and you place an order for new office furniture with a genuine wood desk and ergonomic chair and drawers and compartments galore. You can't wait to get rid of that old scuffed and stained furniture you currently have. But don't turn in the old stuff just yet. For one thing, the promised delivery date is eight weeks out and, if you investigate further, the furniture is likely to be late by another month or so. Why does it take so long? Are skilled craftsmen slaving away at each piece of wood so it looks perfect? A nice thought, but quality has little to do with the delays. Your inconvenience is a result of a clumsy manufacturing process called *batch and queue*. Your desk and office chair are mass-produced in stages. Large batches of standardized material sit in a queue at each stage of the production process and wait for long periods of (wasted) time until they are moved to the next stage of production.

Consider the custom-made office chair that is delivered two months after you order it. The value-added work (i.e., the work actually performed) in the assembly process consists of putting together the upholstery and cover with the standard foam cushions and then bolting together the chair. This takes a few hours at most. Actually making the fabric and foam and frame and parts, which are done in parallel, takes another day at most. Everything else during the two months you are waiting is waste (*muda*). Why is there so much waste? The department making seat covers, the supplier making springs, and the plant making foam are all making big batches of these items and then shipping them to the furniture manufacturer, where they wait in piles of inventory. Then you, the customer, wait for someone to pull them from inventory and build the chair. More wasted time. Add several weeks for the chair to get out of inventory at the plant and through the distribution system to your office and you have been waiting months sitting in that uncomfortable old chair. In a TPS/lean environment the goal is to create "one-piece flow" by constantly cutting out wasted effort and time that is not adding value to your chair. Lean initiatives in companies like Herman Miller and Steelcase are cutting that process of making chairs to days.

In Chapter 3 we summarized the eight non-value-adding wastes that Toyota continually seeks to remove from its processes:

1. overproduction
2. waiting
3. unnecessary transport
4. overprocessing
5. excess inventory
6. unnecessary movement
7. defects
8. unused employee creativity

(In Chapter 10 you will learn about two other sources of waste, *muri* and *mura*, meaning "no value added beyond capability" and "unevenness.")

How do you distinguish the value-added work from waste? Consider an office where engineers are all very busy designing products, sitting in front of the computer, looking up technical specifications, and having meetings with co-workers or suppliers. Are they doing value-added work? The answer is you cannot measure an engineer's value-added productivity by looking at what he or she is doing. You have to follow the progress of the actual product the engineer is working on as it is being transformed into a final product (or service). Engineers transform information into a design, so you look at such things as 1) at what points do the engineers make decisions that directly affect the product? and 2) when do the engineers actually conduct important tests or do an analysis that impacts those decisions? When you start asking these kinds of questions, you're likely to find that typical engineers (or any white-collar professionals) are working like maniacs churning out all sorts of information. The problem is that very little of their work is truly "value added," i.e., work that ends up actually shaping the final product.

Consider the example of an engineering analysis group. They generate and accumulate various complex analyses for a project. Then what happens? The reports sit and wait in an information warehouse (inventory) until someone from another department accesses the reports. If we continue to follow the path of the information, you'll most likely find that any decisions based on this data could take months and go through several people, processes, and/or departments. Or the decision makers may not even know the analysis was done and make the decisions without the information. Your value-added work, which in this case is the flow of information as it is being transformed into a design, is being delayed by a number of inefficiencies because the process is organized around the old rules of batch-and-queue manufacturing. In this example, engineers and departments are mass-producing information that sits around, is inefficiently accessed, and is pushed along to the next stage. This is how most white-collar work (and blue-collar work, for that matter) is organized. What's the alternative? Flow.

Flow means that when your customer places an order, this triggers the process of obtaining the raw materials needed just for that customer's order. The raw materials then flow immediately to supplier plants, where workers immediately fill the order with components, which flow immediately to a plant, where workers assemble the order, and then the completed order flows immediately to the customer. The whole process should take a few hours or days, rather than a few weeks or months.

An example of this is the fact that Toyota engineers new vehicles in Japan in less than one year. Their competitors take over two years. The reason is that Toyota's engineering work is organized into a flow, and efforts are constantly made to reduce waste in this flow. Its engineering work, design decisions, prototype construction, and tool construction seamlessly flow and "communicate" from the beginning to the end of the vehicle design process. No one produces anything before it is needed by the next person or step in the process.

Of course, the ideal of one-piece flow is not reality and Toyota is steeped in reality. So you will not see Toyota just throwing together machines and suppliers and forcing one-piece flow where it does not fit. Taiichi Ohno wrote that it takes time and patience to achieve flow. And as we will see in Chapters 9 and 10, inventory buffers are used judiciously where continuous flow is not possible today. But the ideal of flow provides a clear direction. At Toyota it means that using small lots, having processes close together, and keeping the material moving through processes without interruption is better than producing large batches of stuff and having them sit and wait.

Toyota managers and engineers do not have to do a detailed cost-benefit analysis every time they want to implement something that will improve the flow. Cost is obviously a factor, but the bias is to create flow where it is possible and continuously improve in the direction of better flow. Even when Toyota strategically sets up inventory buffers in places where pure one-piece flow is not possible the focus is still on reducing the inventory over time to improve flow. In fact, inventory buffers in the right places can actually allow for better overall flow across the enterprise.

Traditional Mass Production Thinking

What is the ideal way to organize your equipment and processes? In traditional mass production thinking (the way most companies are organized), the answer seems obvious: group similar machines and similarly skilled people together. So mass production thinking sets up departments of mechanical engineering, electrical engineering, accounting, purchasing, and manufacturing as well as departments for stamping, welding, wire soldering, assembly, and the like. The following were the perceived benefits of grouping similarly skilled people and equipment together:

1. *Economies of scale.* First and foremost, mass production thinking was about squeezing the most production possible at the lowest cost per unit out of every piece of equipment or every worker in a manual operation. Having one huge stamping press to meet the needs of all the factory's products would lead to the smallest capital cost per piece. And then you wanted to run that press flat-out 100% of the time to get the greatest asset utilization. Similarly, by organizing people into departments, you can focus on best practices in each professional specialty and squeeze the highest productivity (or innovation) possible out of each person.

2. *Apparent flexibility in scheduling.* When you put all the welders together in one department, it's easier for the welding department manager to schedule available machines and welders to any job that comes up. If you create one-piece flow cells, you take those welding machines and welders and dedicate them to a one-piece cell, so they're no longer free to do other work that might come up.

In mass production thinking, once you have decided to group all the similar types of people and processes together by department, the next question is how often should you move material or information between departments? Since you have organized your people and equipment by specialty, you must create another specialty, the material handling department or the planning department, to move material. That department is also measured by efficiency. The most efficient way to utilize a person moving material is to get that person to move the most material possible each trip. From the viewpoint of the material handling department, the optimal time to move material from one department to the next is when there is a large batch. The goal is to move the material once a day or, even better yet, once a week.

The best way to schedule an operation that is organized into separate processes is to send individual schedules to each individual department. For example, if schedules are developed weekly, then each department head can decide what to make each day in order to optimize equipment and utilize people for that week. A weekly schedule also provides flexibility for people missing work. You just make less that day and make it up with more production another day in the week. As long as by Friday you meet the production target, everything is OK.

Lean thinking looks at this way of organizing production and sees a company producing a lot of work-in-process (WIP) inventory. The fastest equipment, such as stamping, will build up the most WIP. Material sitting in inventory is caused by the most fundamental waste, overproduction. The mass production system guarantees overproduction in large batches, which in turn guarantees inventory sitting idle and taking up valuable plant space and, more importantly, hiding problems.

Another problem with organizing similar professional specialties and similar manufacturing equipment together into departments is that a product being made for a customer does not live in just one department. It must move across departments to become what the customer wants. Engineering, purchasing, and accounting are all located in different departments. Yet many value streams cross through these departments, causing a delay each time a process enters a new department. In a one-piece flow, you physically line up the processes in the sequence that will produce the customer's order in the shortest time.

Figure 8-1 illustrates a simplified view of a computer maker that is organized into three departments. One department makes computer bases, the second makes monitors and attaches them, and the third tests equipment. (Of course, in the real world there would be many departments and companies in a supply chain making a complete computer.) In this model, the material handling department decided it wants to move a batch size of 10 units at a time. Each department takes one minute per unit to do its work, so it takes 10 minutes for a batch of computers to move through each department. Even without considering material handling time to move between departments, it would therefore take 30 minutes to make and test the first batch of 10 to be shipped to the customer. And it would take 21 minutes to get out the first computer ready to ship, even though only three minutes of value-added work are needed to make that computer.

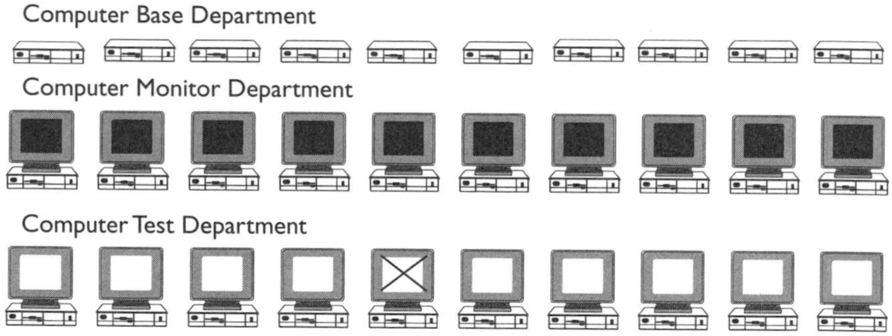

Computer Base Department

Computer Monitor Department

Computer Test Department

- Complete processing of first batch of 10 takes 30 minutes
- First good computer ready in 21 minutes (plus transport time)
- There are at least 21 sub-assemblies in process at a time

Figure 8-1. Batch processing example

The system that Ohno set up does not assume that the ideal batch size is what is most efficient for each individual process or for the material handling department. In lean thinking, the ideal batch size is always the same—one. That is because Ohno was not trying to optimize the utilization of people and equipment in each department. When the Toyota factory was first organized, it was operating this way—like Ford's factories. But this didn't work, because Toyota could not compete with Ford's volume and economies of scale. So Ohno decided to optimize the flow of material so it would move more quickly through the factory. This meant reducing batch size. And the fastest way to achieve this was to blow up departments and "process islands" and create work cells that were grouped by product, rather than by process.

Figure 8-2 illustrates a view of the same computer-making process above, organized into a one-piece flow work cell. If Ohno were to manage this process, he would take the equipment needed to make one base from the base department, the equipment for making a monitor from the monitor department, and a test stand from the test department and then put these three processes next to each other. That is, he would have created a cell to achieve one-piece flow. Then he would have made clear that operators were not allowed to build up inventory between the three operations. For example, the computer base maker would not make the next base until the monitor maker finished building the monitor and mounting it on the last base. In other words, nobody would build more than what is needed immediately. The result is the operators in the cell take 12 minutes to make 10 computers, while the batch flow process takes 30 minutes for 10 computers. And it takes the lean process just three minutes instead of 21 minutes to make the first computer ready to ship. In fact, the three minutes is pure value-added time. What flow has done is to eliminate overproduction and inventory.

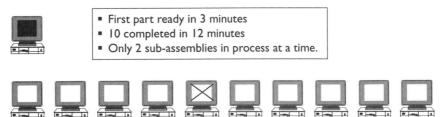

Figure 8-2. Continuous flow example

Why Faster Means Better in a Flow

Often we think that increasing the speed of a process means compromising quality, that faster is sloppier. But flow achieves just the opposite—it generally improves quality. In Figures 8-1 and 8-2 we show one defective computer, with an X on the monitor. That one failed to turn on in the test stage. In the large batch approach in Figure 8-1, by the time the problem is discovered, there are at least 21 parts in process that might also have that problem. And if the defect occurred in the base department, it could take as long as 21 minutes to discover it in the test department. In Figure 8-2, by contrast, when we discover a defect, there can be only two other computers in process that also have the defect and the maximum time it will take to discover the defect is two minutes from when it was made. The reality is that in a large batch operation there are probably weeks of work in process between operations and it can take weeks or even months from the time a defect was caused until it is discovered. By then the trail of cause and effect is cold, making it nearly impossible to track down and identify why the defect occurred.

The same logic applies to a business or engineering process. Let individual departments do the work in batches and pass the batches to other departments and you guarantee major delays in getting work done. Lots of excessive bureaucracy will creep up, governing the standards for each department, and lots of non-value-adding positions will be created to monitor the flow. Most of the time will be spent with projects waiting for decisions or action. The result will be chaos and poor quality. Take the right people who do the value-added work, line them up, and flow the project through those people with appropriate meetings to work on integration and you will get speed, productivity, and better quality results.

Takt Time: The Heart Beat of One-Piece Flow

In competitive rowing, a key position is the coxswain—the little person in the back of the boat who is calling "row, row, row." He or she is coordinating the activities of all the rowers so they are rowing at the same speed. Get a maverick rower who outperforms everyone else and guess what!—the boat gets out of kilter and slows down. Extra power and speed can actually slow the boat down.

A similar thing occurs in any manufacturing or service operation. Make one particular department extra efficient and it can actually bury other departments in excess inventory and paperwork and slow them down, making a mess of things. So there is a need to coordinate activities. When you set up one-piece flow in a cell, how do you know how fast the cell should be designed to go? What should the capacity of the equipment be? How many people do you need? The answer is the *takt* time.

Takt is a German word for rhythm or meter. Takt is the rate of customer demand—the rate at which the customer is buying product. If we are working seven hours and 20 minutes per day (440 minutes) for 20 days a month and the customer is buying 17,600 units per month, then you should be making 880 units per day or one unit every 30 seconds. In a true one-piece flow process, every step of the process should be producing a part every 30 seconds. If they are going faster, they will overproduce; if they are going slower, they will create bottleneck departments. Takt can be used to set the pace of production and alert workers whenever they are getting ahead or behind.

Continuous flow and takt time are most easily applied in repetitive manufacturing and service operations. But with creativity the concepts can be extended to any repeatable process in which the steps can be written out and waste identified and eliminated to create a better flow (see Chapter 21). At the end of this chapter is a case example of creating job summaries in Navy ship repair facilities. There are many other examples my associates and I have worked on in service operations—completing bills of materials for engineering of ships, processing people through a security office of a Navy shipyard, processing new members into a professional association, reimbursing employees for expenses, processing job applicants .... And you can think of many more. Obviously, it's easiest to apply the concepts of takt time and one-piece flow in relatively high-volume and repetitive service operations in which there is some consistency in the cycle time per unit, but the Toyota Way is never satisfied with doing only what is easy.

Benefits of One-Piece Flow

When you try to attain one-piece flow, you are also setting in motion numerous activities to eliminate all *muda* (wastes). Let's take a closer look at a few of the benefits of flow.

1. *Builds in Quality.* It is much easier to build in quality in one-piece flow. Every operator is an inspector and works to fix any problems in station before passing them on. But if defects do get missed and passed on, they will be detected very quickly and the problem can be immediately diagnosed and corrected.

2. *Creates Real Flexibility.* If we dedicate equipment to a product line, we have less flexibility in scheduling it for other purposes. But if the lead time to make a product is very short, we have more flexibility to respond and make what the customer really wants. Instead of putting a new order into the system and waiting weeks to get that product out, if lead times are a matter of mere hours we can fill a new order in a few hours. And changing over to a different product mix to accommodate changes in customer demand can be almost immediate.

3. *Creates Higher Productivity.* The reason it appears that productivity is highest when your operation is organized by department is because each department is measured by equipment utilization and people utilization. But in fact it is hard to determine how many people are needed to produce a certain number of units in a large batch operation because productivity is not measured in terms of value-added work. Who knows how much productivity is lost when people are "utilized" to overproduce parts, which then have to be moved to storage. How much time is lost tracking down defective

parts and components and repairing finished products? In a one-piece-flow cell, there is very little non-value-added activity like moving materials around. You quickly see who is too busy and who is idle. It is easy to calculate the value-added work and then figure out how many people are needed to reach a certain production rate. In every case of the Toyota Supplier Support Center, when they changed a mass-producing supplier to a TPS-style line, they achieved at least a 100% improvement in labor productivity.

4. *Frees up Floor Space.* When equipment is organized by department, there is a lot of bits of space between equipment that are wasted, but most of the space is wasted by inventory—piles and piles of it. In a cell, everything is pushed close together and there is very little space wasted by inventory. By making greater use of the floor space you often eliminate the need to build more capacity.

5. *Improves Safety.* Wiremold Corporation, one of the early adopters of TPS in America, has an exemplary safety record, winning a number of state safety awards. Yet when they worked to transform their large-batch-process company to one-piece flow, they decided not to put in place a special safety program. Art Byrne, the former president and a student of TPS, led the transformation and knew that one-piece flow would naturally improve safety, because smaller batches of material would be moved in the factory. Smaller batches meant getting rid of forklift trucks, which are a major cause of accidents. It meant lifting and moving smaller containers of material, so accidents relating to lifting went away. Safety was getting better because of a focus on flow—even without focusing on safety.[1]

6. *Improves Morale.* Wiremold, in its lean transformation, also found its morale improved in every year of the transformation. Before the transformation, only 60% of employees agreed with various responses about the company being a good place to work. That went up each year, to over 70% by the fourth year of transformation (Emiliani, 2002). In one-piece flow, people do much more value-added work and can immediately see the results of that work, giving them both a sense of accomplishment and job satisfaction.

7. *Reduces Cost of Inventory.* You free up capital to invest elsewhere when it's not invested in inventory sitting on the floor. And companies do not have to pay the carrying costs of the capital they free up. Also your inventory obsolescence goes down.

Figure 8-3 illustrates a traditional shop with machines grouped by type. One tool you can use for charting the path of materials is a spaghetti diagram. When we chart the flow of material through this facility, it ends up looking like a randomly tossed bowl of spaghetti, as in Figure 8-3. Product is moving everywhere. There is no coordination of the product across departments. No amount of sched-

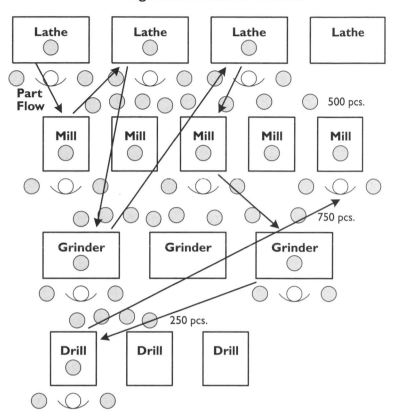

Figure 8-3. Organization by machine type with convoluted flow

uling can control the inherent variation in the system when that system causes materials to move every which way.

By contrast, Figure 8-4 shows a lean cell. The equipment is organized to follow the flow of material as it is being transformed into a product. It is organized in a U shape, which is a particularly good way for efficient movement of people and materials and good communication. You can also arrange a cell to be a straight line or an L. In this case, we show the paths of two people working in the cell. What if demand is cut in half? Put one person in the cell. What do we do if demand doubles? Put four people in the cell. Of course, people need to be multi-skilled to work across different manufacturing processes, a requirement in Toyota plants.

Organization and control

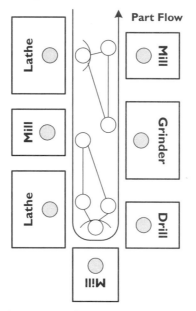

Figure 8-4. U-shaped one-piece flow cell

Why Creating Flow Is Difficult

So, life is good and all your problems and pains simply disappear by creating one-piece flow cells. Not by a long shot! In lean thinking, life will get tougher for a while—at least until you learn how to continuously improve your processes. Ohno explained:

> *In 1947, we arranged machines in parallel lines or in an L shape and tried having one worker operate three or four machines along the processing route. We encountered strong resistance among the production workers, however, even though there was no increase in work or hours. Our craftsmen did not like the new arrangement requiring them to function as multi-skilled operators. They did not like changing from one operator, one machine to a system of one operator, many machines in different processes. Their resistance was understandable. Furthermore, our efforts revealed various problems. As these problems became clearer, they showed me the direction to continue moving in. Although young and eager to push, I decided not to press for quick, drastic changes, but to be patient. (Ohno, 1988)*

One of the comforting things about traditional mass production thinking is that if any one process stops producing—because it takes a lot of time to changeover a machine to a new process, or because a person is out sick, or because the equipment breaks down—the other "separate" process operations can keep on working because you have lots of inventory. When you link operations together in a one-piece flow, your entire cell goes down if any one piece of equipment fails. You sink or swim together as a unit. So why not have some inventory to make life a little more comfortable? Because whether it is a pile of material or a virtual pile of information waiting to be processed, *inventory hides problems and inefficiencies.* Inventory enables the bad habit of not having to confront problems. If you don't confront your problems, you can't improve your processes. One-piece flow and continuous improvement (*kaizen*) go hand in hand! If your competitor challenges itself to adopt the pain and "confusion" of lean thinking, you'll no longer be comfortable hiding behind your inventory—you'll be out of business. As Minoura, former President of Toyota Motor Manufacturing, North America, and a disciple of Taiichi Ohno, explained:

> When they run one-piece production, they can't have the quantity that they want so everybody gets frustrated and doesn't know what to do. But then, within that, they have to find ways to think: what is the way to get the quantity? That is the true essence of TPS and, in that sense, we create confusion so we have to do something different in approaching this problem.

Many companies I have visited make one of two mistakes when implementing flow. The first is that they set up fake flow. The second is that they go backwards from flow as soon as problems occur.

An example of fake flow would be moving equipment close together to create what looks like a one-piece flow cell, then batching product at each stage with no sense of customer takt time. It looks like a cell, but it works like a batch process.

For example, the Will-Burt Company in Orrville, Ohio, makes many products based on steel parts. One of its larger-volume products is a family of telescoping steel masts that are used in vans for radar or for camera crews. Each mast is different, depending on the application, so there is variation from unit to unit built. This company called its mast-making operation a cell and believed it was doing good lean manufacturing. In fact, before I helped lead a lean consulting review of their processes, a production manager warned us that, with the variety of parts they made, we would not have any luck improving the flow.

In a one-week *kaizen* workshop, the current situation was analyzed and this turned out to be a classic case of fake flow.[2] The work time (value added) it took to build one of these masts was 431 minutes. But the pieces of equipment for making each mast were physically separated, so forklifts were moving big pallets of masts from work station to work station. WIP built up at each station. With the WIP, the total lead time from raw material to finished goods was 37.8 days. Most of this was the storage of tube raw material and the storage of finished goods. If you just looked at the processing time in the plant, it still took almost four days from sawing to final welding to do 431 minutes of work. The travel distance of

	Before	**After**
Production Lead Time (dock to dock)	37.8 days	29.2 days
Production Lead Time (saw to weld)	3.75 days	0.8 days
# of Forklife Moves	11	2
Travel Distance (dock to dock per mast)	1,792 feet	1,032 feet
Shop Order Input Time (per mast)	207 minutes	13 minutes

Figure 8-5. Results of lean transformation of mast operation

the mast within the plant was 1792 feet. The solutions were moving the equipment closer together, moving one piece at a time through the system, eliminating the use of the forklift between the operations (a special dolly had to be created to move this large unit at workstation height between two of the operations that could not be placed next to each other), and creating a single shop order for one mast instead of batches of shop orders for a set of masts. The results of these changes were significant improvements in lead time (see Figure 8-5), reduced inventory, and reduced floor space .

One side benefit of the workshop was that the time to set up a shop order was investigated. The batching of shop orders was creating a lot of waste; when that system was eliminated, it reduced this time from 207 minutes to 13 minutes. Figure 8-6 depicts the process flow before and after the one-week *kaizen* workshop. You can see that the "before" situation was really a case of fake flow. Pieces of equipment were sort of near each other, but there was not really anything like a one-piece flow. And the people working in the plant did not understand flow well enough to see that it was fake flow. The "after" situation is a marked improvement that surprised and delighted everyone in the company. They were shocked that it could be done in one week.

The second mistake when implementing flow is backtracking, which occurs as soon as the company realizes that there may be a cost to creating flow. This extra cost can occur in any of the following situations:

- There is a breakdown in one piece of equipment, causing the whole cell to stop production.
- A changeover of another piece of equipment takes longer than expected and delays the whole cell, stopping production.
- To create flow, you must invest in a process (like heat treating) that is currently being sent outside to a supplier and bring it in-house.

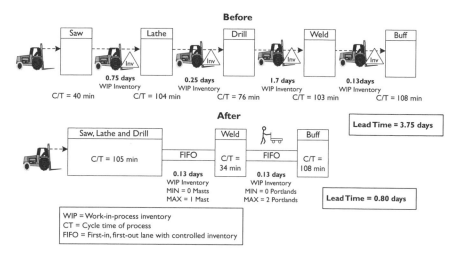

Figure 8-6. Mast making operation before and after one-week lean transformation

In all these cases, I have seen some companies give up on flow. Their thinking is that flow is a good idea when we do a simulation with toy parts to illustrate the benefits of reducing batch size and creating flow. But it is a bad idea when we actually try it in a real operation and it causes some short-term pain and cost. When a cell is set up, it takes discipline to maintain, which often is beyond the capacity of many manufacturing companies, because they don't understand the challenges and pain of continuous improvement. In the long run, the challenges and pain and short-term costs almost always produce dramatically better results.

Toyota's focus in any process is always on creating a true one-piece flow system that is waste free, as embodied in Toyota Way Principle *2. Create continuous process flow to bring problems to the surface*. Creating flow means linking together operations that otherwise are disjointed. When operations are linked together, there is more teamwork, rapid feedback on earlier quality problems, control over the process, and direct pressure for people to solve problems and think and grow. Ultimately, within the Toyota Way the main benefit of one-piece flow is that it challenges people to think and improve.

Because of the focus on thinking, TPS is now being referred to by Toyota as the "Thinking Production System." Toyota is willing to risk shutting down production in order to surface problems and challenge team members to solve them. Inventory hides problems and reduces the urgency to solve them. The Toyota Way is to stop and address each problem as it is exposed. Chapter 11 (on *jidoka*) explains this in more detail.

Case Example: Job Summaries in a Navy Ship Repair Facility

An excellent example of one-piece flow in a service operation was implemented at Puget Sound Naval Shipyard in fall 2001. At this shipyard they do not build ships, but repair Navy vessels from submarines to carriers of various kinds. Every repair situation is unique, so there is heavy involvement of engineering in diagnosing the problem and writing work instructions for the repair. The engineering documentation, including work instructions, is compiled in a folder that goes to the shipyard so skilled mechanics can conduct the repair. This leads to the authorization, funding, and paperwork that mechanics use to do the repair job. The work instructions folder had become a bottleneck in the planning process, in many cases, as well as a cost driver.

To improve the process, a one-week *kaizen* workshop was run. There was a good deal of preparation leading up to the workshop, including preparations for a reorganization and office space assigned to the creation of a cross-functional cell to process work instructions. The workshop focused on mapping the current process and developing a new process. The wastes identified by analyzing the process step by step included rework, redundant systems, different communication vehicles (e.g., spreadsheets), waiting for forms, inspection, excess reviews and signoffs, poor filing systems, lack of needed reference material, excess walking, waiting, and incomplete information.

The solution was to develop a cross-functional work cell to put together the work instructions. As a result, many of the handoffs were eliminated and non-value-added steps were eliminated. A takt time was created, based on the demand for work instructions (demand was fairly easy to predict) and the time available to work on them. A key part of the solution was to take the core people doing the bulk of the work and colocate them in an open office environment. A work cell was physically created in the office so that the key functions required to produce a work instructions folder could pass the package from station to station in record time. The old office arranged people into separate functions and each person had an office with high partitions. In the new work cell, the key people had desks surrounding a round table. The job summaries move around the table from person to person in a one-piece flow. Valued-added time was calculated before and after—with striking results. Note that some non-value-added time is required, e.g., filling out paperwork that adheres to Navy policies even if it is not necessary to get the mechanics what they need. We separate this out from "wait time," which is pure waste. The results of the lean transformation are shown in Figure 8-7.

	Before	After	Improvement
Value-added time (days)	15	15	0%
Required non-value-added time (days)	20	8	60%
Pure non-value-added wait time (days)	62	3	95%
Total lead time (days)	67	26	73%
Travel distance of paperwork (feet)	30,744	2,500-14,000	55-92%
Number of process steps	70	23	67%
Handoffs	58	10	80%

Figure 8-7. Documenting improvement in job summary process

Notes

1. For a detailed analysis of Wiremold and its lean transformation, see Bob Emiliani, David Stec, Lawrence Grasso, and James Stodder, *Better Thinking, Better Results* (Kensington, CT: Center for Lean Business Management, 2002).
2. The *kaizen* workshop was led by Jeffrey Rivera, former senior lean consultant with Optiprise, Inc., and Eduardo Lander, my doctoral student at the University of Michigan.

Chapter 9

Principle 3:
Use "Pull" Systems to
Avoid Overproduction

The more inventory a company has, ... the less likely they will have what they need.

—Taiichi Ohno

Imagine that you find out about a great Internet service where you can get all your dairy products delivered directly to your house at a significant discount. The only hitch is that you have to sign up once and specify a weekly quantity of each item and the company will only guarantee that the delivery will come some time during the week. The company has to schedule weekly shipments of goods to its warehouse, so it wants advance orders locked in to make sure it sells all the inventory that it receives. They will leave it on your front porch in a thermo container so it will stay cold. You specify a typical quantity of eggs and milk and butter that you need in a week. But you are not sure what day of the week the products will come. It may be Monday, but it could be Friday. So you will need to keep enough of all dairy products in your refrigerator to get you through the week. And if the delivery comes on Monday, you will have a refrigerator full of a week's worth of dairy products, plus what comes on Monday—too much to fit in one refrigerator. So you will need to buy a second refrigerator and put it in the garage. And if you go on vacation and happen to forget to cancel the order for that week, you will have a week's worth of bad dairy products on your front porch when you return.

This is an example of an inventory *push* system. In business, goods and services are often pushed onto the retailer whether or not the retailer can sell them right away. The retailer tries to push them onto you whether you need them right now or not. And the result is a lot of inventory of stuff that you do not need to immediately use and most likely the retailer is also holding a boatload of inventory.

Now imagine the Internet service gets a lot of complaints and upgrades its service. They send you a wireless device that has buttons on it for each of your dairy goods. When you open a new bottle of milk or a new carton of eggs, you push the button for that item. The next day they will deliver one unit to replenish what you started using. This means you will have the partially used unit, if you did not finish it, plus one more. Some inventory, but not a lot. If you think you will be using a lot of a product, like milk, then you can get on the Internet or even pick up the phone and they will immediately deliver what you need. On their end, they have renegotiated agreements with their dairy suppliers. When the customer orders more product, that will trigger a signal to dairy companies to send that amount to the retailer. This is an example of a *pull* system. You receive items only when you demand them and the retailer receives product based on actual customer demand. To avoid having items pushed on you, you might even be willing to pay a little more for this "on-demand" service.

Many companies and service organizations within companies work to their own internal schedule. They do what is convenient for them within that schedule. So they produce parts, goods, and services according to their schedule, or plan and push products onto their customers, who have to stockpile it in inventory.

As you already know, the Toyota Way is not about managing inventory; it is about eliminating it. Very early on, Toyota starting thinking in terms of pulling inventory based on immediate customer demand, rather than using a push system that anticipates customer demand. In the Toyota Way, "pull" means the ideal state of just-in-time manufacturing: giving the customer (which may be the next step in the production process) what he or she wants, when he or she wants it, and in the amount he or she wants. The purest form of pull is one-piece flow discussed in Chapter 8. If you can take in a customer order and make a single product just for that order—using a one-piece flow production cell—this would be the leanest imaginable system. That is, it is 100% on-demand and you have zero inventory. But since there are natural breaks in flow from transforming raw materials into finished products delivered to customers, you have to build in some necessary inventory. And we will learn in Chapter 10 that leveling the schedule may even mean holding some finished goods inventory.

The Internet example we used above is not a zero-inventory system. There is inventory, also referred to as a buffer. The (improved) Internet service is asking you to simply tell it when you are starting to use an item so it can replenish what you have started to use. It is replenishing what you are taking away. This is the way most supermarkets work. In fact, supermarkets are simply warehouses, but they operate in a particular way. There is a very specific amount of inventory kept on the store shelves, based on past purchase patterns and expected future demand. Customers come and pull items they want off the shelf. The supermarket clerk periodically looks at what has been taken off the shelf and replenishes that. The clerk is not simply pushing inventory onto the shelf, nor is he or she directly ordering goods from the manufacturer to put on the shelf. The clerk draws from the supermarket's inventory, but it is a small, controlled amount of inventory using a replenishment system. Well run supermarkets are an example of pull. Yes, you have inventory buffers, but instead of pushing material into the inventory buffers based on a schedule, you are merely looking at what the customer is using and replenishing that before it runs out. Similarly, the Toyota Production System is not a zero-inventory system. It relies on "stores" of materials that are replenished using pull systems.

The Principle—Customer Pull and Replenishment

Taiichi Ohno and his associates were fascinated by the importance of the supermarket to daily life in America in the 1950s. It captured the imagination of retailers in Japan and was imported there, where Ohno studied it close up.

Though Ohno recognized from the start that in many cases inventory was necessary to allow for smooth flow, he also recognized that individual departments building products to a schedule using a push system would naturally overproduce and create large banks of inventory. In a push system, the production of goods is based upon a plan (schedule) that's been made in advance, which means production and purchase orders are initiated by *projected* customer demand. The operation keeps building to the schedule and creates waste. But customer demand can change on a dime and things can go wrong. What becomes of the schedule then?

Most mass production departments will try to minimize the equipment changeovers that are necessary for making different types of products with the same equipment. As a result, a specific department may make all of the largest-volume items early in the week before it changes over. Since each department is making what it wants to over the week, there will not be any real coordination between departments. To keep the downstream departments busy, there will be inventory buffers between departments. So the departments working according to independent schedules will be pushing material into these inventory buffers.

As a compromise between the ideal of one-piece flow and push, Ohno decided to create small "stores" of parts between operations to control the inventory. When the customer takes away specific items, they are replenished. If a customer does not use an item, it sits in the store but it is not replenished. There is no more overproduction than the small amount on the shelf and there is at least some direct connection between what customers want and what the company produces. But since factories can be large and spread out and suppliers of parts are a distance away, Ohno needed a way to signal that the assembly line had used the parts and needed more. He used simple signals—cards, empty bins, empty carts called *kanban*. *"Kanban"* means sign, signboard, doorplate, poster, billboard, card, but it is taken more broadly as a signal of some kind. Send back an empty bin—a *kanban*—and it is a signal to refill it with a specific number of parts or send back a card with detailed information regarding the part and its location. Toyota's whole operation of using *kanban* is known as the "*kanban* system" for managing and ensuring the flow and production of materials in a just-in-time production system.

Even today in the world of high-speed electronic communications, you can walk into a Toyota factory making and using thousands of different parts and you'll see cards and other types of *kanban* moving about the factory triggering production and delivery of parts. It is remarkable, simple, effective, and highly visual. Now, throughout the world, companies are learning the power of the *kanban* system. They are turning away from sophisticated computer schedules for many parts of the process. While it can seem like taking a step backward, it has been repeatedly demonstrated that this is a step forward because a company's inventory goes down while the frequency of having the right parts goes up. And all those complex systems for tracking inventory accuracy become unnecessary—waste.

Pull-Replenishment in Everyday Life

One way to demystify the concept of *kanban* is by thinking of simple examples of pull-replenishment systems in everyday life. Like when you decide to buy gas for your car. Does your gas tank get filled according to a schedule? Would you consider simply filling the tank once per week on Monday morning? I doubt it. If you did, you would find you sometimes really do not need gas Monday morning and other times you will run out before Monday. Most likely, when you notice the gas gauge approaching empty, you stop at a gas station. The same pull system behavior goes for most routine things we purchase in our households. The simple trigger is that we notice our inventory is running low on an item and at some point say, "Yep, I better go out and get some more of that."

Not everything can be replenished based on a pull system; some things must be scheduled. Take the example of high-end products, like a Rolex, a sports car, or those killer high-tech golf clubs advertised by Tiger Woods. Whenever you are buying a special or single-use item, you have to think about what you want, consider the costs and benefits, and plan when to get it. In a sense, you create a schedule to purchase, since there is no immediate need for it.

Services are another type of purchase that isn't immediate but has to be scheduled. For example, we recently had our septic tank cleaned. We had no way of telling if it was getting full and needed to be emptied. So we followed the generally recommended (and probably inaccurate) schedule for cleaning the septic tank—a push system. But now there is a device on the market that you can install that detects how full the septic tank is; when it reaches a trigger point, it indicates through a radio signal when to get it cleaned. If we invest in that, we can eliminate the need for a "scheduling system" and replace it with a pull-replenishment system—a signal to replenish (actually, to empty) based on actual usage rather than a vague guess about usage.

Because the pull system corresponds with actual usage or consumption, Toyota is constantly working to achieve the ideal of just-in-time replenishment. Using *kanban*, they are carefully monitoring and coordinating the use and replenishment of thousands of parts and tools, orchestrating specific schedules for replenishment, developing rules for when to pull the trigger to send a replenishment signal, calculating the maximum amount of inventory that will be allowed, and the like. The *kanban*/pull system works better than a schedule system for most business situations. But it still depends on small inventory buffers or "stores of parts"—and inventory is always a compromise. So the goal is to eliminate the "stores of parts" and move to true one-piece flow wherever possible.

Toyota's *Kanban* System—Pull Where You Must

A true one-piece-flow system would be a zero-inventory system where goods just appear when they are needed by the customer. The closest system Toyota has devised to achieve this is the one-piece flow cell that builds to order only at the precise time the product is needed. But when pure flow is not possible because processes are too far apart or the cycle times to perform the operations vary a great deal, the next best choice is often Toyota's *kanban* system.

Rother and Shook (1999), in a widely circulated book about Toyota's Production System called *Learning to See,* say, "Flow where you can, pull where you must." If you want to design lean systems, repeat this phrase every day when you get up to start the day. You can go far with this simple principle. Where it is not possible to create a one-piece flow, the next best thing is to design a pull system with some inventory.

Consider a pull system in a Toyota assembly plant. Orders accumulate from car dealerships. Production control creates a leveled schedule. For example, they make a white Camry, followed by a green Camry, followed by a Red Avalon, and so on. Each of these cars has a whole set of options associated with it. That schedule is sent to the body shop, where stamped steel panels (from a "supermarket" of pre-stamped panels) are welded together into a body. Stamping the panels is a much faster operation than the takt time in assembly plants (e.g., one second per stamped panel versus 60-second takt times in a plant is typical), so putting them into a one-piece flow is not practical. They would be productive one out of every 60 seconds. So a pull system is used. At a certain trigger point when a certain number of steel panels have been used by the body shop, a *kanban* goes back to a stamping press, ordering it to make another batch to replenish the store.

Similarly, when assembly line workers begin to use parts from bins (hinges, door handles, windshield wipers), they take out a *kanban* card and put it in a mailbox. A material handler will come on a timed route and pick it up and go back to a store to replenish what is used on the assembly line. Another material handler will replenish the store based on parts from a supermarket of supplier parts. This will trigger an order back to parts suppliers. And so on. Figure 9-1 illustrates a system like this, where parts in the assembly plant are replenished from a supplier. The process starts at the assembly factory (on the right side of the diagram), then "withdrawal *kanban*" and empty containers are sent by truck back to the supplier to be refilled. The supplier keeps a small store of finished parts in a "parts store," which are used to refill the *kanban*. When parts are withdrawn from the parts store shelves, they must be replenished by sending a *kanban* and an empty container back to the production cell where new parts are built and then sent to refill the "parts store" shelves. Information, orders for parts in the form of *kanban*, flows backward from the customer (the assembly plant). Materials, in this case parts, are sent forward to the customer.

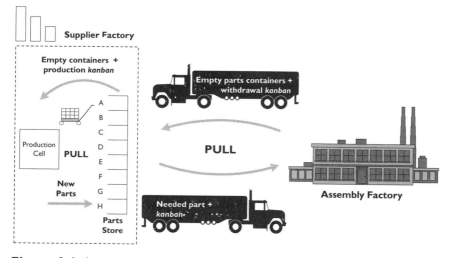

Figure 9-1. Internal and external pull

It is fascinating to watch this work, with so many parts and materials moving through the facility in a rhythm. In a large assembly plant like the one in Georgetown, Kentucky, there are thousands of parts moving about. Alongside the assembly line, there are small bins of parts and small bins are being moved from neatly organized stores. It is hard to imagine how a computer system could do such a good job of orchestrating such a complex movement of parts. When you find out the computer is not doing the orchestration, but rather small, laminated cards moving about, it is shocking.

Yet TPS experts get very impatient and even irritated when they hear people rave and focus on *kanban* as if it is the Toyota Production System. *Kanban* is a fascinating concept and it is fun to watch. I have led many tours of lean plants and you can spend hours talking about the technical details of many different types of *kanban* systems. When is the *kanban* triggered? How are the quantities calculated? What do you do if a *kanban* gets lost? But that is not the point. While you do have to know those things when you set up your system, they are pretty straightforward technically. *The challenge is to develop a learning organization that will find ways to reduce the number of* kanban *and thereby reduce and finally eliminate the inventory buffer.* Remember: the *kanban* is an organized system of inventory buffers and, according to Ohno, inventory is waste, whether it is in a push system or a pull system. So *kanban* is something you strive to get rid of, not to be proud of. In fact, one of the major benefits of using *kanban* is that it is easy to use it to force improvement in your production system. Let's say that you have printed up four *kanban*. Each one corresponds to a bin of parts. The rule is that a bin cannot move unless a *kanban* is traveling with it. Take one *kanban* and throw it away. What happens? There will now be only three bins of parts circulating in the system. So if a machine goes down, the next process will run out of parts 25% faster. It may stress the system and cause some shutdowns, but it will force teams to come up with process improvements.

Push Scheduling Has Its Place

The Toyota Way is not preoccupied with adhering to Principle 3, *Use "pull" systems to avoid overproduction.* There are many examples of push scheduling throughout Toyota. One example is when dealing with parts shipped from Japan to the United States or even moved across the United States. They use traditional scheduling systems to order these parts, with the appropriate lead time to get them to the plant as scheduled. Also the engineering of new products is a tightly scheduled operation, as I have described in Chapter 6.

When Toyota managers do schedule, they are preoccupied with timeliness. In other words, the schedule is not simply a guideline that you should do your best to make, more or less. It is a deadline and you move heaven and earth to make the deadline. So, even in scheduled systems, materials and information move remarkably smoothly. Scheduled systems work best when lead times are very short; for example, ordering parts every day instead of ordering parts once a month. So, when it comes to scheduling, Toyota works to make lead times as short as possible.

These days Toyota is increasingly using computer systems for scheduling. For example, when ordering parts from suppliers, Toyota is moving to electronic *kanban* rather than sorting and sending cards back. In this case, it does not have to be either/or. As we will see in Chapter 13 on visual control, Toyota will often use a computer system for scheduling some operations, but then use manual cues like cards or white boards to visually control the process. For example, the logistics planning backbone of Toyota's Service Parts Distribution Centers is a computerized scheduling system but "process control" whiteboards actually control the operations.

If you are using the Toyota Way to become lean, the lesson here is that you don't have to get hung up imitating Toyota's use of specific tools so you can appear to be lean like Toyota. The Toyota Way is a philosophy and a set of tools that must be *appropriately* applied to your situation. But understand that these principles are something to believe in and strive for. They are part of a greater system that is seeking harmony and perfection to sustain success. As you move on through the chapters in this Section II of the Toyota Way, "*The Right Process Will Produce the Right Results*," you'll continue to see how each of these processes is dependent on the others.

Using Pull in a GM Office

You can effectively use pull-replenishment systems in the office to save money and help avoid shortages of supplies. Most offices use some form of pull system already. Nobody knows exactly how many pencils, erasers, or reams of paper will be used in an office. If there were a standing, scheduled order of all these things, you would guess right in some cases, have too much in other cases, and run out of some critical items. So, in a well-run office, somebody's job is to keep the supply store stocked by looking and seeing what is used. You then replenish that.

General Motors has a Technical Liaison Office in California to organize tours of its joint venture with Toyota—the NUMMI plant. The first place GM employees see on their journey to witness the famous Toyota Production System at NUMMI is this office where some training is conducted. So GM made this a model lean office. In their case, the *kanban* system for supplies is very formal and they rarely run out of anything. There is a place for everything and everything in its place in the store, on desks, by the computer.

In storage areas of supplies, there are little, laminated *kanban* cards that say when they should be triggered. For example, when the aspirin bottle reaches one-quarter full, the aspirin *kanban* is put into a coffee can. They used to have a conventional refrigerator of soft drinks and some drinks were always overstocked while others ran out. Since you could not see through the door, it was easy to hide the mess inside. So they bought a big soda machine with a glass front and took out the payment mechanism. The glass front allows you to easily see the state of soft drink supplies. They put a variety of juices and soft drinks on marked shelves. When a certain soft drink gets to a certain level, you take the *kanban* for that soft drink and put it in a box so it will get reordered.

You might think a pull system in a small office might not be appropriate—it would be a rather elaborate system to maintain for the promised cost savings. You might consider doing a cost-benefit analysis to decide if it is a good use of time. But that is the traditional mass production thinking. The benefits may go beyond the pennies saved. The power of the Toyota Production System is that it unleashes creativity and continuous improvement. And it strives to seek perfection. So putting in these *kanban* systems is likely to intrigue your office workers, get them interested in improving the process of ordering supplies and ultimately finding ways to create flow in their core work. Waste in the office is generally far greater than in factories. A little creative effort to improve the process will have huge multiplier effects.

Chapter 10

Principle 4:

Level Out the Workload (*Heijunka*)

In general, when you try to apply the TPS, the first thing you have to do is to even out or level the production. And that is the responsibility primarily of production control or production management people. Leveling the production schedule may require some front-loading of shipments or postponing of shipments and you may have to ask some customers to wait for a short period of time. Once the production level is more or less the same or constant for a month, you will be able to apply pull systems and balance the assembly line. But if production levels—the output—varies from day to day, there is no sense in trying to apply those other systems, because you simply cannot establish standardized work under such circumstances.

—Fujio Cho, President, Toyota Motor Corporation

Following the lead of Dell Computer and other successful companies, many businesses in America are rushing to a build-to-order model of production. They want to make just what the customers want when they want it—the ultimate lean solution. Unfortunately, customers are not predictable and actual orders vary significantly from week to week and month to month. If you build product as it is ordered, you may be building huge quantities one week, paying overtime, and stressing your people and equipment, but then, if orders are light the next week, your people will have little to do and your equipment will be underutilized. You will also not know how much to order from your suppliers, so you will have to stockpile the maximum possible amount of each item the customers might possibly order. It is impossible to run a lean operation in this way. A strict build-to-order model creates piles of inventory, hidden problems, and ultimately poorer quality and in the end lead times are likely to grow as the factory is disorganized and chaotic. Toyota has found it can create the leanest operation and ultimately give customers better service and better quality by leveling out the production schedule and not always building to order.

Some of the businesses I work with that try to "build to order" are in actuality asking customers to wait six to eight weeks for their "build-to-order" product. A few "special" customers may cut in line and get their orders expedited at the expense of the large majority of customers. But why ruin the pace of your operation to build an order in hand today when the customer will not get the product for six weeks? Instead, accumulate orders and level the schedule and you may be able to reduce production lead times, cut your parts inventories, and quote much shorter standard lead times to all your customers, resulting in greater overall customer satisfaction than a "hurry up, then slow down" build-to-order approach to production.

Toyota managers and employees use the Japanese term *muda* when they talk about waste and eliminating *muda* is the focus of most lean manufacturing efforts. But two other M's are just as important to making lean work, and all three M's fit together as a system. In fact, focusing exclusively on only the eight wastes of *muda* can actually hurt the productivity of people and the production system. The Toyota Way document refers to the "elimination of *Muda, Muri, Mura*" (see Figure 10-1). The three M's are:

- *Muda—Non-value-added.* The most familiar M includes the eight wastes mentioned in earlier chapters. These are wasteful activities that lengthen lead times, cause extra movement to get parts or tools, create excess inventory, or result in any type of waiting.
- *Muri—Overburdening people or equipment.* This is in some respects on the opposite end of the spectrum from muda. Muri is pushing a machine or person beyond natural limits. Overburdening people results in safety and quality problems. Overburdening equipment causes breakdowns and defects.
- *Mura—Unevenness.* You can view this as the resolution of the other two M's. In normal production systems, at times there is more work than the people or machines can handle and at other times there is a lack of work. Unevenness results from an irregular production schedule or fluctuating production volumes due to internal problems, like downtime or missing parts or defects. *Muda* will be a result of *mura*. Unevenness in production levels means it will be necessary to have on hand the equipment, materials, and people for the highest level of production—even if the average requirements are much lower than that.

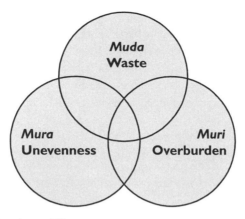

Figure 10-1. The three M's

Let's say you have a production schedule that swings wildly and a production process that is not well balanced or reliable. You've decided to start applying lean thinking and focus only on "eliminating *muda*" from your production system. You start to reduce inventory in your system. Then you look at the work balance and reduce the number of people from the system.[1] Then you organize the workplace better to eliminate wasted motion. Finally, you step back and let the system run. What you'll sadly witness is a system that will run itself into the ground due to spikes in customer demand that force people and equipment to work harder than they efficiently can! When work first begins to flow one piece at a time across work centers, without inventory, the pace and product mix of production jerk all over the place. The only thing you get is erratic one-piece flow. Workers will be overburdened. Equipment will break down even more than before. You will run out of parts. Then you'll conclude, "Lean manufacturing doesn't work here."

Interestingly, focusing on *muda* is the most common approach to "implementing lean tools," because it is easy to identify and eliminate waste. But what many companies fail to do is the more difficult process of stabilizing the system and creating "evenness"—a true balanced lean flow of work. This is the Toyota concept of *heijunka,* leveling out the work schedule. It is perhaps the Toyota Way's most counterintuitive principle. Achieving *heijunka* is fundamental to eliminating *mura*, which is fundamental to eliminating *muri* and *muda*.

Having starts and stops, overutilization then underutilization, is a problem because it does not lend itself to quality, standardization of work, productivity, or continuous improvement. As explained by Taiichi Ohno:

> *The slower but consistent tortoise causes less waste and is much more desirable than the speedy hare that races ahead and then stops occasionally to doze. The Toyota Production System can be realized only when all the workers become tortoises. (Ohno, 1988)*

I have heard this repeated from other Toyota leaders: "We would rather be slow and steady like the tortoise than fast and jerky like the rabbit." U.S. production systems force workers to be like rabbits. They tend to work really hard, wear themselves down, and then take a siesta. In many U.S. factories, workers will sometimes double up on the assembly line, one doing two jobs while the other has free time, and so long as the workers make production quotas for the day, management looks the other way.

Heijunka—Leveling Production and Schedules

Heijunka is the leveling of production by both volume and product mix. It does not build products according to the actual flow of customer orders, which can swing up and down wildly, but takes the total volume of orders in a period and levels them out so the same amount and mix are being made each day. The approach of TPS from the beginning was to keep batch sizes small and build what the customer (external or internal) wants. In a true one-piece flow, you can build Products A and B in the actual production sequence of customer orders (e.g., A, A, B, A, B, B, B, A, B...). The problem with building to an actual production sequence is that it causes you to build parts irregularly. So if orders on Monday are twice those on Tuesday, you must pay your employees overtime on Monday and then send them home early on Tuesday. To smooth this out, you take the actual customer demand, determine the pattern of volume and mix, and build a level schedule every day. For example, you know you are making five A's for every five B's. Now you can create a level production sequence of ABABAB. This is called leveled, mixed-model production, because you are mixing up production but also leveling the customer demand to a predictable sequence, which spreads out the different product types and levels volume.

Figure 10-2 gives an example of an unleveled schedule from an engine plant that makes small engines for lawn care equipment (based on an actual case).

In this case, a production line makes three sizes of engines—small, medium, and large. The medium engines are the big sellers, so these are made early in the week—Monday through part of Wednesday. Then there is a several-hour changeover of the line to make small engines that are made the rest of Wednesday through Friday morning. Finally, the large engines—in smallest demand—are made Friday afternoon. There are four things wrong with this unleveled schedule:

1. *Customers usually do not buy products predictably.* The customer is buying medium and large engines throughout the week. So if the customer unexpectedly decides to buy an unusually large number of large engines early in the week, the plant is in trouble. You can get around this by holding a lot of finished goods inventory of all engines, but this leads to a high cost of inventory, with all its related costs.

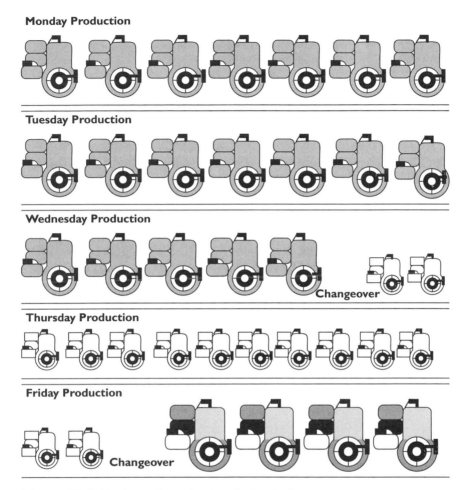

Figure 10-2. Traditional production (unleveled)

2. *There is a risk of unsold goods.* If the plant does not sell all its medium engines built up Monday to Wednesday, it must keep them in inventory.
3. *The use of resources is unbalanced.* Most likely, there are different labor requirements for these different-sized engines, with the largest engines taking the most labor time. So the plant needs a medium amount of labor early in the week, then less labor in the middle of the week, and then a lot of labor at the end of the week. There is potentially a lot of *muda* and *muri*.
4. *Placing an uneven demand on upstream processes.* This is perhaps the most serious problem. Since the plant is purchasing different parts for the three types of engines, it will be asking its suppliers to send certain parts Monday through Wednesday and different parts for the rest of the week. Experience

tells us that customer demand always changes and the engine plant will be unable to stick to the schedule anyway. Most likely there will be some big shifts in the model mix, e.g., unexpected rush order of large engines and the need to focus on making those for a whole week. The supplier will need to be prepared for the worst possible scenario and will need to keep at least one week's worth of all parts for all three engine types. And something called the "bullwhip effect" will multiply this behavior backward through the supply chain. Think of the small force in your wrist creating a huge and destructive force at the end of the whip. Similarly, a small change in the schedule of the engine assembly plant will result in ever-increasing inventory banks at each stage of the supply chain as you move backward from the end customer.

In a batch-processing mode, the goal is to achieve economies of scale for each individual piece of equipment. Changing over tools to alternate between making product A and product B seems wasteful because parts are not being produced during the changeover time. You are also paying the equipment operator while the machine is being changed over. So the logical solution is to build large batches of product A before changing over to product B. But this approach does not allow for *heijunka*.

In the case of the motors, the plant did a careful analysis and discovered the long time to changeover the line was due to moving in and out parts and tools for the larger engine and moving in and out new parts and tools for the smaller engine. There were also different-sized pallets for the different engines. The solution was to bring a small amount of all the parts on flow racks to the operator on the line. The tools needed for all three engines were mounted over the production line. It was also necessary to create a flexible pallet that could hold any size engine. This eliminated the equipment changeover completely, allowing the plant to build the engines in any order it wanted on a mixed-model assembly line. It could then make a repeating (level) sequence of all three engine sizes, so it matched the mix of parts ordered by the customer (see Figure 10-3). There were four benefits of leveling the schedule:

1. *Flexibility to make what the customer wants when they want it.* This reduced the plant's inventory and its associated problems.
2. *Reduced risk of unsold goods.* If the plant makes only what the customer orders, it doesn't have to worry about eating the costs of owning and storing inventory.
3. *Balanced use of labor and machines.* The plant can create standardized work and level out production by taking into account that some engines will require less work and others will require more work. As long as a big engine that takes extra work is not followed by another big engine, the workers can handle it. Once the plant takes this into account and keeps the schedule level, it can have a balanced and manageable workload over the day.

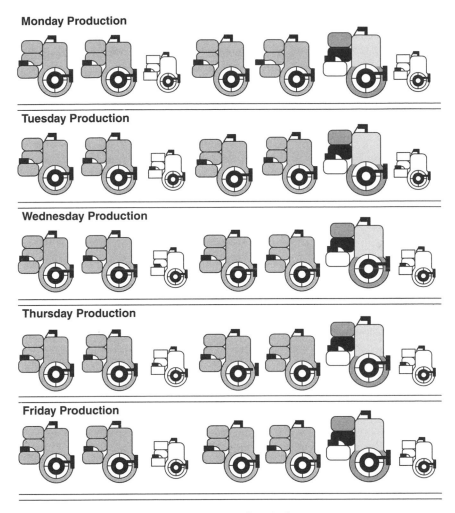

Figure 10-3. Mixed model production (leveled)

4. *Smoothed demand on upstream processes and the plant's suppliers.* If the plant uses a just-in-time system for upstream processes and the suppliers deliver multiple times in a day, the suppliers will get a stable and level set of orders. This will allow them to reduce inventory and then pass some savings on to the customer so that everyone gets the benefits of leveling.

None of this would have been possible if the plant hadn't found a way to eliminate the setup time for changeover.

Though it may seem unrealistic that you could do this in every circumstance, several decades ago Shigeo Shingo proved in his time studies that this was exactly what you had to do. Shingo was not a Toyota employee, but worked closely with Toyota. He was a meticulous industrial engineer who paid attention to every microscopic reach and grasp of the worker. In the Toyota style, he thoroughly analyzed the setup process for large stamping presses and discovered that most of the work performed fell into one of two categories: it was muda or it was something that could be done while the press was still making parts. He called the second category "external setup," as opposed to "internal setup," which was work that had to be done while the press was shut down.

In traditional mass production, the first thing the setup teams did when they performed the changeover of a production line from one model to another was to shut down the press. Shingo wondered how much of the changeover he could perform while the press was still running, so he organized an operator's workplace for that purpose and made other technical improvements until there was no more setup the operator could do while the press was running. Things like getting the next die and tools, preheating the die, and setting it in place beside the press were external and could be done while the press was making parts. When he finally shut down the press, all that was left to do was basically to swap the dies and start it up again. Amazingly, these several-hundred-ton presses that previously took many hours to change over could, it turned out, be changed over in minutes. Think of it like a racing pit crew that quickly services and gets the car back on the track, often in less than a minute.

Over the years changeover has become a kind of a sport in Japan, a manufacturing equivalent of an American rodeo. On one trip I took to Japan in the 1980s, I visited a Mazda supplier of stamped door panels whose team had recently won a prize in a national competition for changing over a several-hundred-ton press in 52 seconds.

Leveling the Schedule—Inventory's Role

Leveling the schedule has profound benefits throughout the value stream, including giving you the ability to plan every detail of production meticulously and standardizing work practices. If you visit a Toyota plant or a Toyota supplier, you will see the great pains taken to level the schedule. The best Toyota suppliers also work on the assumption that Toyota's demand for their parts will be level. This is a risk, because not keeping finished goods inventory means leaving themselves fully exposed to any wild variations in their customer's volume and mix of products. They can do this and still sleep at night because Toyota is a very reliable customer and levels out its production schedule.

For example, Trim Masters is a U.S. supplier in Georgetown, Kentucky that makes seats for the Camry and the Avalon manufactured there. Trim Masters builds and delivers seats just in time, based on a broadcast from the Toyota plant that orders one seat at a time. From the time the orders are placed, Trim Masters has three hours to build the seats, put them on the truck in sequence, and deliver them to the Toyota plant, so they appear on the assembly line in the exact order needed for production. Trim Masters orders parts just in time from its suppliers and keeps very little inventory, with inventory turns of 128 times per month. The Avalons and Camrys take different seats that require different parts, so Trim Masters has to trust Toyota will make the mix of Avalons and Camrys that it projects. If there is a sudden spike in Avalon seat production, Trim Masters will run out of parts and must pay for emergency delivery of parts. This happens routinely for U.S. auto companies, providing many truckers and helicopter pilots a good living on high-priced expedited freight. This happens from time to time with Toyota, but by and large it carefully maintains a leveled schedule and builds what it says it will build.

Most suppliers are not like Trim Masters and must satisfy customers whose demand fluctuates significantly. In these cases, TPS experts will often recommend keeping at least a small inventory of finished goods. This seems to contradict lean thinking. Theoretically, the leanest solution is to build to order and ship just what the customer wants. (If you are going to keep inventory, why keep the most expensive inventory—finished goods? Instead, build to order and store only raw material inventory.) But this reasoning doesn't consider the importance of *heijunka*. A small inventory of finished goods is often necessary to protect a supplier's level production schedule from being jerked around by sudden spikes in demand. It may seem wasteful, but by living with the waste of some finished goods inventory, you can eliminate far more waste in your entire production process and your supply chain, if you keep your production level.

This is one reason why companies that have successfully applied TPS often schedule their production with a combination of building to order and maintaining a pre-determined level of finished goods inventory. The case example at the end of this chapter shows a company that builds high-volume seasonal products to hold in inventory and then builds other products to order. This combination allows the company to level the schedule over the year, have a smooth flow, and build most of its products to order.

"Build to Order" Yet *Heijunka*

Cho's quote at the opening of this chapter suggested customers may have to wait a little longer if they want to order a vehicle specially built for them. He is not willing to sacrifice the quality and efficiency benefits of *heijunka* for the sake of "build-to-order." Yet, other car manufacturers have developed build-to-order systems, potentially giving them a competitive advantage. One of the conventional build-to-order solutions is to keep a lot of finished vehicle inventory in huge dealer lots around the country and swap vehicles among dealers that match custom orders.

So is Toyota satisfied with asking customers to wait while they may be able to get the specific car they want from a competitor? In response to this challenge, Toyota has developed a solution that will allow it to level the schedule and at the same time build to order. They are never satisfied with either/or. Alan Cabito, Group Vice President of Toyota Motor Sales, explained:

The Toyota system's not a build-to-order system. It is a "change to order" system. And the big difference is that we have cars moving down a line that we change specs on. We've always done that. But we're just taking it another big notch up. We pick a car on the line, any car, and change it. And obviously there are guidelines on how many changes you can do in a day, so we consistently have the parts available to do it.

This is all done within the leveled schedule created several months in advance. Cabito explained further the realities of the mixed model production line:

You might have a van unibody and a truck and then you might have another truck, so that the van was every third vehicle. That isn't going to change. You can change the color, which is not simply paint, it's interior and everything else. You can have matching mirrors, etc. There's a lot of complexity to changing color— you have to change virtually all the accessories. And the way that gets managed is on the allowance of how much change can take place. There will be a limit to the number of green, leather-interior Siennas we can make in the same day.

As usual, Toyota experimented with building to order with an actual pilot— the Solara, a sporty coupe version of a Camry—in the Canadian plant. It is relatively low volume. For Solara they achieved 100% "change to order." For the Tacoma truck there are a huge number of engine combinations, and they were able to achieve about 80% "change to order" from dealers who called in with customer requests. Cabito gave me a sales perspective on how this works:

We place a single month's order three times. We'll order it four months out, three months out, two months out. During that time, they set up all the components and suppliers. For July production, the final order will be placed in May. So your order's out there 60 days in advance. Then every week we can change the order in the U.S. plants. Every week we can modify anything that's unbuilt, except for the basic body type.

The important point here is that the Toyota culture does not allow managers and engineers to conclude, "That cannot be done here." The rigid principle of *heijunka* does not stay rigid for long. On the other hand, it is not simply thrown away because of a new trend such as build-to-order. The question is: How can we accommodate the customer's desire to make choices and get the car quickly without compromising the integrity of the production system? In true Toyota Way problem-solving style, the engineers carefully studied the situation, experimented on the shop floor, and implemented a new system.

Heijunka in Service Operations

Leveling out a work schedule is easier in high-volume manufacturing than in typically lower-volume service environments. How do you level schedules in a service operation where service providers are responding to customers and the lead times on service work vary widely case by case? The solutions are similar to the solutions in manufacturing:

1. *Fit customer demand into a leveled schedule.* This is more common in service operations than you may think. Why is it that doctors and dentists schedule procedures and you need to fit into their schedule? So they can level the workload and have a constant stream of income. Time is money in service operations.

2. *Establish standard times for delivering different types of service.* Again, the medical field is instructive. Even though everyone has somewhat different medical needs, doctors and dentists have been able to establish standard times for different types of procedures. And they separate diagnosis from the procedure. You visit, they diagnose you, and then, in most cases, they can predict the time that will be required for your procedure.

Toyota has effectively been able to level the schedule for product development even though lead times are months or even years. In most cases, Toyota will make minor updates to a vehicle every two years, adding features and changing styling, and will do a redesign of the vehicle every four or five years. Toyota product development works according to a matrix, where the rows are the different Toyota vehicles—Camry, Sienna, Tundra—and the columns are years. They decide when each vehicle will be freshened and go through a major redesign. They intentionally level the schedule so a fixed percent of the vehicles are being redesigned in any one year.

Planning when vehicles are scheduled for redesign would be futile if the lead times required to actually design and develop a vehicle were unpredictable. This is where Toyota has a big edge over some of its competitors. While some auto companies let the start of production slip by months or even a year, Toyota is like clockwork. Development milestones are met with virtually 100% accuracy. So the leveled plan becomes reality.

Toyota also has found there is a cadence to the workload requirements over the life of the development project: the workload is relatively light early in the conceptual stage, then builds up as they get to detailed design, and then reduces again in launch. By offsetting different vehicle projects, they know when one is peaking and others are in the light period and can assign the numbers of engineers to products accordingly. They also can flex the number of people needed by borrowing engineers from affiliated companies (suppliers and other divisions of Toyota, such as Toyota Auto Body). Affiliates can come onto projects as needed and then go back to their home companies, allowing an extremely flexible system and requiring minimal full-time employees. This is the result of other Toyota Way principles, particularly standardization. Toyota has standardized its product development system and the product designs themselves to the point that engineers can seamlessly come in and out of design projects, because their engineers have a standardized skill set similar to the Toyota engineers' and years of experience working in Toyota's system. The principle of long-term partnering that we will discuss in Chapter 17 allows Toyota to have a trustworthy and capable set of partners who they can depend on for extra help when needed.

In short, it is possible to level the schedule in service operations. But there are some base requirements. You must follow all of the other Toyota Way process principles—flow, pull, standardization, and even visual management—to get control over lead times. Standardization is critical to controlling lead times and also to bringing people on and off the projects to address peak workloads. You must also develop stable partnerships with outside companies that are capable and that you can trust.

Putting Leveling and Flow Together—A Tough Sell

Every business would like to have a consistent volume over time so there is a consistent and predictable workload. That is an easy sell in concept. But if your sales department does not behave like Toyota Sales by cooperating to avoid spikes in demand, what can you do?

The TPS expert might suggest that a manufacturer hold some finished goods inventory and build at a leveled pace to replenish what the customer takes away in a pull system (discussed in Chapter 9). The manufacturer screams, "But we have 15,000 part numbers!" The expert says, "Look for a smaller number of part numbers that are in big demand and perhaps even seasonal, build those when you have fewer real orders, and then keep those in inventory." That is, use a combination of build-to-stock and build-to-order like the aluminum gutter company in the case study at the end of this chapter. This sounds reasonable to the manufacturer. But then comes the hard sell. The TPS expert says to changeover frequently to level the mix of products built every day. Most manufacturers balk. After all, it is so convenient building in batches, making product A for a while, then retooling, and making product B for a while, and so on. Quick retooling does not seem possible, until an expert shows them how they can do a three-hour changeover in five minutes. Even then, it is difficult for many manufacturers to maintain the discipline of quick changeover. And the real root cause of the problem may be sales promotion strategies that contribute to uneven customer demand. The most sophisticated lean enterprises begin to change their policies in sales to maintain a level customer demand. This requires a deep commitment at the very top of the company, but these organizations quickly find the enormous benefits of *heijunka* make it a worthwhile investment.

It cannot be overstated. To achieve the lean benefits of continuous flow, you need Principle 4: *Level out the workload (Heijunka)*. Eliminating *muda* is only one-third of achieving flow. Eliminating *muri* and smoothing *mura* are equally important. Principle 4 focuses on *muri* and *mura* by leveling your product volume and mix and, most importantly, leveling out the demand on your people, equipment, and suppliers. Standardized work is far easier, cheaper, and faster to manage. It becomes increasingly easy to see the wastes of missing parts or defects. Without leveling, wastes naturally increase as people and equipment are driven to work like mad and then stop and wait, like the hare. Working according to a level schedule applies to all parts of Toyota, including sales. Everyone in the organization works together to achieve it.

Case Example: Building Aluminum Gutters on a Level Production Schedule

These days aluminum gutters for houses, at least in the U.S., are mostly built to order, on-site at the house. Rolls of materials are brought to the job site, where they are cut to length, end caps are formed, and the gutters are installed. A plant in the Midwest makes much of the material that installers use—the rolls of painted aluminum. While these rolls of aluminum are not complex, there is variation in the width of the gutters, the length, and the colors. They also are packaged in different boxes, depending on the customer.

This company originally adopted the build-to-order model. Deliveries were mostly made on time, but the process of getting raw materials, scheduling operations, building the product, moving the finished goods to a warehouse, and then shipping those goods from the dozen or so shipping docks was chaotic, to say the least. There was inventory everywhere. Yet the plant regularly was short of critical materials needed for the gutters ordered. Costs of expediting shipments to large customers were getting higher and higher. People were added and laid off with regularity. A big problem was the seasonality of the business. Big box warehouse stores like Home Depot bought large quantities of gutters in the spring and early summer and then business dropped dramatically for the rest of the year. So a large number of temporary workers were added in the peak season.

The Midwestern gutter plant decided to hire a consultant who used to work for the Toyota Supplier Support Center. The consultant said the unthinkable—the overall operation would be leaner if the plant would build select products to store away in inventory! This meant selectively adding some waste. They followed the consultant's advice.

He knew there is not one type of finished goods inventory, but four types. The first is real built-to-order product that should be set in a staging lane to be put on a truck immediately. The second is seasonal product for high-volume items the plant knows it will sell, that should be built steadily throughout the year and accumulated in a seasonal inventory buffer, which then will be drawn down in the busy spring/summer season. The third is safety stock, which is inventory used to buffer against unexpectedly high demand for products that are not in the seasonal buffer; it is customer-driven variation. The fourth is buffer stock, which is held to cushion against downtime in the factory, so customers will continue to get their product even when machines are down for repair; it is plant-driven variation.

On the consultant's recommendation, each of these four types of inventory was stored in a separate area at the aluminum gutter plant, so that everyone would always be able to see how much inventory of each type was available (Toyota Way Principle #7).

The inventory was replenished by using the *kanban* system (cards instructing the production line to make a certain quantity of a certain end product) explained in Chapter 9. For example, the largest amount of inventory is the seasonal inventory buffer. It is built up during the off-season and reaches a peak just before the spring, when sales are highest. There is a pre-specified amount of seasonal buffer and, based on that forecasted amount, *kanban* is used by the production cell to make only that remaining number of packages needed. In front of the inventory is what looks like a clothesline labeled with months of the year. For example, the amount that should be completed by August, based on a constant level of production over the year, has a sign saying "August." In August, if the inventory pile is larger than should be built by that time, the pile of inventory will have moved beyond the August sign and everyone will know that there is an excess inventory problem needing to be solved.

In *kanban*, discussed in Chapter 9, the information flow begins with the customer order and works backward through the operation. In this company, a final cutting and packaging (one-piece flow) cell gets customer orders that it has to build to order. But when those orders are low, the workers do not have to sit around with nothing to do. They can build to the seasonal inventory buffer or build to replace any safety stock or buffer stock that has been used. The seasonal inventory, safety stock, and buffer stock that need to be built are represented by *kanban* cards. The cards are sorted by a planner into a visual scheduling box called a "*heijunka* box," which levels the schedule. For each product, the box says what to make at 8:00 a.m., 8:10 a.m., 8:20 a.m., etc. Cards are put in the slots and delivered to the production cell. These tell the cell what to make and pace the work of the cell. As the cell uses materials, like the painted aluminum product, a *kanban* is sent back to the prior operation asking it to make more. Pull has been established all the way back to suppliers, like the paint supplier.

At the suggestion of the TPS consultant, other improvements were made, such as standardizing work procedures, reducing changeover time, and putting in error-proofing devices (discussed in Chapters 11 and 12). The result was a very smooth flow of product through the facility, so smooth that all outbound shipping could be handled through two docks with the other 10 closed down. In addition, the plant achieved incredible performance improvements. The overall lead time for making product was reduced by 40%, changeover time was reduced by 70%, WIP of painted product was reduced by 40%, inventory obsolescence was reduced by 60%, and on-time delivery was close to 100%. A typical lean transformation!

Note

1. Toyota would never let go of or demote workers displaced by productivity enhancements. This shortsighted cost-saving move would create ill will toward the company and prevent all other workers from cooperating in future *kaizen* efforts. Toyota always seeks alternative value-added work for workers displaced by production improvements.

Chapter 11

Principle 5:

Build a Culture of Stopping to Fix Problems, to Get Quality Right the First Time

Mr. Ohno used to say that no problem discovered when stopping the line should wait longer than tomorrow morning to be fixed. Because when making a car every minute we know we will have the same problem again tomorrow.

—Fujio Cho, President, Toyota Motor Corporation

Russ Scaffede was the vice president of Powertrain for Toyota when it launched the first American powertrain plant in Georgetown, Kentucky. He had worked decades for General Motors and had an excellent reputation as a manufacturing guy who could get things done and worked well with people. He was excited about the opportunity to work for Toyota and to help start up a brand-new plant following state-of-the-art TPS principles. He worked day and night to get the plant up to the demanding standards of Toyota and to please his Japanese mentors, including Fujio Cho, who was president of Toyota Motor Corporation in Kentucky.

Scaffede had learned the golden rule of automotive engine production: do not shut down the assembly plant! At General Motors, managers were judged by their ability to deliver the numbers. Get the job done no matter what—and that meant getting the engines to the assembly plant to keep it running. Too many engines, that was fine. Too few, that sent you to the unemployment line.

So when Cho remarked to Scaffede that he noticed he had not shut down the assembly plant once in a whole month, Scaffede perked up: "Yes sir, we had a great month, sir. I think you will be pleased to see more months like this." Scaffede was shocked to hear from Cho:[1]

Russ-san, you do not understand. If you are not shutting down the assembly plant, it means that you have no problems. All manufacturing plants have problems. So you must be hiding your problems. Please take out some inventory so the problems surface. You will shut down the assembly plant, but you will also continue to solve your problems and make even better-quality engines more efficiently.

When I interviewed Cho for this book, I asked him about differences in culture between what he experienced starting up the Georgetown, Kentucky, plant and managing Toyota plants in Japan. He did not hesitate to note that his number-one problem was getting group leaders and team members to stop the assembly line. They assumed that if they stopped the line, they would be blamed for doing a bad job. Cho explained that it took several months to "re-educate" them that it was a necessity to stop the line if they want to continually improve the process. He had to go down to the shop floor every day, meet with his managers, and, when he noticed a reason to stop the line, encourage the team leaders to stop it.[2]

The Principle—Stopping the Process to Build in Quality (*Jidoka*)

Jidoka, the second pillar of TPS, traces back to Sakichi Toyoda and his long string of inventions that revolutionized the automatic loom. Among his inventions was a device that detected when a thread broke and, when it did, it would immediately stop the loom. You could then reset the loom and, most importantly, solve the problem to avoid repeating the defect (waste). Like many elements of TPS, a simple invention and simple idea led to profound and broad insights. Quality should be built in. This means that you need a method to detect defects when they occur and automatically stop production so an employee can fix the problem before the defect continues downstream. One of the leading American students of TPS, Alex Warren, former Executive Vice President, Toyota Motor Corporation, Kentucky, defined *jidoka* and how it relates to employee empowerment:[3]

In the case of machines, we build devices into them, which detect abnormalities and automatically stop the machine upon such an occurrence. In the case of humans, we give them the power to push buttons or pull cords—called "andon cords"—which can bring our entire assembly line to a halt. Every team member has the responsibility to stop the line every time they see something that is out of standard. That's how we put the responsibility for quality in the hands of our team members. They feel the responsibility—they feel the power. They know they count.

Jidoka is also referred to as *autonomation*—equipment endowed with human intelligence to stop itself when it has a problem. In-station quality (preventing problems from being passed down the line) is much more effective and less costly than inspecting and repairing quality problems after the fact.

Lean manufacturing dramatically increases the importance of building things right the first time. With very low levels of inventory, there is no buffer to fall back on in case there is a quality problem. Problems in operation A will quickly shut down operation B. When equipment shuts down, flags or lights, usually with accompanying music or an alarm, are used to signal that help is needed to solve a quality problem. This signaling system is now referred to as *andon*. *Andon* refers to the light signal for help.

While it may seem obvious that you should catch and address quality problems immediately, the last thing management in traditional mass manufacturing would permit was a halt in production. Bad parts, when they happened to be noticed, were simply labeled and set aside to be repaired at another time and by another department. The mantra is "produce large quantities at all costs and fix problems later." As Gary Convis, President of the Toyota, Georgetown factory, explained to me:

> When I was at Ford, if you didn't run production 100% of the shift, you had to explain it to Division. You never shut the line off. We don't run 100% of the scheduled time out here. Toyota's strength, I think, is that the upper management realizes what the andon system is all about …. They've lived through it and they support it. So in all the years I've been with Toyota, I've never really had any criticism over lost production and putting a priority on safety and quality over hitting production targets. All they want to know is how are you problem solving to get to the root cause? And can we help you? I tell our team members there are two ways you can get in trouble here: one is you don't come to work, and two is you don't pull the cord if you've got a problem. The sense of accountability to ensure quality at each station is really critical.

So here we have a paradox. Toyota management says it is OK to run less than 100% of the time, even when the line is capable of running full-time, yet Toyota is regularly ranked among the most productive plants in the auto industry. Why? Because Toyota learned long ago that solving quality problems at the source saves time and money downstream. By continually surfacing problems and fixing them as they occur, you eliminate waste, your productivity soars, and competitors who are running assembly lines flat-out and letting problems accumulate get left in the dust.

When Toyota's competitors finally did start using Toyota's *andon* system, they made the mistake of assuming that the line-stop system was hardwired to each and every workstation—push the button and the entire assembly line comes to a screeching halt. At Toyota, the *andon* in all of its assembly and engine plants is called a "fixed-position line stop system." As shown in Figure 11-1, when an oper-

Figure 11-1. The *andon* system on a manual assembly line

ator in workstation five pushes an *andon* button, workstation five will light up in yellow, but the line will continue moving. The team leader has until the vehicle moves into the next workstation zone to respond, before the *andon* turns red and the line segment automatically stops. This is likely to be a matter of 15-30 seconds on an assembly line building cars at one a minute. In that time, the team leader might immediately fix the problem or note it can be fixed while the car is moving into other workstations and push the button again, canceling out the line stoppage. Or the team leader might conclude the line should stop. Team leaders have been carefully trained in standardized procedures on how to respond to *andon* calls.

The assembly line is divided into segments with small buffers of cars in between (typically containing seven to 10 cars). Because of the buffers, when a line segment stops, the next line segment can keep working for seven to 10 minutes before it will shut down, and so forth. Rarely does the whole plant shut down. Toyota achieved the purpose of *andon* without taking needless risks of lost production. It took U.S. auto companies years to understand how to apply this TPS tool. That may be one reason why workers and supervisors were hesitant to stop the line—because it actually stopped the entire line!

The built-in quality created by *jidoka* has never been more important to Toyota than with the Lexus and the necessity of meeting the extremely high expectations of Lexus owners. Until recently, Lexus vehicles were built only in Japan, where the culture and quality systems are undisputedly world-class. But can a Lexus be built in North America and still maintain the unbelievably meticulous levels of quality customers have come to expect? The answer is yes and it is being done in Toyota's Cambridge, Ontario, facility. Among the innovations used to maintain this "pursuit of perfection" are some technologies and processes that are taking *andon* to the next level.

Ray Tanguay, President of Toyota Motor Corporation, Canada, knew that the bar was now higher as he moved from making the Toyota Corolla and Matrix models to the Lexus RX 330. There are many innovations designed into the people, processes, and technologies of the new Lexus line to ensure that Lexus buyers will get Lexus quality. For example, production tools and robots on the line have been designed with built-in sensors to detect any deviation from standard and use radio transmitters to send an electronic signal to team leaders wearing headphone sets. Since not every problem can be caught in process, there is a highly detailed 170-point quality check for every finished RX 330. Tanguay wears a Blackberry personal digital assistant on his belt wherever he goes and every time an error is found on a finished vehicle, a report is instantly sent to Tanguay's Blackberry, along with a digital photo of the problem. Tanguay can transfer the photo to an electronic billboard in the plant so huge displays can be seen by workers and they can be cautious to prevent the same mistake from occurring. While the technology is new, the principle is the same: bring problems to the surface, make them visible, and go to work immediately on countermeasures.

Using Countermeasures and Error-Proofing to Fix Problems

This point has been made earlier in the book, but it bears repeating: the closer you are to one-piece flow, the quicker quality problems will surface to be addressed. This hit home for me personally in a unique opportunity I had in the summer of 1999. General Motors had a program through its joint venture with Toyota, the NUMMI plant, in Fremont, California, in which they sent GM employees for one week of training in TPS. This one week included two days of working on the Toyota assembly line—actually building cars. I was given the opportunity to participate.

I was assigned to a subassembly operation off the main assembly line that made axle assemblies for the Toyota Corolla and the equivalent GM model. In unibody cars, where there is no chassis, there is not a real axle but four independent modules that include the wheel, brakes, and shock absorber. They are built in the same sequence as the cars on the assembly line, put on pallets, and delivered in the order of cars moving down the assembly line. There are about two hours from the time a module is built until it will be attached to the car, so if there is a problem, you have a maximum of two hours to fix it before the main assembly line segment is shut down.

One of the easy "freshman" jobs I had was to attach a cotter pin to hold a ball joint in place. You put in the cotter pin, spread out the ends, and it locked the ball joint in place. This affected braking, so it was a safety item and very important. At one point early in the afternoon, I saw people scrambling around and there were a number of impromptu meetings. I asked the hourly associate next to me what was going on and he explained that a unit had gotten to the assembly line without a cotter pin and it was a big deal. An assembly line worker who installed the subassembly on the car had caught it. The team knew it happened only a couple of hours earlier. I assumed it was my mistake and immediately felt terrible for having missed installing a cotter pin. The team member claimed that it happened while I was on break. Who knows? But his response to my guilt feelings was even more important. He said:

> What is important is that the error went through eight people who did not see it. We are supposed to be inspecting the work when it comes to us. And the guy at the end of the line is supposed to check everything. This should never have gotten to the assembly line. Now we as a team are embarrassed because we did not do our jobs.

The other job I did was the final job on the line—a 100% inspection before loading the axles onto the pallet. The inspection included marking with colored felt-tip pens all the points you are supposed to inspect, including the cotter pin. It turns out that the unit with the missing cotter pin was not marked, so the inspector at the end of the line (which could have been me again—I'm not sure) failed to do a complete inspection. But again, what mattered is that the team went through intense problem solving to identify the root cause and put in place a countermeasure—all within two hours of when the problem occurred.

Although this missing cotter pin went undetected through the entire system of inspection, there were a remarkable number of countermeasures that had already been put in place on the axle line to prevent things like this from occurring. In fact, at every workstation there were numerous *poka-yoke* devices. *Poka-yoke* refers to mistake-proofing (also error-proofing or fool-proofing). These are creative devices that make it nearly impossible for an operator to make an error. Obviously, there was not a *poka-yoke* to detect whether the cotter pin was in place. Nonetheless, the level of sophistication on the line was impressive—there were 27 *poka-yoke* devices on the front axle line alone. Each *poka-yoke* device also had its own standard form that summarizes the problem addressed, the emergency alarm that will sound, the action to be taken in an emergency, the method and frequency of confirming the error-proof method is operating correctly, and the method for performing a quality check in the event the fool-proof method breaks down. This is the level of detail that Toyota uses to build in quality.

As an example, though they did not have a *poka-yoke* to check if the cotter pin was in place, they did have a light curtain over the tray of cotter pins. If the light curtain was not broken by the operator reaching through it to pick up a cotter pin, the moving assembly line would stop, an *andon* light would come on, and an alarm would sound. Another *poka-yoke* device required that I replace a tool (somewhat like a file, used to expand the cotter pin) back in its holder after each time I used it or the line would stop and an alarm would sound. It sounds a bit bizarre—one step removed from getting electric shocks for any misstep. But it is effective. Of course there are ways around the system, and the workers on the line find them all. But at Toyota there is a discipline about following the standard tasks that workers tend to adhere to.

Standardized work (Toyota Way Principle 6) is itself a countermeasure to quality problems. For example, the particular job I had was designed so it could be accomplished in 44.7 seconds of work and walk time. The takt time (line speed in this case) was 57 seconds per job, so there was plenty of slack time; hence it was a freshman job. Yet even for this simple job there were 28 steps shown on the "standard work chart," right down to the number of footsteps to take to and from the conveyor. This "standard work chart" was posted at my job site, where there were visuals that also explained potential quality problems. A more detailed version in a notebook had each of the 28 steps on its own sheet, described in greater detail along with a digital photo of that step being performed correctly. Very little was left to chance. Whenever there is a quality problem, the standard work chart is reviewed to see if something is missing that allowed the error to occur and, if so, the chart is updated accordingly.

Keep Quality Control Simple and Involve Team Members

If American and European companies got anything from the invasion of Japanese products to the U.S. market in the 1980s, it was quality fever. The level of quality consciousness in Japanese companies made our heads spin. They were crafting fine art and we were slapping parts together. But we woke up and worked hard to fix this. J.D. Power's recent surveys of initial quality (during the first three months of ownership) show that the gap between Japanese auto companies and U.S. and European competitors has shrunk to the point of being barely noticeable. But longer-term data shows that the quality differential has not been erased. It has just been hidden. It is relatively easy to inspect an assembled vehicle and fix all the problems before the customer has a chance to see them. But inspected-in quality is often temporary quality.

I have seen a lot of non-public internal quality data on auto companies, including data collected by J.D. Power and the results are striking. Initial quality shows little difference across automakers. But three years out, the gap grows. Five years out, the gap balloons. In the 2003 annual auto issue of *Consumer Reports*, the magazine summarizes its studies of durability. Not surprisingly Acura, Toyota, and Lexus are the top three makes for problems per 100 vehicles during the first three years of ownership, with 25 problems per 100 vehicles for Toyota and Lexus. The U.S. and European makes are mostly at the bottom of the list, with 50, 60, 70 problems per 100—two to three times worse than Toyota and Lexus. Why does the gap persist?

Unfortunately, for many companies the essence of building in quality has gotten lost in bureaucratic and technical details. Things like ISO-9000, an industrial quality standard that calls for all kinds of detailed standard operating procedures, for whatever good they have done, have made companies believe that if they put together detailed rule books the rules will be followed. Quality planning departments are armed with reams of data analyzed using the most sophisticated statistical analysis methods. Six Sigma has brought us roving bands of black belts who attack major quality problems with a vengeance, armed with an arsenal of sophisticated technical methods.

At Toyota they keep things simple and use very few complex statistical tools. The quality specialists and team members have just four key tools:

- Go and see.
- Analyze the situation.
- Use one-piece flow and *andon* to surface problems.
- Ask "Why?" five times.

(Asking "why" five times whenever you uncover a problem will provide root cause analysis of the problem as well as countermeasures to solve it. As discussed in Chapter 20, it's an excellent team tool for keeping the focus on solving problems rather than blaming someone for them, which is just another form of *muda*.)

Don Jackson, VP of manufacturing for Toyota's Georgetown plant, was a quality manager for a U.S. auto supplier before joining Toyota. He had been a stickler for detail and defended the complex quality manuals he had helped write. At Toyota he learned the power of simplicity. As he described it, "Before joining Toyota I made a lot of policies and procedures too difficult to follow. They were doomed for failure." He still participates in some quality audits of suppliers, but his approach and philosophy are now completely different from the more bureaucratic mindset he had before joining Toyota:

You can write a complex procedure that covers the operator, equipment main-tenance, and a quality audit—and theoretically, the process will run forever. But my philosophy is support the team members who are running the process. I want them to be able to know everything because they're the ones producing the product. So those team members have to know that the preventative main-tenance was done on schedule, and their equipment is in good shape by some visual control system. The quality check every hour ... those team members should know that it was done and it was OK every hour or they stop the line. Then finally, they must know what their job requirements are and know that they're getting good built-in quality by some means. So those team members are in total control. I want that team member to know that they have everything they need to build that product correctly ,... man, material, method, machine.

Obviously this audit is very different than the typical quality audit of follow-ing detailed procedures from a manual, perhaps analyzing some statistical data, and maybe even checking to see if the procedures are being followed. Jackson is looking with a different set of eyes—the eyes of the operator controlling the process. He is looking at quality from the point of view of the shop floor—the actual situation (*genchi genbutsu*).

Building in Quality in a Services Environment

You can extend Toyota Way Principle 4: *Build a culture of stopping to fix problems, to get quality right the first time* to the office environment. Of course you are not going to hang *andon* lights over everyone's desk so they can signal in case there is a problem. Clearly the tool of *andon* as it is practiced in manufacturing is designed for very short-cycle, repetitive jobs where immediate help is needed and seconds count. This is the case with some highly repetitive office work, like call centers or data entry departments, and the same tools could be applied. But most kinds of office environments are non-routine work where "stop when there is a quality prob-lem" is a matter of philosophy and personal work habits. In a typical office environ-ment, a person waits and waits for information in order to move along several piles of work in process and then, when the information arrives, often has to sprint madly to meet deadlines, making numerous errors and missing important details along the way. Obviously, this "system" of work needs a different quality model.

Toyota engineering provides one of the better examples of designing in qual-ity within a professional services environment. For example, the extensive use of checklists and standards that will be discussed in Chapter 12 is one way to ensure quality at the source. Also, Toyota's bias toward incremental development—carry-ing over standard components from vehicle to vehicle and focusing on changing selected aspects of the vehicle—also helps greatly. There are many things that

Toyota does that help ensure quality from the start. We will highlight two other areas that illustrate the *jidoka* philosophy in engineering.

First, we saw in the Prius case that at several key junctures in the program the chief engineer was willing to stop and reflect and consider all options (Toyota Way Principle 13) before racing ahead. This was a program of enormous visibility within Toyota and, later, with the public, and the self-imposed deadlines were severe. Timing was of the essence. Yet in the early stages of developing the Prius concept, Uchiyamada saw the team getting bogged down in specific technical details on engine technology. He asked the group to "stop focusing on hardware." The team stepped back and spent several days brainstorming key concepts to describe the 21st-century car and boiling them down to the goal of a "small, fuel-efficient car." Several times throughout the Prius development, Uchiyamada took a "time-out" from the development details to step back and consider where the program was headed.

When my colleagues and students and I originally studied Toyota's product development system, we called it "set-based concurrent engineering" (Ward, Liker, Cristiano, and Sobek, 1995). We noticed that Toyota leaders tended to consider a broad set of alternatives and study them thoroughly before making a final decision. Several leaders explained that the biggest challenge they faced in training young engineers is to slow them down and get them to stop and reflect on all the alternatives they should consider. This is an example of stopping and fixing the problem before racing ahead and causing defects downstream.

A second and related example is in the early stages of development, before the styling department has agreed on the final vehicle design—called "clay-model freeze" in automotive jargon. In traditional auto companies, development engineers think there is nothing to engineer until styling completes the design, because the engineering work would be wasted since key parts of the vehicle could change. Toyota views this time as an opportunity to study alternatives and have them ready to go when the styling design is frozen. It is called the *kentou* (study drawing) phase and the focus in this period is generating hundreds of study drawings, called *kentouzu*.

While the artist is styling in the design studios, engineers are studying many different engineering alternatives in the interior of the car, the exterior, and the engine. They know pretty closely what the main dimensions of the vehicle will be and have made a lot of decisions about aerodynamics, power, and feel of the ride. So they can sketch out these alternatives and share the sketches broadly across specialties. For example, the 2002 Camry headlights were aggressively designed, extending deeply back and cutting into the hood and fender. Body engineers made sketches and determined, based on the checklists of formability in stamping, that it could lead to stamped metal parts that would have quality problems. They suggested to the styling department a redesign of the headlights to avoid the quality problems yet provide the look that styling wanted. Styling approved the changes. Thus, a quality problem that might have haunted manufacturing for years, or even haunted customers several years after they took ownership, was avoided because of this intense study period to design quality into the vehicle very early in the design process.

Building in Quality Is a Principle, Not a Technology

A story I heard from a plant manager at Reiter Automotive (supplier of sound-dampening materials) helped put into perspective what it takes to build in quality. He ran a plant that makes sound-dampening materials in Chicago and supplied them to Toyota. He had a Toyota mentor who was teaching him TPS. The Toyota mentor had suggested they needed an *andon* system to immediately detect quality problems. So the plant manager got his engineers to spec out an *andon* system similar to the kind Toyota uses, with light boards hung from the rafters that are directly hooked up to buttons the operator pushes. This was a relatively small plant compared with the Toyota plant, but he wanted to use the very best to implement this important system. When the Toyota mentor visited and he proudly showed him the elaborate *andon* system they had on order, the mentor said, "No, no, no. You do not understand. Come with me." He then charged off and drove the plant manager to a local hardware store. He picked out a red flag, a yellow flag, and a green flag. He handed them to the plant manager and said, "*Andon*." His point was that implementing *andon* is not the same thing as buying fancy new technology. *Andon* works only when you teach your employees the importance of bringing problems to the surface so they can be quickly solved. Unless you have a problem-solving process already in place and people are following it, there's no point in spending money on fancy technology. Americans tend to think that buying expensive new technology is a good way to solve problems. Toyota prefers to first use people and processes to solve problems, then supplement and support its people with technology.

General Motors early on copied Toyota's NUMMI plant system of team leaders—hourly associates whose primary job is to support team members. But the team leaders spent a good deal of their time in the back room smoking cigarettes or playing cards. What good is pushing the *andon* button if nobody is around to respond? In a later incarnation, GM got smarter. In their Cadillac plant in Hamtramck, Michigan, they put in sophisticated fixed-position stop *andons*. These are full-blown systems. When the button is pushed, the line will keep going until the car enters the next workstation and then the line will automatically stop at a "fixed position." It is very expensive and in the past GM would have rolled this out quickly to show a payoff. Instead, they refused to turn on the automatic stopping capability until a work team had passed an overall lean audit. GM realized that the *andon* system would be effective only when the operators followed standardized work, the *kanban* system was reliably pulling materials to the workstation, workplace discipline was followed, and the team leaders were responding to problems. As a result, each work team struggled to pass the audit so they would have the privilege of having the complete *andon* system turned on. There were celebrations each time a team succeeded.

In the Toyota Way of doing things, what matters when improving quality is enabling the process and the people. You can spend a great deal of money on the latest and greatest *andon* and have no impact whatsoever on quality. Instead, you need to constantly reinforce the principle that quality is everyone's responsibility throughout the organization. Quality for the customer drives your value proposition, so there is no compromising on quality, because adding value to your customer is what keeps you in business and allows you to make money so everyone can continue to be part of the company.

A common Toyota quality tactic is to front-load projects of all kinds, to anticipate problems as early as possible and put in place countermeasures before the problems even occur. Occasionally a time-out is required to reflect on the purpose and direction of the project before moving on. This is done within the context of stretch-timing objectives that are rarely compromised. The Toyota Way is to build into the culture the philosophy of stopping or slowing down to get quality right the first time to enhance productivity in the long run. We saw this repeatedly in the Prius case. Closely related to this philosophy are the problem-solving and organizational-learning approaches of the Toyota Way. It should be clear to the reader by now that all aspects of the Toyota Way—philosophy, processes, partners, and problem solving—support its ability to "build in quality" and satisfy customers.

Notes

1. This quote is a paraphrase from the many times I have heard Russ Scaffede tell this story.
2. This is a classic example of Principle 12: *Go and see for yourself to thoroughly understand the situation (genchi genbutsu)*. Today there are only a handful of companies that are run by a president who will walk the shop floor and teach a philosophical lesson, such as the old Hewlett-Packard Company when Bill Hewlett and Dave Packard did daily walkabouts, called management by walking around (MBWA), to personally engage with the engineers.
3. From *The Toyota Way*, Toyota Motor Company, April 2001.

Chapter 12

Principle 6:
Standardized Tasks Are the Foundation for Continuous Improvement and Employee Empowerment

Standard work sheets and the information contained in them are important elements of the Toyota Production System. For a production person to be able to write a standard work sheet that other workers can understand, he or she must be convinced of its importance.... High production efficiency has been maintained by preventing the recurrence of defective products, operational mistakes, and accidents, and by incorporating workers' ideas. All of this is possible because of the inconspicuous standard work sheet.

—Taiichi Ohno

Whether your employees are designing intricate new devices, styling new attractive products, processing accounts payable, developing new software, or working as nurses, they are likely to respond to the idea of standardizing their work in the same way: "We are creative, thinking professionals and every task we do is a unique project." If you are not in manufacturing, you may be surprised to learn that even workers on the assembly line believe they have a knack for doing the job best their own way and that standards will simply set them back. But some level of standardization is possible and, as we will see, is the backbone of Toyota Way processes.

Standardizing tasks became a "science" when mass production replaced the craft form of production. Much of modern manufacturing and standardization is based on the principles of industrial engineering first set forth by Frederick Taylor, the "father of scientific management."

In the automotive world, plants had armies of industrial engineers who implemented Taylor's approach of time and motion studies. Industrial engineers

(IEs) were everywhere, timing every second of workers' tasks and trying to squeeze every extra bit of productivity out of the labor force. Open and honest workers who shared their work practices with the IEs would quickly find the job standards raised and they would soon be working harder for no extra money. So workers withheld techniques and labor-saving devices they invented and hid them whenever the IEs were around. They deliberately worked slower when the IEs were doing a study, so expectations were set low. The IEs caught on to this and would at times try sneaking up on the operator to watch him or her at work. Often efficiency and time studies that changed the job description and responsibilities led to union grievances and became a major source of conflict between management and workers.

Now companies use computers to accurately monitor human motions and instantly report on productivity of individual workers. As a result, people know they are being monitored, so they will work to make the numbers, often regardless of quality. Sadly, they become slaves to the numbers, rather than focus on a company's mission statement or philosophy. It doesn't have to be this way, as we will see with Toyota's approach to standardized tasks.

Ford Motor Company was one of the early mass-production giants associated with rigid standardization on the moving assembly line, and Toyota's approach to standardized work was partially shaped by Henry Ford's view. While Ford eventually became a rigid bureaucracy that followed the destructive practices of Taylor's scientific management, this was not the view that the founder had of standards. Henry Ford's (1988) perspective, written back in 1926, fits well with the Toyota view:

> Today's standardization ... is the necessary foundation on which tomorrow's improvement will be based. If you think of "standardization" as the best you know today, but which is to be improved tomorrow—you get somewhere. But if you think of standards as confining, then progress stops.

Even more influential than Henry Ford was the methodology and philosophy of the American military's Training Within Industry (TWI) service. This program was established in 1940 during WWII to increase production to support the Allied forces. It was based on the belief that the way to learn about industrial engineering methods was through application on the shop floor and that standardized work should be a cooperative effort between the foreman and the worker (Huntzinger, 2002). During the U.S. occupation and rebuilding efforts of Japan after WWII, a former TWI trainer and his group called "The Four Horsemen" taught Japanese businesses these standardization processes. The Toyota Way of going to the source, observing in detail, and learning by doing were all very much influenced by TWI (Dietz and Bevens, 1970) and became the backbone of Toyota's standardization philosophy.

Standardized work in manufacturing at Toyota is much broader than writing out a list of steps the operator must follow. Toyota President Cho describes it this way:

> *Our standardized work consists of three elements—takt time (time required to complete one job at the pace of customer demand), the sequence of doing things or sequence of processes, and how much inventory or stock on hand the individual worker needs to have in order to accomplish that standardized work. Based upon these three elements, takt time, sequence, and standardized stock on hand, the standard work is set.*

In this chapter, we will see that, like so many organizational practices, the Toyota Way has turned the practice of standardized work on its head. What can be perceived as negative or ineffective becomes positive and effective within the Toyota Way and builds collaborative teams rather than conflict between employees and management. As we will see, standardized work was never intended by Toyota to be a management tool to be imposed coercively on the work force. On the contrary, rather than enforcing rigid standards that can make jobs routine and degrading, standardized work is the basis for empowering workers and innovation in the work place.

The Principle: Standardization Is the Basis for Continuous Improvement and Quality

Toyota's standards have a much broader role than making shop floor workers' tasks repeatable and efficient. The Toyota Way results in standardized tasks throughout the company's white-collar work processes, such as engineering. Everyone in the company is aware of and practices standardization. For example, an engineer can walk into any Toyota factory in the world and see almost identical processes. Toyota also applies standards to the design of products and manufacturing equipment.

Managers have a misconception that standardization is all about finding the scientifically one best way to do a task and freezing it. As Imai (1986) explained so well in *Kaizen*, his famous book on continuous improvement, it is impossible to improve any process until it is standardized. If the process is shifting from here to there, then any improvement will just be one more variation that is occasionally used and mostly ignored. One must standardize, and thus stabilize the process, before continuous improvements can be made. As an example, if you want to learn golf, the first thing an instructor will teach you is the basic golf swing. Then you need to practice, practice, and practice to stabilize your swing. Until you have the fundamental skills needed to swing the club consistently, there is no hope of improving your golf game.

Standardized work is also a key facilitator of building in quality. Talk with any well-trained group leader at Toyota and ask how he or she can ensure zero defects. The answer is always "Through standardized work." Whenever a defect is discovered, the first question asked is "Was standardized work followed?" As part of the problem-solving process, the leader will watch the worker and go through the standardized work sheet step by step to look for deviations. If the worker is following the standardized work and the defects still occur, then the standards need to be modified.

In fact, at Toyota the standard work is posted outward, away from the operator. The operator is trained using the standardized work, but then must do the job and not look up at the standardized work sheet. The standard work sheet is posted outward for the team leaders and group leaders to audit to see if it is being followed by the operator.

Any good quality manager at any company knows that you cannot guarantee quality without standard procedures for ensuring consistency in the process. Many quality departments make a good living turning out volumes of such procedures. Unfortunately, the role of the quality department is often to assign blame for failing to "follow the procedures" when there is a quality problem. The Toyota Way is to enable those doing the work to design and build in quality by writing the standardized task procedures themselves. Any quality procedures have to be simple and practical enough to be used every day by the people doing the work.

Coercive vs. Enabling Bureaucracies—Employee Empowerment

Under Taylor's (1947) scientific management, workers were viewed as machines who needed to be made as efficient as possible through the manipulations of industrial engineers and autocratic managers. The process consisted of the following:

- Scientifically determining the one best way of doing the job.
- Scientifically developing the one best way to train someone to do the job.
- Scientifically selecting people who were most capable of doing the job in that way.
- Training foremen to teach their "subordinates" and monitor them so they followed the one best way.
- Creating financial incentives for workers to follow the one best way and exceed the performance standard scientifically set by the industrial engineer.

Taylor did achieve tremendous productivity gains by applying scientific management principles. But he also created very rigid bureaucracies in which managers were supposed to do the thinking and workers were to blindly execute the standardized procedures. The results were predictable:

- Red tape
- Tall, hierarchical organizational structures
- Top-down control
- Books and books of written rules and procedures
- Slow and cumbersome implementation and application
- Poor communication
- Resistance to change
- Static and inefficient rules and procedures

Most bureaucracies are static, internally focused on efficiency, controlling of employees, unresponsive to changes in the environment, and generally unpleasant to work in (Burns and Stalker, 1994). But in organizational theory, bureaucracies are not necessarily bad. Bureaucracies can be very efficient if the environment is very stable and if technology changes very little. However, most modern organizations try to be flexible and "organic," meaning focused on effectiveness, adaptable to change, and empowering of their employees. Organic organizations are more effective when the environment and technology are changing rapidly. So it would appear, since the world around us is changing at the speed of thought, that it's time to throw out the bureaucratic standards and policies and create self-managing teams to be flexible and competitive. The Toyota Way follows neither approach.

Paul Adler, an organizational theory expert who has studied Toyota's organizational practices, noticed from in-depth studies of Toyota's NUMMI plant in California that the jobs are highly repetitive with short cycle times (e.g., about one minute before repeating). The workers follow very detailed standardized procedures that touch every aspect of the organization. In the workplace, there is a place for everything and everything is in its place. Waste is being eliminated to continually increase productivity. There are a lot of team leaders and group leaders and an extensive hierarchy. There is strict discipline about time, cost, quality ... and safety—virtually every minute of the day is structured. In short, NUMMI has all the characteristics associated with bureaucracy and a very "mechanistic" organization. Wasn't this exactly what Fredrick Taylor's scientific management tried to attain?

But NUMMI also has many of the characteristics associated with flexible organizations referred to as "organic": extensive employee involvement, a lot of communication, innovation, flexibility, high morale, and a strong customer focus. This caused Adler to rethink some of the traditional theories about bureaucratic organizations. He realized that there are not two types of organizations—bureaucratic/mechanistic vs. organic—but at least four, as shown in Figure 12-1. You can distinguish organizations with extensive bureaucratic rules and structures (mechanistic) from those unencumbered by bureaucracy (organic). But often when we think of bureaucracy, we think of a set of rigid rules and procedures. The rules and

SOCIAL STRUCTURE

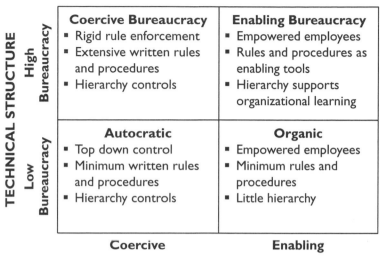

		Coercive	Enabling
	High Bureaucracy	**Coercive Bureaucracy** ▪ Rigid rule enforcement ▪ Extensive written rules and procedures ▪ Hierarchy controls	**Enabling Bureaucracy** ▪ Empowered employees ▪ Rules and procedures as enabling tools ▪ Hierarchy supports organizational learning
TECHNICAL STRUCTURE	**Low Bureaucracy**	**Autocratic** ▪ Top down control ▪ Minimum written rules and procedures ▪ Hierarchy controls	**Organic** ▪ Empowered employees ▪ Minimum rules and procedures ▪ Little hierarchy

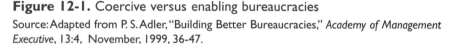

Figure 12-1. Coercive versus enabling bureaucracies

Source: Adapted from P. S. Adler, "Building Better Bureaucracies," *Academy of Management Executive*, 13:4, November, 1999, 36-47.

procedures are all part of the technical structure of the organization. But this ignores the social structure, which can be either "coercive" or "enabling." When you put together the two technical structures with the two social structures, you get the four types of organization and two types of bureaucracy. TPS at NUMMI was proving that the technical standardization when coupled with enabling social structures can lead to "enabling bureaucracy."

Adler (1999) went further in contrasting coercive bureaucracies with enabling bureaucracies. While both carefully design systems and procedures that must be followed, the similarity stops there. Figure 12-2 summarizes how the coercive bureaucracy uses standards to control people, catch them breaking the rules, and punish them to get them back in line. The workers feel like they are part of a chain gang, rather than a home team. By contrast, enabling systems are simply the best practice methods, designed and improved upon with the participation of the work force. The standards actually help people control their own work.

The key difference between Taylorism and the Toyota Way is that the Toyota Way preaches that the worker is the most valuable resource—not just a pair of hands taking orders, but an analyst and problem solver. From this perspective, suddenly Toyota's bureaucratic, top-down system becomes the basis for flexibility and innovation. Adler called this behavior "democratic Taylorism."

The assumption that to be a high-performance organization meant throwing out the mechanistic bureaucratic rulebook and adopting an organic system to

Coercive Systems and Procedures	Enabling Systems and Procedures
Systems focus on performance standards so as to highlight poor performance.	Focus on best practice methods: information on performance standards is not much use without information on best practices for achieving them.
Standardize the systems to minimize gameplaying and monitoring costs.	Systems should allow customization to different levels of skill/experience and should guide flexible improvisation.
Systems should be designed so as to keep employees out of the control loop.	Systems should help people control their own work: help them form mental models of the system by "glass box" design.
Systems are instructions to be followed, not challenged.	Systems are best practice templates to be improved.

Figure 12-2. Coercive versus enabling design of systems and standards

Source: P. S. Adler, "Building Better Bureaucracies," *Academy of Management Executive*, 13:4, November, 1999, 36-47.

empower employees did a great deal of harm to organizations in the 1980s and 1990s. The Toyota Way shows that, to remain competitive year after year and continually stay among the industry leaders, a company must have viable and enabling standards so it can continually improve upon repeatable processes.

Standardizing Work for a New Product Launch

The Toyota Way of handling the chaos of getting an army of people involved in creating and launching a new vehicle is to standardize the work in a balanced way that doesn't give complete control to any group of employees. Having only engineers devise the standards would be a form of Taylorism. On the other hand, having all the workers come to consensus on every step would be overly organic, resulting in chaos. Toyota's innovative approach is to develop a "pilot team." When a new product is in the early planning stages, workers representing all the major areas of the factory are brought together full time to an office area where as a team they help plan the launch of the vehicle. They work hand in hand with engineering and develop the initial standardized work used when the product is first launched. Then it is turned over to the production teams to improve. As Gary Convis, President of Toyota's Kentucky manufacturing operations, explained:

> *Pilot teams are put together, especially when we launch a new model, like we just launched the Camry. Team member voices are heard by way of that link. Usually it's a three-year assignment. We have a four-year model change cycle,*

so we'll have an Avalon model change, then we'll have a Camry model change, and we'll have a Sienna model change. So there are enough big model changes to have these guys go through at least one or two before they rotate back out.

There is a great deal of learning for team members on the pilot team about the design and production of the new vehicle, and when they finish their rotation they are back on the floor as team members, contributing to and improving the standardized work. This is important, because launching a new vehicle is an exercise in coordinating thousands of parts, with thousands of people making detailed engineering decisions that must fit together at the right time.

When my associates and I studied Toyota's product development system, we found that standardization promotes effective teamwork by teaching employees similar terminology, skills, and rules of play. From the time they are hired into the company, engineers are trained to learn the standards of product development. They all go through a similar training regimen of "learning by doing" (Sobek, Liker, and Ward, 1998). Toyota engineers also make extensive use of design standards that go back to when Toyota first started engineering cars. Within each section—door latches, seat-raising mechanisms, steering wheels—engineering checklists have evolved from what has been learned as good and bad design practice. The engineer uses these checklist books from his or her first days at Toyota and develops them further with each new vehicle program. More recently, Toyota has computerized these books.

U.S. companies have tried to imitate Toyota's approach by going right to computers, creating large databases of engineering standards, but without success. The reason is they have not trained their engineers to have the discipline to use the standards and improve on them. Capturing knowledge is not difficult. The hard part is getting people to use the standards in a database and contribute to improving it. Toyota spends years working with its people to instill in them the importance of using and improving standards.

Standardization as an Enabler

The critical task when implementing standardization is to find that balance between providing employees with rigid procedures to follow and providing the freedom to innovate and be creative to meet challenging targets consistently for cost, quality, and delivery. The key to achieving this balance lies in the way people write standards as well as who contributes to them.

First, the standards have to be specific enough to be useful guides, yet general enough to allow for some flexibility. In repetitive manual work, standards are pretty specific. In engineering, since there are no fixed quantities, the standards need to be more variable. For example, knowing how the curvature of the hood of a car will relate to the air/wind resistance of that body part is more useful than knowing a specific parameter for the curve of the hood.

Second, the people doing the work have to improve the standards. There is simply not enough time in a workweek for industrial engineers to be everywhere writing and rewriting standards. Nobody likes following someone's detailed rules and procedures when they are imposed on them. Imposed rules that are strictly policed become coercive and a source of friction and resistance between management and workers. However, people happily focused on doing a good job appreciate getting tips and best practices, particularly if they have some flexibility in adding their own ideas. In addition, it is very empowering to find that everyone is going to use your improvement as a new standard. Using standardization at Toyota is the foundation for continuous improvement, innovation, and employee growth.

Chapter 13

Principle 7:
Use Visual Control So
No Problems Are Hidden

*Mr. Ohno was passionate about TPS. He said you must clean up every-
thing so you can see problems. He would complain if he could not look
and see and tell if there is a problem.*
— Fujio Cho, President, Toyota Motor Corporation

If you walked into most manufacturing plants outside Japan in the 1980s, you
would see a mess. But it was what you would not see that was most important. You would not be able to see around the piles and piles of inventory that
were stacked to the roof. You would not be able to tell whether items were in place
or out of place. Certainly you could not see if there were problems with how work
was being done, as Taiichi Ohno wanted. The accepted dysfunction of the day was
to see no problems and hear no problems until the hidden problems jumped up
and bit you in the face. By that time, it usually wasn't a problem, but a fire-fight-
ing crisis, and managers would spend much of their time jumping from putting
out one fire to the next. In short, crisis management was the accepted mentality
of the day.

The Donnelly Mirrors (now Magna Donnelly) Grand Haven plant, which
produces exterior automotive mirrors, was so disorganized when they began implementing lean manufacturing that no one could see much of anything except waste.
One day a Ford Taurus mysteriously disappeared. It had been in the factory so they
could try fitting it with some prototype mirrors. When it vanished, they even filed
a police report. Then it turned up months later. Guess where it was. In the back
of the plant, surrounded by inventory. Donnelly associates now tell this story to
illustrate how far they have come since implementing lean (Liker, 1997).

Outrageous as the Donnelly story may seem, it dramatizes what many of us deal with in our workplaces daily. Try this little exercise at your own place of work. Go up to a co-worker and ask to see a specific document, tool, or something on his or her computer or the company's intranet. Watch to see if the person can go immediately to one place and pull out the document, locate the tool, or find the information on the computer on the first try. The amount of time it takes, and perhaps the person's frustration level, will most likely tell you at a glance whether your co-worker's way of visually organizing his or her workplace is in control or out of control. Or observe a conference room that is used for important planning meetings. (Some call them "war rooms.") Is it easy to see at a glance the status of what is going on? What do you see when you look at the walls? Are there charts and graphs that tell you if today the managers are ahead or behind schedule on the action items? Are any abnormalities or delays in the project or operation easily visible? That is, are there "visual controls," the ability to see abnormalities at a glance?

The Principle—Clean It Up, Make It Visual

When Americans were making pilgrimages to Japanese plants in the 1970s and '80s, the first reaction was invariably "The factories were so clean you could eat off of the floor." For the Japanese this was simply a matter of pride. Why would you want to live in a pigpen? But their efforts go beyond making the factory look clean and orderly. In Japan there are "5S programs" that comprise a series of activities for eliminating wastes that contribute to errors, defects, and injuries in the workplace. Here are the five S's (*seiri, seiton, seiso, seiketsu,* and *shitsuke,* translated into English):

1. Sort—Sort through items and keep only what is needed while disposing of what is not.
2. Straighten (orderliness)—"A place for everything and everything in its place."
3. Shine (cleanliness)— The cleaning process often acts as a form of inspection that exposes abnormal and pre-failure conditions that could hurt quality or cause machine failure.
4. Standardize (create rules)—Develop systems and procedures to maintain and monitor the first three S's.
5. Sustain (self-discipline)—Maintaining a stabilized workplace is an ongoing process of continuous improvement.

In mass production, without the five S's, many wastes accumulate over the years, covering up problems, and becoming an accepted dysfunctional way of doing business. The five S's together create a continuous process for improving the work environment, as illustrated in Figure 13-1. Start by sorting through what is in the office or shop to separate what is needed every day to perform value-added work from what is seldom or never used. Mark the rarely used items with red tags and move them outside of the work area. Then create permanent locations for each part or tool in the order of how much it is needed to support the operator as if he or she were a surgeon. The operator should be able to immediately reach for each commonly used part or tool. Then shine, making sure everything stays clean every day. Standardize, as described in the previous chapter, to maintain the first three pillars. Sustain keeps the benefits of 5S working by making a habit of properly maintaining the correct procedures. Sustain is a team-oriented continuous improvement technique that managers play a critical role in implementing to support 5S. The 5S programs that are the best sustained, in my experience, are audited regularly, e.g., monthly, by managers, who use a standard audit form and often give symbolic rewards for the best team. One plant awarded the best team with a golden broom, which was rotated when another team got better. In advanced lean plants, work teams audit their own areas weekly or even daily and then managers inspect randomly.

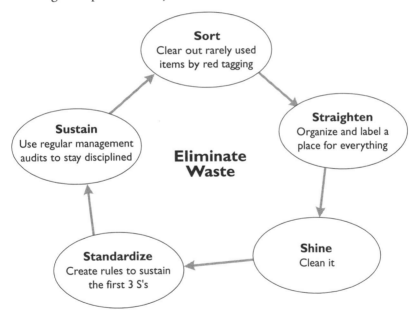

Figure 13-1. The 5 S's

Unfortunately, some companies have confused 5S with lean production. More than one company I have visited has related some version of the following story. "A few years back, management decided to try this lean stuff. They paid a million dollars to a training company who taught us 5S and did a lot of 5S workshops. The place got cleaned up and looked better than it ever had since I started working here.

But we did not save any money, quality did not get better, and eventually management stopped the program. We ended up right back where we started."

The Toyota Way is not about using 5S to neatly organize and label materials, tools, and waste to maintain a clean and shiny environment. Visual control of a well-planned lean system is different from making a mass-production operation neat and shiny. Lean systems use 5S to support a smooth flow to takt time. 5S is also a tool to help make problems visible and, if used in a sophisticated way, can be part of the process of visual control of a well-planned lean system (Hirano, 1995).

Visual Control Systems Are About Improving Value Added Flow

Visual control is any communication device used in the work environment that tells us at a glance how work should be done and whether it is deviating from the standard. It helps employees who want to do a good job see immediately how they are doing. It might show where items belong, how many items belong there, what the standard procedure is for doing something, the status of work in process, and many other types of information critical to the flow of work activities. In the broadest sense, visual control refers to the design of just-in-time information of all types to ensure fast and proper execution of operations and processes. There are many excellent examples in everyday life, such as traffic signals and signage. Because it is a matter of life and death, traffic signals tend to be well-designed visual controls. Good traffic signs don't require you to study them: their meaning is immediately clear.

Visual control goes beyond capturing deviations from a target or goal on charts and graphs and posting them publicly. Visual controls at Toyota are integrated into the process of the value-added work. The *visual* aspect means being able to look at the process, a piece of equipment, inventory, or information or at a worker performing a job and immediately see the standard being used to perform the task and if there is a deviation from the standard. Ask this question: can your manager walk through the shop floor, office, or any type of facility where work is being performed and recognize if standard work or procedures are being followed? If you have a clear standard for every tool to be hung in a certain place and it's made visual, then the manager can see if anything is out of place. This is why a popular 5S activity is to create shadow tool boards. A "shadow" of each tool is painted on the board in the place that tool should be hung; for example, the shape of a hammer shows where the hammer goes, so it is obvious if the hammer is missing. Similarly, having clearly visible indicators of minimum and maximum levels for inventory will help the manager (and everyone else) see if inventory is being managed appropriately. Well-designed charts and graphs that are kept up every day can visually control projects in offices.

Principle 7 of the Toyota Way is to use visual control to improve flow. Deviations from the standard should be deviations from working to takt time, one piece at a time. In fact, many of the tools associated with lean production are visual controls used to make visible any deviations from the standard and to facilitate flow. Examples include *kanban*, the one-piece-flow cell, *andon*, and standardized work. If there is no *kanban* card asking to be filled on a bin, then the bin should not be there. The filled bin without a *kanban* card is a visual signal of overproduction. A well-designed cell will immediately reveal extra pieces of WIP through clearly marked places for the standard WIP. The *andon* cord signals a deviation from standard operating conditions. Standard task procedures are posted, so it is clear what the best-known method is for achieving flow at each operator's station. Observed deviations from the standard procedure indicate a problem. In essence, Toyota uses an integrated set of visual controls or a *visual control system* designed to create a transparent and waste-free environment. Let's look at a most unlikely place where visual control enhances flow—a "lean" mega-warehouse.

Visual Control to Enhance Flow in a Service Parts Warehouse

Automakers in the U.S., as well as Japan, are required by law to keep service parts for vehicles for at least 10 years after they stop making the vehicles. This adds up to having millions of different parts available. Toyota's goal is to have them available just in time, as its manufacturing philosophy preaches.

Hebron, Kentucky, is home of the newest and biggest Toyota service parts facility in the world. This facility ships parts all over North America to regional distribution centers, which ship them to automotive dealers. Contrary to the tenets of JIT, it is a true warehouse, with 843,000 square feet of space and about 232 hourly and 86 salaried associates working there. In 2002 they shipped an average of 51 truckloads of service parts a day, which constituted 154,000 items per day. Parts are brought in from over 400 suppliers all over the United States and Mexico and most of them are put on the shelf until a Toyota dealer needs them. The Hebron facility sends parts to the nine regional parts distribution centers, which then send them to the Toyota dealers. Being global and modern, the facility uses sophisticated information technology, though the basic Toyota principles are apparent, including visual control.

First, the warehouse is organized into cells called *home positions*. The home positions have similar-sized parts stored in the same way, e.g., small parts. Teams of associates are dedicated to home positions. Second, a powerful computer system was custom-designed. The volume of each part was meticulously entered into the computer as was its physical location. A batch of a variety of small parts are all packaged into a standard-sized box to be shipped to a particular regional distribution center. A computer algorithm figures out what parts going to a particular location will just fill the box going to that destination, based on the volumes, and develops a parts-picking route that can be completed in 15 minutes. Pickers have a handheld radio frequency-controlled device with a small screen; it tells them what to pick next and they scan each item as they pick it. Third, visual control is used extensively. Throughout the facility, you will see various types of white boards called "process control boards." These are the nerve centers of the operation. Figure 13-2 illustrates a process control board with actual data from the Hebron facility. The data is handwritten with dry-erase markers. This one was for picking parts in a home position to be put into a box for shipment. It captures an enormous amount of information, including the status of the operation every 15 minutes. It is worth describing how it operates to illustrate the power of visual control to pace an operation and monitor progress vs. takt time.

Each morning before the pickers arrive to work, the parts orders for the day come in by computer. The computer sorts them by home position. Then the algorithm described above assigns parts to 15-minute batches, in this case picking routes. The supervisor of the team fills in the process control boards.

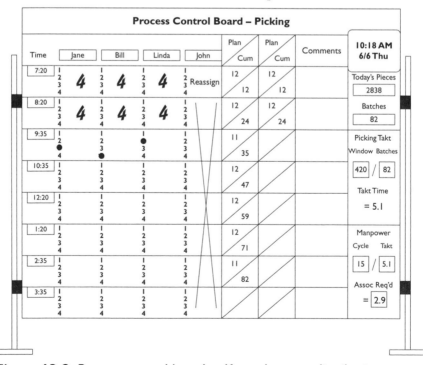

Figure 13-2. Process control board at Kentucky parts distribution center

The supervisor starts with the data to the right. In this case, he wrote in the number of pieces that would be picked for the day—2838—which the computer determined was 82 15-minute batches to be picked. The total "time window" for picking those parts is 420 minutes in the shift, after breaks are taken out. 420 minutes divided by 82 batches gives a takt time of 5.1 minutes per batch—the rate at which boxes must be filled with parts to satisfy the customers. A 15-minute cycle time per batch divided by the takt time of 5.1 minutes means that 2.9 people will be needed to pick the orders for the day.

To the left the team supervisor notes that three of his four team members will be needed to pick parts for that day, so he finds another assignment that day for John. He then writes in the planned number and cumulative number of batches to be picked, spread evenly throughout the shift. There are a few light periods during which there will be 11 boxes filled instead of 12 and those will include break periods. At the beginning of each 15-minute part-picking route, the associates will put a small round magnet on the batch they are picking—a green magnet if they are on time or a red magnet if they are running late. In this case, you can see that Jane is right where she should be, since it is 10:18 a.m., while Bill is ahead and Linda is behind. But in this period the load is light—11 boxes—so they are taking breaks and there is some flexibility. Everyone is OK. At a glance the supervisor knows the status of the operation. Moreover, the board helps to enforce a continuous flow of work throughout the day. Associates will immediately know if they are getting behind and put in extra effort or call for help to catch up. If they try to work ahead of the leveled schedule, it will be clear to the supervisor. *Heijunka* is reinforced daily.

This system at Hebron is quite powerful and is a good example of the ingenuity of Toyota TPS experts who figured out how to create continuous flow in a non-traditional, pick-to-order environment—an environment in which many people would have thrown up their hands and said TPS tools "do not apply here." Despite the complex computer systems, the key tools that govern daily operations are visual management tools. One of the bigger stories at Hebron is how they are building a culture of associate involvement to improve this world-class system (discussed in Chapter 16).

But even before this huge distribution center was built, Toyota's smaller service parts facilities using these same TPS methods led the industry in productivity and facing fill rates and system fill rates—the key indicators that track and measure such facilities. (The *facing fill rate* is the percent of time a part ordered is immediately available at the distribution center assigned to that dealer. The *system fill rate* is the percent of time a part ordered is immediately available somewhere in a Toyota parts distribution center.) For example, from 1992 to 1998 Toyota's parts distribution center in Cincinnati, Ohio, had the highest level of productivity in the industry: the *facing fill rate* was 95% and the *system fill rate* was over 98%. Toyota's fill rates are routinely among the top three in the industry.

Visual Control and Office Work

I have spent a lot of time at the Toyota Technical Center in Michigan, where they engineer vehicles like Camry and Avalon. For much of this time, Kunihiko ("Mike") Masaki was the president there. Masaki had worked in many different engineering and manufacturing organizations during his career at Toyota, all using excellent visual controls, so it seemed quite natural to him that the office environment at the Toyota Technical Center should follow the principles of 5S. Twice a year, Masaki would visit each person at his or her desk and ask to see a file cabinet (as part of Toyota's document retention program). He audited the file cabinets to see that they were organized properly and no documents were there that were not needed. There is a standard way to organize files at Toyota and Masaki was looking for deviations from the standard. A report is then filed and a grade is given. If an area is deficient, associates in the area must prepare a plan for counter-measures and a follow-up review is scheduled to be sure the deficiency is taken care of.

Though this may seem excessive or even intrusive for such mundane activities as filing, for the employee it clearly signals the importance of visual control, especially in the light of the fact that this was the *president* following the Toyota principle of teaching by going directly to the source and seeing for himself (*genchi genbutsu*). More recently, this responsibility has shifted to a vice president and has been expanded to spot auditing of each employee's e-mail organization system, to make sure messages are well organized in folders and old messages are discarded.

One of the biggest visual control innovations in Toyota's globally benchmarked product development system is the *obeya* (big room), which was used in the Prius development discussed in Chapter 6. The system is just a few years old. The chief engineer of a vehicle development project resides in the *obeya*, along with heads of major engineering groups working on the project. It is a very large conference "war room" in which many visual management tools are displayed and maintained by the responsible representatives of the various functional specialties. These tools include the status of each area (and each key supplier) compared with the schedule, design graphics, competitor tear-down results, quality information, manpower charts, financial status, and other important performance indicators. These tools can be reviewed by any of the team members. Any deviation from schedule or performance targets is immediately visible in the *obeya*.

The *obeya* is a high-security area and only appropriate representatives from the functional areas are given access. Toyota has found that the *obeya* team system enables fast and accurate decision-making, improves communication, maintains alignment, speeds information gathering, and creates an important sense of team integration. When I interviewed Ichiro ("Michael Jordan") Suzuki, the chief engineer of the first Lexus, he was at the Toyota Technical Center to teach them the secret to excellent engineering. His focus on this trip was visual management. He emphasized the importance of using visual management charts and graphs everywhere (showing schedule, cost, etc. on one sheet of paper). He also pointed out that "Using an electronic monitor does not work if only one person uses that information. Visual management charts must allow for communication and sharing."

A3 Reports: Capturing All You Need to Know on One Sheet of Paper

When I interviewed David Baxter, vice president at the Toyota Technical Center, he was a bit nervous about a report he was working on. It was the proposed budget for the entire center. The whole time he talked about the report, I was envisioning a large book-like document. Suddenly it dawned on me that he was talking about an 11" x 17" (A3) sheet of paper and how he was going to put the entire budget and its justification on that one sheet of paper. Toyota is very strict about having managers and associates go to great lengths to put key information on one side of an A3-sized piece of paper. Why A3? Because this is the largest paper that can fit through a fax machine. A typical A3 report is not a memo—it is a full report documenting a process. For example, a problem-solving A3 would succinctly state the problem, document the current situation, determine the root cause, suggest alternative solutions, suggest the recommended solution, and have a cost-benefit analysis. This would be on one sheet of paper, using figures and graphics as much as possible. The push in the last few years in Toyota has been for everyone to move to A4 reports (8½" x 11")—the idea that less is more. The ingenious process for developing A3 reports is described in greater detail in Chapter 19.

Keeping It Visual Through Technology and Human Systems

In today's world of computers, information technology, and automation, one of the goals is to make the office and factory paperless. You can now use computers, the Internet, and the corporate intranet to call up large storehouses of data, both written and visual, at lightning speed and share it via various software and e-mail. As we will discuss in the next chapter, Toyota has resisted this information-technology-centric trend. As Suzuki pointed out, going to look at the computer screen is typically done by one person in isolation. Working in a virtual world removes you from hands-on teamwork and, more importantly, usually (unless you do your work on the computer) takes you away from where the "real" work is being performed.

The Toyota Way recognizes that visual management complements humans because we are visually, tactilely, and audibly oriented. And the best visual indicators are right at the work site, where they can jump out at you and clearly indicate by sound, sight, and feel the standard and any deviation from the standard. A well-developed visual control system increases productivity, reduces defects and mistakes, helps meet deadlines, facilitates communication, improves safety, lowers costs, and generally gives the workers more control over their environment.

As the computer, IT systems, and software continue to replace the work of people and companies continue to move whole departments to countries like India that have a workforce steeped in information technology, Toyota will have an increasing challenge to be competitive using its "old" physical human system. How can it continue to make the workplace visual and people-oriented while utilizing the power and benefits of computer technology?

The answer is to follow Toyota Way Principle 7: *Use visual control so no problems are hidden.* The principle does not say to avoid information technology. It simply means thinking creatively using whatever means are the best available to create true visual control. Toyota has already replaced some physical prototype models with digital models on large screens, with high involvement of engineers in critiquing the design. One thing is for certain: Toyota will not readily compromise its principles and goals for something that is merely faster and cheaper, as discussed in the next chapter on new technology. Simply putting everything on the corporate intranet and using information technology to cut costs can have many unintended consequences that can profoundly change or even be detrimental to a company's culture.

The Toyota Way will seek a balance and take a conservative approach to using information technology to maintain its values. This may entail a compromise, such as maintaining a physical visual signal along with a computer in the background, like in the Toyota service parts warehouse in Hebron. Or it may mean using a wall-sized screen to display a 3-D image of a complete vehicle. But the important principle will remain: support your employees through visual control so they have the best opportunity to do a good job.

Chapter 14

Principle 8:
Use Only Reliable, Thoroughly Tested Technology That Serves Your People and Processes

Society has reached the point where one can push a button and be immediately deluged with technical and managerial information. This is all very convenient, of course, but if one is not careful there is a danger of losing the ability to think. We must remember that in the end it is the individual human being who must solve the problems.
— Eiji Toyoda, *Creativity, Challenge and Courage*
Toyota Motor Corporation, 1983

Everyone at one time or another has to search for a job. These days a modern job search cannot ignore the Internet—the technology solution to the problem of finding a job. Yet according to the bible of job searches, *What Color Is Your Parachute?* (Bolles 2003), using the Internet is the absolute worst way to find a job. A survey showed that "96 percent of all online-job-hunters finally found their jobs in ways other than on the Internet. And employers find 92 percent of their new employees in ways other than through the Internet." So what is the best way to find employment? Going to the yellow pages and calling potential employers in your area of interest has an 84% success rate. Knocking on the door of any place that interests you has a 47% success rate. What does this say? Personal contact makes a difference. You could have taken this advice directly out of the Toyota Way playbook.

Over the years, Toyota has tended to lag behind its competitors in acquiring all types of new technology. Notice that I said "acquiring," not "using." Unfortunately, too much of what is acquired by so-called leading edge companies never really gets into actual use. The Toyota Way is to move slowly, because more than one technology has failed to meet their "acid" test of supporting people, process, and values and has been yanked in favor of simpler, manual systems. Toyota is still following this policy in the age of digital technology. Though Toyota does not lead the industry in acquiring technology, it is a global benchmark on how to use value-added technology that supports the appropriate processes and people.

The Principle—Adoption of New Technology Must Support Your People, Process, and Values

At Toyota, new technology is introduced only after it is proven out through direct experimentation with the involvement of a broad cross-section of people. This does not exclude new or cutting-edge technology. It means the technology has been thoroughly evaluated and tested to ensure it provides added value. Before adopting new technology, Toyota will go to great lengths to analyze the impact it may have on existing processes. First, it will go and see firsthand the nature of the value-added work being performed by the workers for the particular process. It will look for new opportunities to eliminate waste and even out the flow. Toyota will then use a pilot area to improve the process with the existing equipment, technology, and people. When it has accomplished as much improvement as possible with the present process, Toyota will ask again if it can make any additional improvements by adding the new technology. If it determines that the new technology can add value to the process, the technology is then carefully analyzed to see if it conflicts with Toyota's philosophies and operating principles. These include principles of valuing people over technology, using consensus decision making, and an operational focus on waste elimination. If the technology violates these principles or if there is any chance it may adversely disrupt stability, reliability, and flexibility, Toyota will reject the technology or at least delay adopting it until the problems can be resolved.

If the new technology is acceptable, the guiding principle is to design and use it to support continuous flow in the production process and help employees perform better within the Toyota Way standards. This means the technology should be highly visual and intuitive. Ideally, it will be used right where the work is being done so it does not require a person in an office to input the data. The important principle is to find ways to support the actual work process while not distracting people from the value-added work. Throughout this analysis and planning, Toyota will broadly involve all key stakeholders in a consensus-building process. Once Toyota has thoroughly gone through this process, it will quickly implement the new technology. Because of this painstaking process, Toyota will typically implement the new technology smoothly without the employee resistance and process disruption that other companies often experience.

People Do the Work, Computers Move the Information

When I teach about Toyota's system, I start with the basics including *kanban*, which is mainly a manual visual process. If there is an information technology specialist in the house, he or she inevitably asks the question, "Isn't there any place for information technology in the Toyota Production System?" I reassure them that they are not out of a job even if their company goes completely lean. But their role may be different. IT will not drive the way Toyota does business and certainly is not allowed to disrupt the values of the Toyota Way.

Toyota is a modern company and, like any modern company, you could paralyze it in no time by shutting down its computer systems. Computers are used to run finances, pay bills, keep track of millions of customer orders and tens of millions of service parts transactions, capture the data for developing new products, and schedule many things. IT is critical to Toyota, but Toyota looks at technology as a tool that, like any other tool, exists to support the people and the process.

For example, at Toyota's service parts operations they continue to use an old software system developed in house years ago under much simpler circumstances. It has continuously evolved over the years and does exactly what is needed today. Jane Beseda, General Manager and VP North American Parts Operations, does not see any burning need to modernize it, but she does plan a gradual transition to newer technology.

In contrast, I had an interesting consulting experience with an America auto parts supplier that had worked with Toyota for years learning the Toyota Production System (TPS). My client's CEO got hooked on the idea of increasing inventory turns as a major corporate "lean" goal. He gave all of the business units aggressive targets for inventory turns, which on the surface would seem to support TPS principles of eliminating waste. It became a corporate mania.

A large group of "supply chain engineers" within the company was tasked with addressing this problem. The background of the leader of the supply chain group was in information technology. His main priority was to bring in new Internet technology to provide "visibility into the supply chain." There are many supply chain software "solutions" promising to radically cut inventory and provide control over the process. They supposedly do this by showing anyone who logs into the Web site how much inventory there is in real time at every stage of the supply chain.

His subordinates were very proud of their boss, who was extremely intelligent and a fast thinker, and they often repeated a story he would tell. He described supply chain visibility software as analogous to a bulldozer. You can dig ditches manually and it will work. But a bulldozer will do the same thing in a fraction of the time. IT was like this—speeding up dramatically work that could be done by hand.

I was floored by this belief. How does keeping track of inventory on the computer give you any control over making it go away? From my TPS training, I knew that inventory is generally a symptom of poorly controlled processes. Ultimately, manufacturing is about making things. I talked to the boss and gave him my perspective. I explained that software may be very fast, but it is not a person or a machine performing work. In fact, true "supply chain visibility" is more analogous to setting up a video camera at the work site and hooking up a remote monitor in another state so you can sit back and watch the ditchdiggers work. To get more productivity out of the work process, you have to change the way the work is done by eliminating waste. Supply chain software by itself does not eliminate waste.

My perspective was confirmed when we did a project in one of their plants. Without any information technology, we were able to cut inventory by 80% on the assembly line. We did this by moving from the system of pushing inventory according to schedules to a manual pull system, using *kanban*. Lead time was reduced by one-third—with no new technology. To eliminate most of the parts inventory required working with a supplier in Mexico—also owned by the same company—that was pushing as much inventory as it could onto this plant so its inventory turns would look good. Improving the process is the only way you can control inventory.

How Information Technology Supports the Toyota Way

I accompanied the University of Michigan's Dean of Engineering on a trip to Japan some years ago and one of our hosts was Mikio Kitano, who at that time was overseeing the Motomachi complex—Toyota's largest industrial complex. My Dean was asking a lot of questions about the use of information technology at Toyota. Kitano seemed a bit impatient. To make a point to the Dean he pulled out a typical information system design flowchart with all the usual IT symbols—information flowing from computer to computer, storage devices, input devices, output devices, and the like. It had been given to him some time earlier by a Toyota IT specialist as a proposal for the Motamachi assembly plant. He said he sent this flowchart back along with the IT guy who brought it to him and told him, "At Toyota we do not make information systems. We make cars. Show me the process of making cars and how the information system supports that." He then pulled out a large process flow diagram that the IT guy had produced in response to Kitano's demand. The top showed the body, paint, and assembly lines representing how Toyota builds cars. The bottom of the diagram showed various information technologies and the way in which they would support the production of cars. As far as Kitano was concerned, the process flow diagram showed IT in its appropriate place—supporting the production lines.

Toyota has had experience with pushing technology that is the latest and greatest, only to later regret it. One example was an experiment 10 years ago in Toyota's Chicago Parts Distribution Center, where the company installed a highly automated rotary-rack system. At the time the warehouse was built, Toyota's dealers placed weekly stock orders for parts. But soon after the warehouse was completed, the company implemented daily ordering and daily deliveries to reduce lead time and lower inventories in the dealerships. When the process changed from a five-day to a one-day shipment cycle, the equipment was inflexible and suddenly outdated, because the fixed conveyor length was designed for larger orders. So the smaller daily orders should have filled the smaller boxes much faster than the larger five-day boxes of parts but the person at the end of the conveyor still had to wait for the parts to come down this long conveyor. The person spent a great deal of time waiting—one of the eight wastes. The benefit of the technology was short-lived and the Chicago facility became one of Toyota's least productive warehouses. In 2002, the company again made a significant investment in Chicago, but this time it was to remove the automation and unwind the computer system that supported it. By comparison, Toyota's most productive regional parts depot is in Cincinnati, where there is very little automation.

Beseda explained:

When you live in the logistics world, nothing moves without information. But, we're conservative in our approach to applying automation. You can kaizen people processes very easily, but it is hard to kaizen a machine. Our processes got far more productive and efficient, but the machine didn't. So, the machine had to come out.

In 2002, Toyota's Parts Distribution Centers completed a two-year systems initiative known as the Monarch Project to improve its demand forecasting and inventory planning. A joint team of logistics experts and information systems specialists spent a year identifying which components of the legacy systems worked well, which components needed an upgrade or replacement, and what new functionalities needed to be added. The focus of the Monarch system is to work behind the scenes supporting a visual system on the floor so people can go and see the actual situation. As Beseda described it:

From the warehouse person's perspective, sitting and looking into a computer screen doesn't tell you everything you need to know. You have to have a feel for the size of the parts and the real situation in the warehouse. The computer recommends an inventory level to the procurement analyst, but it can't tell him if the inventory will make life tough for the person on the warehouse floor because there isn't enough space to store it.

Procurement analysts are located at the parts centers to encourage on-site observation and frequent communication between the inventory group and warehouse operations. The two groups often collaborate to empirically refine the inventory levels of problem parts. The stockkeeper monitors the actual movement of the inventory by putting a large label on each carton and noting the date. If there is demand, the inventory is available to ship. If the dates show that inventory in some cartons is not moving, the stockkeeper and the procurement analyst can safely agree to lower the inventory level. This simple visual control is a practical way to save space and reduce clutter. The procurement analyst relies on the computer-generated stock level, but supplements the system recommendation with his or her own judgment and direct communication with the shop floor.

As Beseda observed:

First work out the manual process, and then automate it. Try to build into the system as much flexibility as you possibly can so you can continue to kaizen the process as your business changes. And always supplement the system information with "genchi genbutsu," or "go look, go see."

IT in Toyota's Product Development Process

In the early 1980s, the trend among automakers was to develop their own internal computer-aided design (CAD) system for designing parts on a computer rather than on paper blueprints. Toyota did this like everyone else, but in a way that preserved and embodied the Toyota problem-solving philosophy. The designers of the new CAD system asked, "What was the specific need for each software module (e.g., styling, die design, component design)? What were the specific conditions of use? What were the software requirements? What options were available? What was the best option?" Often the best option was a low-tech solution. For example, in analyzing stamping dies that stamp out parts, the analysis technology was not sophisticated enough to model the complexity of stamping out the part and verifying the best die design on a computer. So Toyota used a simpler solution that produced a color diagram showing the various stress points on the die. The die designer, working with an experienced die maker, then examined the diagram and made judgments on the design based on experience. In contrast, U.S. automakers implementing CAD systems did this stress analysis using software alone, then made recommendations to the die designers in a throw-it-over-the-wall fashion. The result was that the die engineers often rejected the analysis because the results were impractical or unrealistic.

As their competitors moved to the latest commercial CAD systems, Toyota maintained its homegrown system, to the chagrin of engineers and suppliers. The software is clearly outdated. But it works. Finally Toyota used the principle of "careful consideration in decision making," discussed in Chapter 19) and, after two years of thinking and debating, decided to shift to CATIA (Computer-Aided

Three-Dimensional Interactive Application)—a world-class CAD system used by Boeing and Chrysler and pretty well accepted as the auto industry benchmark. Toyota was slow in implementing CATIA, taking a lot of time to customize it to fit their development process. Ford, in the meantime, quickly adopted a different commercial CAD package, spent hundreds of millions of dollars deploying it internally and with suppliers, and later decided it would rather have CATIA spending millions on that and confusing a lot of people.

Toyota has continued to streamline its product development process, using very specific software solutions, and has gone from 48 months, when it first introduced CAD software in the 1980s, down to less than 12 months to develop a new vehicle. Toyota refers to this approach as "collaborative vehicle development using digital engineering." The phrase says it all. They have found a set of relatively simple technologies that support collaborative work in the Toyota Way of product development.

These collaborative solutions always begin with a specific problem. For example, there was a problem in the old system of too much rework. Data from prototypes, vehicle evaluations, and pre-production tests were fed back to engineering in the form of a series of problems to solve. But these shortcomings were discovered and fixed at the next process step, not in the place where they originated. This went against the principle of *jidoka* (see Principle 5), so Toyota changed the process. The new paradigm was to learn to do a lot of the testing and visualization digitally up front in the design process, thereby avoiding this downstream rework. This is absolutely necessary to get to a new vehicle design in less than one year.

Now complete assemblies, for example the instrument panels, are done digitally in three dimensions. This method builds on the standardization that Toyota does in vehicle design. For decades Toyota engineers kept detailed checklists of good and bad design features. Now these are stored electronically in a "know-how database" that allows the product to be designed with quality from the start. There is also detailed data on proper sequences in the assembly plant that a person can look at in the earliest stages of design. Engineering animation allows the engineers to watch animated versions of people putting together the vehicle to anticipate ergonomic problems and avoid them in the earliest design stage. Multi-point TV conferencing allows engineers throughout the world to watch the vehicle go together digitally and solve many of the problems that in the past would be done standing around an actual car being assembled.

The point here is that Toyota did not go into a poorly functioning development process and try to fix it using the most sophisticated computer technology. They took a finely tuned development process, based on exceptionally well-trained engineers and excellent technical leadership, and surgically inserted information technologies to enhance it. These were all proven technologies that

Toyota carefully evaluated prior to going live. Moreover, they did it maintaining the collaborative design process and the strong value placed on visualization of the actual situation in the design process.

The Role of Technology—Adapting It Appropriately

In industry today, the watchword is flexibility. Everyone wants to be as flexible as possible and Toyota is no exception. Originally, what allowed Toyota to compete with global players was its flexibility. To Toyota, flexibility does not mean pushing the latest and greatest technology onto operations and struggling to make it work. Toyota follows Toyota Way Principle 8: *Use only reliable, thoroughly tested technology that serves your people and processes.* Again, "testing" involves both existing technology and new or cutting-edge technology that Toyota has thoroughly evaluated and piloted to prove that it works.

One example of this is in the body shop, where the automotive body is welded together. This has been one of the few places for years where a lot of robotics is used and with great success. But it is also the place that most limits flexibility in making cars. Ultimately, all of the large panels that make up a vehicle must be held in place and welded together just right. There are complex fixtures that hold the parts of the body in place. Originally these fixtures were specific to a particular car body. To produce a different car body required changing all of the fixtures manually, which took weeks of hard work. Flexible body shops were a major innovation that allowed multiple car bodies to be made in the same shop. And this also allowed for a much more rapid changeover from one year's model to the new model. Toyota eventually learned to do this without stopping the line—called a "running change" in the industry.

Nevertheless, Toyota's body shop still was not very flexible, because it used very expensive pallets that were designed to hold the body parts in place for different cars. For example, there would be a Camry pallet and an Avalon pallet. And you could not change the mix of Camry and Avalons that could be run (e.g., going from 70% Camry to 80% Camry) without building new pallets and changing the mix of pallets—an expensive and time-consuming proposition. Now, instead of the car body riding on a customized pallet, it is being held in place by robots that can be programmed for each car body. The bodies ride on something like a ski lift. The earlier pallet system held the body together from the outside in and had fixtures sized and positioned differently for each vehicle. The new system has a programmable fixturing device that holds the parts together from the inside out—a radical new concept that improves flexibility. And it takes up about half the space. Toyota calls this new global standard the "blue sky system." Among other things, it is not as tall as the old system and has allowed for more "blue sky" in the body shop, which used to be dark and dingy and now is very open and bright—for the people working there. They also call it the Global Body Line, since it is being introduced as a new standard in every Toyota plant in the world. Different car models can be run back to back and the mix can be changed instantly through a change in programming. It is a true one-piece flow and will be a key contributor to Toyota's move toward "build to order."

Often when manufacturers implement new systems like this, it is a disaster—disrupting production, creating quality problems, and keeping maintenance busy fighting fires for years. But Toyota implemented the "blue sky technology" systematically, module by module, replacing pieces of the old equipment as it was running. They never missed a beat. As Don Jackson, Vice President of Manufacturing at Toyota's Georgetown, Kentucky, operation, explained:

> At Toyota Georgetown, we were the seventh plant to get the new blue sky system. And it takes up roughly half the space of the old line. So we actually put two new body shops in the place of one to support our two assembly lines. But we had to do that during mass production at full production capacity. We didn't have any space. So every week we moved a piece of the line off-line and we put a new piece in. And we had 13-14-year-old equipment, so it was pretty challenging trying to make sure it ran the next Monday.
>
> For example, to create a place for the new underbody welding, we had to clear out some restrooms and some area where we could make a space and start assembling there. We would use part of the old line and part of the new line in parallel until we changed it over. And once we had the first line in, we had an empty space to put new equipment in. So, then we were OK, but the first year it was interesting.

I asked Jackson how Toyota could pull this off—launching an entire new body shop while continuing to make cars without any production losses, while maintaining 96% uptime, when most U.S. body shops are lucky to run at 80-85% uptime. He gave a typical Toyota answer:

> Well, probably one of the big things is attention to detail. I probably stand myself, even at the vice president level, at least six or seven hours on the floor a day. And a big part of this is genchi genbutsu—go and see activity—and doing the "five whys" problem investigation. Why are we only running 90%? If the management tools are all on the plant floor in a visual fashion, then you don't have to look at a computer or go to somebody's desk. It's visual, and you can manage the floor from the actual floor. So that's what I'm trying to make sure happens.

What we see here is a blend of sophisticated technology for flexible body

welding combined with human approaches to management. Despite being programmable, the new "inside out" approach is far simpler and has led to greatly
reduced equipment maintenance cost and less downtime of the system. And even
with a complex computerized system, team associates use simple visual displays to
help them assess what is going on. The global body line meets Toyota's acid test
for new technology—lean, simple, and speedy. It has resulted in 50% fewer
processes to weld the body together, 70% less investment to change over the line
for a new vehicle, and 75% less time to go from launch to meeting Toyota's high-
quality targets.

It is interesting to note that I attended a presentation at the University of
Michigan by Toyota's North American president who described this system to a
room full of experts on "reconfigurable" manufacturing technology. Their immediate question was: "how could you anticipate all the benefits of this new technology and cost justify it?" His answer made it seem obvious. They did some
rough calculations and based on one changeover in the next few years the system
would pay for itself. "It was easy to justify," he said. The experts were shocked as
many had struggled to do careful cost justifications and their companies demanded a one year payback or they would not make the investment. At Toyota, the
decision makers are typically very experienced engineers who have worked on the
floor. If it seems clear that the new technology has been thoroughly evaluated and
will pay for itself in the long term the decision to adopt it seems easy and obvious.

Just as Toyota refuses to push parts made in one department onto another
department, Toyota refuses to allow an information technology department or
advanced manufacturing technology department to push technology onto departments that do the value-added work of designing and building cars. Any information technology must meet the acid test of supporting people and processes and
prove it adds value before it is implemented broadly.

Section III

Add Value to the Organization by Developing Your People and Partners

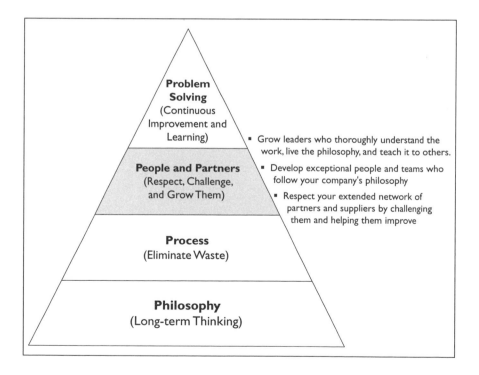

Problem Solving
(Continuous Improvement and Learning)

People and Partners
(Respect, Challenge, and Grow Them)

Process
(Eliminate Waste)

Philosophy
(Long-term Thinking)

- Grow leaders who thoroughly understand the work, live the philosophy, and teach it to others.
- Develop exceptional people and teams who follow your company's philosophy
- Respect your extended network of partners and suppliers by challenging them and helping them improve

Chapter 15

Principle 9:

Grow Leaders Who Thoroughly Understand the Work, Live the Philosophy, and Teach It to Others

Until senior management gets their egos out of the way and goes to the whole team and leads them all together ... senior management will continue to miss out on the brain power and extraordinary capabilities of all their employees. At Toyota, we simply place the highest value on our team members and do the best we can to listen to them and incorporate their ideas into our planning process.

—Alex Warren, former Senior VP
Toyota Motor Manufacturing, Kentucky

The *Automotive News* wraps up each year by recognizing the biggest newsmakers in the industry. The Newsmakers of 2002 (December 20, 2002) included Bill Ford (CEO of Ford), Robert Lutz (GM Executive VP), Dieter Zetsche (Chrysler Group President), Carlos Ghosn (Nissan President), and Fujio Cho (President of Toyota). The contrast between Cho's accomplishments and those of several other recognized leaders was very revealing of differences in culture across companies. Here are some direct quotes from the issue:

Bill Ford (Ford CEO): Talks up revitalization, brings back Allan Gilmour, promotes David Thursfield, and stars in TV commercials. But it's tough out there. Ford Motor stock remains mired in the $10 range.

Robert Lutz (GM Executive VP): At 70, former Marine pilot inspires GM's troops and revolutionizes (and simplifies) product development, giving car guys and designers a bigger voice.

Dieter Zetzsche (Chrysler Group President): Turns the Chrysler group around a year early with three quarters in the black.

Carlos Ghosn (Nissan President): Perennial newsmaker produces more incredible results at Nissan. U.S. market share moves up again. Ghosn truly deserves to be called the "Mailman." He delivers.

Fujio Cho (Toyota President): Toyota president presides over rise in operating profit to industry record. Takes lead on hybrids. Grabs 10 points of U.S. market. Joins with Peugeot for plants in Eastern Europe.

All of these leaders have made a remarkable impact on their companies. What the non-Toyota leaders have in common is that they were brought in from outside to turn around ailing companies. They each, in turn, brought in a group of their own handpicked outside lieutenants to help in the turnaround. They also reorganized and brought their own philosophy and approach to transform the company. Bill Ford, a Ford employee and family member, is the exception. However, those inside Ford would agree that he had an atypical career path for a Ford CEO; for example, he quit the company in 1995 after serving in 17 mid-level management jobs. He was brought in to save a company teetering on the brink of bankruptcy and relieve former President Jacques Nasser. None of these non-Toyota leaders naturally progressed through promotion to become presidents and CEOs at these companies. They abruptly came in from the outside to change the culture, to shake up and change the direction of a company that was going bad.

In fact, it seems the typical U.S. company regularly alternates between the extremes of stunningly successful and borderline bankrupt. The solution to severe problems is often to bring in a new CEO who will take the company in a radically new direction. This roller-coaster ride is exciting and even works in bursts. Then, when something goes wrong, someone else preaching a still newer direction replaces him or her. It is business leadership like the hare in the fable, not slow and steady like the tortoise.

In contrast, Cho grew up in Toyota and was a student of Taiichi Ohno. He and Ohno provided a theoretical basis for the Toyota Production System (TPS) and the Toyota Way principles in order to teach them throughout the company. Cho was the leader of the Georgetown, Kentucky, plant, Toyota's most important venture in the United States. He was a board member and came into his new role when the company was already successful. He moved into the position naturally and built on the momentum that had been ongoing for decades. His accomplishments were the result of years of work and preparation by his predecessors. At Toyota, the new president or CEO does not need to come in and take charge to move the company in a radically new direction to put his imprint on the company. The leadership role of Cho focuses on something entirely different.

The Principle—Growing Your Leaders Rather than Purchasing Them

Even when Toyota promoted someone from an unusual part of the company to save it from impending doom, there has never been a sudden change of direction. Perhaps this is the concept of eliminating *muri* (unevenness) at work at the executive level. It seems that, throughout Toyota's history, key leaders have been found within the company, at the right time, to shape the next step in Toyota's evolution. They have been there across the enterprise—in sales, product development, manufacturing, and design.

Hiroshi Okuda was the first non-Toyoda family member to take the reins in decades and came at a time when Toyota needed to globalize the company aggressively. After this aggressive period, Fujio Cho, in a calmer, quieter way, continued the globalization of Toyota, building on his experiences in the United States and focusing on reenergizing the internal Toyota Way culture. Despite major differences in personal style, neither of these leaders deviated from the basic philosophies of the Toyota Way. Behind the scenes, the Toyoda family has always been there, carefully grooming and selecting the new leaders. Perhaps it is no coincidence that there has always been an internal leader ready to step up to the plate.

Toyota does not go shopping for "successful" CEOs and Presidents because their leaders must live and thoroughly understand the Toyota culture day by day. Since a critical element of the culture is *genchi genbutsu*, which means deeply observing the actual situation in detail, leaders must demonstrate this ability and understand how work gets done at a shop floor level within Toyota. According to the Toyota Way, a superficial impression of the current situation in any division of Toyota will lead to ineffective decision-making and leadership. Toyota also expects its leaders to teach their subordinates the Toyota Way, which means they must understand and live the philosophy.

Another important leadership tenet of the Toyota Way is the effort leaders make to support the culture year after year so it can create the environment for a learning organization. In Western companies with revolving door leaders, no one leader is in place long enough to build a mature culture to match their personal vision. (Some of the most successful companies are exceptions as we will discuss in Chapter 22.[1]) So changing the culture each time a new leader comes into office necessarily means jerking the company about superficially, without developing any real depth or loyalty from the employees. The problem with an outsider leading radical shifts in the culture is that the organization will never learn—it loses the ability to build on achievements, mistakes, or enduring principles. This affects the ability of leaders to make effective changes. On the other hand, in Deming's terms, Toyota uses "constancy of purpose" throughout the organization, which lays the groundwork for consistent and positive leadership as well as an environment for learning.

There is no doubt that Toyota's leadership culture was shaped by the personalities, values, and experiences of its founders in the Toyoda family. There is a long line of distinguished and remarkable leaders from this family, beginning with Sakichi Toyoda, who built Toyota Automatic Loom into one of the premier loom manufacturers in the world, and his son Kiichiro Toyoda, who founded Toyota Motor Company. As discussed in Chapter 2, they helped to shape the Toyota Way. Among their profound impacts on the company, they epitomized the spirit of innovation that drives Toyota and the hands-on philosophy of Toyota leaders. The characteristics of Toyota leadership, particularly the drive to meet seemingly impossible targets and the requirement to understand the work by getting your hands dirty, evolved from the leadership of these two company founders.

Eiji Toyoda, nephew of Sakichi Toyoda, was the president and then chairman of Toyota Motor Manufacturing during the company's most vital years after the war and through its growth into a global powerhouse. He played a key role in selecting and empowering the leaders who shaped sales, manufacturing, and product development. He seemed to have a sixth sense for identifying individuals who possessed the profound leadership qualities needed to shape Toyota's future. Arguably, a maverick like Taiichi Ohno would never have survived, let alone prospered, within a conservative company like Toyota without the executive sponsorship of Eiji Toyoda (Womack, Jones, and Roos, 1991). But Toyoda was like the owner of a basketball team who needed someone like Ohno to turn the franchise around, a headstrong and passionate coach with a bold vision, a disciplinary motivator who knew the game of manufacturing inside and out and could teach it to others.

First American President of Toyota Motor Manufacturing

Given that the Toyota Way is to make decisions slowly, thoroughly considering alternatives (see Chapter 19 on *nemawashi*), it was not surprising that Toyota took a very long time to establish NUMMI, its first American plant, and then took its time setting up Toyota, Georgetown. While in each case Toyota relied on American leaders, there was a Toyota "coordinator" from Japan mentoring them behind the scenes and the top executive was from Japan. So it was big news when Gary Convis was named the first American President of Toyota Motor Manufacturing in Kentucky in 1999. His selection into this critical position—leading Toyota's largest manufacturing plant outside Japan—represented a coming of age for Toyota in the United States. It took Toyota executives about 15 years to develop Convis into someone they could trust to carry the banner of the Toyota Way, but the result was a true Toyota leader.

His first job out of Michigan State University was in GM's Buick division, where he worked in engineering and production for three years. He moved from GM to Ford in 1966. He was not a job hopper and stayed with Ford, moving steadily up the manufacturing organization over 18 years, when an opportunity came up to be interviewed to help lead Toyota's joint venture with GM as general manager of the NUMMI plant. Ford was struggling, and it seemed like a good time to explore new pastures. Little did Gary know that this was not just a career move. His life, personal philosophy, and way of looking at the world would change dramatically as he learned to understand the Toyota Way. After 15 years as a student of TPS, Gary is as upbeat, energized, and humble about learning from Toyota as if he was a new employee coming to his first orientation.

I learn all the time, but I don't think I'll finish developing as a human being. One of my main functions now is growing other Americans to follow that path. They call it the DNA of Toyota, the Toyota Way and TPS—they're all just very integrated.

Like other Toyota executives, Convis stresses on-the-job experience more than brilliant theoretical insights, which underscores Toyota executives' proclamation, "We build cars, not intellectuals." The fact is they are as apt to talk philosophy as they are nuts and bolts. But the philosophy driving the principles of the Toyota Way is always rooted in the nut-and-bolts practice. Gary talks in the self-deprecating, but at same time proud way that is characteristic of his Japanese brethren:

I got where I am because of trial and error and failure and perseverance. That trial and error was on the floor under the direction of my Japanese mentors. I'm very proud to have grown up with Toyota. Some people would look at 18 years and say, "Well, gee, you spent 20 years in the auto industry before the 18 you just spent with Toyota; you're sort of a slow bloomer!" But this business, I don't think it's one where there are fast bloomers. There's a lot to be said for experience and, if you enjoy what you're doing, it's not a long day, it's a fun day, and it's something you look forward to doing tomorrow.

Convis met and learned from all of the most famous leaders in Toyota who helped create TPS. So when I met with him, I was surprised he didn't want to talk about the nuts and bolts of JIT and *jidoka*. He wanted to talk about the philosophy of TPS and the importance of culture. He pulled out a diagram (see Figure 15-1) that he had obviously put together thoughtfully so he could present what he had learned about TPS through years of actually living it. Though the technical focus includes short lead times and is prominently featured in the definition, of equal prominence is "engaging people toward goals." Convis sees TPS as a three-pronged beast, where only one prong includes the technical tools often associated with lean production—JIT, *jidoka*, *heijunka*, etc. According to Convis, these are just technical tools and they can be effective only with *the right management and the right philosophy—the basic way of thinking*. At the center of TPS is people.

Toyota Production System = Operations Management System to achieve goals of highest quality, lowest cost, shortest lead time via engaging people toward goals.

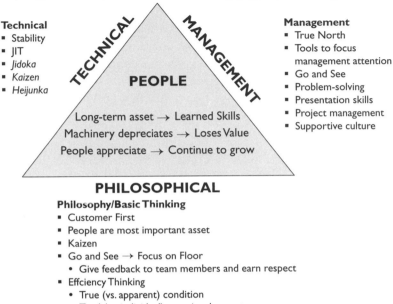

Technical
- Stability
- JIT
- Jidoka
- Kaizen
- Heijunka

PEOPLE

Long-term asset → Learned Skills
Machinery depreciates → Loses Value
People appreciate → Continue to grow

Management
- True North
- Tools to focus management attention
- Go and See
- Problem-solving
- Presentation skills
- Project management
- Supportive culture

PHILOSOPHICAL

Philosophy/Basic Thinking
- Customer First
- People are most important asset
- Kaizen
- Go and See → Focus on Floor
  - Give feedback to team members and earn respect
- Effciency Thinking
  - True (vs. apparent) condition
  - Total (vs. individual) team involvement

Figure 15-1. A Toyota leader's view of the Toyota Production System
Source: Gary Convis, President of TMMK.

The practice of *genchi genbutsu* is easy to adopt as a corporate policy and new hires can be sent out to the shop floor to "go and see" and then report back on what they see. But at Toyota, this is not simply a lesson for the neophyte to learn. The executive or manager must go, see, and really understand the actual situation at the working level. Managers are not just managing technology or tasks; they are promoting the culture. The absolute core of the Toyota philosophy is that *the culture must support the people doing the work*. Management must demonstrate a commitment to quality every day, but ultimately quality comes from the workers. And you cannot tell people they are important and then risk their health and safety to make production goals that day. This leads to a complex set of interrelated philosophies and practices, as Convis described:

> *Basically people will do what upper management wants them to do. So if that's consistent, if they're not whipsawed and being governed by different priorities, they learn what is truly important and what is not.... The two priorities are very clear—quality first, safety first. Extra effort. Extra caring. It's that kind of culture that we hope to create, by the way we manage our business.*

First Lesson of Management—Putting Customers First

Shotaro Kamiya was to Toyota Motor Sales what Ohno was to the Toyota Production System. His leadership defined the sales philosophy of Toyota. Like most Toyota leaders, Kamiya could be described as a self-made man. Unlike most Toyota employees today, who are hired directly out of school, he joined Toyota as sales manager in 1935, when Toyota Motor Company was first being formed. Toyota needed to hire experienced people and Kamiya had worked at Mitsui Trading Company (a close partner to Toyota) and had a lot of international experience in the U.S. and Europe. Kamiya ended up creating the Toyota dealer network in Japan and was also responsible for expansion of Toyota into sales in the U.S. Eventually he became the honorary chairman of Toyota. One famous quote from Kamiya reflects the "customer first" philosophy he preached and ingrained in others throughout his career:

> *The priority in receiving benefits from automobile sales should be in the order of the customer, then the dealer, and lastly, the manufacturer. This attitude is the best approach in winning the trust of customers and dealers and ultimately brings growth to the manufacturer.*

Unlike the use of auto showrooms in the United States to boost sales, Japan's tradition is door-to-door sales. In Japan, auto companies have extensive data on customers and know when to come knocking at the door. For example, when Mika is about to become of age to drive, there will be a salesperson contacting her to outfit her with just the right Toyota for her needs. The personal attention creates a bond between customers and the company. If customers need auto repairs, they are likely to call the salesperson for help rather than deal with an impersonal maintenance department. This supports the goal of Toyota to have customers for life … and for the lives of their descendants.

Toyota used this practice of door-to-door sales, and later its dealerships, as a way to teach new employees how to see and understand things from the customer's perspective. I asked Toshiaki "Tag" Taguchi, president and CEO of Toyota Motor, North America, if he could remember any special experience in his life when he really learned what the Toyota Way was all about. He recalled an early experience selling Toyota cars:

> *The first assignment I got as a freshman trainee …, I had to go through various operating departments of Toyota Motor Sales Company and three of us were sent to the dealerships to see if factory people would benefit by spending a few months at dealerships. So I spent about five months at the dealership in Nagoya, where I visited house to house carrying brochures, and sold a total of*

nine new and used cars during that time. But the point was learning about our customers. I think Toyota is trying to give freshmen an opportunity to learn about themselves. Even today, freshmen have a baptism to go to the dealership for a month or two to learn."

Going to the source to see and understand (*genchi genbutsu*) extends to understanding what customers want. It is not sufficient for leaders to pore over marketing data or listen to marketing presentations and get an abstract sense of the customer. Selling door to door is one way to get inside the heads of customers and develop a visceral sense of what purchasing a Toyota means to customers.

The Chief Engineer: The Critical Link to Innovation, Leadership, and Customer Satisfaction

In a traditional auto company, it is difficult to pin down where the real responsibility for a new vehicle development program lies. Many departments and many executives have partial responsibility. If you want to find who has responsibility for a new vehicle development program at Toyota, find the chief engineer (CE), because the buck stops there. In many ways, the CE epitomizes the Toyota approach to leadership (as seen in Chapter 5 and 6).

Traditionally, the importance of a person at a company directly relates to how many departments or direct reports he or she has. This is the hierarchy of top-down management. Judging by this standard, the Toyota's CE is a very unimportant person. Although thousands of Toyota associates work on a new vehicle program, the CE has perhaps only a half-dozen people formally reporting to him. This is because Toyota uses a matrix organization structure in engineering. (See Figure 15-2 from Cusumano and Nobeoka, 1998.)[2]

Vehicle centers I, II, and III each focus on a family of products—rear-wheel drive cars, front-wheel drive cars, and utility vehicles/vans. The functional groups within each center, like body engineering and chassis engineering, are technical specialty (functional) groups with their own general managers. The general managers control the engineers by assigning them projects, generating their performance evaluations, and the like. The CE controls the vehicle program and is responsible for the results, but not the people who work on the project. The CE has to depend on all of the functional groups to supply the people and get the work done. While it is an American adage that managers must have authority commensurate with their responsibility, the CE system works contrary to this belief and the role would be uncomfortable for most U.S. managers.

John Shook, former Toyota manager and a lifelong student of TPS, described this system to me as "responsibility without authority" and a common practice within Toyota. At Toyota, formal authority is typically one level up from the

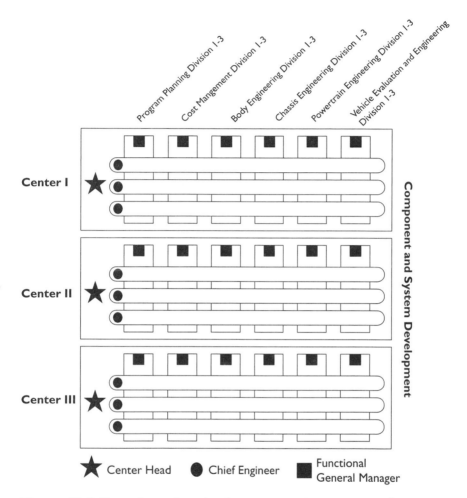

Figure 15-2. Toyota's product development matrix organization[3]

responsibility. This forces the person responsible, who has no formal authority, to defend his or her ideas, work through other people, and convince the person with formal authority that the ideas are correct. The only defense for taking action is to present the real facts of the situation to the formal authority. This process forces managers either to uncover the facts and develop a compelling case for their position or to go out on a limb and prove they are right through demonstrated success. For example, in the case of the development of the first Lexus, Ichiro Suzuki pushed the Lexus beyond the original conception of senior executives as a vehicle only for the American market and pushed its performance characteristics beyond what the senior executives in charge of the functional groups thought was possible.

Why does the CE system work at Toyota? Clark and Fujimoto (1991), who wrote an influential book on Toyota's product development system, referred to the CE as a "heavyweight project manager." This is in contrast to U.S. companies, where project managers are often "lightweights" with little real authority. But the CE does not have formal authority in the American sense by design. The checks and balances of the system force the CE to sell his or her ideas. On the other hand, the CE is a powerful and influential person who is empowered through multiple sources, including:

- *Being blessed by top executives at Toyota.* The CE has the ear of these executives and they are committed to getting the CE the resources to succeed.
- *Controlling the vehicle program.* The functional groups where the engineers reside are all in support roles to the development process, which is controlled by the chief engineer and which is the birthplace of all the exciting new design programs.
- *Leading the program.* CEs are selected for this honorific position because of a history of excellence in leadership. Moreover, they get to do it again only if they are successful on the last program.
- *Having proved that you are an exceptional engineer.* You also rise to this position because you have demonstrated exceptional technical engineering capability. CEs have much broader training and exposure across several engineering specialties than most other engineers at Toyota.
- *Being a critical link between engineering and customer satisfaction.* Toyota has managed to build a culture of individuals focused on customer satisfaction and they recognize the CE as a critical link in that commitment.

I think that the phrase "heavyweight project manager" does not do justice to the important role the chief engineer plays. Suzuki was known as the Michael Jordan of chief engineers. This reputation came from repeated technical achievements that demonstrated remarkable technical skills and engineering intuition. At Toyota, the CE is someone who is in the trenches of engineering and knows how to "play the game." He or she exemplifies what an excellent engineer is through actions and leadership.

The Common Themes of Leadership at Toyota

Toyota leaders have a distinctive approach and philosophy that fits the Toyota Way. The two-dimensional leadership matrix in Figure 15-3 helps depict what distinguishes leadership at Toyota from leadership at other companies. On the one hand, leaders can either rule by top-down directives or use a bottom-up involving style to develop people so they can think and make the right decisions on their own. We have seen repeatedly that Toyota leaders are passionate about involving people who are doing the value-added work in improving the process. Yet encour-

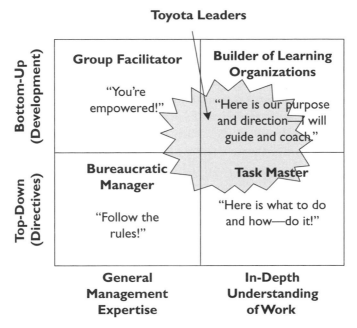

Figure 15-3. Toyota leadership model

aging employee involvement by itself is not enough to define a Toyota leader. A second dimension requires an "in-depth understanding of the work" in addition to general management expertise. It was fashionable in the U.S. in the 1980s to think of the typical successful manager as an MBA who could walk into any business and instantly run it by looking at the numbers and using general management and leadership principles to whip the organization into shape. No self-respecting Toyota manager would subscribe to this notion.

The least effective manager in this model is top-down and has only general management expertise—the bureaucratic manager. This characterizes a large portion of U.S. managers. How effective can you be if you are trying to run the organization through command and control without any intimate understanding of what is going on? Your only choice is to make a lot of rules and policies and measure performance relative to those rules and policies. This leads to metrics-driven management that takes the focus away from satisfying customers or building a learning organization.

The bottom-up leader who wants to develop employees but does not really understand the work is called the group facilitator. The belief is that if a leader has strong facilitation skills, he or she can motivate employees to work together toward common goals. Facilitators are catalysts but cannot teach or guide the junior people on the content of the work. Leaders like these can be great at motivating teams and helping them to develop. But can they really coach or mentor others in what they do not understand? They don't even have the expertise to judge excellent work and contributions from subordinates.

The next type is a top-down leader with a strong understanding of the work—an expert in the field—who lacks people skills and can be a tough taskmaster. The taskmaster treats subordinates like puppets, pulling all the strings at the right time, a major burden since one missed pull of a string might cause the work process to collapse. This type of leader is likely to be distrustful of others with less experience. Like the bureaucratic manager, he or she will give orders, but orders to do specific tasks exactly as ordered. This is the definition of micro-management.

By contrast, the Toyota leaders, by having a combination of in-depth understanding of the work and the ability to develop, mentor, and lead people, are respected for their technical knowledge as well as followed for their leadership abilities. Toyota leaders seldom give orders. In fact, the leaders often lead and mentor through questioning. The leader will ask questions about the situation and the person's strategy for action, but they will not give answers to these questions even though they have the knowledge.

We show the Toyota leader as partially in all four of the quadrants in Figure 15-3. Each of these forms of leadership has a role at the appropriate time and place. But his or her primary leadership role is as builders of a learning organization—a distinctive strength of Toyota's culture. The roots of Toyota leadership go back to the Toyoda family who developed Toyota Way Principle 9: *Grow leaders who thoroughly understand the work, live the philosophy, and teach it to others.*

If we look at all of the great leaders in Toyota's history we see they share several common traits:

- Focused on a long-term purpose for Toyota as a value-added contributor to society.
- Never deviated from the precepts of the Toyota Way DNA and lived and modeled themselves around this for all to see.
- Worked their way up doing the detailed work and continued to go to the *gemba*—the actual place where the real added-value work is done.
- Saw problems as opportunities to train and coach their people.

A common phrase heard around Toyota is "Before we build cars, we build people." The leader's goal at Toyota is to develop people so they are strong contributors who can think and follow the Toyota Way at all levels in the organization. The leader's real challenge is having the long-term vision of knowing what to do, the knowledge of how to do it, and the ability to develop people so they can understand and do their job excellently. The payoff for this dedication is more profound and lasting to a company's competitiveness and longevity than using a leader merely to solve immediate financial problems, make the correct decision for a given situation, or provide new short-term solutions to bail a company out of a bad situation. A company growing its own leaders and defining the ultimate role of leadership as "building a learning organization" lays the groundwork for genuine long-term success.

Notes

1. Jim Collins, *Good to Great* (New York: HarperBusiness, 2001).
2. Michael A. Cusumano and Kentaro Nobeoka, *Thinking Beyond Lean: How Multi-Project Management Is Transforming Product Development at Toyota and Other Companies* (New York: Free Press, 1998).
3. Reprinted with the permission of The Free Press, a Division of Simon & Schuster Adult Publishing Group, from *Thinking Beyond Lean: How Multi-Project Management is Transforming Product Development at Toyota and Other Companies* by Michael A. Cusumano and Kentaro Nobeoka. Copyright © 1998 by Michael A. Cusumano and Kentaro Nobeoka. All rights reserved.

Chapter 16

Principle 10:
Develop Exceptional People and Teams Who Follow Your Company's Philosophy

Respect for people and constant challenging to do better—are these contradictory? Respect for people means respect for the mind and capability. You do not expect them to waste their time. You respect the capability of the people. Americans think teamwork is about you liking me and I liking you. Mutual respect and trust means I trust and respect that you will do your job so that we are successful as a company. It does not mean we just love each other.
— Sam Heltman, Senior Vice President of Administration
Toyota Motor Manufacturing, North America
(one of the first five Americans hired by Toyota, Georgetown)

Form vs. Function of Teams

General Motors has had a unique opportunity through its joint venture with Toyota at the NUMMI plant to learn the Toyota Production System firsthand. In recent years, they have been doing quite well in applying TPS. But that was not always the case.

In the early stages of the joint venture, GM tried to carbon-copy TPS throughout the organization. Among the things GM copied was the work group structure, which consists of small work groups of four to eight people that use an hourly team leader to act in a support and coordination role for the group. The hourly team leader does not perform a manual job unless someone is missing. About three or four work groups report to the first-line supervisor, called the *group leader*, a salaried position. These two leadership roles are central to solving problems and implementing continuous improvements (*kaizen*).

At GM the team leaders in particular were in a new role. They added a layer on the organizational chart, so their existence needed to be justified. So at some point an executive wanted to know how the groups were performing. GM conducted a time study to measure how the GM team leaders were using their time throughout the company as well as a parallel study for NUMMI team leaders. The overarching difference between GM and NUMMI team leaders is that GM team leaders didn't really understand their role. In fact, only 52% of the time the GM team leaders were doing anything that you could regard as work, while NUMMI team leaders were actively supporting the assembly line workers and spent 90% of their time doing work on the shop floor. Some of the things the NUMMI team leaders were actively doing:

- 21% of their time was spent filling in for workers who were absent or on vacation. GM team leaders did this 1.5% of the time.
- 10% of their time was spent ensuring a smooth flow of parts to the line. GM team leaders were at 3%.
- 7% of their time was spent actively communicating job-related information. This was virtually absent at GM.
- 5% of their time was spent observing the team working, in order to anticipate problems. This did not happen at all at GM.

Basically, GM team leaders focused on emergency relief of workers (e.g., so workers could use the restroom) and quality inspection and repair. When there were no immediate problems and no fires to put out, they went to a back room for a break. What GM was lacking was obvious: it did not have the Toyota Production System or the supporting culture. It merely copied and appended the work group structure onto traditional mass-production plants. The lesson was clear: don't implement work teams before you do the hard work of implementing the system and culture to support them.

The Principle: Developing Excellent Individual Work While Promoting Effective Team Work

Talk to somebody at Toyota about the Toyota Production System and you can hardly avoid getting a lecture on the importance of teamwork. All systems are there to support the team doing value-added work. But teams do not do value-added work. Individuals do. The teams coordinate the work, motivate, and learn from each other. Teams suggest innovative ideas, even control through peer pressure. Nevertheless, for the most part, it is more efficient for individuals to do the actual detailed work necessary to produce a product. Teams can coordinate in meetings, but in most cases, not a whole lot of the detailed work gets done if individuals spend all their time in meetings.

Toyota has established an excellent balance between individual work and group work and between individual excellence and team effectiveness. While teamwork is critical, having individuals work together in a group does not compensate for a lack of individual excellence or understanding of Toyota's system. Excellent individual performers are required to make up teams that excel. This is why Toyota puts such a tremendous effort in finding and screening prospective employees. It wants the right individuals to train and empower to work in teams. When Toyota selects one person out of hundreds of job applicants after searching for many months, it is sending a message—the capabilities and characteristics of individuals matter. The years spent carefully grooming each individual to develop depth of technical knowledge, a broad range of skills, and a second-nature understanding of Toyota's philosophy speaks to the importance of the individual in Toyota's system.

Toyota's assumption is that if you make teamwork the foundation of the company, individual performers will give their hearts and souls to make the company successful. Originally, the Toyota Production System was called the "respect for humanity system." As you will read on, you will see that the Toyota Way is not about lavishing goodies on people whether they have earned them or not; it is about challenging *and* respecting employees at the same time.

Launching a Toyota Facility in North America: One Shot at Getting the Culture Right

By the time Toyota began setting up its service parts facility in Hebron, Kentucky, the management team had learned from experience that a successful startup depended much more on creating a Toyota culture than on building a facility with the right technology. Years earlier, Toyota set up a global service parts distribution center in Ontario, California. While a lot of planning and thought went into the launch of the Ontario, California, facility and how to develop the people there, the management team believed it could build on that experience and improve on the launch. The long-term vision for Hebron was to have a service parts operation driven by empowered work teams, as is the case in Japan. But the experience at Ontario taught them that "empowering" employees too quickly when setting up the facility can be premature. Until individuals and teams really understand the Toyota Way and TPS, they are not in a position to be empowered.

I visited the Hebron facility about three years after it was launched. Management was still in the process of slowly implementing work teams and granting autonomy to workers. What are these people doing that is so complex that they need over two years to be ready to contribute as work teams? According to the manager of the facility, Ken Elliott, "We are not building a warehouse; we are building a culture. This is why we have been as successful as we are." He believed it was worth the time to develop the culture early on because "we have one shot at this to get the culture right."

At Hebron, they began building a culture by using a three-stage process to select the best associates. It took about one year to do the bulk of the hiring. First was the written application process. Getting people to apply was not difficult. An announcement was made to the local press that Toyota would be opening the facility and there would be new jobs. The resulting newscast, not a paid advertisement, resulted in 13,500 applicants for 275 jobs. Second, from this pool they randomly selected a subset to attend a job fair where there were opportunities for informal meetings and assessments. Third, a random sample of those who passed the job fair were invited to three one-hour meetings for interviews. Randomness was used to ensure fairness and diversity. After a background check, drug test, and physical exam, the finalists were offered jobs.

The early stages of the selection process were designed to winnow down the applications to a reasonable number. The job fair was designed using Toyota Way principles. The goals were both to educate the applicants in Toyota's philosophy and to see who fit in. The fair included presentations on Toyota's history and culture and that of service parts operations, a realistic videotape of what it is like to work in the facility, a review of Toyota benefits, an overview of the selection process, and finally a written test. The most important process was the third stage of face-to-face interviews to determine whether Toyota could mold the individual's values and personal characteristics into the Toyota Way. In the year prior to full launch, 37 associates were hired to be on the design team to develop the operational processes and 20 others were assigned to support roles. These hourly associates then helped in the interviewing of other hourly associates who would later join their teams. Some associates had to wait a year or more to get their actual job offer. Yet this process was relatively quick and informal compared with the process at other facilities, like Toyota, Georgetown, where aptitude tests were given and applicants were put on teams to solve problems while being videotaped and then often waited one to two years to get their job offers.

Elliott had learned from his experience at the Ontario facility the importance of ramping up gradually and systematically. So, the Hebron team developed a four-phase implementation process over an 11-month period.

In phase one, the facility operated at a very low volume level, so there was a lot of slack time to get the job duties and responsibilities right. The teams worked out the basic operational procedures, often in a crude form, tested standard operating procedures, and trained and taught some more. In phase two, management picked the best suppliers to ship low-volume parts to the operation, and there were only a few resulting problems receiving the parts on time. In phase three, the teams added smaller suppliers that were not as sophisticated in their manufacturing and logistics systems. This added variability to the process, which further challenged associates. In phase four, they finally brought high-volume suppliers on line. At each phase, management took the time to teach more of the Toyota Way. This staged process also allowed for bringing on hourly associates gradually over time, so all 230 did not have to be trained at the same time. Even within each of these phases, there were multiple live simulations before going live with a new process. Each stage posed new challenges, but the earlier stages built a set of skills and routines, along with confidence.

The result was a very smooth ramp up. Using metrics like fill rate (percent of parts available when customers wanted them), the Hebron facility was the best launch of any such Toyota facility in North America.

Developing Teams at Toyota: Not a One-Minute Proposition

One surprise I had when I was visiting the Hebron operation was the frequent reference to "situational leadership" that they had learned from Ken Blanchard, famed author of *The One-Minute Manager*. This was only one of a number of leadership models they had learned from, but it at first struck me as incongruous with the Toyota philosophy. They showed me an evolutionary model of high-performance work teams that they had gotten from a Blanchard workshop that helped them think about the gradual process of developing work teams.

This prompted me to read *The One Minute Manager Builds High Performing Teams* (Blanchard, Carew, and Parisi-Carew, 2000). The book is similar to others in the "One Minute Manager" series. The basic premise is that groups have to develop over time and cannot jump from a bunch of individuals to a high performing team immediately. Blanchard describes four stages of team development:

Stage 1: Orientation. The group needs strong direction from the leader and must understand the basic mission, rules of engagement, and tools the members will use.

Stage 2: Dissatisfaction. The group goes to work, which is a lot less fun than talking about great visions of success, and the members discover it is harder than they thought to work as a team. In this stage, they continue to need strong direction (structure) from the leader but also need a lot of social support to get through the tough social dynamics they do not understand.

Stage 3: Integration. The group starts to develop a clearer picture of the roles of various team members and begins to exert control over team processes. The challenge is for the group to learn about roles, goals, norms, and team structure. The leader does not have to provide much task direction, but the team still needs a lot of social support.

Stage 4: Production. The group puts it all together and is functioning as a high-performing team with little task support or social support from the leader.

It was clear to me that what Toyota was doing with this simple model was combining TPS thinking with the situational leadership model into something new and different and much more powerful. The book by Blanchard et al. focuses on people coming together in task forces and holding meetings. This is what I normally think of as temporary problem-solving groups. Toyota was building work teams that were doing finely tuned work every day in addition to making improvements to the work process as problem-solving groups. It was much more than task force meetings.

Combining the concepts of situational leadership with the highly evolved work processes of TPS led to something new that you could not teach in one minute. In fact, in Blanchard's book, one of his stages seems to happen in a few meetings, such as stage 3, Integration, which can even happen in even one well-facilitated meeting. Hebron was taking three years to get to stage 4. Were they stuck in stage 3 with slow managers and mentally inferior workers? Quite the contrary. As we saw earlier in the book, TPS is based on a particularly challenging technical process—the ideal of one-piece flow. Flow involves extremely tight coordination between each step in the process and this coordination helps build effective work teams.

Figure 16-1 illustrates the effects of flow on team functioning. In the top half, we have traditional batch-and-queue manufacturing. Each worker is doing his or her job at his or her own pace and building to inventory—in this case overproducing and creating waste. Under this system, the next operator in the process is oblivious to any problems occurring upstream or downstream. As long as there is inventory of incoming parts and the workers are allowed to build up as many parts as they want in the outbound queue, they can work happily along, regardless of what their associates are doing. Even if a worker produces a defect, it may not be caught in this shift and operators in the next shift can worry about it. If the next worker catches it, he or she can just put it aside and take a good part from the large pile of inventory. The person sitting down at Station C has the good job and probably has waited years to get that cushy job.

Now the one-minute manager comes along and says it's time to become a team. (You can substitute for Blanchard any team-building program you may have experienced.) So everyone piles into the conference room to work on improving productivity. What is likely to happen is that the team will focus on reducing the amount of time it takes to perform the value-added processes, the work they perform, or work on creature comforts like the lighting and putting in a water cooler. In the batch-and-queue process, the workers work individually, so it is natural that they focus only on their individual tasks.

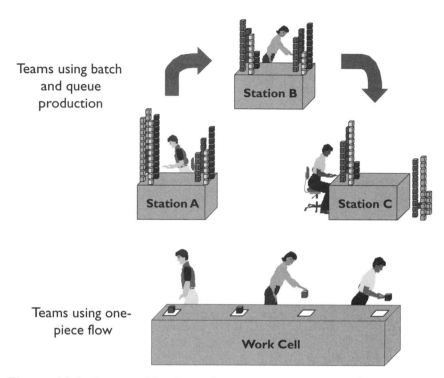

Teams using batch and queue production

Station B

Station A

Station C

Teams using one-piece flow

Work Cell

Figure 16-1. Teams and batch production versus one-piece flow

Now let's consider the case of a TPS expert coming in and analyzing the batch-and-queue operation in Figure 16-1. The expert would immediately observe that there is no flow and that there is a great deal of waste. The first task of the TPS expert might be to improve the flow and eliminate most of the inventory that is getting in the way of tying together operations. The squares are *kanban* squares: as long as there is a piece in the square, stop building. The expert would want the flexibility of staffing the cell with one, two, or three people, depending on the demand, so eventually all team members will need to learn every job and rotate. To reduce the number of people in the cell and have each person doing multiple jobs, the expert must get rid of the cushy chair. You can't have workers stopping and sitting in the chair. What you need is a team creating value for customers, doing only what needs to be done. We can see the "dissatisfaction" stage coming up fast and furious from that worker who lost the chair. In addition, there may be more dissatisfaction when the new flow reveals that the work can be done using two workers, not three.

In fact, the very stages described by Blanchard apply nicely to the process of implementing TPS and work teams, as the Toyota service parts management team had learned, though the process takes years and not minutes. When the service parts operation was set up, apart from a small group of leaders who had experience with TPS, the concepts were all new to the recently hired associates. In stage 1, the leadership group explained the vision, orienting team members, and did various simulations, which were fun. Morale was high. The team members got some awareness training in TPS, but could not really understand it. At this point, the leadership group had to be very directive.

As the team slowly ramped up production under management's direction, there were natural problems and setbacks. Stage 2 kicked in and morale went down a bit. The team needed a lot of social support from the group leaders, along with continued direction. However, unlike Blanchard's model, the group leaders could not focus only on social support and stop being directive, especially since they were still removing waste and making jobs more interdependent. So a combination of directiveness and social support was still needed while associates removed waste and contributed new ideas to improve the technical process.

After three years, the group leaders finally felt the associates had matured to the point that, in some home positions, they could assign some associates to team leader roles and move the group toward being more self-directed. They were in Blanchard's stage 3. The move toward stage 4 is continuing to evolve over years.

The way I see it, the difference between the one-minute version of situational leadership and the Toyota version is the difference between holding meetings with action items and actually working as a team in a tightly coordinated, complex work system. The individuals in the coordinated system are executing standard operating procedures and there is a need for tight synchronization across associates to get the job done right. This type of team building does not happen in a conference room across a few well-facilitated meetings.

Work Groups Are the Focal Point for Solving Problems

In a conventional automotive plant, white-collar or skilled-trade staff is responsible for problem solving, quality assurance, equipment maintenance, and productivity. By contrast, shop floor work groups are the focal point for problem solving in the Toyota Production System (see Figure 16-2).

The associates who perform the value-added jobs are the most familiar with the actual work and the actual problems that affect the work. Since Toyota exists to add value for its customers and it is team members who do the value-added work, the team members are at the top of the hierarchy. The rest of the hierarchy is there to support them. The next line of defense is the *team leader*, an hourly employee who worked on the line but has an opportunity for a small promotion. The team leader cannot take disciplinary action but is there to support the team

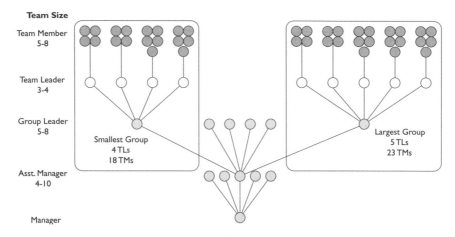

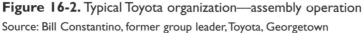

Figure 16-2. Typical Toyota organization—assembly operation

Source: Bill Constantino, former group leader, Toyota, Georgetown

members. The first-line supervisor is the *group leader*, who is responsible for leading and coordinating a number of groups.

By the standards of many companies, Toyota has an organizational structure that looks very inefficient—lots of leaders for a small number of workers. Team leaders typically have just four to eight workers they support and most of the time the team leaders are not doing production jobs. Group leaders typically have three or four groups.

This concept of bottom-up management and employee empowerment is a cliché in many companies, but Toyota takes this very seriously. The small span of control of the team leaders is more a matter of necessity. In some respects, the TPS bottom-up management is even more challenging for teams, because TPS continuously takes the waste out of the value stream, that is, the inventory is taken out of the process, and it takes out waste from every job position. On the other hand, traditional job layouts are designed with waste built in, or at least little systematic thought has been given to making the layout efficient and synchronized with other processes. This waste is a cushion from the perspective of the worker. Now, remove that waste and replace it with additional value-added tasks. Suddenly the worker has to be on his toes. This would arguably be inhumane if it were not for the team leader system. The team leader is like an on-the-spot physician ready to jump in any time there is a problem, such as when there is a call for help through the *andon* system (Chapter 11). The team leader is also a safety valve, always walking the line and watching to see if there are any problems emerging, such as parts getting low or someone getting behind who needs assistance or relief.

The roles and responsibilities for team members, team leaders, and group leaders are summarized in Figure 16-3 (courtesy of Bill Costantino, one of the first group leaders at the Toyota plant in Georgetown, Kentucky). Noteworthy is the progression of responsibilities from team members to group leaders. *Team members* perform manual jobs to standard and are responsible for problem solving and continuous improvement. *Team leaders* take on a number of the responsibilities traditionally done by "white-collar" managers, though they are not formally managers and do not have the authority to discipline other team members. Their prime role is to keep the line running smoothly and producing quality parts. *Group leaders* do many things that otherwise would be handled by specialty support functions in human resources, engineering, and quality. They are integral to major improvements of the process, even introducing new products and processes. They regularly teach short topics. If needed, they are also capable of getting on the line and performing the jobs. There is no such thing as a hands-off leader at Toyota.

Team Member (TM)
- Perform work to current standard
- Maintain 5S in their work area
- Perform routine minor maintenance
- Look for continuous improvement opportunities
- Support problem-solving small group activities

Team Leader (TL)
- Process start-up and control
- Meet production goals
- Respond to *andon* calls by TM
- Confirm quality—routine checks
- Cover absenteeism
- Training and cross-training
- Work orders for quick maintenance
- Insure standardized work is followed
- Facilitate small group activities
- On-going continuous improvement projects
- Insure parts/materials are supplied to process

Group Leader
- Manpower/vacation scheduling
- Monthly production planning
- Administrative: policy, attendance, corrective actions
- Hoshin planning
- Team morale
- Confirm routine quality and TL checks
- Shift to shift coordination
- Process trials (changes in process)

Figure 16-3. Toyota roles and responsibilities (continued on next page)

- TM development and cross-training
- Report / track daily production results
- Cost reduction activities
- Process improvement projects: productivity, quality, ergonomics, etc.
- Coordinate major maintenance
- Coordinate support from outside groups
- Coordinate work with up-stream and down-stream processes
- Group safety performance
- Help cover TL absence
- Coordinate activities around major model changes

Figure 16-3. Toyota roles and responsibilities (continued)

This same basic system of team leaders and group leaders applies throughout Toyota. The Hebron service parts warehouse is moving in this direction. You also see something similar in engineering. The equivalents of the team leaders are first-grade engineers who have mastered a specific technical area and take on the role of supporting and developing junior engineers in their specialty. At Toyota, when you are at the working levels of high-volume production—whether it is producing parts, engineering drawings, quality plans, or sales—there is always an immediate mentor there to support you day to day. Nobody is cut loose to figure it out for himself or herself, though the mentorship style is to give challenging assignments and let you struggle until you "pull the andon" and call for help.

At Toyota, Everything You Learned in School About Motivation Theory Is Right

Most of us at some point in our education learned about human motivation. If you took a class, you may recall a dizzying array of different theories and theorists and no clear way of figuring out who was right or wrong. Which motivation theory does Toyota, implicitly, subscribe to? As it turns out, all of them. All of the theories are used to great effect at Toyota, though often with a bit of a twist on the original theories.

Figure 16-4 summarizes Toyota's approach to the five most prominent motivation theories. The first two theories assume people are primarily motivated internally: intrinsic characteristics of the job itself motivate them to work hard and do quality work. The next three theories assume people are primarily driven by external factors—rewards, punishments, and measurement toward goals. Toyota uses all of these approaches to motivate associates. We will discuss each in turn.

Internal Motivation Theories	Concept	Toyota Approach
Maslow's Need Hierarchy	Satisfy lower level needs and move employees up the hierarchy toward self actualization.	Job security, good pay, safe working conditions satisfy lower level needs. Culture of continuous improvement supports growth toward self actualization.
Herzberg's Job Enrichment Theory	Eliminate "dissatisfiers" (hygiene factors) and design work to create positive satisfiers (motivators).	5S, ergonomics programs, visual management, human resource policies address hygiene factors. Continuous improvement, job rotation, and built-in feedback support motivators.
External Motivation Theories		
Taylor's Scientific Management	Scientifically select, design standardized jobs, train, and reward with money performance relative to standards.	All scientific management principles followed but at the group level rather than individual level and based on employee involvement.
Behavior Modification	Reinforce behavior on the spot when the behavior naturally occurs.	Continuous flow and *andon* creates short-lead times for rapid feedback. Leaders constantly on the floor and providing reinforcement.
Goal Setting	Set specific, measurable, achieveable challenging goals and measure progress.	Sets goals that meet these criteria through *hoshin kanri* (policy deployment). Continuous measurements relative to targets.

Figure 16-4. Classic motivation theories and the Toyota Way

Internal Motivation Theories

Maslow's Hierarchy of Needs. Abraham Maslow's need hierarchy looks at motivating people as equivalent to satisfying their internal needs. Your highest level of motivation will be to do the things that better you as a person—called "self-actualization." But there are a few steps you have to take before you can get there. Humans can work on higher-level needs like self-actualization only if lower-level needs are satisfied—physiological (e.g., having enough food to eat), safety and security (e.g., feeling safe from harm), and social approval (having others you care about think well of you). These factors are all external to you. There are then two higher-level needs—self-esteem (you feel good about yourself) and the ultimate self-actualization—striving to develop yourself.

When you work for Toyota, your lower-level needs are covered. You are well paid, you have job security, and you are working in a safe, controlled environment. The work group can help satisfy social needs along with a myriad of social activities at work and after work. Toyota's culture emphasizes the use of challenging work situations to build self-confidence in their people for experimenting and accomplishing exceptional feats that can move in the direction of self-actualization.

Herzberg's Job Enrichment. Frederick Herzberg's theories are similar to Maslow's, but they focus on characteristics of work that are "motivators." He said that what Maslow called lower-level needs are really "hygiene" factors. Their absence will cause dissatisfaction, but providing a person more and more of them will not positively motivate. For example, a clean and bright work environment, nice eating facilities, and good pay and benefits can help keep people in the job, but more hygiene factors do not make people work harder. If you really want to motivate people, you have to go beyond the hygiene factors and enrich jobs so they are "intrinsically" motivating. People performing the work need feedback on how they are doing. They need to perform a whole piece of work, one in which they can identify with the product of their work. They also need a degree of autonomy.

Toyota has done a good job of providing for the hygiene factors through job security with safe and attractive work environments. Nevertheless, on the face of it, an assembly line is anything but enriching. People do the same mindless task repeatedly and are responsible only for a tiny piece of an overall product. However, TPS adds a great deal to make the tasks more intrinsically motivating and Toyota has specifically worked on designing assembly lines to improve job enrichment. Some of the features that make the job more enriching include job rotation (which gives the work group ownership over a subsystem of the vehicle), various kinds of feedback on how workers are doing at their jobs, the *andon* system (which allows the worker to be proactive in solving problems), and a good deal of work group autonomy over the tasks. Toyota became interested in job enrichment in the 1990s and redesigned its assembly lines so that parts that make up a subsystem of the vehicle are installed in one specific area on the assembly line. Rather than a work group assembling electrical systems and then putting in floor mats and then door handles, a work group might focus almost exclusively on the electrical system under the hood. For white collar workers, Toyota organizes teams around complete projects from start to finish. For example, the design of the interior of the vehicle is the responsibility of one team from the design phase through production. Having the responsibility of participating in the project from beginning to end enriches and empowers the employee.

External Motivation Theories

Taylor's Scientific Management. Taylorism is the ultimate in external motivation. People come to work to make money—end of story. You motivate workers by giving them clear standards, teaching them the most efficient way to reach the standard, and then giving them bonuses when they exceed the standard. The standards are for quantity, not quality. In Chapter 12, we discussed how Toyota's system is also based on standardization, but workers have responsibility for improving standardized work. Basically, Toyota turned scientific management on its head and turned over control of standardization to work teams. While Taylor strictly focused on individual incentives for productivity, Toyota distributes work to teams. Groups, not individuals, take on responsibility. Performance measures are about how the group is doing.

Behavior Modification. Behavior modification is the more generalized approach of using rewards and punishments to motivate. In behavior modification, we recognize that there are many things that people find rewarding and punishing, that go beyond money. It could be praise from a supervisor or peer. It could be winning an award. The important point is that the positive or negative reinforcement comes as quickly as possible after the action.

Toyota's system based on continuous flow and the *andon* system is ideal for powerful behavior modification. Feedback is very rapid. The best kind of negative feedback is impersonal and people find out how they are doing without a supervisor even telling them—by uncovering quality problems immediately. As for praise or reprimands from supervisors, the group leaders are right there on the floor in a perfect position to give immediate feedback to associates. In addition, they are trained to do it.

One example of a splashy reward system developed by Toyota in the United States is the perfect attendance award used in all U.S.-based manufacturing facilities. Attendance is critical within Toyota, because associates are very skilled and part of a team, and staffing is lean. The perfect attendance system rewards perfect attendance—zero unexcused absences in a year. Those who make the perfect attendance club are invited to a big banquet held at a major convention center. About a dozen brand-new Toyota vehicles are paraded on stage. A lottery picks winners who drive home the vehicles with taxes and fees all fully paid. About 60% to 70% of Toyota associates get into the perfect attendance club—not a single day of missed work or lateness. The total cost of this one-night extravaganza to Toyota for getting thousands of associates to come to work on time every day is peanuts.

Goal Setting. Put simply, people are motivated by challenging but attainable goals and measurement of progress toward those goals—like playing a game. Toyota's visual management systems plus policy deployment mean that teams always know how they are doing and always are working toward stretch improvement targets.

Policy deployment sets challenging, stretch goals from the top to the bottom of the company. Careful measurements every day let work teams know how they are performing.

People Drive Continuous Improvement

Toyota invests in people and in return it gets committed associates who show up to work every day and on time and are continually improving their operations. On one of my visits, I found that in the past year at the Toyota, Georgetown, assembly plant associates made about 80,000 improvement suggestions. The plant implemented 99% of them.

So how can you get your employees to work diligently to do their jobs perfectly and strive to improve every day? Build a system that follows Toyota Way Principle 10: *Develop exceptional people and teams who follow your company's philosophy* by first looking at the system dynamics of your organization. Building excellent people who understand and support your company's culture is not a matter of adopting simple solutions or an afterthought of applying motivational theories. Training exceptional people and building individual work groups needs to be the backbone of your management approach, an approach that integrates your social systems with your technical system. Throughout this book, you have seen how one-piece flow drives positive problem-solving behaviors and motivates people to improve. However, you need a social system and culture of continuous improvement to support this behavior.

Of course, you cannot pull a ready-made culture out of a wizard's hat. Building a culture takes years of applying a consistent approach with consistent principles. It includes the foundational elements of Maslow. People must have a degree of security and feel they belong to a team. You must design jobs to be challenging. People need some autonomy to feel they have control over the job. Moreover, there seems to be nothing as motivating as challenging targets, constant measurement and feedback on progress, and an occasional reward thrown in. The rewards can be symbolic and not all that costly. In the end, building exceptional people and teams derives from having in place some form of a "respect for humanity system."

Chapter 17

Principle 11:
Respect Your Extended Network of Partners and Suppliers by Challenging Them and Helping Them Improve

Toyota is more hands-on and more driven to improving their own systems and then showing how that improves you.... Toyota will do things like level their production systems to make it easier on you. Toyota picks up our product 12 times per day. They helped move presses, moved where we get the water from, trained our employees. On the commercial side they are very hands-on also—they come in and measure and work to get cost out of the system. There is more opportunity to make profit at Toyota. We started with Toyota when we opened a Canadian plant with one component and, as performance improved, we were rewarded, so now we have almost the entire cockpit. Relative to all car companies we deal with, Toyota is the best.

—an automotive supplier

Auto industry suppliers consistently report that Toyota is their best customer—and also their toughest. We often think of "tough" as difficult to get along with or unreasonable. In Toyota's case, it means they have very high standards of excellence and expect all their partners to rise to those standards. More importantly, they will help all their partners rise to those standards. This chapter explains how this unusual approach to supplier relationships works.

Let's start with an example of an *ineffective* (but sadly typical) approach to supplier relationships. In 1999, one of the Big Three U.S. auto companies, which I'll call "American Auto," decided it wanted to make its supplier relationships the best in the industry. American Auto was tired of hearing how great Toyota and Honda were at teaching and developing their suppliers to be lean. For years,

American Auto had worked to improve its relationships with suppliers, but when suppliers were asked who the leaders were in supplier development, it was uniformly Toyota and Honda. Their goal was to develop a supplier development center that would become the global benchmark for best practice. Even Toyota would benchmark American Auto.

This became a highly visible project within American Auto's purchasing department, with champions for its success at the vice president level. From the start the vice presidents already had a vision for their supplier development center. In fact, one vice president already had preliminary blueprints for building a supplier development center that would have state-of-the-art instructional technology. Their building would be the biggest and best, and suppliers would come together to learn best practices, including lean manufacturing methods.

The first step in the project was to collect data on the current situation by interviewing about 25 suppliers to American Auto. Most of these suppliers already had internal lean manufacturing programs and many had surpassed American Auto on lean. The main message from the supplier interviews was clear and consistent:

> *Tell American Auto not to waste their money building a big expensive building to train us, but instead to get their own house in order so they can be a capable and reliable partner we can truly work with. Fix their broken product development process and ask them to implement lean manufacturing internally. We will even help teach American Auto.*

The following quote from a supplier provides a flavor of a very consistent message:

> *The problem is American Auto has inexperienced engineers who think they know what they are supposed to do. I would rather have those who realize they need to learn and train them. It is not clear if it is the reward system that causes them to get aggressive and adversarial. I have worked with American Auto for almost 18 years and saw the wave of good people back then who were trying to help you. Now relationships have deteriorated tremendously. It used to feel good working with the American Auto people. Today, I do not trust them. Even people I worked with and trusted are finding ways to manipulate suppliers. It is almost sad.*

Clearly American Auto needed to do a great deal of work before any benefit would come from constructing a fancy supplier development center. The basic problems were inherent in the weaknesses of American Auto's own internal systems, the lack of development of their own people, and their focus on carrot-and-stick management without understanding their supplier's processes. They needed to earn the right to be leaders before they could expect their suppliers to be followers and learn from them. They were a long way off and, in fact, headed in the wrong direction.

Ultimately, cost-cutting killed the whole effort to build a supplier development center. That was 1999 and, if anything, things have deteriorated even further at American Auto. American Auto is not unusual in my experience in companies that want to jump right to the benefits of a streamlined, efficient supply chain without doing any of the hard internal development needed to get there.

In the meantime, Toyota has spent decades building a strong lean enterprise in Japan and has a fast start at building a world-class supplier network in North America. Suppliers are reacting positively to Toyota's demanding but fair partnership approach. For example, the OEM Benchmark Survey, a survey of auto suppliers by John Henke of Oakland University that is the principal measure of supplier relations in the American auto industry, ranks Toyota number one. In 17 measures from trust to perceived opportunity, the 2003 survey places Toyota first, followed by Honda and Nissan, while Chrysler, Ford, and GM are fourth, fifth, and sixth. And Toyota's scores keep getting better, with a 7% improvement over 2002.[1]

A survey conducted by J.D. Power of automotive suppliers found that Nissan, Toyota, and BMW are the best North American automakers in promoting innovation with their suppliers (*Automotive News*, Feb. 24, 2003). Honda and Mercedes also finished above average in fostering innovation, while the Chrysler group, Ford, and General Motors all were rated below average.

Toyota has been rewarded time and time again for its serious investment in building a network of highly capable suppliers that is truly integrated into Toyota's extended lean enterprise. Much of the award winning quality that distinguishes Toyota and Lexus results from the excellence in innovation, engineering, manufacture, and overall reliability of Toyota's suppliers. And Toyota's suppliers are integral to the just-in-time philosophy, both when it is working smoothly and when there is a breakdown in the system.

While many companies would abandon just-in-time when the first crisis hits, Toyota works its way through the rare crises working hand in hand with suppliers. For example, February 1, 1997, a fire destroyed an Aisin factory.[2] Aisin is one of Toyota's biggest and closest suppliers. Normally Toyota dual sources parts but Aisin was the sole source for something called a "p-valve" which is an essential brake part used in all Toyota vehicles worldwide—at that time 32,500 per day. Toyota's vaunted JIT system meant only two days of inventory were available in total in the supply chain. Two days and disaster would strike—evidence that JIT is a bad idea? Instead of faltering, 200 suppliers self-organized to get p-valve production started within 2 days. Sixty three different firms took responsibility for making the parts piecing together what existed of engineering documentation, using some of their own equipment, rigging together temporary lines to make the parts, and keeping Toyota in business almost seamlessly. The power of the supply chain is far more than information technology. It is the power of ingenuity and relationships.

The Principle: Find Solid Partners and Grow Together to Mutual Benefit in the Long Term

Go to a conference on supply chain management and what are you likely to hear? You will learn a lot about "streamlining" the supply chain through advanced information technology. If you can get the information in nanoseconds, you should be able to speed the supply chain to nanosecond deliveries, right? What you are not likely to hear about is the enormous complexity of coordinating detailed, daily activities to deliver value to the customer. You are not likely to hear about relationships across firms—about how to work together toward common goals. Yet, this is the heart of what has made Toyota's partnership with suppliers a global benchmark.

When Toyota started building automobiles, it did not have capital or equipment for building the myriad of components that go into a car. One of Eiji Toyoda's first assignments as a new engineer was to identify high-quality parts suppliers that Toyota could partner with. At that time they did not have the volume to give a lot of business to suppliers. In fact, some days they did not build a single vehicle because they did not have enough quality parts. So Toyoda understood the need to find solid partners. All that Toyota could offer was the opportunity for all partners to grow the business together and mutually benefit in the long term. So, like the associates who work inside Toyota, suppliers became part of the extended family who grew and learned the Toyota Production System.

Even when Toyota became a global powerhouse, it maintained the early principle of partnership. It views new suppliers cautiously and gives only very small orders. They must prove their sincerity and commitment to Toyota's high performance standards for quality, cost, and delivery. If they demonstrate this for early orders, they will get increasingly larger orders. Toyota will teach them the Toyota Way and adopt them into the family. Once inside, you are not kicked out except for the most egregious behavior.

This is not to say that respect for the extended network of supplier partners is analogous to being soft and an easy target. Toyota's view is that, just as it challenges its own people to improve, it needs to challenge its suppliers. Supplier development includes a series of aggressive targets and challenges to meet those stretch targets. Suppliers want to work for Toyota because they know they will get better and develop respect among their peers and other customers. But no supplier I know that has Toyota as a customer believes it is easy to please. From Toyota's perspective, having high expectations for their suppliers and then treating them fairly and teaching them is the definition of respect. Treating them softly or beating them up without teaching them would be very disrespectful. And simply switching supplier sources because another supplier is a few percentage points cheaper (a common practice in the auto industry) would be unthinkable. As Taiichi Ohno said:

> *Achievement of business performance by the parent company through bullying suppliers is totally alien to the spirit of the Toyota Production System.*

How Ford and Toyota Took Different Approaches to a Logistics Partnership

An excellent example of the contrast in approaches between Toyota and its competitors is in how Toyota approached the logistic challenges in building manufacturing and supply chain capabilities in North America. How can Toyota assembly plants get just-in-time delivery of parts multiple times per day to U.S.-based plants when they are spread across the U.S. and Canada? One part of the solution was to use cross-docking (some call these "break-bulk" facilities). In this case, the cross-dock takes in deliveries of supplier parts a few times a day and reconfigures them into different mixes of products so they are shipped as mixed truckloads of the right number of parts for one to two hours of production. The cross-dock allows for efficient pickup of parts from suppliers and for just-in-time delivery to the assembly plant. Cross-docks are quite common in many industries, for example, in the food industry, and normally cross-docking is subcontracted out as a commodity. What is distinct about Toyota's cross-dock is the care with which Toyota's partner, Transfreight, manages it and the care with which Toyota painstakingly teaches that partner to use TPS. From Toyota's perspective, the cross-dock is an extension of the assembly line—part of the lifeblood of the value stream that gets parts just in time from suppliers onto vehicles and finally to customers. It is all part of the flow.

Ford Motor Company, in the mid-1990s, developed the Ford Production System, which was modeled after the Toyota Production System. Most of the early focus was on implementation inside the four walls of the plant, but later in the 1990s they began to focus on "synchronous material flow" outside the plant—mainly getting parts to the plant just in time in small lots with frequent deliveries. So Ford did what many large U.S. companies do in this situation. In the late 1990s, they hired an outside executive and gave him the task. The executive they hired had worked in logistics for General Motors and had some exposure to NUMMI (though he had not worked there). He fit the Ford model of an aggressive, hard-driving leader who issues orders and expects action or heads to roll. He recognized that he had to change the way the assembly plants were set up to accept just-in-time deliveries and deliver parts in small quantities, so he hired a large group of experts on pull systems in the factory (over 20 of them) to straighten out

Ford's internal logistics. They worked in the assembly plant, pulling inventory off the assembly line and in some cases repacking parts from large 4' x 4' x 4' containers into small containers holding one hour's worth of parts. They then put in pull systems to replenish the assembly line. This still left the assembly plants with large inventories of parts from suppliers in the wrong-sized containers, but that was supposed to be taken care of by a separate external logistics initiative, so they didn't worry about it.

This Ford executive decided to handle the external part of the logistics process by hiring it out to a third-party logistics firm, sort of like Toyota's supplier, Transfreight. He put out a request for bid that had aggressive cost-reduction targets for cutting logistics costs (10% per year) and offered the whole of North America to the company that would meet the target price. Penske Logistics won the bid and set out to get to smaller lot deliveries of parts to the assembly plant. They took on responsibility for getting 167,000 production parts from 900 suppliers to Ford's engine and assembly plants. They designed and managed the entire transportation network, dealt directly with the carriers, handled disciplinary issues, and paid bills.

The Ford executive issued the marching orders: "every part every day." He meant he wanted every part currently delivered weekly or monthly to the assembly plants to be delivered at least once every day. This was a "take no prisoners" order. Ironically, he called the project "Nirvana" and the centerpiece was the deal negotiated with Penske Logistics. Ford stood to save hundreds of millions of dollars in transportation and inventory costs. As a result, the Ford executive was promoted to vice president of Ford's material planning and logistics.

Penske Logistics set up a business unit with its own executive dedicated to the Ford business. Penske did not own many of the assets associated with Ford's business, such as trucks or cross-docks, but instead was acting as a broker, making the appropriate arrangements from Ford's end and the logistics end. Penske had full-time analysts and traffic people who were setting up the appropriate transportation logistics and then managing it on an ongoing basis. This put Penske in an intermediary position in which it needed to both negotiate with Ford assembly plants on things like delivery times and part quantities and negotiate with transportation service providers. In the assembly plants, the plant managers had inventory reduction targets and arranged to set up much smaller, Toyota-style "parts supermarkets" and free up warehouse space for other business.

Overall, the effort seemed to have all the trappings of duplicating Toyota's system ... on the surface. But the results were nothing short of a disaster. In an interview with a Penske manager responsible for design of the transportation network in fall 2002, we learned:

"Every part every day" was great for the plants, because it hollowed out the

buildings and they were making money with that space. But it cost logistics $100 million more per year. After a while, it got so distasteful to Ford that the VP in charge left and we were tasked with going back to the old system of delivering large batches of parts weekly and monthly. We have been working on that for eight months. Ford senior management is baffled at why we cannot do it in eight weeks. But it will take more like one year. The goal is to get back to pre-Nirvana freight costs. By the end of Nirvana, we had the capability of shipping 95% of parts every day. With the new vision, Ford management would like to see it around 60% and currently we have it at around 80%. It was unrealistic to go from non-JIT to JIT and expect cost savings. I do not know where the savings were supposed to come from. We just completed a study of delivery network improvement. We think it will save Ford $8 million per year. But what will it do to the plants? It is going to put in more inventory and they are not happy about that.

There is a lot embedded in this case example that illustrates how Ford, under then CEO Jacques Nasser, had a supplier management approach totally in contrast with that of Toyota. Ford was well-intentioned in trying to learn from TPS in moving to just-in-time in its parts supply network. What did Ford do wrong from the perspective of the Toyota Way?

- Ford tasked an executive hired from the outside to manage a multi-billion-dollar logistics network, and he was able to make major decisions based on his own vision.
- This executive did not understand the "Ford Way" and had only a superficial understanding of how to get to a just-in-time logistics network. For example, Toyota would never try to move "every part every day." That makes sense for some parts but not others.
- He handed off an amazing amount of responsibility to an outside vendor with which Ford did not have a strong partnership—at least not in this area and on a project of this magnitude.
- The outside vendor was purely a logistics management company and in fact did not have any real expertise in the Ford Production System. They knew how to move freight, and that is the only "network" they wanted to optimize—freight costs.
- The outside vendor never understood or believed in the mission of Nirvana and thought Ford was making a mistake that could only lead to higher costs.
- Ford put an outside company between its plants and the logistics network, guaranteeing political battles between different functions that want to sub-optimize for their own benefit.

The last point is an important one. Toyota works hard to break down barriers among functions so everyone is working toward a common goal. By hiring an outside logistics vendor that has the sole objective of reducing cost in the transportation network, Ford was almost guaranteeing conflict and suboptimization. As the Penske manager explained:

> *We (Penske) are playing in the middle between the plants and the parts delivery network. The plants want what is best for them. Optimizing delivery costs may not be the cheapest for a given plant. A plant may want parts from a specific supplier delivered to it five times a week. If I go there once a week with a truckload of volume, I save money for the delivery network but inconvenience that plant. Plants always want JIT delivery. But the delivery network may be going to less frequent, less expensive deliveries. I talk to the plants in numbers and they talk to me in numbers. If my numbers are bigger than theirs. I win and the network wins.*

The results were that Ford never really got to just-in-time and an enormous amount of money was wasted. The logistics network Penske was rebuilding after Nirvana still represented a compromise. For example, when plants emptied out their warehouse space, they put in more production and reduced the amount of space available for holding inventory for less frequent deliveries. As a result, Penske had to rent warehouse space near the plants.

In contrast, Toyota did not simply hand off responsibility to Transfreight for cross-docking, but rather slowly and deliberately built Transfreight into part of the extended enterprise *over a 10-year period*. Transfreight was a joint venture formed in 1987 between TNT Logistics and Mitsui Trading Company—part of the Toyota family of companies in Japan. TNT Logistics had an existing logistics network and Toyota's goal was to keep as much as possible of North American auto supply in North America. Mitsui's role was to be a silent partner but to give Toyota control over the joint venture. (Actually, it was 50-50 ownership.) With intense involvement by TPS experts from Toyota, the first cross-dock was set up. A Toyota advisor from Japan even toured the first cross-dock with the Transfreight plant manager and drew on the floor what the system should look like.

The purpose of the cross-dock is to take in deliveries from distant suppliers a few times a day, temporarily store the pallets of material, and then load trucks for the assembly plant with mixed loads going out about 12 times per day. The assembly plants get frequent JIT deliveries and trucks are full from suppliers to the cross-dock and from the cross-dock to the assembly plant.

The cross-dock is designed using all of the principles of the Toyota Production System (Karlin, 2003).[3] It is a flow-through facility, associates are involved in continuous improvement, visual indicators and mistake-proofing devices are everywhere building in quality and reliability, and truck drivers have clearly defined roles in picking up and delivering within tight time windows, including making quality checks. Nothing is left to chance. The system is set up using many of the principles of the service parts operations distribution system we discussed in Chapter 8 on flow.

Because of the tight coordination among parts suppliers, Transfreight, and the assembly plants, there is a carefully orchestrated flow of parts moving toward the assembly plants and the returnable containers coming back from the assembly plants through the cross-docks. It is basically a one-for-one exchange of full containers for empty returnable containers. Toyota works hard in the assembly plant to level the schedule, which also levels the delivery of parts through the network to the assembly plant. This leads to a very even flow of parts from suppliers through the cross-dock to the assembly plant and creates a balance between parts sent to the assembly plant and the returnable containers sent back to suppliers.

Toyota started small with one cross-dock and one assembly plant and over a decade built up Transfreight so it serves most of their North American cross-docking needs. Transfreight has added additional customers beyond Toyota and is a profitable enterprise. The results:

- Toyota achieved its goal of just-in-time deliveries in North America despite the great distances.
- The costs of transportation went down considerably after the cross-docking system was in place. Before the cross-docking, there were expensive milk runs from supplier to supplier over great distances, with the trucks only partially full. Now trucks are almost always very full in either direction.
- Toyota saves money on returnable containers, using the minimum number because of the balance between parts going to the assembly plant and empty containers returned every day.
- Transfreight is continually improving and reducing costs, like other Toyota operations.

Not only has Transfreight successfully solved Toyota's problem of JIT logistics in North America, but it has become a successful international company and an exemplar of lean logistics. On two occasions, Transfreight has won Toyota's Truckload Carrier of the Year Award. Toyota has continued to give Transfreight additional business as it has expanded globally to plants in West Virginia, Indiana, California, France, the United Kingdom, and Spain.

It is interesting to note that TNT Logistics did not understand the value of Transfreight and was unable to transfer the remarkable lean logistics system to its own operations. Mitsui, on the other hand, saw Transfreight's stellar reputation in the trucking and logistics industry and its profitable growth. TNT and Mitsui discussed their positions and came to a mutually agreeable settlement in which

Mitsui bought out TNT's half of Transfreight. Effective June 27, 2002, Mitsui became the sole shareholder in Transfreight.

Partnering with Suppliers While Maintaining Internal Capability

Toyota is very careful when deciding what to outsource and what to do in house. Like other Japanese automakers, Toyota outsources a lot, about 70% of the components of the vehicle. But it still wants to maintain internal competency even in components it outsources. These days a management buzzword is "core competency." Toyota has a clear image of its core competency, but seems to look at it quite broadly. This goes back to the creation of the company, when Toyota decided to go it alone instead of buying designs and parts of cars from established U.S. and European automakers.

As we discussed in Chapter 2, one of the philosophical roots of Toyota is the concept of self-reliance. It states in the Toyota Way document: "We strive to decide our own fate. We act with self-reliance, trusting in our own abilities." So handing off key capabilities to outside firms would contradict this philosophy. Toyota sells, engineers, and makes transportation vehicles. If Toyota outsourced 70% of the vehicle to suppliers that controlled technology for them and all its competitors, how could Toyota excel or distinguish itself? If a new technology is core to the vehicle, Toyota wants to be an expert and best in the world at mastering it. They want to learn with suppliers, but never transfer all the core knowledge and responsibility in any key area to suppliers.

In Chapter 6 the Prius was discussed. One of the core components of the hybrid engine is the insulated gate bipolar transistor IGBT (a "semiconductor switching device [IGBT] boosts the voltage from the battery and converts the boosted DC power into AC power for driving the motor").

Toyota engineers were not experts at semiconductors, but rather than outsource this critical component, Toyota developed it and built a brand-new plant to make it—all within the tight lead time of the Prius development. Toyota saw hybrid vehicles as the next step into the future. They wanted "self-reliance" in making that step. Once they had that internal expertise, they could selectively outsource. Senior managing directors insisted on making the transistor in-house because they saw it as a core capability for future hybrid vehicle design and manufacture. Toyota wants to know what is inside the "black box." They also did not want to trust other companies to put the effort they knew they could apply into cost reduction.

In Chapter 6 we mentioned how Toyota decided to work with Matsushita to outsource the battery technology, which is at the center of hybrids and future energy-efficient vehicles. Toyota sorely wanted to develop this capability in-house, but finally did not have the time. Rather than simply handing off responsibility to Matsushita, Toyota established a joint venture company—Panasonic EV Energy. This was not their first experience working with Matsushita. The Electric Vehicle Division of Toyota had already co-developed with Matsushita a nickel-metal hydride battery for an electrical version of the RAV4 sport utility vehicle, so they had a prior relationship and a track record of successfully working together.

Even with this past history of working together, the joint venture tested the company's differing cultures. Yuichi Fujii, then General Manager of Toyota's Electric Vehicle Division and Prius Battery Supervisor, at a point of frustration, said (as quoted in Itazaki, 1999):

I have a feeling that there is a difference between an auto maker and an elec-tric appliance maker in the way they feel the sense of crisis about lead time. A Toyota engineer has it in his bones to be fully aware that preparing for pro-duction development should occur at a particular point in time. On the other hand, I feel that the Matsushita engineers are a little too relaxed.

There were also some concerns about Matsushita's quality control discipline and if the level of quality required for this new, complex battery was too high for what Matsushita was used to. Fujii was reassured when he found a young Matsushita engineer one day looking pale. He learned he had been working until four in the morning to finish some battery tests. Yet he had come back in the next day to "make sure of just one thing" (Itazaki, 1999, p. 282). At that point Fujii realized that there was a "Matsushita style" that could work together with Toyota's style. Ultimately, the two corporate cultures did complement each other and pro-duced a world-class hybrid vehicle battery.

Even when Toyota chooses to outsource a key component, the company does not want to lose internal capability. Witness Toyota's relationship with Denso. Formerly, Nippon Denso (Japan Electronics) was a division of Toyota. It spun off as a separate company in 1949 and grew into one of the largest global parts sup-pliers in the world. Denso essentially grew up with Toyota as a partner and is still partly owned by Toyota in the Japanese *keiretsu* (set of interlocking corporations). Denso was the electrical and electronic parts supplier of choice for Toyota and acted like it was still a division of Toyota. As a general rule, Toyota wants to have at least two suppliers for every component, but it broke this rule often in its rela-tionship with Denso, making Denso its sole supplier. So in 1988, when Toyota opened an electronics plant in Hirose and made a major effort to recruit electrical engineers, it was a shock to the industry. Why this seeming reversal of policy?

First of all, Denso had become so big and powerful that there were some well-known strains in the relationship with Toyota, such as Denso getting a bit too cozy with Toyota's competition, including Toyota's archrival, Nissan. Second, and more importantly, Toyota recognized that electronics was becoming an ever-increasing part of a vehicle—including computerization and the trend toward electrical vehicles. About 30% of total vehicle content these days is electronics-related and electronics technologies change at a much faster rate than traditional automotive technologies. Toyota believed that it needed to truly master any core technology internally in order to manage its suppliers effectively (e.g., understand true costs) and to continue to learn as an organization to stay at the forefront of the technology. Toyota determined that electronics had become so central to the automotive business that only an intensive program of "learning by doing could infuse its entire organization with the skills and values essential to making electronics a genuine core competence." Now it is estimated that about 30% of Toyota recruits are electrical engineers (Ahmadjian and Lincoln, 2001).

Working with Suppliers for Mutual Learning of TPS

One way that Toyota has honed its skills in applying TPS is by working on projects with suppliers. Toyota needs its suppliers to be as capable as its own plants at building and delivering high-quality components just in time. Moreover, Toyota cannot cut costs unless suppliers cut costs, lest Toyota simply push cost reductions onto suppliers, which is not the Toyota Way. Since Toyota does not view parts as commodities to be sourced on the market through open bidding, it is critical that it works with highly capable suppliers that are following TPS or an equivalent system. There are many methods Toyota uses to learn with its suppliers and, in the Toyota Way style, these are all "learning by doing" processes, keeping classroom training to a minimum. The important learning happens through real projects on the shop floor.

All key suppliers are part of Toyota's supplier association. These are core Toyota suppliers that meet throughout the year sharing practices, information, and concerns. There are committees that work on specific things, including joint projects. In the U.S., BAMA (Bluegrass Automotive Manufacturers Association) was created in the Kentucky area, since Toyota suppliers started there. This has now expanded to a national association. Members of BAMA can participate in many activities, including study groups that meet to develop greater skills in TPS. These are called *jishuken* or voluntary study groups.

The *jishuken* was started in 1977 in Japan by the Operations Management Consulting Division (OMCD). OMCD is the elite corps of TPS experts started by Ohno in 1968 to improve operations in Toyota and its suppliers. This now includes about six senior TPS gurus and about 50 consultants—some of these are fast-track, young production engineers on a three-year rotation who are being groomed to be manufacturing leaders. Only the best TPS experts have directed OMCD. About 55-60 of Toyota's key suppliers (representing 80% of parts in value) were organized into groups of four to seven suppliers by geography and type of part. They rotate across companies, working on three- to four-month projects in each company one by one. They choose a theme and go to work. Representatives of the other suppliers visit regularly and make recommendations. The OMCD TPS expert visits the plant every week or so to give advice. OMCD uses an annual conference to share learnings. The projects involve radical transformation, not incremental improvement, often tearing up the floor and creating once-piece flow, leveling the schedule, and the like, to create huge improvements in cost, quality, and delivery. Strict targets are set and achieved.

Kiyoshi Imaizumi, an executive with Araco Corporation, which is one of Toyota's most sophisticated suppliers in Japan, was assigned to the U.S. to lead Trim Masters, Inc., a Toyota/Araco/Johnson Controls joint venture. Imaizumi explained that *jishuken* in Japan can be very "severe." It is teaching TPS in the spirit of the harsh approaches originally used by Taiichi Ohno.

> *Toyota's suppliers'* Jishuken *in Japan is completely different from that in the U.S. It is compulsory. You cannot say no. Toyota picks suppliers to participate. From each supplier they pick three to five members. Toyota sends their own TPS expert to the target plant and they review this plant's activity and give a theme, e.g., this line must reduce 10 people from the plant. The supplier's member has one month to come up with a solution. The TPS expert comes back to check to see if the supplier has met the target. Then the Toyota TPS expert verbally abuses the supplier participants. In the past some of the participants had a nervous breakdown and quit work. Toyota has a gentler version of TPS in the U.S. Once you clear Toyota's jishuken in Japan, you can feel so much more confidence in yourself. One of the former Trim Masters presidents went through this and became so confident he never compromised anything with anybody.*

Toyota has gradually changed its style to one that is more supportive and less punitive, particularly in the U.S., when they learned from experience that the punitive approach does not work. They have set up similar *jishuken* activities with American suppliers (called "plant development activities"), trying various configurations. They found they had to group suppliers by skill level with TPS, since there was such a wide range.

The closest thing in America to OMCD is what occurs at the Toyota Supplier Support Center (TSSC) run by Hajime Ohba, a former member of OMCD. A variation on the theme of OMCD was created to fit the American culture, with the focus still on projects. Suppliers, and even companies outside of the auto industry, like Viking Range and Herman Miller, had to petition to be accepted as clients. The service was originally free, but then became a pay-for-service consulting firm. The TSSC identifies a business need and then picks a product line to do a project. The project consists of developing a "model line." A typical model line includes component assembly and a manufacturing process that makes parts that go to the assembly line. A full TPS implementation is done with all the elements of JIT, *jidoka*, standardized work, Total Productive Maintenance, etc.

The TSSC results have been spectacular. As of 1997 the TSSC had completed 31 projects, getting impressive results in every single case. They had reduced inventory an average of 75% and improved productivity an average of 124%. Space was reduced, quality improved, and emergency freight shipments eliminated (Dyer, 2000). But there were compromises along the way.

As he did in Japan, Ohba tried the OMCD approach of giving vague instructions and then expecting the plants to leap into action. Only after this would he provide guidance with pointed questions and challenges. What he discovered with U.S. companies is that they wanted more guidance and needed more visits to keep the projects going. Projects that might take two to three months in Japan were dragging on for four or six months and complete implementation could take nine months or more. Some of the companies did a good job of propagating TPS to other parts of the plant, but most did not. And few companies spread TPS across plants. Even the "star" suppliers that the TSSC worked with closely fell back to a lower level of TPS unless Ohba's group made continued visits, pumping them up and doing more projects. Unfortunately, while TPS experts could force installation of TPS principles with extraordinary results on selected lines, they could not inoculate the suppliers with Toyota Way genes. The explanation by Ohba was quite simple. Companies that failed to continue implementing TPS after seeing dramatic improvements were led by executives who were not serious and committed. It was not shop-floor resistance but top management that was responsible.

Saving "Sick" Suppliers Through TPS

The TSSC by design is not part of the business relationship with suppliers. It is there to educate through projects. Toyota purchasing has its own quality and TPS experts to work with suppliers when there are problems, the most severe of which is when a supplier shuts down the Toyota assembly plant because of a quality or production problem. Don Jackson, who later became vice president of manufacturing in Georgetown, Kentucky, was a quality manager in purchasing and created a system of evaluating and classifying suppliers.

Before joining Toyota, when Jackson worked for a supplier to the Big Three American automakers, he was shocked at how little hands-on assistance or monitoring was provided. He recalls, "I was successful in shutting down Ford for a day. No one ever visited my plant—even though I shut down the plant for a day." He was determined that would not happen at Toyota. Suppliers are rated from one (like when a plant burns down) to five (exemplary TPS supplier). If a supplier puts a Toyota assembly plant in danger of shutting down, it will be a two. Toyota will then send a team of people swarming through the supplier's plant and the supplier must develop an action plan to address all of their concerns. A level two typically means severe probation for a year.

Jackson came up with a "supplier improvement committee" in 1998 to work on problem suppliers. He explained:

> *I didn't realize it stood for SIC. The Japanese called it the "sick supplier club." It was funny, but it was sort of true! We had some real successes and one of the suppliers is going to get the outstanding quality award from the NUMMI plant this year. I am especially proud of that.*

It is interesting how the "help" Toyota provided spread beyond technical issues to a human resource audit. As Jackson explained:

> *My Human Resources department approached me and said, "We'd like to support you in the supplier improvement committee." At first I rejected the offer. I said a quality audit is all we need. But after I went on several visits to local suppliers I realized the issues were much deeper than quality of the process or the tooling of the process. It was a lot of the human side. You know, salary was too low or overtime was too high, working conditions were poor, there was no training or development plan. There was not good management. So I went ahead and had HR join me on audits of a couple of these critical suppliers. We did a very deep analysis of their organization. We looked at the turnover ratio, what they paid people, how they decide what the pay scale should be in the area. The HR team would investigate training, development, did they have an opinion survey? Etc. So for "SIC" suppliers, HR would do the HR investigation, quality would do a quality audit, production engineering would examine the manufacturing side.*

Another example of Toyota's approach to "SIC" suppliers is the case of Trim Masters (TMI) and its just-in-time Nicholasville, Kentucky, seat plant, which makes about 250,000 seat sets a year for Avalon and Camry. (See the case study at the end of the chapter.)

In 1995, one year after the Nicholasville plant was brought on line, Steve Hesselbrock took over as Director of Operations for all TMI plants. His first year was anything but a honeymoon. Nicholasville was completely dependent on its computer technology to get the vehicle sequence from Toyota and convert it into a sequence for the plant's seat assembly line. They had a manual backup system, but it never worked. The computer system went down one day for only three hours, but with TMI's very lean system it was enough to shut Toyota's assembly line down. Immediately a crew of supplier quality experts from Toyota descended on the TMI plant and swarmed through it daily for two weeks. TMI was given a level-two designation in Toyota's purchasing supplier rating, which meant they were put on watch and had to report monthly on improvements based on a true root cause analysis and clearly defined countermeasures. The Toyota experts ended up visiting the plant a few times a week for six months, then monthly.

A typical response to this problem might be "The computer went down, for heaven's sake—fix it and implement a true manual backup system and be done with it." In fact, TMI had delivery problems in the past and Toyota considered this to be yet one more symptom of a deeper problem. Toyota's solution: analyze every aspect of the business, including quality planning, employee selection and training, team structure, problem-solving processes, pull systems, standardized work, supplier management—basically recreate the business.

TMI did just that and now J.D. Power routinely rates it as the top automotive seat supplier in the country on quality, a model TPS supplier exceeded only by its parent company in Japan. TMI also runs a manual system every month to be ready for any computer malfunctions. In a very big way, TMI's crisis and level two rating was the best thing that every happened to it. Whereas other companies would threaten problem suppliers—"Fix the problems or we will drop you"—Toyota nurses them out of their "sickness" in a very holistic way.

Developing an Extended Learning Enterprise Means Enabling Others

While musing over American Auto's debacle with suppliers and wondering why it wanted to take an elevator to the top without stopping at any of the floors in between, I began to conceptualize the problem as a pyramid or hierarchy. Thinking back to college social psychology, I thought of Maslow's needs hierarchy, discussed briefly in the last chapter, which assumes humans can work on higher-level needs like self-actualization (developing themselves) only if lower-level needs are satisfied. So I developed a supplier version of the need hierarchy (see Figure 17-1).

The message from suppliers was that they were not interested in supplier development help from American Auto until some more fundamental issues were fixed. As a starting point, they wanted fair and equitable commercial relations. A lot of American Auto's practices were simply unfair. For example, American Auto had adopted the Toyota practice of target pricing, setting targets for suppliers instead of relying on competitive bidding, but they had not executed it effectively. One supplier explained:

> We have gone through a different target cost process for every group we deal with (in American Auto). If you are above target, they cannot issue a purchase order. We have gone around and around and reached launch without a purchase order.

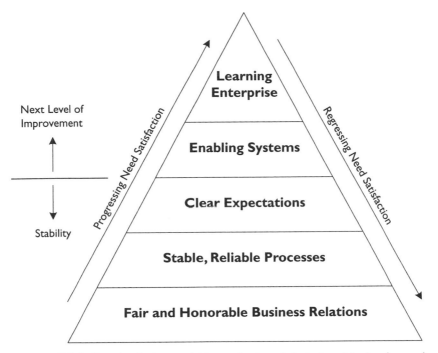

Figure 17-1. Supply chain need hierarchy (modeled after Maslow's need hierarchy)

Another supplier complained how inconsistent American Auto is in the target setting process:

> If we meet the target too early in the design process, they will change the target. So there is absolutely no incentive to make the target early. There is no target-setting process. It is done differently every time. It even is different across programs within the same platform. It depends on who is in the room.

American Auto also has developed a long and complex process of certifying that a supplier's process is capable from a quality perspective. Although it was burdensome, suppliers accepted it—but American Auto kept changing it. In fact, it would change multiple times during a new vehicle program and each time the supplier certification process would extend out. Until they were certified, suppliers did not get paid for tooling. Typical of most manufacturing businesses, American Auto is responsible for paying for the costs of tooling, dies, and special equipment used to make the parts. This can run into millions of dollars. In some cases, suppliers got all the way to the production phase and were producing new parts for months that were passing all the quality tests, but since they were not quality certified, they were not paid for the tooling.

This comes back to the concept of "coercive" versus "enabling" bureaucracy discussed in Chapter 12. Both American Auto and Toyota are very bureaucratic in their dealings with suppliers. By this, I mean there are extensive standards, auditing procedures, rules, and the like. While suppliers view American Auto as highly coercive, Toyota, which uses similar quality methods and procedures, is viewed as enabling. For example, an American automotive interior supplier described working with Toyota in this way:

> *When it comes to fixing problems, Toyota does not come in and run detailed process capability studies 15 times like American Auto. They just say, "Take a bit of material off here and there and that will be OK—let's go." In 11 years I have never built a prototype tool for Toyota. Knee bolsters, floor panels, instrument panels, etc. are so similar to the last one it is not necessary to build a prototype. When there is a problem, they look at the problem and come up with a solution—focus on making it better, not placing blame.*

By contrast, a supplier gave the following highly emotional description of American Auto:

> *In the climate we have today versus days past, we are successful if we do not get the crap beat out of us. We may execute on a program or a change and may be performing under the most demanding circumstances (e.g., attempting something we had said could not be done) and we execute 99.9% flawless. But if it is not 100% you get killed. We used to get appreciation for busting our butt for making the last-minute change. Now we are happy if we do not get any licks during the course of the week. It used to be a reward system and now it is purely a punitive system.*

The supply chain need hierarchy in Figure 17-1 suggests that, until the relationship has stabilized to the point where the business relationship is fair, processes are stable, and expectations are clear, it is impossible to get to the higher levels of enabling systems and truly learning together as an enterprise. And you can come down the hierarchy as fast as you can go up. American Auto was making progress up the hierarchy in the early to mid-1990s and then went sharply down in the late 1990s and into the 21st century. Toyota in the meantime has been moving steadily up. For American Auto to become a benchmark for supplier relations, they will need to do much more than build a supplier development center. To begin to approach Toyota, they will need to remake their internal culture, become a learning organization, and break down the chimneys that provide contradictory policies to suppliers.

Toyota Way Principle 11 is *Respect your extended network of partners and suppliers by challenging them and helping them improve.* What really cements Toyota as the model for supplier relations is its approach to learning and growing together with its suppliers. It has achieved, in my view, something unique: an extended learning enterprise. This is, to me, the highest form of the lean enterprise.

Case Example: Trim Masters, Inc.—JIT Auto Seats Like the Toyota Textbook Says

In 1994 Trim Masters, Inc. (TMI) was established as a joint venture operation to supply Toyota's Georgetown plant. It was part of Toyota's effort to purchase parts in the U.S. and to get JIT delivery to Toyota assembly plants in North America. The Toyota Way does not allow Toyota to buy parts from just anybody. Toyota views the suppliers as long-term partners and they must meet Toyota's exacting standards for quality, cost, and delivery. So, to get the localization and the expertise they demanded, Toyota arranged for a joint venture to be created with ownership by Toyota Tsusho, Araco, their long-term interior parts supplier in Japan, and Johnson Controls. Johnson Controls (JCI) is the single largest shareholder, with 40%, but Toyota and Araco (of which Toyota owns 75%) together have controlling interest. Toyota had earlier contracted with Johnson Controls to supply seats for its vehicles and worked closely to teach TPS to Johnson Controls. That plant still makes a large percentage of Toyota's seats, but Toyota likes to have at least two suppliers in competition, to keep them motivated to improve *and reduce cost.*

So Toyota set up TMI as a joint venture to supply seats for the opening of its new plant in Georgetown, Kentucky. TMI's seat plant is in Nicholasville, Kentucky. Araco runs the show on getting TMI's operation together, while JCI is more or less a silent partner. Toyota encourages TMI to follow TPS—building only the seats needed on the assembly line, in the exact order in which they are needed. Even Araco, one of Toyota's premier seat suppliers and veteran TPS practitioner, sometimes keeps finished goods inventory in Japan, but Toyota wants TMI to do better than that. From the time the auto body comes out of Toyota's paint shop and starts down the assembly line, TMI has about four hours to receive Toyota's order for the sequence of seats it needs, build the seats, and ship them to Toyota. Then the seats travel down a spur to the main assembly line just in time to mate up with the exact car they were built for. This is a very challenging system and not for the weak of heart! Any slight hiccup risks shutting the Toyota plant down, at a cost of tens of thousands of dollars a minute. For one thing, most of TMI's parts come from suppliers that are delivering to TMI throughout the day. A problem from one of them can shut TMI down in a couple of hours. Also, seats are complex assemblies and appearance counts. A bad batch of leather, a tiny scratch on any one of dozens of pieces of plastic, a spring mechanism that is not precise, etc., and Toyota will reject the seat.

But the Toyota Way is to patiently teach TPS to its suppliers to meet its exacting standards. And though TMI has had its share of struggles, the results have been outstanding. Lean expert Jim Womack likes to say that the amount of regular inventory turnover is the acid test of true leanness—the more, the better. Ask Hesselbrock, Director of Operations for all TMI plants, what the Nicholasville inventory turns are and you will think he is making it up: 135 turns per month! When I saw this on an overhead slide, I thought I was very clever in spotting the error. This should be per year, right? No, it is per month. The plant brings in over 750 part numbers of raw materials. Some come from Japan, some from Mexico, and most from the U.S. and Canada. If delivery of raw materials stopped at any point in time, the plant would have to stop making seats in one and a half hours.

For example, every seat needs foam, which comes in large containers from a sister company, Foamex. There are 75 varieties of foam, so too much inventory would take up a small warehouse. So there is typically only one and a half hours of foam on the floor and 45 minutes of safety stock. TMI receives 12 truckloads of foam every day coming in every one and a half hours. When I visited the seat plant in 2000, they were averaging just under 40 parts per million defects to Toyota. Toyota expects a maximum of 50 defective seats per million. There are 100 parts on every seat and about 1000 seats per day. Any part could be defective; if so, the whole seat is considered a defect. When I was last there in the summer of 2002, they were down in the range of 20-30 parts per million defects. TMI has since launched a new seat plant to provide seats for the Lexus RX330 in Cambridge, Ontario, which has a requirement of single-digit parts per million defects maximum—true Six Sigma quality.

The seat plant in Nicholasville looks much like a Toyota supplier's plant in Japan. Final seat assembly is done on a one-piece-flow moving assembly line. There are about one to two hours of parts along the line, neatly arranged in small bins on flow racks. The only schedule for the plant is the broadcast order Toyota sends out after the car body has been painted, stating the exact sequence of seats required to mate up with the cars. Every 55 seconds (the takt time of the Toyota plant) an order comes in. So TMI knows only 55 seconds in advance what to work on next. They queue up 10 broadcast orders for seat sets, they reverse the sequence that Toyota has requested (to adjust for the fact that they load finished seats on the truck in reverse sequence), and then send the orders out to the assembly line and to other sequencing processes in the TMI plant. Some large components—such as seat frames, seat covers, and foam—are sequenced to the seat assembly line and smaller components—like nuts and bolts—are stored in a parts supermarket and brought to the line based on a kanban system. TMI also uses a pull replenishment system with its own suppliers.

They have almost 800 different parts coming into the plant, some from Mexico and Japan. Obviously, for the distant plants more inventory is held and TMI uses a schedule to bring in these parts. For example, they keep 40 hours of Mexico parts in safety stock and hate every hour of it.

But TMI's work is never done. Toyota in 2001 challenged its suppliers to reduce the price of components by 30% for the next new major model introduction in 2004—about 10% price reduction per year. One of the rumors is that Toyota, through its joint venture with Peugeot, got insight into what other automakers pay for parts. While other companies might have gone shopping around to other companies for lower prices, in the true Toyota Way fashion of using operational excellence as a strategic weapon, Toyota saw no reason why its current suppliers with the TPS couldn't match or beat world-class costs.

Though TMI is already quite lean in labor costs, its reaction has been quite positive and productive. They launched a major *hoshin kanri* initiative to achieve the target. *Hoshin kanri* means "policy deployment." It starts with high-level objectives and then cascades these objectives down to every function in the organization. It is part of the Toyota Way approach to management, a give-and-take process of communicating between top to middle management and sometimes supervisors and team leaders. One of *hoshin kanri*'s greatest strengths is its ability to translate high-level, executive-level goals into quantitative, achievable actions. Simply put, policy deployment is a system that encourages employees to analyze situations, create plans for improvement, conduct performance checks, and take appropriate action. For this purpose, Trim Masters has a war room with objectives for every function in the organization to reduce costs, as well as cross-functional projects. Every policy deployment chart ends with measurable objectives, measures, and a point person responsible for achieving the results. TMI holds weekly meetings to discuss progress in each area.

One reason TMI never panics about the high demands placed on it is because it is always working closely with Toyota. Toyota realizes that TMI has limited control over costs, and some of the biggest cost savings can be achieved jointly in the product design stage through value engineering. Value engineering is a systematic, cross-functional team approach to examine the design factors that affect the cost of new products and then redesign the product to achieve the required standard of quality at the *target cost* set by Toyota. TMI and Toyota working together can greatly reduce cost by changing the engineering of the seat prior to production. In addition, Toyota purchasing representatives come to the plant regularly to review their process and progress and, to date, have been very pleased with the effort. TMI realizes that, with a sincere effort and good results, it will be treated fairly and well.

TMI is a U.S. success story in implementing TPS under rather severe circumstances—just-in-time building and delivery with no inventory in sequence to the assembly plant. But ask the senior managers if they are a model lean facility and they will just laugh. They know how far they have to go to get to the level of sophistication they see in their parent company in Japan.

Notes

1. Source: Robert Sherefkin and Julie Cantwell Armstrong, "Suppliers Prefer Japanese," *Automotive News*, May 12, 2003, pp. 1 and 50.
2. Nishiguchi, T. and A. Beaudet, 1998, "The Toyota Group and the Aisin Fire," *Sloan Management Review*, Fall, pp. 49-59.
3. Jennifer Karlin, *Defining the Lean Logistics Learning Enterprise: Examples from Toyota's North American Supply Chain*, unpublished doctoral dissertation, University of Michigan, Ann Arbor, September 2003.

Section IV

Continuously Solving Root Problems Drives Organizational Learning

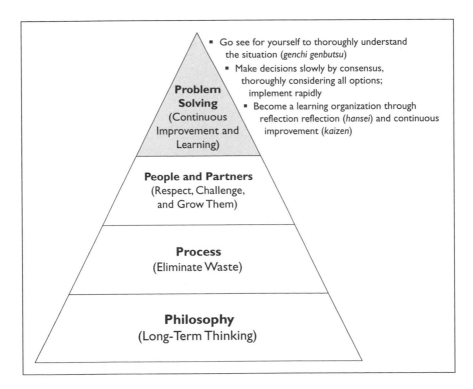

- Go see for yourself to thoroughly understand the situation (*genchi genbutsu*)
- Make decisions slowly by consensus, thoroughly considering all options; implement rapidly
- Become a learning organization through reflection reflection (*hansei*) and continuous improvement (*kaizen*)

Problem Solving (Continuous Improvement and Learning)

People and Partners (Respect, Challenge, and Grow Them)

Process (Eliminate Waste)

Philosophy (Long-Term Thinking)

Chapter 18

Principle 12:
Go and See for Yourself to Thoroughly Understand the Situation (*Genchi Genbutsu*)

Observe the production floor without preconceptions and with a blank mind. Repeat "why" five times to every matter.
—Taiichi Ohno (as quoted in The Toyota Way document)

In my Toyota interviews, when I asked what distinguishes the Toyota Way from other management approaches, the most common first response was *genchi genbutsu*—whether I was in manufacturing, product development, sales, distribution, or public affairs. You cannot be sure you really understand any part of any business problem unless you go and see for yourself firsthand. It is unacceptable to take anything for granted or to rely on the reports of others.

I have often heard the following story, or a variant, from managers of Toyota's Georgetown, Kentucky, plant. Reflecting back on the early days when Fujio Cho was the first president of the Georgetown plant, the stories begin with the managers' visits to the factory floor in the morning. On the way in, they notice Cho standing and watching an operation. They pass nearby him, expecting Cho to notice and greet them, but he doesn't respond. He just stands and stares, as if off into space. They walk even closer. He continues to stare. They go about their business, then happen by 15 minutes later. Cho is standing and staring. They wonder if he is ill or frozen to the ground at that point. Finally, Cho relaxes, as if coming out of a trance, notices he is not alone, and says, "Good morning" with a smile. Later there are some orders from the president's office to tighten up some part of the Toyota Production System in the plant.

So what was Cho doing? The only way he could truly understand the state of

TPS in the plant was to go and see for himself. "Are they following the standard work procedures?" "Is it a level flow and just-in-time?" "Are parts being delivered before they are needed?" He must personally observe the flow of material to the line to answer these questions. He must look to see if workers on the line are using the *andon* to call for help and stop the line if necessary. "And how are the team leaders and group leaders responding?" Applying decades of skill, he can see all of this … for himself. He is a black belt of seeing and understanding TPS. He knows that what he sees firsthand would not show up in written reports and tables of numbers, though he wants to see those also. Tables and numbers may measure results, but they do not reveal the details of the actual process being followed every day.

The Principle: Deeply Understanding and Reporting What You See

Literally translated, *Genchi* means the actual location and *genbutsu* means the actual materials or products. But *genchi genbutsu* is interpreted within Toyota to mean *going to the place to see the actual situation for understanding*. *Gemba* is a term that has become more popular. It refers to "the actual place" and means about the same thing as *genchi genbutsu*. The first step of any problem-solving process, development of a new product, or evaluation of an associate's performance is grasping the actual situation, which requires "going to *gemba*." Toyota promotes and expects creative thinking, and innovation is a must, but it should be grounded in thoroughly understanding all aspects of the actual situation. This is one of the behaviors that really distinguishes someone trained in the Toyota Way—they take nothing for granted and know what they are talking about, because it comes from firsthand knowledge.

It would be relatively easy for management attempting to learn from the Toyota Way to mandate that from this day forward all engineers and managers will spend a half hour observing the floor to understand the situation. But this would accomplish very little unless they had the skill to analyze and understand the current situation. There is a surface version of *genchi genbutsu* and a much deeper version, which takes many years for employees to master. What the Toyota Way requires is that employees and managers must "deeply" understand the processes of flow, standardized work, etc., as well as have the ability to critically evaluate and analyze what is going on. (This may include some analysis of data.) In addition, they must know how to get to the root cause of any problems they observe and communicate it effectively to others. As Tadashi ("George") Yamashina, president of the Toyota Technical Center, explained:

> It is more than going and seeing. "What happened? What did you see? What are the issues? What are the problems?" Within the Toyota organization in North America, we are still just going and seeing. "OK, I went and saw it

and now I have a feeling." But have you really analyzed it? Do you really understand what the issues are? At the root of all of that, we try to make decisions based on factual information, not based on theory. Statistics and numbers contribute to the facts, but it is more than that. Sometimes we get accused of spending too much time doing all the analysis of that. Some will say, "Common sense will tell you. I know what the problem is." But collecting data and analysis will tell you if your common sense is right.

When Yamashina joined the Toyota Technical Center as president, he laid out his 10 management principles (see Figure 18-1), which include principles three and four that relate to *genchi genbutsu*:

3. Think and speak based on verified, proven information and data:
    - Go and confirm the facts for yourself.
    - You are responsible for the information you are reporting to others.
4. Take full advantage of the wisdom and experience of others to send, gather or discuss information.

Always keep the final target in mind
- Carefully plan for your final target
- Have a clear purpose for meetings

Clearly assign tasks to yourself and to others

Think and speak based on verified, proven information and data
- Go and confirm the facts for yourself (*genchi genbutsu*)
- You are responsible for the information you are reporting to others

Take full advantage of the wisdom and experiences of others to send, gather or discuss information (form of *genchi genbutsu*)

Share your information with others in a timely manner
- Always consider who will benefit from receiving the information

Always report, inform and consult (Hou/Reng/Sou) in a timely manner

Analyze and understand shortcomings in your capabilities in a measureable way
- Clarify the skills and knowledge that you need to further develop yourself

Relentlessly strive to conduct kaizen activities

Think "outside the box," or beyond common sense and standard rules

Always be mindful of protecting your safety and health

Figure 18-1. President's management philosophies—Mr. Yamashina, Toyota Technical Center

Ohno Circle—Watch and Think for Yourself

There are many stories about the famous Ohno circle. I was fortunate to speak in person with Teruyuki Minoura, who at the time was president of Toyota Motor Manufacturing, North America. He had learned TPS directly from the master and part of his early education at Toyota was standing in a circle:

Minoura: Mr. Ohno wanted us to draw a circle on the floor of a plant and then we were told, 'Stand in that and watch the process and think for yourself,' and then he didn't even give you any hint of what to watch for. This is the real essence of TPS.

Liker: How long did you stay in the circle?

Minoura: Eight hours!

Liker: Eight hours?!

Minoura: In the morning Mr. Ohno came to request that I stay in the circle until supper and after that Mr. Ohno came to check and ask me what I was seeing. And of course, I answered, (reflecting) I answered, "There were so many problems with the process...." But Mr. Ohno didn't hear. He was just looking.

Liker: And what happened at the end of the day?

Minoura: It was near dinner time. He came to see me. He didn't take any time to give any feedback. He just said gently, "Go home."

Of course, it is difficult to imagine this training happening in a U.S. factory. Most young engineers would be irate if you told them to draw a circle and stand for 30 minutes, let alone all day. But Minoura understood this was an important lesson as well as an honor to be taught in this way by the master of TPS. What exactly was Ohno teaching? The power of deep observation. He was teaching Minoura to think for himself about what he was seeing, that is, to question, analyze, and evaluate.

These days we often depend upon computers to analyze and evaluate data. For example, in a Six Sigma quality improvement initiative, we collect data and run it through our statistical package—correlations, regression, analysis of variance. Some of the results we get are statistically significant. But do we truly understand the context of what is going on or the nature of the problem?

Data is of course important in manufacturing, but I place the greatest emphasis on facts.

—Taiichi Ohno

To Ohno the big difference was that data was one step removed from the process, merely "indicators" of what was going on. What you want to do is verify the on-the-scene facts of the situation. Ohno's approach was very much like that of a forensic scientist investigating a crime scene.

Think and Speak Based on Personally Verified Data

David Baxter is a vice president at the Toyota Technical Center. At one point he was responsible for evaluating supplier parts. When Toyota launched a version of the Camry in 1997, they had a wire harness problem. Yazaki Corporation, a parts supplier to Toyota in Japan, supplied the problem wire harness. What happened next is not typical of most companies. Yes, a quality engineer from Yazaki called Toyota to explain what corrective action they were taking. Yes, Yazaki sent an engineer to the Camry plant. But then the president of Yazaki actually went out to the Camry plant in Georgetown personally, to watch how workers assembled the wire harness onto the vehicle.

What would a U.S. executive of a parts supplier do in this circumstance? Well, one data point is a story told by Jim Griffith, also a vice president of the Toyota Technical Center, who took over the parts evaluation function from Baxter. A problem similar to the wire harness problem occurred with a U.S. parts supplier. In this case, the vice president of the business unit that serves Toyota came out to the Toyota Technical Center to discuss what he was doing to solve the problem. He was very reassuring, explaining, "I am deeply sorry about this. Do not worry. This will get my personal attention. We are going to solve this problem. There are no excuses." When Griffith asked him what the problem was and what his plans were, he responded, "Oh, I do not know yet and I do not get into that kind of detail. But do not worry. We are going to get to the bottom of this and solve the problem. I promise." Griffith looked exacerbated as he told the story:

> And I was supposed to feel better about that? It would be unacceptable in Toyota to come to a meeting like that so poorly prepared. How could he give us his assurance if he did not even go and see for himself what the problem was? ... So we asked him to please go back and do this and then return when he truly understood the problem and countermeasure.

Another Baxter story reveals the benefits of taking time and effort to see for yourself. It is about an early assignment to evaluate the capabilities of an outside test lab, let's call it Detroit Labs, which was highly reputable and had been in business since the early 1900s. Toyota brought in some previously tested struts from Japan and wanted Detroit Labs to test them, using the same test standards used in Japan. As Baxter explained:

> I went on visits with my Japanese mentor, who was an exceptional test engineer. We took the struts to Detroit Labs and compared their test results with the known data in Japan. For us the issue was not whether their results came out exactly the same or different, but we wanted to see if they had a good procedure and a good way to do the test. Even when we went to the test company

to do this, we were not satisfied looking at pictures and failed parts. We wanted to see the parts under failed tests and to see how the data was being compiled. My mentor would ask most of the technical questions to understand in detail how they had done the testing. What we concluded was they had a very good process and procedure for implementing the tests, but their technical capability did not meet our expectations. They did not use engineering analysis techniques that met Toyota standards. For example, they did a fatigue test and reported the number of cycles and load, but in addition, we were interested in how the load was oriented and we thought they should be controlling the frequency in applying the load (during the durability test) and they did not do that. So we were not pleased with their approach to testing and analysis.

Of course, the Toyota team had further discussion with them and gave them feedback, which is part of *genchi genbutsu*. Detroit Labs responded by saying Toyota did not tell them to do the test in this way. Part of the Toyota Way evaluation was to determine whether Detroit Labs would take the initiative to test the struts thoroughly on their own, which they hadn't. Not only that, they had a negative attitude about it. Baxter concluded:

Had we not gone to see the testing ourselves, we would not have been able to confirm that lack of understanding on their part. We would have only seen it in the results and it would have been vague. We were not interested in pass-fail but the process to control the test. The data itself turned out OK—their test of how the part failed confirmed our tests from Japan. Previous tests indicated it would fail. They found out and confirmed what we knew, so got the right answer. At GM (former employer), I would have said, "They got the same answer, so let's use them." But they were doing a test to a prescribed procedure rather than doing actual engineering the way Toyota expects. They were doing a task and not thinking deeply. From this experience, I started to understand what a learning company is all about.

See America, Then Design for America

The 2004 Sienna is what Toyota considers a major redesign—a new and improved version of its highly ranked minivan. Toyota engineered it to be bigger, faster, smoother, quieter, and about $1,000 cheaper. Toyota also designed in many small but important enhancements that make life easier for the North American driver. Many of these enhancements were the result of *genchi genbutsu*.

The chief engineer job of developing this Sienna was assigned to Yuji Yokoya. The primary markets are the U.S. and Canada with some sales in Mexico. Yokoya had worked on Japanese and European projects, but never a North American vehicle. He had seen various parts of North America, but not specifically with the eyes of a chief engineer developing a vehicle for North America. So he felt that he did not really understand the North American market. Other managers may have hit the books on marketing data, but that is only one thing you do at Toyota. Yokoya went to his director and requested he be permitted to make a trip. He said, "I want to drive all 50 states and all 13 provinces and territories in Canada and all parts of Mexico."

Andy Lund was an American program manager at the Toyota Technical Center assigned to assist Yokoya. He had an opportunity to take part of the trip through Canada with him. He related the following example of Yokoya's determination to go and see a small town in Canada called Rankin Inlet in Nunavut:

> *He arrived at a very small airport and tried to reserve a car, but there were no rental car companies there or in the whole town. So Yokoya-san called a taxi and a minivan-type taxi picked him up. He tried to speak to the taxi driver to make a request, but the driver did not speak English well enough for Yokoya-san to understand. Eventually the taxi driver's son came out and translated. The taxi driver agreed to Yokoya-san's request to hire the car but drive it himself. As it turned out, the town was so small Yokoya-san drove the taxi through the only roads in minutes and was done.*

Yokoya achieved his goal of driving in every single U.S. state, including Alaska and Hawaii, and every part of Canada and Mexico. In most cases they were able to rent a Toyota Sienna, looking for ways to improve it. As a result, he made many design changes that would make no sense to a Japanese engineer living in Japan. For example:

- The roads in Canada have a higher crown than in America (bowed up in the middle), perhaps because of the amount of snow they get. They learned driving in Canada that controlling the "drift" of the minivan is very important.
- When driving on a bridge over the Mississippi River, a gust of wind blew him very hard and Yokoya realized that side-wind stability was very important. Driving through the crosswinds of Ontario, he was alarmed how easy it was for trucks to blow the minivan aside. If you drive any place with a crosswind, the newer Sienna is much better.
- When he was driving the narrow streets of Santa Fe, Yokoya found it hard to turn the corner with the previous Sienna and improved the turning radius by 3 feet. This is a huge accomplishment, since the new version is also significantly bigger.
- By practically living in the Sienna for all these driving trips, Yokoya learned the value of cup holders. In Japan, distances are usually shorter. You may buy a can of juice, but it is more common in the culture to drink this outside of the car. In America, on a long trip, he learned it was common for

one person to have one-half empty cup of coffee or bottle of water and one full one. You don't want to wait until you stop and have already run out. Therefore, you really need two cup holders per person, or even three, if a person wants a cup of coffee plus two bottles of water. There are 14 sturdy cup and bottle holders in the Sienna. And there are numerous compartments and pockets for those long trips as well.

- Yokoya also noted the American custom of eating in vehicles rather than taking the time to stop and eat. In Japan it is very uncommon to eat in the car, partly because the roads are narrower and trucks wind in and out, so you need to focus on the road and periodically take a break from the stress. The luxurious American highways lead to more relaxed driving, using cruise control. So he learned the value of having a place for hamburgers and fries by putting in a flip-up tray accessible from the driver position. This option had been previously adopted by Toyota minivans in Japan but is even more useful for the North American market.

The original concept for a longer minivan also came from *genchi genbutsu*. Dr. Akihiko Saito, who was responsible for all of R&D for Toyota globally, believed in the design philosophy that "small is smart." The philosophy is to adopt the smallest possible exterior to minimize the weight of the vehicle while achieving the appropriate interior volume. During a visit to the Toyota Technical Center in Ann Arbor, he took a trip to Home Depot. He just stood in the parking lot and watched—like he was in the Ohno circle. What Saito saw were Americans buying large things, like 4' x 8' plywood, and putting them into the back of their pickup trucks and Honda Odysseys. Back at the technical center, he also saw how a sheet of plywood fit into the Honda Odyssey but not the previous generation Sienna. Mr. Saito approved the size to accommodate the 4' x 8' plywood for the new Sienna on the spot.

Leaders Are Not Excused from *Genchi Genbutsu*

Kiichiro Toyoda learned from his father the importance of getting your hands dirty and learning by doing. He insisted on this from all of his engineers. A famous story about Toyoda has become part of Toyota's cultural heritage (Toyota Way document, p. 8):

> One day Kiichiro Toyoda was walking through the vast plant when he came upon a worker scratching his head and muttering that his grinding machine would not run. Kiichiro took one look at the man, then rolled up his sleeves and plunged his hands into the oil pan. He came up with two handfuls of sludge. Throwing the sludge on the floor, he said: "How can you expect to do your job without getting your hands dirty!"

For some reason, sludge in oil pans seems to creep into a number of Toyota stories. When I visited Jim Press (COO of Toyota Motor Sales, U.S.A.), he related the following story:

> *Our dealers see executives from Japan more often than domestic dealers see executives from Detroit. I recall when I was with Dr. Shoichiro Toyoda on a visit, in the mid-'70s. And we had just introduced a four-speed automatic transmission. It was very unusual to have an automatic transmission fail, if ever. It seemed indestructible. We were visiting a dealership. And the dealer complained about the fact that a car just came in with a transmission that had failed. Dr. Toyoda, in his pressed suit, walked over to the technician, got in a dialogue with him, walked over to the oil pan where he'd drained the oil from the transmission, rolled his sleeve up and put his hand in this oil, and pulled out some filings. He put the filings on a rag, dried them off, and put them in his pocket to take back to Japan for testing. He wanted to find out if the filings were the result of a failed part or if it was residue from the machining process.*

In most large U.S. companies, the president is like the king. The king is not someone who you casually run into and strike up a conversation with. One can judge rank in these U.S. fiefdoms based on office size, windows, furniture quality, carpet quality, how difficult it is to get an appointment, and yearly bonuses.

When I last visited Toyota in Georgetown, Kentucky, to interview President Gary Convis, I also had to go through public affairs and secretaries. A secretary led me into a luxurious conference room in the front office and offered me something to drink. Convis was late, which is also quite typical of visits like these. So I wandered a bit under the pretext of going to get coffee. The executive offices were quite spartan for someone of his rank and stature. But what was odder was that the vaunted 5S of Toyota was in disarray here. There were boxes every place and his assistant was busily packing boxes. When I asked what she was doing, she explained, a bit disgruntled, that "the boss wanted to be near the shop floor so he could be where cars are being made, so he moved to one of the offices in the middle of the plant with windows overlooking the assembly line." His assistant seemed a little annoyed that she had to leave the nice front-office facilities with their outside windows. But she seemed to understand, pausing and then explaining: "He is the most shop-floor-oriented president we have had." This is quite a compliment when past presidents included the likes of Fujio Cho.

When I interviewed Don Jackson, vice president of manufacturing of the Georgetown plant, he spent more time with me than we had scheduled. He had several calls that he did not take. Finally he got one that got his attention, and it wasn't from higher up.

Jackson: [Yeah, I'll be right down. Just a second, OK? Bye.] I am sorry. I have a team member concern meeting. I have to be there.

Liker: Is this something you usually handle?

Jackson: Yes. The group leader or superintendent could handle it. But I want to investigate it for myself. And I want them to see that this is important to me. I want the team member to see that.

Liker: I've heard about the concept of managers spending their time on the floor. Is that true even up to your level? Do you really have that much time to spend on the floor?

Jackson: Typically my average day is 10 to 12 hours. I usually start out on the production floor around 8:00 and I pick an area of the plant I visit in the morning to sort of assess the last 24 hours of what took place. And from that point on, I'm pretty much confirming different parts of the operation or the annual plan activity throughout the plant. Part of the annual planning process is milestones and how you'll achieve efficiency improvements or quality improvements or supplier improvements. So, based on our annual plan, we are following those items up. And I do weekly department head reviews on the floor. The team members are pretty motivated by that. I actually come, see their improvements, and give them some suggestions.

Liker: So you spend a lot of time here on site, as opposed to traveling.

Jackson: Well, when I was managing quality, I spent probably 50% of my time visiting suppliers and then 50% in the plant, but now probably about 95% in the plant.

Liker: One last question. Many companies bring in managers from outside the company. Can a Toyota plant manager be hired from another company?

Jackson: I think that would be pretty difficult. I recently hired a person from General Motors and I brought him in at the department head level. It's really the first time it's been done here at Georgetown. He was pretty unique. He grew up through Saturn, spent a couple of years at NUMMI, so he had a little bit of experience hands-on versus maybe operating from his office. I think a lot of the plant managers at a company like Ford, for example, are looking at the financial side and looking at more of the manpower and efficiency from a computer screen versus on-the-floor management. And our philosophy is management on the floor. If you can manage from the floor operation, then that's the same way the group leader will manage and the same way the assistant manager will manage. Then they're in control. And I'm spending that much time on the floor because I'm trying to develop the staff in my department.

Hourensou—Rapid *Genchi Genbutsu* for Executives

As president of Toyota, Cho had to learn to rely more on trust than he did in the days of running a few manufacturing plants. He doesn't have the time to go and see everything for himself. Instead, he surrounds himself with people he trusts and, by default, goes and sees secondhand through them.

But he also uses a method called *hourensou* to keep in touch with what is going on. It seems almost antithetical to *genchi genbutsu*, but—if practiced right—it can be an efficient way for an executive to accomplish the same thing. *Hourensou* is a Japanese word made up of three parts: *hou* (*hou koku*—to report), *ren* (*ren-raku*—to give updates periodically), and *sou* (*sou dan*—to consult or advise). To serve some of the *genchi genbutsu* functions, senior management uses *hourensou*, which is common within top Japanese companies.

Since Toyota executives know the importance of keeping involved at a detailed level and see as a key role the training and developing of subordinates through questioning and carefully targeted advice, they make a big effort to find efficient ways to get information fed to them and to give feedback and advice. There is no one magic bullet for accomplishing this, but one important approach they use is to have subordinates who learn how to communicate efficiently give reports daily on key events that happened during the day. When they can, the executives will still travel to where the work is being done.

For example, Yamashina, as president of the Toyota Technical Center (TTC), has responsibility for five areas: the main technical center in Ann Arbor, Michigan; the prototyping center in Plymouth, Michigan; the Arizona proving grounds; the technical center in California; and design engineers at Toyota's manufacturing plants. Yamashina schedules meetings with all the departments in TTC once a month, which includes all levels, and travels from site to site to have these meetings in remote locations. Different individuals have an opportunity to report on the status of their projects and prepare what they will say for that monthly meeting. Though Yamashina has a great understanding of what is happening and can, on a regularly scheduled basis, get feedback and give advice, this is not enough. He also insists that each vice president and general manager give him a report on the day, a little update, instead of waiting until the end of the week. This gives Yamashina an opportunity to share live information he got that day from other parts of the company.

While Toyota is not the most computerized company in the world, they are learning to use e-mail effectively for *hourensou*. As Yamashina explained:

> *One young engineer explains his test through e-mail and its purpose and asks if others have any experience with similar tests. Suddenly a very experienced engineer sends an e-mail saying, "I tried that test under similar circumstances*

and the test did not work." His advice to the young engineer is to find another way to perform the test or stop the test. If there were no system to share the information, probably that young engineer will waste a lot of time and energy. So using e-mail is a type of training or consulting or reporting system from top to bottom and bottom to top. I insist that those who report to me send me a daily journal. So I get 60-70 e-mails from VPs or general managers per day. I insist that they make bullet points in the messages. What are the key things you are doing? It has to be designed in such a way that others will read it. That stimulates thinking and sharing information. It is part of how Toyota does learning.

The first reaction of U.S. managers to *hourensou* is that it is another form of micro-management, that is, until they begin to practice and experience the benefits at Toyota. According to several managers I spoke to, over time it becomes an essential part of their management repertoire. How could they manage effectively without it?

The Way of *Genchi Genbutsu* Is Ingrained in a Country's Culture

It is easy to point to dramatic examples of *genchi genbutsu*, like driving all over North America to develop the Sienna minivan or standing in a circle all day in the factory, but what is most important is how it becomes incorporated into the collective psyche of all employees. It is really part of the culture when it simply becomes the natural way of doing things. Though this is the Toyota Way in Japan, Toyota must work hard to implement it in its overseas operations. For example, Bruce Brownlee, general manager of external affairs for the Toyota Technical Center, is one of the few American members of the management staff who grew up in Japan and speaks Japanese fluently. He explains:

We use genchi genbutsu more casually outside of engineering. For example, when I organize a press event at a hotel, I always take time to go in advance and look at the hotel. I want to understand what to expect. Often there are surprises and we want to solve the problems in advance. Or, if there is an important dinner, say for a visiting director, I will go to the restaurant in advance and perhaps eat there. We may ask to see the kitchen. In one case, a highly rated restaurant did not have a quiet back room where we could meet and the service was not what it was reputed to be, so we went to a different restaurant. When Dr. Saito (senior executive of R&D) visited, he wanted to see the Getty Museum, so we checked it out in advance. We wanted to understand exactly what to expect.

Earlier in the chapter, I quoted Yamashina, who lamented that "within the Toyota organization in North America, we are still just going and seeing" (*genchi genbutsu*). Obviously, building a Toyota Way culture overseas is a slow process and Toyota works diligently on it. But are they in any way hampered by the American culture? Interestingly, there is some evidence that they may be, if you look at a fascinating book by Richard E. Nisbett of the University of Michigan, *The Geography of Thought: How Asians and Westerners Think Differently ... and Why*. The book compares East Asians (Korea, China, and Japan) and Westerners (Europe, United Kingdom, and North America). A series of experiments provide concrete evidence that, when looking at the same scene, what Westerners typically see are general categories of objects at a somewhat superficial level, while Asians typically see objects and relationships between objects at a more detailed level.

In one study, Japanese and American students at the University of Michigan were briefly shown pictures of aquariums that contained fish, frogs, and the usual plants, rocks, etc. He then asked them to recall what they had seen. The Japanese remembered 60% more background elements than did the American students and referred twice as often to relationships involving the background objects (e.g., "the little frog was above the pink rock").

Nisbett and his associates concluded that "Westerners prefer abstract universal principles; East Asians seek rules appropriate to a situation."[1] And the East Asians see the same situation in more detail than the Westerners. Now consider Yokoya traveling all over North America to figure out how to redesign the Sienna. If he is experiencing the journey with much greater resolution due to his Japanese heritage and the skills developed in Toyota's culture of *genchi genbutsu*, he undoubtedly got a whole lot more out of the trip than a Western engineering project leader would. He was not just "going and seeing," but understanding the situation at a very deep level and using this deep understanding to make decisions about the direction of the next Sienna minivan.

The implication of Toyota applying Principle 12: *Go and see for yourself to thoroughly understand the situation (genchi genbutsu)* for learning overseas is both exciting and a bit scary. Thinking through the fine details of strategy and operations is clearly central to the culture that has helped Toyota become one of the world's most successful companies. So the Toyota Way principles are something every company should try to learn from and apply. However, if some of these principles are more truly hardwired into the East Asian cultural DNA, it will be more difficult for Westerners to emulate. Or, at least it will require greater effort and practice for Westerners to get really good at it.

We will return to this theme in the last chapter of the book when we consider what companies can learn from the Toyota Way. In the meantime, we have set the stage for examining more closely in the next two chapters how Toyota uses the detailed knowledge that comes from *genchi genbutsu* to make carefully reasoned decisions and ultimately become a true learning organization.

Note

1. Sharon Begley, "East Versus West: One Sees Big Picture, Other Is Focused," *The Wall Street Journal*, March 28, 2003.

Chapter 19

Principle 13:

Make Decisions Slowly by Consensus, Thoroughly Considering All Options; Implement Rapidly

If you've got a project that is supposed to be fully implemented in a year, it seems to me that the typical American company will spend about three months on planning, then they'll begin to implement. But they'll encounter all sorts of problems after implementation, and they'll spend the rest of the year correcting them. However, given the same year-long project, Toyota will spend nine to 10 months planning, then implement in a small way—such as with pilot production—and be fully implemented at the end of the year, with virtually no remaining problems.
—Alex Warren, former senior vice president,
Toyota Motor Manufacturing, Kentucky

If you have bought a house, you probably signed a zillion documents at closing, trusting and hoping that they were all standard documents that wouldn't come back to haunt you. Your lawyer may even have reviewed the documents and told you that everything was in order. This seems like a natural way of doing business to most companies, but not if you are following the Toyota Way.

Richard Mallery was engaged by Toyota in 1989 as its lawyer to help acquire 12,000 acres just northwest of Phoenix. Today it is the Toyota Arizona Proving Ground, where vehicles are driven on test tracks and evaluated. The acreage comprised the northern one-fourth of the Douglas Ranch. Mallery has handled much larger transactions and, from his perspective, the acquisition was routine. A Stanford law school graduate and attorney since 1964 in a prestigious law firm, he knew his stuff and assumed he would handle his relationship with Toyota just like he would with any client. But he had not worked for a client like Toyota. As

Richard explained:

> *I came away with a far more complete knowledge of the legal history of*
> *Arizona and the development of its statutory and common law than I ever*
> *had before (laughing), because I had to answer all of the Toyota team's ques-*
> *tions. I could not just point to the title policy and say either, "That is how we*
> *have always done it" or "Do not worry, the seller will indemnify us." The*
> *Toyota team wanted to dig deeper and know the complete background and*
> *history leading up to the decision in order to make the best possible reasoned*
> *decision. To answer all of their questions, I became a student again and*
> *learned a lot about the federal system that established Arizona first as a ter-*
> *ritory and then as a state.*

Toyota wanted to know how the seller acquired title and how title traced back
to the original owner, the federal government. Having now worked with Toyota
for 14 years, Mallery concludes, "Toyota stands out as the preeminent analyst of
strategy and tactics. Nothing is assumed. Everything is verified. The goal is getting
it right." His learning from working with Toyota has spilled over to how he works
with other clients as well:

> *I am more inclined to ask the penetrating question: why do you do it that*
> *way? Do not just tell me what you do—the standard operating procedures. I*
> *want to know why. I also challenge conventional assumptions. I learned more*
> *about due diligence and strategic planning as legal counsel for Toyota than*
> *with any other client I have had in 40 years of practice.*

The Principle: Thorough Consideration in Decision Making

Many employees outside Japan who have joined Toyota after working for another
company have had to face the challenge of learning the Toyota approach to problem solving and decision making. Because Toyota's process of consensus decision
making deviates so dramatically from the way most other firms operate, it is a
major reeducation process. New employees wonder how an efficient company like
Toyota can use such a detailed, slow, cumbersome, and time-consuming decision-
making process. But all the people I have met who have worked for or with Toyota
for a few years are believers in the process and have been greatly enriched by it—
even in their personal lives.

For Toyota, *how you arrive at the decision is just as important as the quality of*
the decision. Taking the time and effort to do it right is mandatory. In fact, management will forgive a decision that does not work out as expected, if the process
used was the right one. A decision that by chance works out well, but was based

on a shortcut process, is more likely to lead to a reprimand from the boss. As Warren explained in this chapter's opening quote, Toyota's secret to smooth and often flawless implementation of new initiatives is careful, upfront planning. Underlying the entire process of planning, problem solving, and decision making is careful attention to every detail. This behavior is associated with many of the best Japanese firms and Toyota is a master at it. No stone is left unturned. In fact, every stone is inspected under a microscope. Mallery had an eloquent explanation:

> *There is a classic theory of beauty that comes out of Greek and Roman art: God is in the details. Even the frieze on the Parthenon that is high above the spectators on ground level is perfect because their gods would see it. I think Toyota's excellence is in the details.*

Thorough consideration in decision making includes five major elements:

1. Finding out what is really going on, including *genchi genbutsu*.
2. Understanding underlying causes that explain surface appearances—asking "Why?" five times.
3. Broadly considering alternative solutions and developing a detailed rationale for the preferred solution.
4. Building consensus within the team, including Toyota employees and outside partners.
5. Using very efficient communication vehicles to do one through four, preferably one side of one sheet of paper.

We already discussed *genchi genbutsu* in the last chapter and we will be discussing five- why analysis in the next chapter. So we will focus here on steps three through five.

Broadly Consider Alternative Solutions with a Set-Based Approach

As a young Toyota engineer, you attack a problem with relish. You carefully identify the cause of the problem, taking care to do a thorough five-why analysis. You then think and think and come up with a brilliant solution. You detail the solution and run in to share it with your mentor. Instead of evaluating the idea on its merits and congratulating you, he asks, "What other alternatives have you considered? How does this solution compare with those alternatives?" You are stopped dead in your tracks, as you were convinced you had the best approach.

When my colleagues and I started to study Toyota's product development system, we noticed a distinguishing feature of Toyota, compared not only with U.S. auto companies but also with other Japanese companies, like Mazda and Nissan. Toyota senior engineers and managers were trained to think in sets of alternative solutions. Moreover, they could think concurrently about how things like the design of the product and the manufacturing system fit together. We called this "set-based concurrent engineering" (Ward et al., 1995). It seemed paradoxical that considering such a broad array of alternatives required so much time and delayed decisions, yet Toyota was consistently faster in product development than its competitors.

There are many examples of this in the Prius development discussed in Chapter 6:

1. In developing the new suspension needed for Prius, Uchiyamada decided to hold a competition. Instead of using trial and error and testing one suspension alternative at a time, the competition led to over 20 different suspensions tested simultaneously.

2. There were many hybrid engine technologies to choose from. The team began with 80 different hybrid types and systematically eliminated engines that did not meet the requirement, narrowing it down to 10 types. The team carefully considered the merits of each of these and then selected the best four. Each of these four types was then evaluated carefully through computer simulation. Based on this, they were confident in the one alternative selected.

3. The styling of the vehicle was also based on a competition among design centers in California, Europe, Tokyo, and Toyota City. Over 20 designs were put forward in the first wave of the competition, which were narrowed down to five sketches and then four life-sized models. Two were then selected as exceptional and each was revised based on feedback from a wide range of employees until one was finally selected.

Recall that there was extreme time pressure in the development of Prius. For any of these decisions, Uchiyamada could have asked for an opinion up front on the best choice and then developed the one option and refined it through iteration. But the iterative approach, what we called "point-based," might have completely missed a much better alternative. Part of spending the 80% of time planning that Warren spoke of in the opening quote is considering a broad range of alternatives before deciding on one. Senior managers at Toyota have told us that one of the hardest and most important lessons they teach young engineers is to delay decisions until they have considered a broad array of alternatives. One of the advantages of getting many opinions from many different people (through *nemawashi*, discussed next) is that many alternatives are brought to light that can then be systematically evaluated.

Getting on the Same Page Through *Nemawashi*

Toyota Way Principle 13 includes the important process of *nemawashi*: *Make decisions slowly by consensus, thoroughly considering all options; implement rapidly.* The process of *nemawashi* is often used to describe how junior people build consensus by developing a proposal and circulating it broadly for management approval. In the *nemawashi* process, many people are giving their input and this generates consensus. By the time the formal proposal comes up for a high-level approval, the decision is already made. Agreements have been reached and the final meeting is a formality. Though this is a typical process at Toyota, there are many different ways to achieve consensus. If suppliers or other parties could be affected by a decision, their input is required as well.

For example, in 2002 Toyota became aware that a planned mega-development near its Arizona Proving Ground threatened the long-term water supply of the entire surrounding area. Toyota took legal action to stop the developers and worked to get a citizens committee organized to protest the plan. But instead of taking an adversarial approach, Toyota tried to get consensus from all the parties involved—the developer, the surrounding towns, and their local governments. And they searched for a solution all could benefit from. Ultimately, the developers agreed to set aside 200 acres and pay several million dollars in infrastructure costs to create a groundwater replenishment site. Basically, for every gallon of water they used they would purchase a gallon to replace it in the aquifer. As Mallery, who led the consensus-building process, explained:

> *The Mayor, the developers, and the citizens' committee—all of the contending parties agreed that Toyota had served each of them well and had satisfied all of the parties from each of their perspectives. The town ended up with a more responsible, long-term solution to groundwater subsidence concerns, the problem was solved for the developers, who would have had to address it eventually—maybe 30 years from now. And it helped the surrounding communities that are concerned about irresponsible growth. Everyone came away with greater respect for Toyota—not only what Toyota did but how Toyota did it. It is the what and the how that makes the difference—protecting the land for the next 50-100 years, not just for the short term.*

In simple terms, Toyota turned conflict into consensus and created a win-win environment for all parties. From the perspective of a lawyer, this is very unusual. Once you go to court, get involved with local politicians, and take sides politically, the usual assumption is that you are fighting against somebody to win. You win; they lose. Toyota was not satisfied with this, as Mallery explained:

Achieving consensus—it's a belief in reason. Let's work it out. It's a combination of reason and pragmatism with this overlay of integrity and excellence. We were in a political campaign, but Toyota had no thoughts of smearing anybody. There was no negative campaigning.

Now let's translate this consensus-building behavior into a company's day-to-day business. Inside the company, everyone is supposedly on the same team. There is no reason to act in an adversarial way. Yet, the most common problem I hear in large corporations is the "chimney" phenomenon. Many different groups are in their own chimneys and seem to care more about their own objectives than about the company's success. These groups could be functional departments like purchasing, accounting, engineering, and manufacturing or they could be project teams that are implementing new software or even implementing lean manufacturing. These groups often seem to act as though they want their particular department or project to get all the resources and their perspective to dominate in decisions—they want to win at all costs, even if other groups lose in the process.

Not so in Toyota. The same process used to gain consensus with these outside community groups in Arizona is used every day to get input, involvement, and agreement from a broad cross-section of the organization. This does not mean all parties get what they personally want, but they will get a fair hearing.

There are a variety of decision-making methods all used at Toyota in different situations. These range from a manager or expert making a decision unilaterally and announcing it to group consensus with full authority to implement the decision they agree to. As shown in Figure 19-1, the preferred approach at Toyota is group consensus, but with management approval. But management reserves the right to seek group input and then make a decision and announce it. This is done only if the group is struggling to get consensus and management must step in or if there is an urgent need for a quick decision. The philosophy is to seek the maximum involvement appropriate for each situation.

One example of the *nemawashi* process is the way the broad circulation of ideas works in the early stages of product development. Before the styling of a vehicle is even determined, Toyota puts an enormous amount of effort into evaluating the early designs and thinking through all possible engineering and manufacturing issues. Each design is meticulously analyzed and countermeasures are developed through "study drawings." These are sketches that include possible problems and alternative solutions. When the study-drawing phase is completed, the collective drawings across all engineering departments are put together into a binder called the K4 (shorthand for *kozokeikaku—a Japanese word referring to a structure plan—the study drawings that collectively address the structure and integration of the vehicle*). One day I met with Jim Griffith, who at the time was VP of Technical Administration. He looked frazzled. I asked him why and he said he just

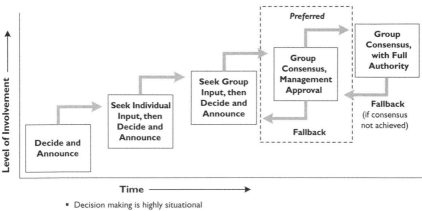

- Decision making is highly situational
- Philosophy is to seek maximum involvement for each situation

Figure 19-1. Alternative Toyota decision making methods

had gotten a K4 on a new vehicle to review. Griffith is not an engineer, so I asked why an administrator would get this document. He seemed surprised I would ask and said that Toyota is always looking for broad input and he, too, will have opinions about the vehicle.

He was frazzled because this was clearly a challenging task for a non-engineer and he felt obliged to take it seriously and come up with some useful input. As it was, there were well over one hundred signatures required on the K4. Jim was a vice president and very well established in a company with lifetime employment, so he could have just blown off the assignment. But he knew that if the chief engineer was asking for a non-engineering opinion and he had to sign off on the document, there was a reason. The process matters and every member must take the process seriously. Perhaps he might see things that others missed. In any event, he knew his opinions would count.

One way new engineers learn about *nemawashi* is through the freshman project. They are given a very challenging project, something they are unprepared for and could not possibly do on their own. For example, one American stamping engineer responsible for setting up the process of stamping body panels was given the assignment in his first year of designing what is called a "checking fixture." This is a complex device that clamps a body panel (like the outer part of a door) down on specific points and checks that the measurements are accurate. Stamping engineers generally have to learn how to use these, but not design one. It requires understanding the design of the part, understanding the critical quality points, and designing something complex from scratch. The young American stamping engineer did not have a clue how to start. He was not given any rulebook. So he struggled and thought about it and finally started asking questions. In the process of asking questions, he had to talk to many engineers from different departments—body engineering, quality, vendors. In the process he learned a lot about quality and design and met people whom he would continue to draw on as resources throughout his career. The assignment forced him to learn *nemawashi* by doing it.

Communicate Visually on One Piece of Paper to Arrive at Decisions

With all this communication going back and forth to build consensus, one might think that Toyota takes forever to get anything done. Yet we know how efficient and speedy Toyota is, so it should not be surprising that they have communication down to a science. The most time-consuming and difficult way to understand complex ideas is to have to decipher a lengthy report filled with technical descriptions, business jargon, and tables of data. More efficient is the visual approach— "a picture is worth a thousand words." Acting on the fact that people are visually oriented, new employees at Toyota learn to communicate with as few words as possible and with visual aids. The A3 report discussed in Chapter 13 (in which all necessary information to make a complex decision is presented on one 11" x 17" piece of paper) is a key part of the process of efficiently getting consensus on complex decisions

Figure 19-2 is one example of an A3 report developed at the Toyota Technical Center in 1996. It is the final report for an extensive analysis of using purchasing cards for small purchases to avoid lengthy and expensive approvals.

The A3 is read from the top left down and then into the second column. Analysis of the current situation revealed that 40% of the purchases in the technical center were for under $500, but represented only 4% of the dollars spent. Yet, the time to process and approve these tiny purchases took as long as for major purchases. The proposal was to use purchasing cards and the benefits in time and money saved are clearly spelled out in the report. A plan is proposed to pilot the program along with details of who will issue the cards and what uses would be blocked out on the card. The plan includes a timeline for full implementation once the pilot is complete.

This A3 report was conceived when a cross-functional purchasing team and team leader were assigned to study the problem. They had learned the Toyota Way of approaching an assignment like this and knew that *nemawashi* was mandatory. If they went off on their own, did a study, and came back with a lengthy report and executive summary, they would face resistance to their ideas and their solution might not be implemented. So, throughout the process they involved everyone they could think of who might be affected by this decision,

PURCHASING CARD IMPLEMENTATION

To: Jim Griffith, VP ADM
Joe Fukunaga, CTO
Date: August 20, 1996

CURRENT SITUATION

Cost to process PO (labor & mat'l):
Purch. Dept. - $37.00   Tech. Dept. - $27.00   AFD - $39.00   TOTAL = $103.00/PO

Cost to process Invoice (labor & mat'l):
Purch. Dept. - $0.00   Tech. Dept. - $27.00   AFD - $27.00   TOTAL = $54.00/Invoice

1995
# of Purchases:	<= $250.00 - 813	<= $500.00 - 1200	<= $1,000.00 - 1525
# of Invoices:	<= $250.00 - 2316	<= $500.00 - 2740	<= $1,000.00 - 3026
Time Required:	<= $250.00 - 5525 Hrs.	<= $500.00 - 7184 Hrs.	<= $1,000.00 - 8489 Hrs.

TTC Purchase Order Analysis

(Bar chart: Percentage of Total vs. Purchase Order Dollar Amount (core); legend: ■ Percentage of Purchase Orders □ Percentage of Purchase Order Dollars)

PROPOSAL

Implement use of purchasing credit cards for purchases <= $500.00 to incur the following savings and increases in efficiency:
- Labor hours saved - Tech Groups, Purchasing, AFD
- Labor & Material Cost savings.
- Reduced P.O., RFP, Expense Reports, Invoice paperwork.
- Customer Service to T/A's through reduction of time spent on completion of paperwork.
- Ease of performing spot transactions - Test Trips, Emergency Purchases, Etc.
- Helps to maintain existing ADM & AFD headcount while TTC grows over next 5-10 years.
- Reallocated time used on higher ticket buys, priority projects, etc.

LABOR & MAT'L SAVINGS:

	P.O.	INV.
Current Cost/Transaction	$103.00	$54.00
Purchasing Card Costs	$20.00	$20.00
Savings/Transaction	$83.00	$34.00

TIME SAVINGS:

	P.O.	INV.
Current process:	3300 Hrs	3900 Hrs
Purchasing Card:	650 Hrs	1550 Hrs
Potential Annual Time Savings	2650 Hr/Yr*	2350 Hr/Yr*

*Approx. 1/3 of time savings is to Tech Grps.

PLAN

- Pilot program starting with Facilities, Purchasing, Tech. Grp. (AA-PED; LA-LAPT; TAPG-VEA)
- Dept. GM determines which T/A's are issued cards for specific dept. purchases.
- Purchasing is issued cards.
- Acceptable business related purchases using card:

Small Tools	Seminars	Photo Processing & Film
Auto Supplies	Office Supplies	Postage
Minor Equip. Repairs	Printing Services	Copy Services
Electrical Supplies	Safety Supplies	Bldg. Maint. Supplies
Catering	Florists	Coffee Services
Hardware	Signage	

- Unacceptable uses of card (blocked):

Cash Advance	Travel & Entertainment	Independent Contract Services
Computer Hardware	Personal Use	Capital Purchases
Jewelry, Furriers		

IMPLEMENTATION

1. Card user obtains approval from Dept. Manager for each purchase.
2. Card user contacts vendor, places order & provides vendor with appropriate information.
3. Goods shipped as specified and labeled "Purchasing Card" - Cardholder Name.
4. Goods received per standard receiving procedure with following exception: packing list & receipt is forwarded to card user.
5. All packing lists & receipts are retained by requestors and matched against monthly statement.
6. Card user reviews statement, attaches appropriate packing lists & receipts, records JRN #'s, signs and forwards to Dept. Manager.
7. Dept. Manager reviews statement for accuracy and initials and dates statement.
8. Dept. Manager forwards to AFD. AFD audits statement & supporting docs. for compliance, sales tax, 1099.
9. AFD pays from master invoice received directly from the purchasing card bank.

CONTROLS

The following controls are set up prior to the card being issued:
- Monthly dollar limits per card
- Single transaction limits ($500.00)
- Limited number of transactions per card per day
- Merchant Category Blocking (i.e. cash advances, jewelry stores, appliances, entertainment, etc.)

TTC requires all card users to sign a P-Card Agreement stating that all use of the card will be for business purposes and within the procedures set forth.

TIME LINE

9/3	9/4-9/20	9/16-11/15	11/18-3/31	11/18-3/31	4/1-4/15	4/16-4/18	4/21-5/30	6/2/97
Present at CTR Mtg.	Policy Guidelines, Issuer Selection & Supplier Enrollment	Training for Pilot Program - Purch/AFD, Management, Cardholders	Pilot Program	Concurrent Revisioning of Policy & Procedure	Audit & Analyze 3 Month Pilot Program	Report Results of Audit	Training - Corporate Wide	Corporate Wide Implementation

From: AFD & Purchasing

Figure 19-2. Example of an A3 report

not just the purchasing department but also the general managers and vice presidents who were used to having control over their budgets through the approval process. Suddenly they were going to have to relinquish this control and risk overrunning their budget. Employees would have to learn new procedures for purchasing items and would obviously be lobbying for as much flexibility and the highest spending limit possible. And so on. So all of the affected parties saw A3 reports in various stages being circulated and modified to incorporate their ideas. While seeking consensus is a cumbersome process, it goes much faster when all the different opinions, scenarios, and numbers are communicated on one side of one sheet of paper.

Embedded in an A3 report is Toyota's problem-solving process, which is based on the Deming Cycle. Deming said any good problem-solving process should include all of the elements of planning, doing, checking, and acting (PDCA). (We will discuss the Deming Cycle further in the next chapter.) When Toyota teaches A3 report writing, one of the prerequisites is taking its course on PDCA.

Figure 19-3 shows how the A3 proposal incorporates PDCA. In the spirit of *genchi genbutsu*, the A3 report starts with one step before planning—a thorough understanding of the current situation, the values, expectations, policies, reason for the current system, etc. Once you lay this groundwork, you are ready for the Deming Cycle steps—the plan, doing or implementing the plan, then checking and acting.

The checking and acting stages are critical and often overlooked in problem solving. Notice the timeline for the purchasing card report in Figure 19-2. A pilot program is created and then, three months into the pilot, the audit and analysis (check) and then a report on the results of the audit. This will include countermeasures to any problems discovered. Then you act by implementing the pilot corporate-wide. Once everything is in place, the process of continuous improvement kicks in and continues operating well beyond this timeline.

After months of study and great pains in writing and refining the A3 report so it included only critical and visual information, the team presented the report to the decision makers for the final decision. This was the executive board presided over by the president of the technical center. They had exactly five minutes on the agenda. They presented the report, which was largely ceremonial, as everyone had seen it multiple times. There was a little discussion. And then the decision makers formally approved the proposal.

Alan Cabito, Group VP of Sales Administration, went to work for Toyota as his first job out of school, so he only knew the Toyota way. But he was able to observe differences in the way Toyota communicated when he started working

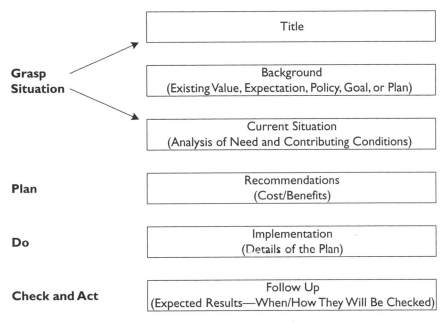

Figure 19-3. Plan-Do-Check-Act in the proposal process

with General Motors on the NUMMI plant in the 1980s:

> *Their (General Motors') solution to making a decision was to write a memo. I haven't written a memo in I don't know how many years—maybe 20. I walk over to someone and I sit down and we talk about the issue. And ultimately, I try to get them to buy in or to make it their idea. But you never write a memo. A memo to me is like a directive, as opposed to an A3 PDCA document that has in it an evaluation that everybody can see and understand. To me an A3 is a learning process. A memo's not a learning process.... In the GM world, at least to those people who came here, memos were a way of finding a direction, and then expecting everybody to follow it without any communication necessary.*

One of the benefits of the A3 communication format and a disciplined approach to problem solving is that Toyota runs its meetings very efficiently. The discipline of the A3 process helps to accomplish effective meetings. There are several prerequisites to an efficient meeting:

1. *Clear objectives prior to the meeting.* These are sometimes reflected in an agenda, but the agenda needs to be very focused on clear tasks and deliverables.
2. *The right people at the meeting.* People expected to show up need to show up.

3. *Prepared participants.* All participants know what they should prepare for the meeting and have done it.
4. *Effective use of visual aids.* The A3 format is extremely effective.
5. *Separate information sharing from problem solving.* Share information as much as possible prior to the meeting so that the focus of the meeting can be on problem solving.
6. *The meeting starts and ends on time.*

I have been in too many meetings in many companies where the vast majority fail on all six points. The meeting has a vague purpose, some people do not show up, nobody does any preparation except, perhaps, the person running the meeting, visual aids are ad hoc, most of the meeting is about sharing information, and the meeting starts late and ends late. Now, this is a time-consuming, cumbersome, and wasteful way to arrive at decisions.

A Great Deal of Learning up Front Makes for Easier Decision Making

Andy Lund, program manager for the 2004 Toyota Sienna, explained to me why he always uses *nemawashi* when he is making decisions and preparing to present his recommendations:

> For some decisions I may think I already know the answer and do not need input from others. There may be a department that is not directly involved and I think they probably do not have much to contribute. I may in fact find the right answers on my own, but I will have a hard time presenting it because the group I skipped will challenge my recommendations and ask why I did not consider this and that and the presentation will become a debate. But through nemawashi they will agree with the presentation because they have already agreed with it. So I will go and talk to that department in advance anyway and generally I am pleasantly surprised because I get new information.

By going through lengthy and thorough information gathering and analysis in decision making, what does Toyota achieve?

1. It uncovers all the facts that, if not considered, could lead to a great deal of pain and backtracking further down the road. Execution tends to be flawless by most standards.
2. It gets all the parties on board and supporting the decision so any resistance is worked out before implementing anything. The cost of addressing this resistance when implementation begins is likely to be many times the cost of addressing it in the planning stage. Dick Mallery could not believe that every concerned party, even Toyota's opponents, ended up thanking

Toyota for solving their problems.

3. It achieves a great deal of learning up front before anything is even planned or implemented.

The last point leads us to the next chapter and the final Toyota Way principle, which focuses on Toyota's greatest accomplishment—becoming a true learning organization. We will see that the Problem-Solving layer of the 4P model (see Figure 1-1) is actually intertwined with the other three layers: Process, Partners, and Philosophy. We already saw in this chapter that we could not really understand *nemawashi* without understanding *genchi genbutsu* and the Deming cycle of problem solving. In fact, new employees cannot learn even a seemingly simple tool like an A3 report without first understanding these three processes.

Chapter 20

Principle 14:

Become a Learning Organization Through Relentless Reflection (*Hansei*) and Continuous Improvement (*Kaizen*)

> *We view errors as opportunities for learning. Rather than blaming individuals, the organization takes corrective actions and distributes knowledge about each experience broadly. Learning is a continuous company-wide process as superiors motivate and train subordinates; as predecessors do the same for successors; and as team members at all levels share knowledge with one another.*
> —The Toyota Way document 2001, Toyota Motor Corporation

The beginning of the 21st century has continued the turbulence, uncertainty, and intense competition of the end of the 20th century. Long gone are the days when a company could set up shop, make a product well, and then milk that product for years, hanging on to its original competitive advantage. Adaptation, innovation, and flexibility have knocked this old business approach off its pedestal and have become the necessary ingredients for survival as well as the hallmarks of a successful business. To sustain such organizational behavior requires one essential attribute: the ability to learn. In fact, the highest compliment we can pay to a business in today's business environment is that it is a true "learning organization."

Peter Senge popularized this concept in his book, *The Fifth Discipline*, over a decade ago, defining a learning organization as a place (Senge, 1990):

> *... where people continually expand their capacity to create the results they truly desire, where new and expansive patterns of thinking are nurtured, where collective aspiration is set free, and where people are continually learning how to learn together.*

Senge focuses on "new patterns of thinking" and learning to learn. In other words, a learning organization does not only adopt and develop new business or technical skills; it puts in place a second level of learning—*how to learn* new skills, knowledge, and capabilities. To become a true learning organization, the very learning capacity of the organization should be developing and growing over time, as it helps its members adapt to a continually changing competitive environment.

Of all the institutions I've studied or worked for, including world-class companies and major universities, I believe Toyota is the best learning organization. The reason is that it sees standardization and innovation as two sides of the same coin, melding them in a way that creates great continuity. For example, as we discussed in Chapter 12, Toyota has judiciously used stability and standardization to transfer individual and team innovation into organization-wide learning. It is one thing for individual employees to come up with innovative ways to do things. But to be transferred to organization learning, the new way must be standardized and practiced across the organization until a better way is discovered. This is the foundation for the Toyota Way of learning—standardization punctuated by innovation, which gets translated into new standards.

Throughout this book, we have emphasized that the Toyota Way is far more than tools and techniques. TPS itself is designed to push team members to think and learn and grow. Toyota evolved out of innovation, originally in making looms and then in automobile design, and ever since, the leadership has worked hard to keep this innovative spirit alive. We saw, for example, how Toyota used the Prius project to revitalize a maturing product development process. Lexus also pushed the organization to new levels of quality and excellence. However, breakthrough innovation is only one aspect of the Toyota Way. Possibly the most important aspect is Toyota's relentless application of the more "mundane" process of continuous improvement, which results in thousands of little lessons learned. The Toyota Way involves the company learning from its mistakes, determining the root cause of problems, providing effective countermeasures, empowering people to implement those measures, and having a process for transferring the new knowledge to the right people to make it part of the company's repertoire of understanding and behavior. This chapter will describe how Toyota accomplishes this.

The Principle: Identify Root Causes and Develop Countermeasures

Unlike most companies, Toyota does not adopt "programs of the month" nor does it focus on programs that can deliver only short-term financial results. Toyota is process oriented and consciously and deliberately invests long term in systems of people, technology, and processes that work together to achieve high customer value. "Systems" are not information systems but work processes and appropriate procedures to accomplish a task with the minimum amount of time and effort. The philosophy of Toyota and its experience support the belief that if it focuses on the process itself and continual improvement, it will achieve the financial results it desires.

As you learned in Section II, The Right Process Will Produce the Right Results, continuous improvement (*kaizen*) can occur only after a process is stable and standardized. When you make processes stable and have a process to make waste and inefficiencies publicly visible, you have an opportunity to learn continually from your improvements. To be a learning organization, it is necessary to have stability of personnel, slow promotion, and very careful succession systems to protect the organizational knowledge base. To "learn" means having the capacity to build on your past and move forward incrementally, rather than starting over and reinventing the wheel with new personnel with each new project.

Ultimately, the core of *kaizen* and learning is an attitude and way of thinking by all leaders and associates—an attitude of self-reflection and even self-criticism, a burning desire to improve. Westerners view criticism and admitting to a mistake as something negative and a sign of weakness. Westerners are often eager to blame others when something goes wrong. The attitude of "the buck stops here" is the exception, not the rule. It is just the opposite within Toyota. The greatest sign of strength is when an individual can openly address things that did not go right, take responsibility, and propose countermeasures to prevent these things from happening again.

Getting to the Root Cause by Asking "Why?" Five Times

An integral part of *kaizen* is Toyota's famous five-why analysis. I recall interviewing Yuichi Okamoto, a former Toyota Technical Center vice president, about the secret to the success of Toyota's product development system. I was expecting a description of a sophisticated process similar to the TPS. Instead, he answered with an underlying tone of sarcasm, "We have a very sophisticated technique for developing new products. It is called five-why. We ask why five times."

The reason for Okamoto's sarcasm is that there are no complex tools and techniques to explain Toyota's success in product development. Many people are surprised when I give talks and tell them that Toyota does not have a Six Sigma program. Six Sigma is based on complex statistical analysis tools. People want to know how Toyota achieves such high levels of quality without the quality tools of Six Sigma. You can find an example of every Six Sigma tool in use somewhere in Toyota at some time. Yet most problems do not call for complex statistical analysis, but instead require painstaking, detailed problem solving. This requires a level of detailed thinking and analysis that is all too absent from most companies in day-to-day activity. It is a matter of discipline, attitude, and culture.

Taiichi Ohno emphasized that true problem solving requires identifying "… 'root cause' rather than 'source;' the root cause lies hidden beyond the source." For example, you might find that the source of a problem is a supplier or a particular machining center—the problem occurs there. But what is the root cause of the problem? The answer lies in digging deeper by asking why the problem occurred. Asking "Why?" five times requires taking the answer to the first why and then asking why that occurs. Typically, the process of asking "Why?" leads upstream in the process. It may be a defect that occurs in assembly, but the root cause is upstream in the raw material supplier, where the variation in the thickness or hardness of steel affects how the part is stamped, which then affects the way it is welded, which then affects the ability in assembly of the fastener to hold the part in place.

Figure 20-1 provides a hypothetical example of five-why analysis that Toyota uses in internal problem-solving training. The problem is oil on the shop floor. In this example, each why brings us further upstream in the process and deeper into the organization. Note that the countermeasures are completely different depending on how deeply we dig. For example, cleaning up the oil would simply be a temporary measure until more oil leaked. Fixing the machine would be a little longer term, but the gasket would wear out again, leading to more oil on the floor. Changing the specifications for gaskets could solve the problem for those particular gaskets, but there is a deeper root cause that would still go unresolved. You

5 Whys is a method to pursue the deeper, systematic causes of a problem to find correspondingly deeper countermeasures.

Level of Problem	Corresponding Level of Countermeasure
There is a puddle of oil on the shop floor	Clean up the oil
Because the machine is leaking oil	Fix the machine
Because the gasket has deteriorated	Replace the gasket
Because we bought gaskets made of inferior material	Change gasket specifications
Because we got a good deal (price) on those gaskets	Change purchasing policies
Because the purchasing agent gets evaluated on short-term cost savings	Change the evaluation policy for purchasing agents

Figure 20-1. "5-Why" investigation questions
Source: Peter R. Scholtes, *The Leader's Handbook*, McGraw-Hill, 1998.

could purchase other parts at lower cost, based on inferior materials, because purchasing agents are evaluated based on short-term cost savings. Only by fixing the
underlying organizational problem of the reward system for purchasing agents can
we prevent a whole range of similar problems from occurring again in the future.

A five-why analysis of a real problem within the Toyota Technical Center
(TTC) provides another illustration. The manager of information systems developed a plan to convert to a new e-mail system with new features such as extended
external e-mail capability and room scheduling. He devised the plan by identifying
the weaknesses of the current e-mail system and compiling new capabilities that
users wanted. Through a bidding process, the manager found an e-mail system he
was pleased with and got approval to purchase it. When they installed the e-mail
system, the manager sent out manuals to all employees and had them sign a letter
confirming they had received one. One month later, the manager received many
complaints from employees who did not understand all of the functions and found
the manual too difficult to read. The manager met with the technicians and system
analysts and they decided as a countermeasure to provide training. The training was
viewed as helpful, but one month later, the manager still had numerous complaints
about the same problem of understanding functions and the poor manual.

What was the real root cause of the e-mail complaints? Figure 20-2 shows the
result of the five-why analysis at TTC. In this case, the surface problem was that
employees were not happy about their understanding of the e-mail system and the
poor manual provided. As they got deeper and deeper into the root cause, they discovered that the manager had not followed the Toyota Way principles of *genchi
genbutsu* and *nemawashi* discussed in Chapters 18 and 19 and this chapter. The
manager had not done enough work going directly to the source and studying how
people use e-mail or the manual. He did not develop a deep understanding of the
situation (*genchi genbutsu*) and he failed to pilot the process. A well-executed A3
reporting process could have avoided the problems. When they dug even deeper,
asking "Why?" TTC discovered this failure to follow principles occurred because
senior management failed to create a culture that supported the Toyota Way. The
final countermeasure resulting from the e-mail incident was to include training
and a great deal of follow through by senior management to build a culture supporting the use of good internal processes that follow the Toyota Way.

What is the real learning point of these two cases? To keep asking why until the
root cause(s) are determined. Take countermeasures at the deepest level of cause
that is feasible and at the level that will prevent reoccurrence of the problem.

"Practical Problem Solving" in Seven Steps

At Toyota, a five-why analysis is often used as part of a seven-step process they call
"practical problem solving." (See Figure 20-3.) Before the five-why analysis can

What is the problem?	Employees are frustrated and complaining about the new e-mail system.
Why?	Employees do not understand how to use the functions of the system.
Why?	The employees didn't receive adequate training on the new system, a manual they can use, and didn't give input on their needs for the new system functions.
Why?	The I.S. manager had a poor planning process: didn't ask employees about their needs on system functions, didn't plan for training up front, didn't notify employees using multiple communication channels, didn't review the manual with employees (pilot group).
Why?	The manager didn't get direction and support from his boss, or receive planning process training.
Why?	The company as a whole does not have effective internal processes in place, nor is it disciplined in using good process.
Why?	Senior management hasn't worked to create a work culture that encourages and reinforces effective internal processes.

Figure 20-2. "5-Why" analysis of e-mail problems
Source: Toyota Technical Center, Ann Arbor, Michigan

begin, "practical problem solving" requires you to clarify the problem or, in Toyota terminology, "grasp the situation." Trainers who teach this methodology within Toyota have found the most difficult part to learn is grasping the situation thoroughly *before* proceeding with five-why analysis. Grasping the situation starts with observing the situation with an open mind and comparing the actual situation to the standard. To clarify the problem, you must start by going to where the problem is (*genchi genbutsu*). This may include prioritizing a number of different problems in a Pareto analysis. The *Pareto diagram* uses bar graphs to sort problems according to severity, frequency, nature, or source and displays them in order of size to show which problems are the most important. It is probably the most often used statistical analysis tool within Toyota—simple, but powerful.

At this point you also want to set targets for improvement. Then you make a first attempt at identifying the point of cause (POC). Where is the problem observed? Where is the likely cause? This will lead you upstream toward the general vicinity of the root cause, which you can discover through five-why analysis. The ultimate purpose of the exercise is to generate and implement a countermeasure and evaluate the results. Only at this point, if the countermeasure is

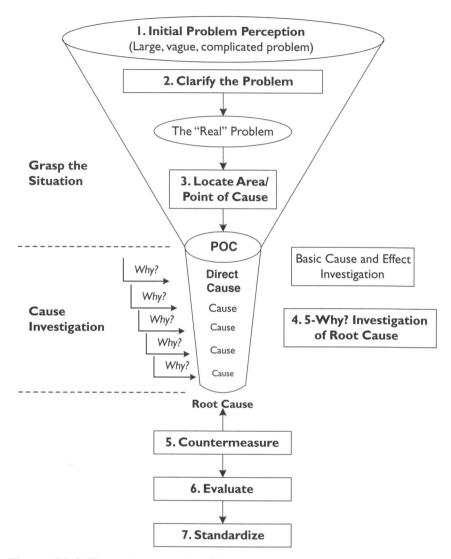

Figure 20-3. Toyota's practical problem-solving process

effective, does it become part of a new standardized approach.

The seventh step—standardizing the new process—is very important at Toyota. As mentioned in this chapter and discussed in Chapter 12, standardization and learning go hand in hand and are the basis for continuous improvement. If you do not standardize the improved process, the learning up to that point falls into a black hole, lost, forgotten, and unavailable for further improvements.

Tools, techniques, and metrics aside, Toyota's greatest emphasis is on thinking through problems and solutions. At Toyota, it is said that problem solving is 20% tools and 80% thinking. Unfortunately, I've learned from many Six Sigma programs that some companies get caught up in using all the great and new sophisticated analysis tools, where problem solving seems to be 80% tools and 20% thinking.

Hansei: Responsibility, Self-Reflection, and Organizational Learning

Teamwork never overshadows individual accountability at Toyota. Individual accountability is not about blame and punishment, but about learning and growing. A key to learning and growing, not only within Toyota but in Japanese culture, is *hansei*, which roughly means "reflection." *Hansei* is a bit of Japanese culture that Toyota recently has been working to teach to its overseas managers. It is one of the most difficult things they have ever had to teach, but it is an integral ingredient in Toyota's organizational learning.

For many years after setting up shop in the U.S., the Japanese leadership intentionally did not introduce *hansei*. They realized it was a distinctly Japanese concept and too alien to the American culture. George Yamashina, who runs the Toyota Technical Center, explained it as something like the American "time-out" for children, though in Japan *hansei* has a broader meaning.

> *In Japan, sometimes the mother and the father say to the children, "Please do the Hansei." Some child did a bad thing. It means he or she must be sorry and improve his or her attitude—everything is included, spirit and attitude. So once the child is told, "Please do the Hansei," he understands almost everything about what the mother and the father want him to do.*

Translated as *reflection,* Toyota finally introduced *hansei* to its U.S. managers in 1994. According to Yamashina, it had to be introduced at some point:

> *Without* hansei *it is impossible to have* kaizen. *In Japanese* hansei*, when you do something wrong, at first you must feel really, really sad. Then you must create a future plan to solve that problem and you must sincerely believe you will never make this type of mistake again.* Hansei *is a mindset, an attitude.* Hansei *and* kaizen *go hand in hand.*

Mike Masaki, president of the Toyota Technical Center from 1995 to 2000, found it very challenging to get Americans to understand the value of reflection—they take the implied criticism personally and negatively. In 1997 he lamented:

> *Wherever Mr. (Akihiro) Wada (then executive VP of global R&D) goes, he critiques. I do the same thing at TTC. For example, I recently reviewed a pro-*

totype of the next-generation Avalon body. I pointed out that these parts are very bad and the Americans had an uncomfortable reaction. In Japan the reaction is "I should have designed this better—I made a mistake!" The U.S. designer's expectation is that "I did a good job so I should be rewarded." This is a big cultural difference. In Japan we would not point out the good things, but would focus on the negative.

At Toyota, even if you do a good job successfully, there is a *hansei-kai* (reflection meeting). Bruce Brownlee, General Manager at the Toyota Technical Center, helped clarify this, drawing on his experience as an American who grew up in Japan:

Hansei is really much deeper than reflection. It is really being honest about your own weaknesses. If you are talking about only your strengths, you are bragging. If you are recognizing your weaknesses with sincerity, it is a high level of strength. But it does not end there. How do you change to overcome those weaknesses? That is at the root of the very notion of kaizen. If you do not understand hansei, than kaizen is just continuous improvement. Hansei is the incubator for change—that whole process. We want to overcome areas of weakness. It also explains why we (Toyota) spend little time talking about successes. We spend more time talking about our weaknesses. If anything, perhaps a weakness for Toyota is that we do not celebrate our successes enough.

Toyota is continually "reflecting" on *hansei* as well. By implanting *hansei* into an alien culture, at first in the U.S., Toyota has an opportunity to watch it germinate and develop in a new way. The Americans have embraced *hansei* to a degree, but there are certain traditional elements they have rejected and new elements they are adding. Andy Lund, a program manager for the Toyota Sienna, also grew up in Japan as a missionary's child. He explained how *hansei* is being adapted to the American culture:

The hansei view of feeling deeply sorry and admitting shame is a traditional Japanese view, but I did not experience it when I was growing up in Japan. Here at TTC we are using a more gentle version. If individuals do commit a mistake, they will learn from the mistake and from having to report to Yamashina-san. It may be difficult for them. When you have to prepare an A3 report for the president, you learn so much more. He will be looking not only at the error you made but how you reflect on it.... You will of course get advice, but the preparation for the meeting is when the team member will learn so much. Part of on-the-job training is to provide opportunities for your team associates to present to the president. We try to give all team associates a chance to present to the president what they have learned, and they will get feedback from the president about dotting every "i" and crossing every "t," but to bring shame is not the goal.

When I first started doing interviews at the Toyota Technical Center a decade ago, U.S. managers often used the term "the obligatory negative" in discussing their Japanese coordinators. The Americans felt that, whatever work they showed the coordinators, it was obligatory to find a mistake or expose a weakness. Lund believes this is a cross-cultural misunderstanding of *hansei*:

> *People who have not been to Japan may not understand that the objective is not to hurt that individual but to help that individual improve—not to hurt the program but to show flaws to improve the next program. If you understand that deeply, you can get through that constructive criticism. No matter how good a program or a presentation someone makes, we believe there is always something that can be improved, so we feel it is our obligation. It is not an "obligatory negative" but an obligatory opportunity to improve—it is the heart of kaizen.*

Hansei is not simply a philosophical belief system at Toyota, but a practical tool for improvement. For example, TTC holds formal and scheduled *hansei* events at key milestones in a vehicle program as well as after it launches the vehicle and the program ends. Like other companies, Toyota conducts design reviews to identify problems with the vehicle. But the *hansei* is a reflection on the *process* of developing the vehicle. *Hansei* is the check stage of PDCA. It is used most often at the end of a vehicle program, but TTC is starting to move it further upstream so there are several *hansei* events at key junctures in the program.

When Lund led a *hansei* event after the prototype phase of the 2004 Sienna model, he began by collecting information from a wide range of participants in the vehicle development process. He then was able to consolidate what he learned into four themes. The themes are really root causes. He asked "Why?" five times for many different problems that surfaced during the development of the Sienna and moved upstream in the process. All the process flaws could be explained by these four root causes.

For example, some parts on the prototype vehicle were late and therefore older parts had to be used to build the Sienna prototype. Other parts were not as high-quality as Toyota would have liked. A thorough five-why analysis revealed that, in the quest for introducing the perfect vehicle to market, Toyota had insisted that every part be as perfect as possible at each prototype phase. This insistence resulted in the practice of last-minute revision requests, such that if the design engineers had an improvement on a part just prior to the prototype, they were requested by program management to get the latest revision onto the prototype so they could test the best ideas. The result was that the design engineers did not complete some prototype parts in time. Lund concluded,

> *We missed a great opportunity to test parts, even if they were not the most up-to-date versions. The reflection was not so much that there were late changes,*

because if the market changes we always need to change the vehicle. But we learned the value of being able to freeze the part at some point so we can test a complete vehicle and learn as much as possible at that point.

Lund immediately communicated the four root cause problems he observed, along with countermeasures, to other program managers across the company who had not yet reached the prototype stage on their projects. One benefit of having a regular and short product-development cycle is that when you learn something, there are several vehicles coming right behind it, so you have an opportunity to apply immediately what you learned to improve the process and product.

Process vs. Results Orientation: The Role of Metrics

Believing they can get any behavior they can measure, companies wishing to emulate Toyota's system often ask me about its metrics. To their inevitable disappointment, they learn that Toyota is not particularly strong at developing sophisticated and common metrics across the company. Toyota measures processes everywhere on the factory floor, but prefers simple metrics and does not use many of them at the company or plant level.

There are at least three types of measures at Toyota:

1. *Global performance measures—how is the company doing?* At this level, Toyota uses financial, quality, and safety measures very similar to those used by other companies. When I queried whether the listing of Toyota Motor Company on the N.Y. Stock Exchange made them more short-term-focused, they assured me that was not the case. They did say that now they must report financial results quarterly, when in the past they used to report annually. They found the quarterly reporting very useful. Prior to this, they were arguably less sophisticated in financial measurement than other companies listed on the stock exchange.
2. *Operational performance measures—how is the plant or department doing?* Toyota's measurements seem to be timelier and better maintained than what I have seen at other companies. The people doing the work at the work group level or the project manager's level painstakingly track progress on key metrics and compare them with aggressive targets. The metrics tend to be specific to a process.
3. *Stretch improvement metrics—how is the business unit or work group doing?* Toyota sets stretch goals for the corporation, which are translated into stretch goals for every business unit and ultimately every work group. Tracking progress toward these goals is central to Toyota's learning process.

Again, Toyota does the tracking at the work group and project level. The measures are very particular to what the teams are trying to accomplish.

I recall talking to Wayne Ripberger, who at the time was the VP of Powertrain manufacturing for Toyota in Georgetown. I asked what they measure at the plant level to track its performance. I was expecting insights into the golden metrics that drive any manufacturing plant. He said they track total cost for plant operations, a few simple quality measures like parts per million defects, and productivity. They of course keep track of safety by measuring accidents and do some employee morale surveys. There was nothing new here, except for one thing. Ripberger explained that the one measure he found most useful as a manager was the number of *andon* pulls made by each department, to stop the production line. The departments regularly graph the data, noting the problems that caused each of the *andon* pulls, and use Pareto analysis to identify the most common reasons. Then they go to work on countermeasures. Obviously you must have a well functioning andon system before this metric makes any sense. But when in place, this metric provides great insight into the actual day-to-day problems faced in the production process.

The difference between Toyota and many other companies is that Toyota is process oriented. In one study I worked on with Tom Choi[1], we tried to understand why some companies had vital continuous improvement programs while others had superficial programs that died before they got going. We discovered the top management in the companies with vital programs had a *process orientation*, while the unsuccessful companies had *results-oriented* managers. The results-oriented managers immediately wanted to measure the bottom-line results of the continuous improvement program. The process-oriented managers were more patient, believing that an investment in the people and the process would lead to the results they desired.

In short, developing standard, global metrics is not a high priority at Toyota. They do it as simply as possible. More important to them are the metrics driving problem solving and supporting their process orientation. The most important learning measurements track progress toward stretch improvement goals, which is the process called *hoshin kanri*.

Hoshin Kanri—Directing and Motivating Organizational Learning

The adage that "you get what you measure" is in a sense true at Toyota as well. Toyota long ago realized that the key to organizational learning is to align objectives of all of its employees toward common goals. The underlying value system of Toyota's culture does that to a great degree. But to get everyone involved in continuous improvement in a way that adds up to huge corporate improvements requires aligned goals and objectives and constant measurement of progress toward those objectives. The important insight here is that simply setting specific, measurable, challenging goals and then measuring progress is highly motivating—even when there is no tangible reward associated with success. It's approached like a game or sport. Playing tennis or even solitaire is simply not as much fun if you are not keeping score.

Toyota managers have become masterful at setting challenging goals jointly with their subordinates and are passionate about measurement and feedback. This is the basis for *hoshin kanri* (also discussed in the Trim Masters case example, Chapter 17). *Hoshin kanri*, sometimes called "policy deployment," is Toyota's process of cascading objectives from the top of the company down to the work group level. Aggressive goals start at the executive level and then each level in turn develops measurable objectives for the year, designed to support the executive-level goals. At Toyota, these objectives must be measurable and very concrete. Vague goal statements are not acceptable. Figure 20-4 shows how the process cascades down throughout the organization and follows the PDCA process.

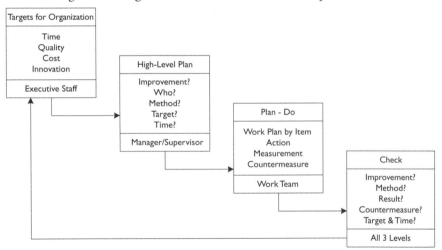

Figure 20-4. Policy deployment process (*hoshin kanri*)

For instance, all of Toyota's service parts facilities use *hoshin kanri* to develop three-year stretch goals to support the goals of Jim Press, COO of Toyota Motor Sales, who is ultimately supporting the objectives of Toyota's CEO. At the Hebron, Kentucky, facility, when you walk into the lobby, one of the first things you see on the wall is a big matrix that shows all of the target metrics for the facility for this three-year period. For the three-year period ending 2003, the baseline measures were taken in 2000 and targets are expressed as percent improvements over the baseline. You can see the annual targets through 2003 as well as monthly targets and actual achievements. The targets are all aggressive stretch objectives like the following:

- Reduce packaging costs as a percent of sales by 47%.
- Reduce transportation costs as a percent of sales by 25%.
- Reduce inventory by 50%.
- Reduce parts per million defects by 75%.
- Reduce OSHA recordable incidents per 200K hours by 50%.

At the bottom of the chart, you can see at a glance how the facility is doing on each metric. Red is less than 50% achieved, yellow is 50%-89% achieved, and green is over 90% achieved. The matrix I saw was as of June 2002, about halfway into the process, and they had achieved many of the three-year targets ahead of schedule. I also met with a group leader who showed me his objectives and measures for the day, which included detailed measures to support the overall facility-level objects that a computer program tracked. Unlike many companies I visit, where the posted performance metrics are months out of date, everything the group leader showed me was updated daily.

The policy deployment measures and actions become more specific as you move down the hierarchy from senior executives to working level team members, while progress reports flow upward from the lower levels to the senior executives. Every team member knows his or her small number of specific objectives for the year and is working on them throughout the year. The process of *hourensou* we discussed in Chapter 18 is one way senior managers are updated. They go to the source and talk to the workers as well. There are also formal review sessions. At the Toyota Technical Center, each team member has meetings three times per year to review progress toward the *hoshin kanri* objectives. The check and act part of PDCA are critical to turn the planned goals into effective action.

Creating a Learning Organization Is a Long-Term Journey

Anyone who has participated in creating a learning organization knows that it is a major undertaking. It has taken Toyota well over a decade to build an organization in North America that bears even a resemblance to the learning enterprise it built over several decades in Japan. Moving people from firefighting and short-term fixes to long-term improvements by adapting Toyota Way Principle 14: *Become a learning organization through relentless reflection (*hansei*) and continuous improvement (*kaizen*)* is an ongoing process at Toyota.

Even the Toyota Production System itself embodies the learning cycle of Plan-Do-Check-Act (PDCA). (See Figure 20-5.) You can see how the cycle relates to creating one-piece flow, surfacing problems, creating countermeasures, and evaluating results. An effective learning organization will then check to be sure the countermeasure is doing its job and then reduce inventory to create even more flow, which will surface new problems.

PDCA usually applies to fairly detailed work processes, but Figure 20-6 suggests that a learning enterprise is continually using PDCA at all levels of the company, from the project, to the group, to the company, and ultimately across companies.

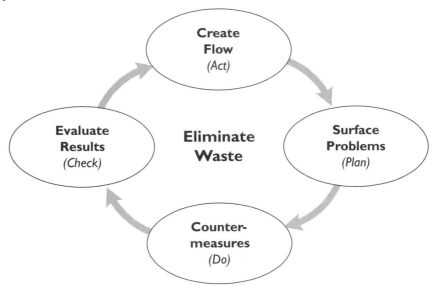

Figure 20-5. Creating flow and PDCA

Transforming a company into a learning enterprise is a daunting task. It has taken Toyota most of a century to get to where it is today. After reading in this chapter how Toyota doesn't have a golden set of metrics, uses *hansei*—a culturally foreign method for self-reflection, and depends on the straightforward tools of five-why, PDCA, and policy deployment, you must be scratching your head as to how you could emulate their success at all. The final part of this book addresses this complex issue of learning from the Toyota Way. Read on if you are thick-skinned.

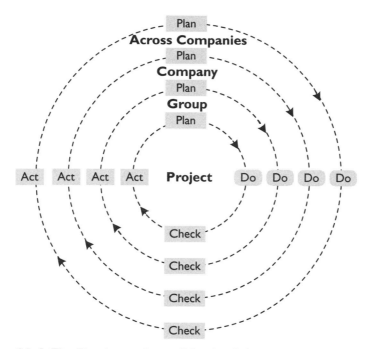

Figure 20-6. The Deming cycle at all levels of the enterprise

Note

1. Thomas Y. Choi and Jeffrey K. Liker, "Bringing Japanese Continuous Improvement Approaches to U.S. Manufacturing: The Roles of Process Orientation and Communications," *Decision Sciences*, Vol. 26, No. 5, September-October 1995.

Part Three

Applying the Toyota Way in Your Organization

Chapter 21

Using the Toyota Way to Transform Technical and Service Organizations

Applying the Toyota Production System outside the shop floor can be done, but this takes some creativity. Certainly, the basic principles can be applied to administrative processes. We sent some associates from our kaizen promotion office to dealers to help them. They have been able to reduce the time it takes to inspect the vehicle and do routine repairs, like changing parts or changing oil, in some cases from 60 minutes to 10 minutes. This is very good for us and makes our customers very happy. There are many more opportunities that we need to work on using our creativity.

—Fujio Cho, president of Toyota Motor Corporation

Manufacturing companies throughout the world have applied the Toyota Production System on the shop floor to varying degrees, and interest in TPS or "lean manufacturing" continues to grow. As companies experience extraordinary improvements on the shop floor, it is natural to ask how this can apply to technical and service operations. Many service companies that initially look at Toyota are attracted most by the technical TPS principles of flow and how they can apply it to a highly variable and often chaotic process. You can sum up the prospect of applying lean in-service operations by the reactions of three categories of people:

1. *Lean zealots.* Manufacturing companies that have implemented lean with any degree of success have experienced people who led the transformation. These people invariably become lean zealots who eat, breathe, and sleep lean. Understanding the power of the lean philosophy through actual experience, they naturally look at the enormous waste in administering techni-

cal and service operations in their companies and want to go at it like kids in a candy store.

2. *Executive decision makers.* Rarely do executive decision makers have a very deep understanding of TPS or appreciate the power of the process or the philosophy. But they love the results. So if TPS works so well in manufacturing, why not try it in engineering, purchasing, accounting, and so on? Even executives of service industries like hospitals have heard of the benefits of lean in manufacturing and want to know if they too can get in on the benefits. Often this means an assignment delegated down to a less than enthusiastic manager to check it out.

3. *Ordinary people.* Managers, supervisors, or ordinary workers in technical and service organizations are so immersed in doing their jobs it is difficult for them to see the flow in their work. To them, what goes on in the repetitive work in factories is as different from their lives as night is from day. The idea that you can apply some management fad about lean "flow" to their daily work seems ludicrous at best.

Unfortunately, for the first and second categories of people who are enthusiastic about applying lean concepts, there are no ready-made models of success in lean technical or service organizations to push the idea past resisters and the natural organization inertia. Cho admits that Toyota has a lot more opportunity to implement TPS principles beyond its manufacturing and is working on it. But there are already many examples inside of Toyota of Toyota Way principles spread well beyond manufacturing. For example, we have discussed throughout the book how Toyota has continually refined its product development process to become the industry's best in lead time. Toyota has figured out how to view product development as a repeatable process that it can continuously improve. Recognizing that any process is repetitive at some level is the starting point.

In this chapter I will address only *one* of the four layers in the Toyota Way 4P model—the Process layer, which focuses on the technical principles of the TPS. The final chapter will address how manufacturing *and* service organizations can learn from the broader set of Toyota Way principles.

The Problem of Identifying Flow in Service Organizations

In technical and service organizations, people are sitting at desks, working at computers, walking about, sitting around conference rooms, and generally busy moving from task to task. It is very difficult to understand the workflow in the same way you can map a physical product as it is being transformed. In service organizations, the work is often organized around projects that vary widely in size, complexity, number of people involved, and lead time. But if you start with the customer, define value, and then map the process that adds value to the customer, identifying workflow can be more manageable.

My associates and I have done over one hundred *kaizen* events on technical and business processes and it is always eye-opening for the teams how much waste is uncovered once they start mapping the value stream. Another eye-opener is the discovery that the bulk of these processes are fairly repetitive and standardizing them is possible.

Figure 21-1 illustrates a hypothetical account verification value stream. Waste in this case is mostly information waiting in queues for someone to act on it. People are working on their own timelines and there is no coordination among processes. This causes batches of stuff to build up before being shipped to the next process, where they may sit and wait. Often this is information inventory, rather than physical inventory, so it is more difficult to determine the amount. The key importance of physical inventory is how it causes a delay in the process, not the amount of physical inventory itself. And so it is for information inventory—when information is produced before it is used and builds up waiting, the main issue is time delays, just as with physical inventory.

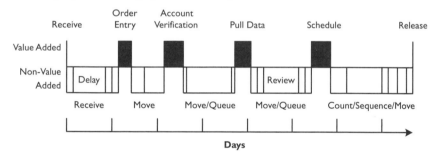

Figure 21-1. A non-lean flow in an account verification process

The ideal of TPS is one-piece flow. However, as we have seen earlier in the book, the benefits of flow really come from tightly linking processes to bring problems to the surface, as shown in Figure 21-2. When you link processes in a flow, problems cannot hide in inventory or in queues waiting to be processed. When one department immediately gets the information it needs just in time from a supporting department, two things happen:

1. If the supporting department gets behind, it will shut down the receiving department and will get immediate attention.
2. There will be rapid feedback from the receiving department if there is a problem with the information provided by the supporting department.

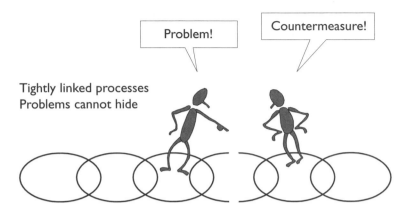

Figure 21-2. TPS flow environment
Source: Glenn Uminger, Toyota Motor Manufacturing, North America

Thus, problems will surface immediately, which will lead to the problem-solving process and organizational learning discussed in Chapter 20. Creating lean flow is the technical backbone of TPS in both service and manufacturing organizations.

There are five steps to creating flow in technical and service organizations:

1. Identify who the customer is for the processes and the added value they want delivered.
2. Separate out the repetitive processes from the unique, one-of-a-kind processes and learn how you can apply TPS to the repetitive processes.
3. Map the flow to determine value added and non-value added.
4. Think creatively about applying the broad principles of the Toyota Way to these processes using a future-state value stream map.
5. Start doing it and learn by doing using a PDCA cycle and then expand it to the less repetitive processes.

Canada Post Corporation: Lean in Repetitive Service Operations

Canada Post Corporation (CPC) is the equivalent of the U.S. Postal Service. It has a commercial mandate and leaders at this government-owned corporation operate with the same corporate governance as a private company. The profits are reinvested in the company to secure its ability to grow or are turned over to the Canadian government in the form of a dividend.

CPC has about 57,000 employees with 22 main sorting plants. Customers can access their services at 900,000 points in Canada—more points than all Canadian bank branches combined. They deliver to over 13 million delivery addresses domestically. Their revenues are approximately $6 billion Canadian. In the mid-1990s, CPC began applying lean methods to its sorting and delivery operations. The sorting operations are the central nervous system of the whole process. Mail comes in from all over Canada and abroad, it is sorted, it goes on trucks and airplanes, and it is distributed all over the world.

Before the lean effort started in 1995, the situation was dreadful. The sorting facilities were more like warehouses. The focus in these facilities was on automation and faster sorting equipment. Yet most of the waste was between these value-adding processes and was being ignored. Steve Withers, an executive within Canada Post, held the unusual title of Senior Advisor of Lean. He described the situation as follows:

We had a complete batch mentality in how we laid out our plants. In many cases, we were using equipment that could not be started up until we had a large enough batch. Mail went like lightning through sorting machines—then it was moved and stored; there was very little flow. The engineering philosophy was bigger, faster, and more expensive equipment in plants, which led to incredible point velocities (and more wasteful movement and storage). We had elaborate forecasting and inventory control systems, with people wandering the plant floor to expedite the flow. We color-coded everything to prioritize what to process next. But visibility was terrible and mail was often stored in overhead buffer systems that employees couldn't see. We had huge sorting facilities—much bigger than needed, populated with fast sorting machines and inventory everywhere. Some plants had thousands of pieces of material-handling equipment. This led to large travel distances, poor quality, and long lead times, but quick sorting.

As it was, CPC ended up going through three stages in its lean transformation. The first was "point *kaizen,*" trying things here and there at various points in the value stream. The second was a big-picture value stream focus that systematically analyzed the value stream and implemented changes. By 2003 they were starting their journey into the third phase—building a lean enterprise.

In the first phase, applying TPS methods was a process of trial and error—do a project here, apply this tool there—but even then CPC made huge, impressive gains with lean methods. At its Ottawa sorting facility, CPC mapped the current state of the value stream for the facility on a wall, showing how letters, advertisements, and parcels went all over the place in the facility. They discovered that from the moment an incoming letter entered the facility to when it left the facility it traveled 167 meters, was stored and removed eight times, took 26 hours of total lead time to process, and the value-added time of sorting (actual work) was only 12 seconds. In short, according to Withers: "Mail was sorted in *seconds*, transported in *minutes*, staged in *hours*, and delivered in *days*. The plant was a warehouse."

As a result, in 1997 the Ottawa facility removed inventory and moved some operations to arrange the equipment in more of a continuous process flow. This was in a three-story facility and they were able to free up enough space to empty out a whole floor of the building. This allowed them to move several letter carrier depots into that space and sell buildings or get out of leases, saving millions of dollars. Among the results:

- 28% reduction in travel time for the mail
- 37% reduction in lead time
- 27% reduction in storage (staging)

Here is another example. In 1996 each area in CPC's Hamilton mail-sorting facility was a stand-alone work center and supervisors concentrated on completing the tasks in their own areas. The Hamilton facility was operating 24 hours a day, seven days a week, and still not meeting the commitment to postal customers. Finally, out of necessity, a team was formed to fix the process and in 1997 the plant brought in an external lean consultant.

The first objective was to improve the flow from one process to the next. The facility created a continuous-flow cell for processing one type of package, pulling pieces of equipment out of departments and putting them into a flow. It reassigned supervisors from process islands to flow cells. The operation was paced in 15-minute intervals (similar to the Toyota service parts operations, chapter 13). The result was a huge improvement in flow, but the floor layout still led to excessive material movement. In 1998, the major focus was changing the layout to streamline the material movement within cells. In 1999, the facility expanded the cells to include a large sorting process that was still done in large batch sizes because equipment changeover required 30-40 minutes. A project was done to minimize the changeover activity. By reducing the changeover time to *zero*, the run batch sizes and the transfer batch sizes were reduced to a fraction of the previous sizes. This allowed much less inventory and thus reduced lead times. In 2000, the focus was on refinement and stabilizing the operation.

Under the unwavering leadership of the Hamilton plant director, Mike Young, there were continuing flow improvements in 2001. But the major emphasis was on the "rate and repair" process. The rate is when people fail to pay postage, so the item has to be rated for the amount of postage due. The repair process deals with items damaged during processing. There was a specialty department that did rating and repair under a batch process. Jim Womack, during a visit, once referred to it as the "parcel hospital." Items from all three shifts were taken to the "hospital" on the second shift, where three operators did the rating and repair. Items damaged on an off-shift could wait 16 hours to be worked on. Often work was done during weekends. The solution to this problem included creating a mobile rate-and-repair station and staffing each shift with a flexible-sized rate-and-repair team. The result was a space savings and higher customer satisfaction because of shortened lead times. (Note that previous work done on improving flow also meant that there was far less damage—resulting in substantially reduced repair work.)

A transformation of this magnitude even in one facility is not an overnight process and requires a continual cycle of improvement and stabilization. It also requires focused leadership all the way from the top, which CPC had. As a result, today the lean enterprise has become the operating philosophy of CPC and, as it continues to apply it to all its facilities, the benefits are profound. For the past eight consecutive years since starting on the lean journey, Canada Post Corporation has turned a significant profit, far exceeding the profits before lean. In total, it has returned almost $300 million Canadian to the Canadian government in the last five years, and customers are getting their mail faster.

Developing and Implementing Value Stream Maps Through *Kaizen* Workshops

Obviously, CPC is not a pure technical or service organization and has some similarities to a manufacturing process. So where can you find an example of TPS being successfully applied to less repetitive technical or service organizations? The answer is that examples will be hard to find.

You could spend your time looking for such an example or you could follow the Toyota Way of analyzing your own situation, developing innovative solutions, and applying lean in your own way. As Cho's quote in Chapter 1 says, "We place the highest value on actual implementation and taking action." The first action to take on the road to improvement of any complex service operation is to create a macro value stream map of the entire system.

A proven method used in lean manufacturing is *value stream mapping*, which was adapted by Mike Rother and John Shook (1999) from Toyota's material and information flow diagrams. The value stream map captures processes, material flows, and information flows of a given product family and helps to identify waste in the system. Value stream mapping evolved from a tool Toyota now calls the "material and information flow diagram" that Taiichi Ohno's operation management consulting division used in helping manufacturing suppliers learn TPS. It was the best place to start for suppliers to understand their current situation so they could then map a future state vision that included *kanban*, production leveling, changeover times, etc. Processes are represented as boxes. Arrows connect the boxes. In the original version, tombstones (for dead material) represent inventory between processes. Overall, lead time is represented and broken into value-added time and non-value-added time.

Even though there are no physical transformations for many service and business operations, one can easily modify this methodology by making more of an "information flow diagram." Morgan (2002) developed a version that effectively maps product development value streams (see Figure 21-3). The mapping was modified to capture such critical things as decision points, feedback loops, and project review events (*hansei* events). The events are placed on a project timeline, showing when events take place. Since different organizational functions come into play at different times, the processes are arranged by the function responsible for them, for example "body engineering" and "die-processing" in the diagram. Like value stream mapping for manufacturing, boxes represent processes and triangles represent inventory. Inventory in this case is information waiting to be processed. The hours of queue times are shown in boxes beneath the "inventory" triangles between processes. The processes have some key indicators like the task time (TT), time in system (TIS), and the value ratio of value added to total lead time (VR). Many wastes are represented on the value stream map. In addition to the queue times, we see engineering changes (e/c), rework, and time resolving various issues that result from not doing things right the first time. The cross-hatched arrows connecting processes depict that everything is "pushed" onto the next process in batches.

Service processes are often complex and involve hundreds or thousands of activities. If you try to map everything all at once, it leads to a mess. However, by developing a big-picture, macro value stream map of the current system, you bring everyone together to agree on all the waste in the processes. A macro-future state map can then identify the big picture version and help identify where the biggest opportunities are for reducing waste in the value stream. From this you can identify the most obvious five to 10 high-level phases to work on in great detail to begin to eliminate waste. For example, a shipbuilder created a macro value stream map for the detail design phase for a class of ships. While the overall process seemed too overwhelming to improve, it identified seven subprocesses that were relatively repetitive and therefore perfect candidates for improvement, such as performing engineering analysis. Once you have identified repetitive and manageable processes, an organization is ready to get the maximum return from any *kaizen* effort. It is here that you can get your team's hands dirty improving processes on a more detailed level.

The more detailed subprocesses can then be worked on in a project format and using *kaizen* workshops to blitz activity in short periods of time. The *kaizen* workshop is one key tool for change in any service organization. I describe here a format that my associates and I have successfully used many times to illustrate the issues and what you can accomplish. The workshops are typically one-week events where participants analyze the current process, develop a lean vision for the process, and, most importantly, begin implementation.[1]

Participants in the event must include the manager responsible for the process being improved ("process owner"), who is the team leader of the event, along with the people who actually do the work within the process. It is also advisable to

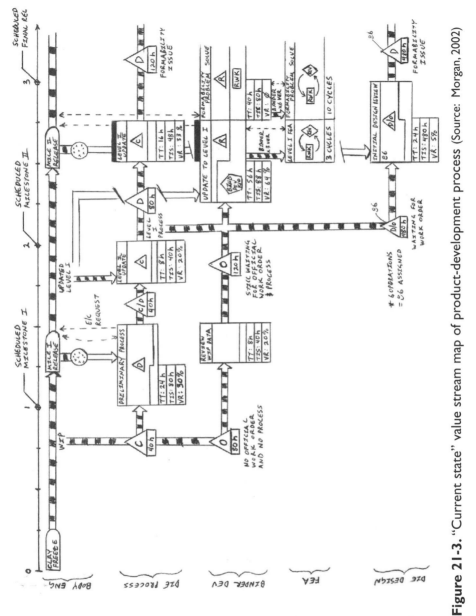

Figure 21-3. "Current state" value stream map of product-development process (Source: Morgan, 2002)

include customers and suppliers of the process in the event. However, whenever possible, you should limit the team size to no more than 15 people, to keep the workshop discussions and implementation manageable. There are three phases to a *kaizen* workshop: preparation, the actual workshop, and sustaining and continuous improvement after a workshop. We will discuss each of these.

Phase One: Preparation for the Workshop

There are five essential pre-workshop things to do to facilitate the flow of the workshop and effectively use participants' time.

1. *Clearly define the scope.* Determine the start point or trigger that begins the process and what the final deliverable product(s) to the customer is.
2. *Set objectives.* The process owner must set measurable objectives for the team to achieve. The goals must clearly align with the overall corporate objectives. At the very least, specific goals should be set to reduce lead time, improve quality, and reduce cost. The targets should be aggressive, to ensure that participants are challenged to come up with innovative process changes versus simply tweaking the existing process.
3. *Create preliminary current state map.* Have a subgroup of three or four participants walk through the current process prior to the event to document the steps of the process, the time it takes to perform the task (task times), and wait times between processes. If there isn't available data for some processes, this allows time to collect it prior to the workshop. This is the most important part of the pre-work activities, as it saves valuable workshop time over starting with a blank sheet.
4. *Collect all relevant documents.* While creating the preliminary current state map, the subgroup should collect samples of forms and documents used at each step. In addition, copies of all standard procedures affected by the process should also be available for the workshop.
5. *Post a preliminary current state map in the team room.* Each task in the process is listed on its own separate sheet (8.5"x 11" preferred) of paper and posted on butcher-block paper on a wall. Some teams list the tasks on large Post-its®. Space is left among task boxes to allow for notes and modifications during the workshop.

Now you are ready for the actual workshop.

Phase Two: The *Kaizen* Workshop

The session begins with a review of the scope of the process to be improved and a review of the objectives with the team. Some training is provided on basic lean concepts, particularly the concept of value added and non-value added. Figure 21-4 shows the flow of a typical service *kaizen* workshop.

Step 1. *Who is the customer?* The first step in any improvement process is to have the team identify the customer's needs and the processes that support or add value to deliver on that need. Only then can the team clearly define value and assist in noting which tasks in the process are truly value added.

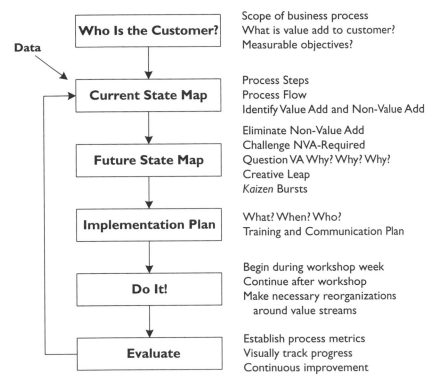

Figure 21-4. Flow of "above shop floor" *kaizen* workshop

This process can be more complex than you might think. I helped lead one workshop involving an entire accounting department. They had identified a number of subprocesses, such as accounts payable, accounts receivable, employee expense reimbursement, etc. In the case of employee expense reimbursement, who was the customer? Was it the employee who wanted to be reimbursed? Was it the organization that wanted a controlled procedure to prevent fraud? Was it the Internal Revenue Service, which has standards for appropriate documentation for travel expenses? As it turned out, all three were customers and we then had to consider their collective *value* systems.

Step 2. *Analyze current state.* Participants physically walk through the process (whenever possible) for purposes of *genchi genbutsu.* During the walk, participants should discuss the process with the employees to obtain insights on how the process works, to surface issues, and to solicit ideas for improvement. The walk-through also gives participants a better sense of the travel distances and the physical stop points in the flow of the product. Following the walk, the team can then begin a detailed analysis of the preliminary current state map. Based on the data collected on the walk-through and the knowledge of the team, the processing steps are modified and/or added as required. In addition, the team validates all data, which includes task times, wait times, quality levels, etc. The final and most important part of this step is to identify what is value added. Again, this can be quite complex and even controversial. For this step it is critical to use the *three* Toyota categories:

- *Value Added. What is the actual transformation process core to the service that the customer is paying for?* This could be an information transformation, like engineering or accounting. Or it could be a transformation in the customer, e.g., hair styling, surgery, educating the customer.
- *Non-Value Added. What is pure waste?* For example, all wait times are non-value added, as are walk times, rework, and unused information.
- *Non-Value Added, but Required.* Ohno called this "non-value added work" or, sometimes, incidental work. The question to ask is "What is required under today's conditions even though it does not add value from the customer's perspective?" This can include inspections, control systems to check that procedures are being followed, documentation, etc.

Using the required non-value added category can help avoid divisions and a conflicted workshop. Nobody wants to consider what they do non-value added. In the accounting example mentioned above, the whole department can be considered non-value added from the perspective of the customers of the Society of Automotive Engineers (SAE). People who pay for a professional society's services do not think they are buying its internal accounting services. Yet accounting serves a critical function to any business. If the business goes out of business because of poor accounting, it cannot serve customers at all.

So what is the value add? It always comes back to how you define the customer. Take the process of employee reimbursement. The employee is a customer and wants to be paid fast with minimum hassle. If SAE as a business entity is a customer of internal accounting, then the policies, controls, and monitoring put in place add value from SAE's perspective, even though employees would rather they all go away. If the IRS is a customer of SAE, then following any IRS-imposed rules and forms is part of the value added of accounting. In the employee reimbursement case, the group decided the employees being reimbursed for expenses were the first customers and SAE as a business is the second customer. The IRS is not really a customer, but filling out IRS forms is a *required* non-value added. Because of the complexities and challenges in determining who the customer is, it is important that people do not prematurely jump to solutions to problems during the current state analysis. You can capture any ideas for improvement on a flip chart for the future state discussion.

When analyzing the current state, you are typically following a given product through a process (e.g., a drawing, a bill, a purchase order). However, all service processes deal with varying volumes of transactions. Consequently, it is important to capture the *number of transactions per period* and the *variety of products* that flow through the process. This will help shed light on why there are delay points in the process and assist in locating the bottlenecks. Once the team has completed documenting the current state, the next step is to calculate the summary metrics of the business process. These are some common measures calculated at this stage:

- Lead time: total time the product stays in the system
- Value-added ratio: sum of value-added time divided by lead time
- Travel distance of the product
- Travel distance of people doing the work
- Productivity: people hours per transaction
- Number of handoffs
- Quality rate: percent of products that go through the process the first time with no defects

After the team calculates the metrics, it revisits the objectives that were determined in the preliminary stage to see if they are still plausible and whether they should add objectives. At this point, the team is ready to work on developing a lean future state.

Step 3. *Develop future state vision.* Before diving into changing the current process or sketching out a new process, it is vital to draw out all ideas for improvement from the participants. A great way to achieve this is to use group brainstorming and have participants write their ideas on sticky notes. The facilitator collects the ideas, reads them aloud, and posts them on the relevant area of the current state map. After team members post their ideas, the team evaluates each idea to see if it will help toward achieving one or more of the stated objectives. Some ideas that surface may be outside the scope of the workshop but may have merit. The team captures these ideas on a "parking lot" and forwards them to the appropriate process owners. Some of these ideas may need to be explored in another *kaizen* workshop. The team captures all ideas pertinent to creating the future state vision on a list and moves to the next stage of drawing the future state map of the process, incorporating lean principles. The role of the lean facilitator at this point is to challenge participants to create a future state vision that eliminates waste, improves first-time quality, and optimizes the flow through the entire process and to lay out the new flow of tasks. Afterwards, task times and wait times are calculated (or estimated) for the new tasks. The major lean concepts that should be a part of the future state vision include the following:

- Create one-piece flow. As much as possible, have information move through the system seamlessly rather than in batches.
- Arrange work centers (e.g., organizational structures) to align with value streams to support customers in a one-piece flow.

- Use cross-functional teams, co-located if possible, when needed to avoid handoffs.
- Identify a value stream or case manager who is responsible for the service from start to finish from the customer's perspective, like the chief engineer in Toyota's product development system.
- Level (load level) the number of transactions whenever possible to balance workloads.
- Build in quality in the process rather than inspect it (e.g., eliminate unnecessary approvals, checking, review cycles).
- Standardize the tasks and clearly document work on standardized worksheets.
- Eliminate redundant systems, such as reconciliation across different people.
- Include visual displays and controls to make work status easy to see and understand (minimize tracking).

Once the team completes the future state map, the new process metrics are calculated and compared with the current state metrics to quantify the expected savings. At this stage, the future state vision is presented to senior management and the owners of other affected processes for immediate approval. Once all have agreed upon the future state vision, the team may proceed to the next step, implementation.

Step 4. *Implementation: do it!* The next phase of the above shop floor *kaizen* workshop is to start to make the future state vision a reality. The future state map is divided into segments and participants are broken into subgroups to work on each segment. A project plan is developed with what, when, and who. Implementation activities during the workshop can include:

- Re-layout of work areas to facilitate one-piece flow
- Workplace organization (5S and visual displays)
- Creation of standard work instructions
- Revision of corporate procedures
- Redesign forms and documents
- Problem-solving activities to uncover root causes of quality problems
- Specifications or even some changes for any information technology required to support the improved process
- Training people in the new process

Clearly, you may not complete some activities during a one-week *kaizen* workshop, such as creating a database or obtaining customer approval on changes in specifications. You capture these ongoing items in a project plan that will serve as the work plan for the sustaining team after the workshop. Each item in the plan should have a sustaining team member's name assigned to it and a firm completion date. The sustaining team typically consists of the workshop team leader and a subgroup of the participants whose skills are needed to complete the transition to the future state vision.

Step 5. *Evaluate: measuring performance.* The last phase of the *kaizen* workshop is to establish metrics that will track progress toward the future state and ensure that gains achieved during the workshop are indeed sustained over time. Most of the metrics should be the same as those captured in the *kaizen* workshop. The current state metrics provide the baseline and the future state metrics provide the targets. Then you need to implement a simple tracking system that ideally should be based on the metrics data collection currently in place. You should assign a person for each metric to collect and collate the information. Figure 21-5 provides a sample form for establishing metrics.

Metric	Unit of Measure	Baseline	Target	% Improved	Owner
Lead Time	Days				
Delivery	% on time				
Quality	# of deficiencies per project				
Productivity	Hours per project				

Figure 21-5. Sample process improvement metrics

You post the current and future value stream maps, process metrics, project plan, objectives, and other communications on a "lean status board" in the main work area to serve as the visual display to communicate to all employees the progress that is taking place. Data should be posted on the lean status board at least once a month (weekly is preferred). It is advisable to keep the number of metrics to a minimum. Remember that tracking metrics takes time away from people doing their work. It is also important at this stage to discuss the existing metrics and *immediately* eliminate ones that are superfluous or drive behaviors that are counter to the implementation of the lean future state vision.

Phase Three: After the Workshop—Sustaining and Continuous Improvement

Following the workshop, the sustaining team will continue to drive the future state. This is the check-act part of the Plan-Do-Check-Act (PDCA) cycle. The team meets on a weekly basis to do the following:

- Review the status of the open action items from the project plan.
- Review process metrics to ensure improvements are being achieved.
- Discuss additional opportunities for improvements.
- Continue to improve the process.

Senior management should do monthly reviews of the lean status board to evaluate metrics, open items on the project plan, and resolve any roadblocks to implementation. They should also provide recognition to the team as it achieves key milestones in implementation. This is part of the *hourensou* process discussed in Chapter 18.

A Northrop Grumman Ship Systems Service Process *Kaizen* Event[2]

Northrop Grumman Ship Systems Ingalls shipyard in Mississippi began aggressively implementing lean in its operations areas in the summer of 2000. Since engineering is critical to shipbuilding, it soon expanded its transformation to lean to include engineering processes.

The issue of label plates, the responsibility of engineering, had been a perennial problem in getting compartments of the ship approved by the Navy and the cost of achieving compliance. There are label plates all over the ship describing what things are and issuing warnings of various sorts. Label plates are a very visible aspect of a ship and must have the correct wording and be posted in the correct location. The perception in the yard was that it was "just a label plate," as most are easy to fabricate and install. However, a ship has 40,000 or more label plates, so management clearly saw that it was a significant process and important to its customer.

Based on the value stream map, the physical manufacturing processes for making the various types of label plates were relatively simple but the information flows required to make the label plates crossed several functions and took a relatively long time to reach the label plate department. Given that problems appeared to cross over functions and there was a potential to improve customer satisfaction while reducing costs, Ingalls management agreed to support a lean event to improve the label plate process led by lean consultant John Drogosz. The results of the *kaizen* workshop were:

- Lead time reduction of 54%
- Rework reduction of 80%
- Productivity improvement of 29%
- Standardized work/process for label plates

The team achieved these results by dividing into subgroups during the week to implement the necessary changes. These changes made during the workshop included:

- Incorporating label plate comments earlier onto system diagrams to eliminate rework downstream.
- Use of a single database to maintain consistent data throughout the construction and trials of the ship.
- Standardizing work for all tasks to minimize variation.
- Problem-solving sessions completed to find the root cause of rework.
- Mistake proofing and changes in standard work used to eliminate most of the rework.
- Engineering trials of some new materials to improve durability of plates.

At the end of the week, the team established metrics and posted a lean status board in its area to track the improvements. The process was audited four months after the *kaizen* workshop and the team was consistently meeting or beating the expected results. The team continued meeting regularly and morale greatly improved in the area. The stress level of people working on the process greatly diminished, since they rarely needed to make replacement plates and run to the ship to put them on as they so frequently had done in the past.

Visual Control of Engineering at Genie Industries

A central issue for many service processes is controlling the process. Some successful *kaizen* workshops have focused on creating the system of tracking and controlling the process using visual controls. Genie Industries is an example of this.

Genie makes many different kinds of lift devices, like the hoist device phone company service people use to work on telephone poles. Genie has aggressively implemented lean throughout its operations and credits lean with keeping it afloat in a down cycle in the industry in the late 1990s and then helping it grow to the number-one producer in this market segment. In this lean improvement period, Genie went from five or six inventory turns per year to 45 turns annually over a three-year period. Total cost has been going down at a rate of 5% per year.

Most of Genie's products are highly engineered, many of them to a specific customer order, so engineering can become the bottleneck in getting customers what they want when they want it. A key part of the improvement process in engineering was simply moving the front offices to the shop floor, where engineers and manufacturing team leaders sit together. The approach was to organize around value streams, get product engineers together with manufacturing, and use simple visual systems to manage the process.

The nerve center of engineering is now a conference room with visual displays on the wall. The two core processes visually represented in the room are engineering changes to existing products (e.g., to customize a product for a particular customer) and new product development. In the past, Genie ran both of these processes through computer schedules. However, it took too long, never met the schedule, and ended up generating 14 copies of each change order that circulated to a bunch of offices. Now they manage both processes through manual visual schedules posted where the team meets weekly to review progress.

For engineering change orders they use a large magnetic board. Magnetic strips identify the number and description for each live change order and serve as the title of a row for that change order. Time is measured across the rows, so you can see when the change order was initiated, when it is due to be complete, and if it is on time or late. A maximum of seven days is allotted to do the necessary research to determine what the change will involve and commit to a completion date. Part of the magnetic board has a "countdown" folder with slots for completion due dates out 1-7 days, 8-14 days, 15-23 days, and 24-30 days and a slot for those still in research mode waiting for a commitment date. The master version of the engineering change notice is kept in the appropriate slot and moves as time passes. There is also an engineering change-notice process flowchart showing the steps and responsibilities. Through this process, the time to incorporate change orders into the product was reduced from 120 days to 30 days or less.

They also use a visual system for new product development, which is essentially a large Gantt chart on the wall with sticky notes showing tasks. When a task is complete, a big X is put over the task. Each project takes about a year, and the chart covers much of the wall. There are some spreadsheets in the computer backing it up, but no complex, Web-enabled, collaborative product development system. What is on the wall is the main tool for managing the engineering projects. Since the lean effort, engineering costs have been driven down at a rate of 10% per year.

It's All About Supporting the Core Value Stream

I have illustrated throughout the book applications to service operations. Some of the specific, detailed tools of TPS may be harder to apply.

It would not make sense, for example, for a lawyer to sit at his or her desk waiting for a material handler to deliver a *kanban* asking for the next legal brief. However, most lawyers have many repetitive processes that can benefit from a value stream perspective. Analyze the process from the customer's perspective, draw a current state map showing the waste, define the future process flow in a future state map, develop an implementation plan along with roles and responsibilities, track progress visually, and focus on continuously improving the process. To be effective, it may be necessary to reorganize around value streams. These simple steps will take you a long way.

As I have stated since Chapter 1, the key to applying TPS in any environment is to focus on the value-added operations and work to eliminate waste. As you have learned in this chapter, this is a bit more challenging for a service operation, because defining the customers and understanding their needs can be tricky. But with extra effort, it can be done.

When Glenn Uminger, an accountant, was given the assignment to set up the first management accounting system for the Toyota plant in Georgetown, Kentucky, he was advised that he must first understand the Toyota Production System. He spent six months in Japan and in other U.S. plants learning by doing—actually working in manufacturing. It became evident to Uminger that he did not need to set up the same complex accounting system he had set up at a former company. He explained:

> *If the system I set up in the parts supplier I previously worked for was a 10 in complexity, the Toyota system I set up was a 3. It was simpler and far more efficient.*

The system was simpler because Uminger took the time to understand the manufacturing system, the *customer* for which he was a *supplier* of services. He needed to build an accounting system that supported the real needs of the actual manufacturing system that Toyota set up. Through *genchi genbutsu*, he developed a deep understanding of the Toyota Production System in action. He learned that Toyota's system is based on pull and has so little inventory that the complex inventory tracking systems his former company used were unnecessary. And the arduous and expensive task of taking physical inventory could be greatly streamlined. Toyota does physical inventory twice per year and uses the work teams to facilitate it. Tags are prepared for the work teams for inventory counting and the team leader does a count in 10 minutes at the end of the shift and writes the numbers on the tags. Someone from accounting collects the tags and enters them in the computer. That same evening the inventory count is completed. They spend a few hours twice a year and it is done!

Because of his experience of implementing the accounting system at the Toyota plant, Uminger had developed such a deep understanding of TPS that they put him in charge of creating a TPS office to do projects to improve operations in the plant and teach TPS. He then became the material logistics manager to apply TPS to the logistics network and became responsible for that network for all of North America.

The point is that it is impossible to define value in a service operation without first understanding its *core value stream*. Some service operations are the core value stream, as we saw in the case of the Canada Post Corporation. In a legal office, the lawyers are part of the core value stream. Once you define the core value stream, then all support service operations must view their roles as supporting the core value stream. The leaner the core value stream, the leaner the support operations can be. Generally, it is recommended to start by applying TPS to the core value stream and then branch out to the support functions.

In the final chapter, we will discuss how to learn the broader lessons of the

Toyota Way and apply them to your company. It is this broader philosophy—the way Toyota leads people and partners, solves problems, and learns—that is the most difficult for organizations to adapt, develop, and sustain.

Notes

1. This material is based on work I first did applying lean to business process-es in the Society of Automotive Engineers with my associate John Drogosz of Optiprise, Inc.
2. The label plate case is modified from an article by my associate John Drogosz, "Applying Lean Above the Factory Floor," *Journal of Ship Production*, Vol. 18, No. 3, August 2002.

Chapter 22

Build Your Own Lean Learning Enterprise, Borrowing from the Toyota Way

One man did his part, and the other his, and neither even had to check to make sure both parts were getting done. Like the dance of atoms Alvin had imagined in his mind. He never realized it before, but people could be like those atoms, too. Most of the time people were all disorganized, nobody knowing who anybody else was, nobody holding still long enough to trust or be trusted, just like Alvin imagined atoms might have been before God taught them who they were and gave them work to do.... It was a miracle seeing how smooth they knew each other's next move before the move was even begun. Alvin almost laughed out loud in the joy of seeing such a thing, knowing it was possible, dreaming of what it might mean—thousands of people knowing each other that well, moving to fit each other just right, working together. Who could stand in the way of such people?

—Orson Scott Card
Prentice Alvin: The Tales of Alvin Maker, Book Three

I n the series by renowned science fiction and fantasy writer Orson Scott Card, Alvin can see the tiniest bits of matter and detect when they are out of their natural pattern, e.g., bones broken or a fault in a piece of iron. He can see the correct pattern in his mind and make the matter reform itself back into the correct pattern, thus healing the bone or making the iron strong again. In the quote above, Alvin is learning how this works, through the ordering of atoms that otherwise aimlessly move about until somehow they learn a pattern—learn where they are supposed to stay in relation to other atoms. He observes two men who appear to be strangers, but then realizes that they fit together in a pattern because for years they had been secretly working together to free slaves. This breakthrough in his thinking leads him to realize that social bonds between people can be as powerful as physical bonds between atoms—creating a whole much greater and stronger than the sum of the individual parts.

The lesson and secret of the Toyota Way is just as clear as this: it creates bonds among individuals and partners such that they "move to fit together just right, working together" toward a common goal. It is in stark contrast to most companies, which are made up of individuals who are, in Alvin's words, "disorganized, nobody knowing who anybody else is, nobody holding still long enough to trust or be trusted." The question is how to get to there from here.

A Commitment from the Top to Build a Total Culture from the Ground Up

The toughest and most basic challenge for companies that want to learn from Toyota is *how to create an aligned organization of individuals who each have the DNA of the organization and are continually learning together to add value to the customer.*

Will Rogers, American social commentator, said, "We are a great people to get tired of anything awful quick. We just jump from one extreme to another." I am afraid that is what most companies are doing with lean manufacturing. It is just one more thing to jump into and one more thing to jump away from when the next fad comes along. If there is anything to learn from Toyota, it is the importance of developing a system and sticking with it and improving it. You cannot become a learning organization by jumping willy-nilly from fad to fad.

The Toyota Way model was intentionally built from the ground up, starting with a philosophy. And the philosophy starts with the chief executives of the organization. What should their goal be? To build an enterprise for the long term that delivers exceptional value to customers and society. And this requires long-term thinking and continuity of leadership. It may take decades to lay the foundation for radically transforming the organization's culture.

What do we know about changing a culture?

1. Start from the top—this may require an executive leadership shakeup.
2. Involve from the bottom up.
3. Use middle managers as change agents.
4. It takes time to develop people who really understand and live the philosophy.
5. On a scale of difficulty, it is "extremely" difficult.

What if the top does not understand and embrace the new philosophy? I asked Gary Convis, president of Toyota Motor Manufacturing, Kentucky, the following question: "If you were a middle manager or even a vice president passionate about implementing the Toyota Way in your company and the senior executives did not strongly support it, what would you do?" His answer was blunt:

I would be out looking for better pastures (laughter), because the company may not be around long enough for me to get my pension. Actually, that's a good question. Now, there could be a change in the top management. Maybe somebody up in the board recognizes that lean is not happening and needs to. Like General Motors did. ... I think the board said, "Wait a minute, we've been giving these guys rope and we've been giving them time and we don't see the direction." At some point in time they decided enough is enough. The new direction was set and new priorities were set and resources were established.

So a prerequisite to change is for top management to have an understanding and commitment to leveraging the Toyota Way to become a "lean learning organization." This understanding and commitment extends to building the lean systems and culture and, the most difficult for Western companies, sustaining and constantly improving the system. These are really two different skills, and even Toyota struggles with the balance, particularly in overseas operations.

This insight led me to develop the model shown in Figure 22-1, which illustrates the minimum level of leadership commitment needed to start on the lean journey—to learn from Toyota's model of a lean learning enterprise. Answer these three questions:

1. *Are top executives who run the company committed to a long-term vision of adding value to customers and society in general?* If the commitment is simply to short-term profitability, the answer is "No," so go directly to the short-term tools box (the equivalent of "go directly to jail" in the game Monopoly).
2. *Are top executives who run the company committed to developing and involving employees and partners?* This includes key suppliers. If people are viewed as expendable labor and suppliers are viewed as sources of cheap parts, the answer is "No," so go directly to the short-term tools box.
3. *Will there be continuity in top leadership's philosophy?* This does not mean the same people need to run the company forever, but they need to develop their successors with the company's DNA to continue the philosophy. If leaders turn over every time there is a crisis or if the company is bought out every decade with a new cast of characters installed as leaders, the answer is "No," so go directly to the short-term tools box.

As Figure 22-1 illustrates, if the answer is "No" to any of these three questions, top leaders should pick and choose from whatever tools are out there to improve processes for the short term, make a bundle of money, and go do something else. This is tantamount to admitting the company will never be a learning enterprise, or a great company, and is interested only in cutting and slashing waste to look

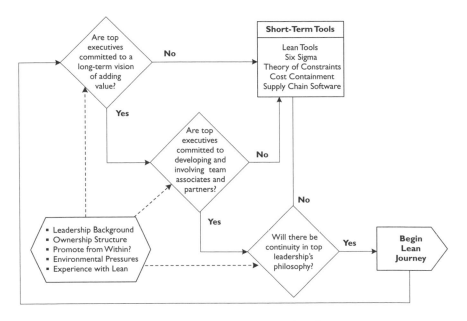

Figure 22-1. Top leadership's "commitment to lean" journey

good for the short term. But beware, because whatever tools are implemented, they deteriorate over time and the company will suffer in the long term. As Convis said, nobody's retirement income will be secure.

Note that there is a feedback loop from "begin lean journey" back to the original question of top leadership's commitment to a long-term vision that has to be continually challenged. Let's consider two examples that illustrate the importance of sustained leadership commitment. One was a great success but is now on the way to deteriorating because of a top leadership change and the second is a work in progress.

The Importance of Sustained Leadership Commitment: Two Examples

The first example is the Wiremold Corporation, which was showcased by Womack and Jones in *Lean Thinking* as a lean exemplar and more recently has been documented in detail by Emiliani et al. (2003) in *Better Thinking, Better Results*. Wiremold makes "cable-management solutions" that enclose various kinds of cables. This was a family-owned business, started in 1900 in Hartford, Connecticut, and the family made considerable investments in the early 1980s in Total Quality Management and various lean tools. They got positive results, but realized they were only scratching the surface.

So they hired Art Byrne as CEO, who had a great deal of success in leading lean transformations. Byrne was an exemplary leader in the spirit of the Toyota Way. For example, he taught TPS to employees directly and personally led *kaizen* events. He hired some experienced lean leaders to report to him and developed others. He enjoyed a great deal of autonomy in running the company. He started with the shop floor, beginning with simple local changes, and then moved to link together operations. Then he worked on the supporting infrastructure of information technology, accounting, purchasing, etc. He also acquired related companies and led lean conversions for those. Business was booming and the company was never more profitable.

Having accomplished so much, Byrne decided it was time to retire and, shortly after that, the family decided to cash in the greatly enhanced value of the company. In June 2000, Wiremold became part of the Legrand Group, a global company that did not understand lean manufacturing. Recognizing that the new focus was on short-term cost reduction and not on the lean enterprise, most of the lean leaders Byrne had developed left the company—years committed to learning and progress in building a lean enterprise stopped.

The second example is a work in progress. Merillat is a leader in the manufacture of household cabinets for kitchens and other uses. Merillat also had dabbled in Total Quality Management and lean methods and decided to get serious. In this case, the CEO realized the need for a first-rate lean leader with the autonomy to run operations. He hired Keith Allman, whose superior leadership skills had helped successfully transform a plant at Donnelly Mirror to the Donnelly Production System with outstanding results (Liker, 1998).

With the enthusiastic support of the CEO, Allman has systematically worked to transform Merillat into a lean enterprise and has made major strides in the manufacturing area as well as the support structures. Ask Allman what it will take to keep the lean journey going and he is very clear. "My role is to drive a system to develop people and promote from within. Leadership development is the key to sustaining a lasting system and culture that drives continuous improvement." Allman does not own the company, nor is he the CEO. This means that what he's accomplished is not guaranteed to last unless he develops a successor and the ownership remains stable and continues to support the lean direction. While Allman cannot control the ownership of the company, he can take the opportunity he has to develop a lean leader. He believes he needs to develop the lean successor from within the company.

Collin's best selling book on eleven "great" American *Fortune* 500 companies that had stock returns 6.9 times the general market over a fifteen year period found these companies had specific types of leaders (referred to as "level 5 leaders").[1] The CEOs were unusually ambitious, but for the company, not for themselves. They had an extraordinary will to make the company succeed, yet equally extraordinary personal humility. Personal aggrandizement or enrichment was not the goal. And they worked tirelessly to develop a successor who they set up for success. In short, they were a lot like Toyota's leaders.

Figure 22-1 shows a set of factors that will influence whether top executives are committed to the lean vision. These include:

1. *Ownership structure.* Obviously, who owns the company and how it is financed has a major influence on the ability of the company to focus on long-term objectives. Looking good to Wall Street for the quarter may conflict with long-term investments in excellence. Toyota clearly has a unique situation in being such a large company with a good deal of family control and a *keiretsu* structure of interlocking ownership among like-thinking organizations that grew up together. And being publically traded so far has not hampered Toyota's long-term perspective.

2. *Promote from within.* Develop future leaders from within or there is no chance of sustaining long term. When Toyota has brought in outside leaders, this has been only at the upper-middle-management level, such as general managers, with mixed success. But the culture is so strong and there are so many people with the Toyota Way DNA that any "outside" manager will be pressured to learn the Toyota Way or decide to leave.

3. *Environmental pressures.* Unfortunately, there are factors beyond the control of any lean leader that can make it difficult to sustain the lean learning enterprise. One is the market, which can take major downturns or the market for the particular product the company makes can deteriorate. Other factors are wars, radical new technologies, government policy changes, and on and on. Clearly, Toyota has survived and prospered in many different business and political environments and its strong culture and philosophy have helped it navigate through these treacherous environments.

4. *Experience with lean.* The leaders I mentioned above, Art Byrne and Keith Allman, along with many others too numerous to list here, have all had very positive experiences with real TPS. The best lean leaders in my experience worked for Toyota, for someone who worked for Toyota, or for a company that worked closely with Toyota—the common theme being direct exposure to the Toyota gene pool. Obviously, as more and more companies develop real lean systems, there are broader opportunities for learning lean thinking outside Toyota and its affiliates.

So what can you do if you are not the CEO and top management is interested only in short-term financial results? There are three things I know of:

1. Find greener pastures, as Convis suggests.

2. Participate in playing the game of applying tools for short-term gains and hope you share in the gains.
3. Work to build a successful lean model and educate top management by blowing them away with exceptional results.

The third alternative is frankly going to be the most common position of those with a passion for lean. Allman and Byrne were fortunate in coming in with experience, having strong support from the leaders and owners of the firm, and being able to bring in other passionate lean leaders one or more levels below them. Even then, they did not have complete control over the company. If they had not succeeded in impacting the bottom line, they would have lost their support in a hurry.

In both these cases—Wiremold and Merillat—lean leaders had unique opportunities to come in and seriously transform the company with the backing of the very top executives. They were successful as far as they got and produced stunning results. Merillat is a work in progress and we do not know where it will be in 10 years. The Wiremold story took a sad turn when the company was bought by a company that did not understand or support lean. It suffered a serious setback. On the other hand, the lean systems are still there and many people have adopted them as standard operating procedures. Some remnants will remain should the new owners realize the company's vitality was because of the lean philosophy and choose to rebuild what they allowed to degrade.

Sadly, few top executives today have the requisite understanding of lean thinking that you truly need from the outset to support a learning enterprise. The majority of companies will require a more radical makeover by new top leaders who know how to leverage the Toyota Way. Until then, the "true believers" of lean will simply have to do their best by creating, step by step, lean models that executives can learn from. But no matter what the approach, it will take time for new leaders to understand lean and for the old system and culture to evolve beyond the batch-and-queue wasteland of the past. Even within Toyota, Convis noted:

> The Toyota Way and the culture—I think it takes at least 10 years to really become in tune with what is going on and be able to manage in a way that we would like to sustain. I don't know as you can come into Toyota and in three or four years have it in your heart and your spirit with a deep understanding.

Six Sigma, Lean Tools, and Lean Sigma: Just a Bunch of Tools?

There are many "tools" approaches to organization improvement. One very popular program, which General Electric adopted with great success, is Six Sigma, an extension of Total Quality Management (TQM). Six Sigma refers to a goal of 3.4 defects per million units produced,[2] and the focus is on training green belts, black belts, and master black belts. The training includes classroom sessions on the tools and a project purporting to save $100,000 or more. A presentation on the project is given to top executives as the last stage before earning the credential.

At the same time Six Sigma was spreading, companies were also selectively applying various lean tools in manufacturing and having some success with that. While Six Sigma focused on improving the value-adding processes—e.g., find the source of the quality problems or downtime on the machine center and put in countermeasures to fix it—lean focused on the whole value stream and creating flow among the value-adding operations. There is an obvious case for a harmonious marriage between Six Sigma, which fixes individual processes, and lean, which fixes the connections among processes.

Recently a new hybrid was born, Lean Sigma. I do not believe lean tools or Six Sigma tools or a marriage of the two will get a company to a lean learning enterprise. The following example from a company I worked closely with will clarify my concern about Six Sigma, lean tools, and Lean Sigma.

The CEO of a large automotive parts supplier wanted the Six Sigma program because of the great success of GE and Jack Welch. He worked with a group of senior managers and executives to pick the right consultants to do the training and determine how many certified Six Sigma black belts were needed. The leadership team reasoned that recent college graduates with high grade-point averages would be best suited to learn the complex statistical methods that are part of Six Sigma and decided to recruit bright young stars to become black belts. They recruited aggressively, offering a five-digit bonus and a brand-new car when they completed the Six Sigma program and achieved the required dollar savings. Needless to say, they attracted some topnotch young recruits.

Unfortunately, these young recruits had little if any manufacturing experience and stepped into these rust-belt factories with the mission to "fix processes" when these factories had been operating for decades with a well-established culture. Word got out about the hefty incentives for the recruits, which caused some managers and engineers to wonder why they should help these "youngsters" successfully complete a project when there wasn't any payoff for them. The employees with an affinity for lean claimed that the projects being turned in as Six Sigma projects were actually lean projects—cells, pull, etc.

In my view, by treating lean and Six Sigma as two tool kits and then setting up a situation in which different groups in the company go to war over whose tool kit is bigger and better, the company created a self-defeating improvement program. In this particular case, there was enough dissent over the large incentives for the Six Sigma recruits, as well as the awareness that experienced employees were actually helping them, that management ended up not giving out any of the cars.

In the end, the company turned current employees into additional black belts. There still remained an uneasy tension between lean and Six Sigma, especially with internal lean zealots who viewed Six Sigma merely as tool kits. And the plant managers wondered what to do with the young black belts when they needed to move them into operational jobs, as their salaries were too high for the lower-level positions they were really suited for based on experience.

This is not to say the company should throw out Six Sigma or lean tools. Both are extremely powerful tool kits, but in the end, they are just tools. What companies need to be told over and over is that lean tools represent only one aspect of the broader philosophy of the Toyota Way. It seems like this is the most difficult lesson to get across to companies that want to "go lean." Figure 22-2 contrasts the myth of TPS as a set of tools to make short-term improvements on the shop floor with true TPS as the basis of a total management philosophy, based on a presentation by a Toyota manager (Glenn Uminger).

Myth What TPS Is Not	Reality What TPS Is
▪ A tangible recipe for success ▪ A management project or program ▪ A set of tools for implementation ▪ A system for production floor only ▪ Implementable in a short- or mid-term period	▪ A consistent way of thinking ▪ A total management philosophy ▪ Focus on total customer satisfaction ▪ An environment of teamwork and improvement ▪ A never-ending search for a better way ▪ Quality built in process ▪ Organized, disciplined Workplace ▪ Evolutionary

Figure 22-2. Myth versus reality of TPS

In reality, the training of internal Six Sigma and lean "experts" serves to reinforce the superficial tool orientation in the vast majority of companies. We will see in the next section how Toyota has mentored international associates over five to 10 years to bring them to a deep understanding of the Toyota Way. Even Convis says it took 10 years of living in Toyota for him to begin to understand and he is still learning every day. Yet companies seeking to benefit from TPS and Six Sigma typically train employees for one to two weeks, ask them to do a project, and anoint them as experts.

Why Changing Culture Is So Difficult

Culture change is a complex topic in its own right and the subject of many books. This became most evident to Toyota in its efforts to globalize in the 1980s. To Toyota, globalization did not mean purchasing capacity in other countries. Globalization meant exporting the Toyota culture to build autonomous divisions in other countries that reproduced the DNA of Toyota.

What is culture? There are many definitions, but one thing is for sure: what you see and hear when you walk into a company for the first time are only surface manifestations of culture. Figure 22-3 depicts a TPS view of culture as an iceberg. What many visitors to Toyota and its affiliates see when they visit are surface features such as *kanban*, high employee suggestion rates, clean floors, lots of charts and visuals, cells, and teams. The most common question I have heard when taking groups on tours of Toyota plants is "How do you reward your people to get them so involved?" A reward system itself is simply a surface manifestation of culture. It is a human resource tool—something easy to manipulate and only the tip of the iceberg.

Below the surface is the Toyota Way culture. In fact, Toyota takes a "textbook" approach to developing culture. Edgar Schein, one of the leaders in analyzing and understanding culture, defines culture this way:[3]

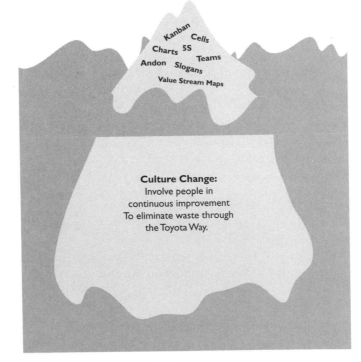

Figure 22-3. Iceberg model of TPS

The pattern of basic assumptions that a given group has invented, discovered, or developed in learning to cope with its problems of external adaptation and internal integration, and that have worked well enough to be considered valid, and, therefore, to be taught to new members as the correct way to perceive, think and feel in relation to those problems.

This is a remarkably apt description of the Toyota Way culture in a number of ways:

1. The Toyota Way has a depth that goes to the level of basic assumptions of the most effective way to "perceive, think, and feel" in relation to problems. Things like *genchi genbutsu*, recognizing waste, thorough consideration in decision making, and the focus of Toyota on long-term survival are the DNA of Toyota.

2. The Toyota Way was "invented, discovered, and developed" over decades as talented Toyota managers and engineers, like Ohno, "learned to cope with its (Toyota's) problems of external adaptation and internal integration." The history of Toyota is very important because we understand the challenges and context that led to active on-the-floor problem solving, not theoretical, top-down exercises.

3. The Toyota Way is explicitly "taught to new members." Toyota is, in fact, doing seminars on the Toyota Way, but that is a limited part of the learning process. The Toyota Way is explicitly taught the way you should transmit culture—through action in day-to-day work where leaders model the way. As Jane Beseda of Toyota Sales explained:

The Toyota Way matches everything that they (team members) do every hour of the day. So they are swimming in this culture and this philosophy. We're always doing kaizen *projects. It's a part of who we are.*

Regarding this third point, Toyota in Japan hires almost all of its new employees fresh out of school, in some cases from a Toyota City technical high school, where students begin to learn the Toyota Way while still in school. Toyota is their first job … and typically their last. Therefore, they do not have to unlearn past practices from other companies with conflicting approaches. Aspects of the Toyota Way are, in fact, intertwined with Japanese culture, which is relatively homogenous. For example, *hansei, hourenso, kaizen,* and *nemawashi* are characteristics of top Japanese companies and not peculiar to Toyota.

We can look to Toyota's globalization as an object lesson in what it takes to build a culture. When Toyota began seriously globalizing in the 1980s, most broadly in the U.S., they quickly realized the challenges of creating the Toyota Way in a culture that was alien to many of their values. Toyota's approach to spreading the culture to global operations has been intensive and very costly. The most intensive effort has been in Toyota's largest market outside Japan—North America. In this case:

1. All U.S. senior managers were assigned Japanese coordinators. The coordinators had two jobs: coordinating with Japan, where there are continuous technical developments, and teaching U.S. employees the Toyota Way through daily mentorship. Every day is a training day, with immediate feedback shaping the thinking and behavior of the U.S employees.

2. Toyota used trips to Japan, which turned out to be one of the most powerful ways to influence the cultural awareness of U.S. employees. We discussed in Chapter 7 the importance of sending group leaders and union officials from NUMMI to Japan to work in Toyota factories.

3. Toyota used the TPS technical systems, or "process" layer of the Toyota Way, to help reinforce the culture Toyota sought to build. For example, we discussed how large batch manufacturing with lots of inventory supports the Western culture of short-term firefighting and ignoring systems problems. By creating flow across operations using TPS and lean product development in its overseas operations, Toyota is helping change this behavior and shape the culture it seeks to nurture.

4. Toyota sent over senior executives to engrain the Toyota DNA in new American leaders. This started with managers from Japan and has evolved to homegrown managers in North America like Gary Convis and Jim Press.

The journey for Toyota is by no means over. Toyota is continually adapting its culture to local conditions. Here are example adaptations from the Toyota Technical Center (TTC) in Ann Arbor, Michigan:

1. Being more flexible about work hours. In Japan, Toyota engineers historically worked as needed, even if it was 15 hours a day, nights, weekends. TTC has become more flexible, to the point of putting in flex-time systems.

2. Performance-based rewards. Traditionally, Toyota in Japan pays a large portion of salary in semi-annual bonuses, but these are tied to company performance, not individual performance. In TTC they developed an individual bonus system based on performance.

3. *Hansei* events at TTC have been modified to provide more positive feedback in addition to critiques and opportunities for improvement.

Companies moving into lean will not have to take their employees to Japan to learn the culture, but will need to make serious long-term investments to educate and change their culture so employees can adapt to and use many of the Toyota Way principles.

I was personally involved in one encouraging example of true culture change when in January 2000 my colleague Jeff Rivera and I began consulting with Ford's

Cuautitlan assembly plant, outside Mexico City. The site had four assembly lines in one plant, making four different vehicles, from small cars to full-sized trucks to commercial-grade trucks and about 9000 parts. It was more like a city of auto parts than an assembly plant, with parts streaming in once a week across the border.

Our focus was on material flow. We used *kaizen* workshops to get teams in the plant to reorganize parts and tools for best presentation and efficiency. We then followed up with pull systems to get parts to the line from a supermarket of parts. The operators loved it and in each case there were large gains in efficiency. The internal lean coaches became very committed to the process. But we faced continual resistance from senior management in the plant who did not see any direct labor reduction savings. As a result, once the workshops were completed, there was little follow-up activity. When Ford began struggling financially, it pulled product from the plant. By fall 2001, rumors floated that Ford was going to close it. Eventually, the internal lean coordinators we trained were let go. I feared that was the end of the story.

Then I learned in fall 2002 that Ford Production System (FPS) experts were flocking to see the Cuautitlan plant. Miraculously, the plant had become a model for FPS, a version of TPS. Operators were heavily involved in continuous improvement and the plant was performing at one of the highest levels in North America. Because of the high level of quality and efficiency at Cuautitlan, Ford gave the plant new products to build. How did this sudden turnabout to FPS occur?

1. The director of manufacturing for Ford of Mexico, who brought us in and was a believer in TPS, realized he had to get more hands-on when there were rumors of shutting down the plant.

2. He brought in new plant management, including an assistant plant manager from Hermosillo, Mexico, who had an understanding of TPS. (The Hermosillo plant was originally set up by Mazda, using a production system similar to TPS.)

3. The Cuautitlan plant began focusing on cultural change, not simply FPS tools and checklists. This included mandatory training for all managers on the core disciplines of FPS and a test. Managers who failed the test were let go. Managers who passed were required to implement what they had learned.

4. Management effectively used policy deployment (*hoshin*), including putting it into a Web-based system so everyone knew his or her objectives. Performance was monitored daily, so that every problem that occurred was immediately conveyed to the appropriate level of management for immediate action.

In other words, this was a top-down process with real teeth in it. Management was taking a tougher approach than Toyota has taken in its U.S. operations. But it was necessary in an environment that had grown complacent and needed radical change in the culture. Management was changing the culture by aligning objectives, measurements, and visual systems to reinforce the appropriate behavior every day.

13 Tips for Transitioning Your Company to a Lean Enterprise

We can learn a great deal from the few companies out there run by experienced and talented lean leaders who have really been successful at effecting change at the cultural level. It is clear there are a variety of ways of doing this. At Wiremold, the CEO, Art Byrne, started by personally leading *kaizen* events to shake up the organization with radical change in high-opportunity areas. Keith Allman at Merillat took a two-pronged approach. He hired a few young and talented lean change agents to work quietly on creating model lines (discussed below). For the rest of the company, he personally taught courses on lean and on the specific tools he wanted them to implement in the first year. (He started with 5S.) Each year he rolled out an additional level of tools and management changes, teaching the employees along the way while putting in management objectives committed to implementing the tools. Top experts in the field were brought into the company to teach other tools, like value stream mapping and standardized work.

Despite different approaches, both lean leaders started immediately with action in their core value streams. In a manufacturing plant, this means the shop floor. In a product development organization, it means the product development process. In a bank, it means the core business processes that affect the bottom line, like loan transactions.

Here are 13 general tips on what works in transitioning a company into a lean enterprise:

1. *Start with action in the technical system; follow quickly with cultural change.* Most companies attempting a lean transformation focus on the "process layer" of the 4P model and this is, in fact, the right approach, as the technical systems of lean drive the Toyota Way behaviors, such as surfacing problems that employees must learn how to solve. But the social and technical systems of TPS are intertwined; if a company wants to change the culture, it must also develop true lean leaders who can reinforce and lead that cultural change. The best way a company can develop this is through action to improve the company's core value streams, supported by committed leaders who reinforce culture change. Leaders must be involved in the value stream mapping and shop floor transformation so they can learn to see waste.

2. *Learn by doing first and training second.* I have been involved in many corporate start-ups of lean and someone will inevitably say, "Before we can get

started with all these radical changes, we need to inform people of what we are doing through training courses." This has led to elaborate corporate training programs with PowerPoint™ presentations. Unfortunately you cannot PowerPoint™ your way to lean. The Toyota Way is about learning by doing. I believe that in the early stages of lean transformation there should be at least 80% doing and 20% training and informing. The best training is training followed by immediately doing ... or doing followed by immediate training. The Toyota approach to training is to put people in difficult situations and let them solve their way out of the problems.

3. *Start with value stream pilots to demonstrate lean as a system and provide a "go see" model.* In Chapter 17 we learned about the model lines that the Toyota Supplier Support Center implements in companies to teach lean. Within a value stream, defined by a product family, a model is created. By model, I mean implementing the whole system of tools and ultimately human resource practices so other employees from your company can go and see lean in action without having to go to some other company. For a plant, this usually means creating one lean product line, beginning with raw materials received and ending with finished goods. In a service organization, it is one complete business process from start to finish within the company boundaries. The go-and-see model line should become a singularly focused project with a great deal of management attention and resources to make it a success and an object lesson in management commitment.

4. *Use value stream mapping to develop future state visions and help "learn to see."* In Chapter 21, we discussed how value stream mapping is a method for clearly showing in diagram form the material and information flow. When developing the current state map, future state map, and action plan for implementation, I always recommend using a cross-functional group consisting of managers who can authorize resources and doers who are part of the process being mapped. The team learns together as they see the waste in the current state, and in the future state they come together to figure out how to apply the lean tools and philosophy. I have spent endless hours debating with individuals over whether lean can apply to their particular situation since they do not have the high volumes and repetitive processes of Toyota. I have never had that debate in a value stream mapping workshop, because the mapping creates a language and tool for the team to actually pick apart a specific process, see the waste, develop a lean vision, and apply it to that particular process. Value stream mapping should be applied only to specific product families that will be immediately transformed. I know many cases where top management mandated mapping an entire plant and all the products in it and the result was a lot of value stream wallpaper in the conference room.

5. *Use* kaizen *workshops to teach and make rapid changes.* As described in Chapter 21, the *kaizen* workshop is a remarkable social invention that frees up a cross-functional team to make changes in a week that otherwise can drag on for months. Selecting the right people for the team is critical, as is setting aside the time for those individuals and giving them a lot of management support. Using a talented and experienced facilitator who has a deep understanding of lean tools and philosophy with a specific problem to tackle makes all the difference in what you can accomplish. However, the *kaizen* workshop should not become an end in itself. In many companies, "lean efforts" revolve around having numerous workshops: the more the better. This leads to "point *kaizen*"—fixing individual problems without straightening out the core value stream. *Kaizen* workshops are best used as one tool to implement specific improvements guided by a future state value stream map.

6. *Organize around value streams.* In most organizations, management is organized by process or function. In a factory, there is a manager of the paint department, a manager of the assembly department, and a manager of the maintenance department. In a bank, there may be a manager of order processing, a manager of order fulfillment, a manager of customer complaints, etc. In other words, managers own steps in the process of creating value for customers and nobody is responsible for the value stream. In *Lean Thinking*, Womack and Jones recommend creating value stream managers who have complete responsibility for the value stream and can answer to the customer. In the Delphi plant described at the end of this chapter, they organized around five product families. A manager is responsible for each product family (value stream) and has control of all the resources needed to make the truck cockpit—including maintenance, engineering, and quality. In the second edition of *Lean Thinking* (2003), they have modified this as possibly a matrix organization where there are still heads of departments but also value stream managers, similar to Toyota's chief engineer system. The message remains the same: someone with real leadership skills and a deep understanding of the product and process must be responsible for the process of creating value for customers and must be accountable to the customer.

7. *Make it mandatory.* If a company looks at lean transformation as a nice thing to do in any spare time or as voluntary, it will simply not happen. We saw that the transformation at Cuautitlan was the result of a shift from management suggesting lean to making it mandatory with consequences for not buying in.

8. *A crisis may prompt a lean movement, but may not be necessary to turn a company around.* A sinking ship certainly mobilizes management and the work-

force into getting serious about lean, as we saw at Cuautitlan. On the other hand, Wiremold and Merillat were not on the chopping block, yet senior management proactively championed improvement. What is important is that lean leadership is focused on long-term learning.

9. *Be opportunistic in identifying opportunities for big financial impacts.* I have emphasized throughout the book that Toyota focuses on improving processes, confident that this in turn will improve financial results. However, when a company does not yet believe in the lean philosophy heart and soul, it is particularly important to achieve some big wins. By picking the right product family and with experienced lean expertise, a serious effort has about a 100% chance of making huge and visible improvements that will impress any executive.

10. *Realign metrics with a value stream perspective.* "You get what you measure" has become a truism in most companies. But metrics are used very differently by Toyota compared to most companies. They are an overall tool for tracking progress of the company and they are a key tool for continuous improvement. At most companies they are mainly a tool for short-term cost control by managers who do not understand what they are managing. For example, companies track indirect/direct labor ratios and call to the carpet those with unfavorable ratios. The way to make the ratio look good is to have lots of direct labor and keep those people busy making parts, even if they are over-producing or doing wasteful jobs. Creating a team leader role for support like Toyota's structure means damaging that ratio and a short path to the unemployment line. The first step therefore is to eliminate non-lean metrics that are wreaking havoc with those seriously invested in improving operational excellence. The next step is to measure a variety of value stream metrics from lead time to inventory levels to first-pass quality and treat these metrics as seriously as labor productivity and other short-term cost metrics.

11. *Build on your company's roots to develop your own way.* Toyota has its way. You need to have your way. When Toyota works with companies to teach TPS, they insist that the companies develop their own system. It is OK to borrow some of the insights from the Toyota Way and I recommend adopting the basic principles in this book. But you need to put them into your language in a way that fits your business and technical context. The Toyota Way evolved through some inspired leaders who provided a very rich cultural heritage. Your company probably has a rich heritage as well. A large majority of business start-ups fail within the first three years. If you are reading this book hoping to improve your company, most likely you are one of the survivors. Someone did something right to get you to this point. Build on that. When

we first started working with Ford to help develop the Ford Production System, we held seminars for senior management and handed out copies of Henry Ford's book, *Today and Tomorrow*. This book inspired generations of Toyota senior managers, yet astonishingly few Ford managers had ever read the book. Build on your company's heritage to identify what you stand for.

12. *Hire or develop lean leaders and develop a succession system.* We discussed what it means to be a Toyota leader in Chapter 15. Leaders must thoroughly understand, believe in, and live the company's "way." All leaders must understand the work in detail and know how to involve people. If the top is not driving the transformation, it will not happen.

13. *Use experts for teaching and getting quick results.* The word "*sensei*" is used in Japan with some reverence to refer to a teacher who has mastered the subject. A company needs a *sensei* to provide technical assistance and change management advice when it is trying something for the first time. This "teacher" will help facilitate the transformation, get quick results, and keep the momentum building. But a good teacher will not do it all for you. If you want a lean organization, you need to get lean knowledge into your company, either by hiring experts with a minimum of five years' lean experience or by hiring outside experts as consultants. An expert, whether internal or external, can quick-start the process by educating through action, but to develop a lean learning enterprise you need to build internal expertise—senior executives, improvement experts, and group leaders who believe in the philosophy and will spread lean throughout the organization over time.

Having said all this, the question remains, can a company transform and sustain a culture to become a lean learning organization? If a company can maintain continuity of leadership over time, I see no reason why it cannot profit by implementing its version of the Toyota Way principles. It will not be easy. Typical obstacles may be reluctant top managers who do not understand, managers willing to try lean tools but are not committed to following through, a management shakeup from committed lean leaders to anti-lean managers, a market that goes sour, or a buyout.

We also mentioned there may be cultural barriers to following the Toyota Way. There are a litany of cultural traits that differ between Japanese and Americans and French and Germans, etc. For example, we saw that the philosophies underlying *hansei* that Toyota considers necessary for *kaizen* are rooted in Japanese upbringing. And there is even some evidence that Asians more naturally do *genchi genbutsu* and observe things in greater detail. Yet, the Toyota Way is working and prospering within Toyota affiliates around the world albeit with a great investment of time and energy by Toyota in developing its unique culture. And the Toyota Way is evolving as it adapts to other cultures, probably making Toyota an even stronger company.

Even though there are plenty of uncertainties and challenges, my advice is start adopting your version of Toyota Way principles. As you have seen in this book, it is very feasible and there are successes to emulate. If Toyota is any example, the rewards and results will far outweigh the great effort required. You will simply be the best in your business because you will be using operational excellence as a strategic weapon. Good luck on your journey!

Case Example: Transforming Delphi to a Lean Culture

Delphi was a division of General Motors composed of several mass production operations that produced in-house parts for GM. Costs were high and quality was not competitive. General Motors spun it off and named it "Delphi," a separate company, in May 1999. For a while, it retained the high-cost structure of General Motors, including a UAW contract requiring higher wages than other parts suppliers.

Almost immediately after Delphi went public, J.T. Battenberg, Delphi's president, strongly endorsed creating the Delphi Manufacturing System, based on the principles of TPS. John Shook and other former Toyota managers and TPS experts assisted Delphi in the transformation. While it took years to penetrate the old-line union culture of these former GM divisions, the pieces slowly began coming together, moving from the application of isolated tools to building systems, to transforming the culture of Delphi toward a lean enterprise. UAW-negotiated wages could not be reduced, but there were opportunities for productivity improvements, quality improvements, space savings, and inventory savings.

One of Delphi's many success stories was its Adrian, Michigan, plant, which made instrument panels for light trucks. Adrian was in competition with low-cost and high-quality Delphi manufacturing in Mexico. At some point in the 1990s, it became clear the plant was on the "fix, sell, or close list" since it was not profitable. But the plant decided to fight for its survival and saw the Delphi Manufacturing System as the only way to be successful.

During the summer of 2002, when I spent time in the plant, it was making 6,000 automotive instrument panels a day for seven GM plants, which was less than half its capacity. The plant had made many of the lean changes, one of the most dramatic being the removal of the overhead conveyor system. There had been a half mile of power and free chain conveyor overhead that these instrument panels circulated around on, which carried a ton of inventory. Moreover, because it was up in the sky, it could easily be ignored. Problems were hidden up there. As part of the future state value value stream map, they decided to tear it down. Removing the overhead conveyor system freed up four maintenance people who were just keeping it running. They were then reassigned to preventive maintenance for the plant. Assembly of the instrument panels was reorganized into cells by product family. *Kanban* was implemented to control the flow of parts from molding to assembly and purchased parts to the line. Various clever mistake-proofing devices were put in to reduce defects. *Andon* systems were installed so operators could call for help. The place was cleaned up and organized through a 5S program. Material began to flow and costs began to come down.

A milestone in the lean transformation came when the plant introduced *heijunka* (leveled production scheduling). In the past, it built in big batches of each model of instrument panel. This contributed to the large buildup in inventory and general chaos in the plant. When the plant implemented one-piece flow, it still built in batches and had no way to control the erratic schedule from the customer, which varied dramatically in volume and mix from day to day. With the help of a lean consultant, who had worked with Toyota, it implemented *heijunka* to control production and smooth out these peaks and valleys. The plant kept a small store of finished goods instrument panels and replenished this based on a simple visual system: a big box with slots (*heijunka* box) was used to visually schedule the production for the day, based on changing over to different products throughout the day. An order for parts was pulled from the *heijunka* box every 26 minutes and, based on what the card said, instrument panels were loaded on a train of carts, which triggered the scheduling of new panels to be made. To support this, setup times were dramatically reduced and eventually supported four color changes a day.

Perhaps more important than implementing these TPS tools, the entire plant was reorganized from functional units to five value streams, each focused on a particular part family of instrument panels—mostly by customer and type of truck. All the operators responsible for building an instrument panel, from raw material to finished goods, reported to a value stream production manager. The production managers moved out of the front offices and relocated to the floor within their value stream. Maintenance, which had been located around the periphery of the plant, was reassigned to and physically located within the value streams. The main support functions for each value stream were matrixed. For example, quality specialists were assigned certain value streams but also reported to a quality manager. The result was a shift from focusing on maximizing production of individual departments and pointing fingers of blame to maximizing throughput and quality of value streams.

Back in 1986, the plant had embraced a team problem-solving program. It was a mess. There were multiple leaders and different departments had different concerns, often at cross-purposes. It became a session for venting complaints and ultimately there was little action. When the plant took the lean approach, the improvement process relied heavily on value stream mapping as a visioning tool. Each of the five value stream organizations created 90-day visions, using value stream mapping to draw the vision. Based on the 90-day new value stream map, a detailed action plan was created with assignments and due dates. A cross-functional team in each value stream would meet every week to assess progress in implementing the action plan. Problem solving became unified and focused on a shared vision. Every quarter, they updated the future state map to bring it to the next level of lean.

Up-to-date metrics kiosks were posted in each manufacturing area. The metrics defined by the Delphi Manufacturing System focused on lean characteristics such as productivity (parts/labor hour), product cost, first-time quality, total process cycle time, overall equipment effectiveness (a measure of equipment uptime), *andon* response time, and scrap. There were specific targets for improvement for these metrics for each value stream each quarter. Since the measures were by value stream and the plant was organized that way, all of the resources were under one value stream manager to improve the process. Just improving the "first-time quality" paint process alone saved $2 million annually.

A separate metric for the overall plant measured productivity improvements of direct, indirect, and salaried labor. Double-digit productivity improvements each year have became commonplace. Prior to the lean transformation, the plant was losing money every month; in less than two years of lean, the plant was profitable at about $2 million per month. If you tour the facility today, you may be surprised to find that your tour guide is an hourly worker, or a union representative, or perhaps even the plant comptroller. These people all seem to be interchangeable and it is often hard to tell who is who. They are all talking the same language of DMS and value stream improvement. They apparently impressed their largest customer, General Motors. According to Mike Schornack, who ran manufacturing and was instrumental in leading the lean transformation (April 2003):

> *We were given some great news last week. The Adrian plant was awarded the GMT-900 instrument panel business. This is replacement work for the current IP and the largest IP business platform in the world. There is no doubt in my mind that we won this business because of our lean transformation. There were many GM tours through our facility before the business was awarded. Every group was impressed with the plant, the metrics, and the positive attitude of our people. The system really works!*

Notes

1. Collins, J. *Good to Great* (New York: HarperBusiness, 2001).
2. In reality, statistically six sigma calculates out to .002 failures in one million chances or one defect per five million parts produced. But Motorola adopted the convention of 3.4 parts per million (David L. Goetsch and Stanley B. Davis, *Quality Management: Introduction to Total Quality Management for Production, Processing, and Services*, Fourth Edition [Upper Saddle River, NJ: Prentice Hall, 2003]).
3. Edgar H. Schein, "Coming to a New Awareness of Organizational Culture," in James B. Lau and Abraham B. Shani, *Behavior in Organizations* (Homewood, IL: Irwin, 1988), pp. 375-390.

Bibliography/Chapter References

Preface

Liker, Jeffrey K. (Ed.). *Becoming Lean: Inside Stories of U.S. Manufacturers.* Portland, OR: Productivity Press, 1997.

Sobek, Durward K., II, Jeffrey K. Liker, and Allen C. Ward. "Another Look at How Toyota Integrates Product Development." *Harvard Business Review*, Vol. 76, No. 4, July-August 1998, pp. 36-50.

Ward, Allen C., Jeffrey K. Liker, John J. Cristiano, and Durward K. Sobek II. "The Second Toyota Paradox: How Delaying Decisions Can Make Better Cars Faster." *Sloan Management Review*, Vol. 36, No. 3, Spring 1995, pp. 43-61.

Chapter 1

Ohno, Taiichi. *Toyota Production System: Beyond Large-Scale Production.* Portland, OR: Productivity Press, 1988.

Womack, James P., and Daniel T. Jones. *Lean Thinking: Banish Waste and Create Wealth in Your Corporation.* New York: Simon & Schuster, 1996.

Womack, James P., Daniel T. Jones, and Daniel Roos. *The Machine That Changed the World: The Story of Lean Production.* New York: HarperPerennial, 1991.

Chapter 2

Ford, Henry. *Today and Tomorrow.* Garden City, NY: Doubleday, Page & Company, 1926. Reprint Edition. Portland, OR: Productivity Press, 1988.

Fujimoto, Takahiro. *The Evolution of a Manufacturing System at Toyota.* New York: Oxford University Press, 1999.

Reingold, Edwin. *Toyota: People, Ideas, and the Challenge of the New*. London: Penguin Books, 1999.

Smiles, Samuel. *Self-Help: With Illustrations of Character, Conduct, and Perseverance*. New York: Harper & Brothers, 1860. Published as *Self-Help* (Peter W. Sinnema, editor). New York: Oxford University Press, 2002.

Toyoda, Eiji. *Toyota: Fifty Years in Motion*. Tokyo: Kodansha International, 1987.

Womack, James P., and Daniel T. Jones. *Lean Thinking: Banish Waste and Create Wealth in Your Corporation*. New York: Simon & Schuster, 1996.

Womack, James P., Daniel T. Jones, and Daniel Roos. *The Machine That Changed the World: The Story of Lean Production*. New York: HarperPerennial, 1991.

Chapter 3

Womack, James P., and Daniel T. Jones. *Lean Thinking: Banish Waste and Create Wealth in Your Corporation*. New York: Simon & Schuster, 1996.

Chapter 5

Reingold, Edwin. *Toyota: People, Ideas, and the Challenge of the New*. London: Penguin Books, 1999.

Chapter 6

Itazaki, Hideshi. *The Prius That Shook the World: How Toyota Developed the World's First Mass-Production Hybrid Vehicle*. Translated by A. Yamada and M. Ishidawa. Tokyo: The Kikkan Kogyo Shimbun, Ltd., 1999.

Ward, Allen C., Jeffrey K. Liker, John J. Cristiano, and Durward K. Sobek II, "The Second Toyota Paradox: How Delaying Decisions Can Make Better Cars Faster," *Sloan Management Review*, Vol. 36, No. 3, Spring 1995, pp. 43-61.

Chapter 7

Cusumano, Michael A. *The Japanese Automobile Industry: Technology and Management at Nissan and Toyota*. Cambridge, MA: Council on East Asian Studies/Harvard University Press, 1985.

Dyer, Jeffrey H. "How Chrysler Created an American Keiretsu." *Harvard Business Review*, Vol. 74, No. 4, July-August 1996.

Shook, John. Presentation at 8th Annual Lean Manufacturing Conference, University of Michigan, Dearborn, May 6-8, 2002.

Chapter 8

Emiliani, Bob, David Stec, Lawrence Grasso, and James Stodder. *Better Thinking, Better Results: Using the Power of Lean as a Total Business Solution*. Kensington, CT: Center for Lean Business Management, 2002.

Ohno, Taiichi. *Toyota Production System: Beyond Large-Scale Production*. Portland, OR: Productivity Press, 1988.

Chapter 9

Rother, Mike, and John Shook. *Learning to See: Value Stream Mapping to Add Value and Eliminate Muda*. Brookline, MA: Lean Enterprises Institute, Inc., 1999.

Chapter 10

Ohno, Taiichi. *Toyota Production System: Beyond Large-Scale Production*. Portland, OR: Productivity Press, 1988.

Chapter 11

Ward, Allen C., Jeffrey K. Liker, John J. Cristiano, and Durward K. Sobek II. "The Second Toyota Paradox: How Delaying Decisions Can Make Better Cars Faster." *Sloan Management Review*, Vol. 36, No. 3, Spring 1995, pp. 43-61.

Chapter 12

Adler, Paul S. "Building Better Bureaucracies." *Academy of Management Executive*, 13, 1999, pp. 36-49.

Burns, Tom, and George M. Stalker. *The Management of Innovation*. New York: Oxford University Press, 1994.

Ford, Henry. *Today and Tomorrow*. Garden City, NY: Doubleday, Page & Company, 1926. Reprint Edition. Portland, OR: Productivity Press, 1988.

Huntzinger, Jim. "The Roots of Lean: Training Within Industry: The Origin of Kaizen." *Target*, Vol. 18, No. 1, First Quarter 2002.

Imai, Masaaki. *Kaizen: The Key to Japan's Competitive Success*. New York: McGraw-Hill, 1986.

Ohno, Taiichi. *Toyota Production System: Beyond Large-Scale Production*. Portland, OR: Productivity Press, 1988.

Sobek, Durward K., II, Jeffrey K. Liker, and Allen C. Ward. "Another Look at How Toyota Integrates Product Development." *Harvard Business Review*, Vol. 76, No. 4, July-August 1998, pp. 36-50.

Taylor, Frederick W. *Scientific Management*. New York: Harper & Row, 1911. Reprint Edition. New York: Harper and Brothers, 1947.

Chapter 13

Hirano, Hiroyuki. *5 Pillars of the Visual Workplace: The Sourcebook for 5S Implementation*. Translated by Bruce Talbot. Portland, OR: Productivity Press, 1995.

Liker, Jeffrey K. (Ed.). *Becoming Lean: Inside Stories of U.S. Manufacturers.* Portland, OR: Productivity Press, 1997.

Chapter 14

Bolles, Richard Nelson. *What Color Is Your Parachute? A Practical Manual for Job-Hunters and Career-Changers.* Revised edition. Berkeley, CA: Ten Speed Press, 2003.

Toyoda, Eiji. "Creativity, Challenge and Courage," Toyota Motor Corporation, 1983

Chapter 15

Clark, Kim B., and Takahiro Fujimoto. *Product Development Performance: Strategy, Organization, and Management in the World Auto Industry.* Boston: Harvard Business School Press, 1991.

Cusumano, Michael A., and Kentaro Nobeoka. *Thinking Beyond Lean: How Multi-Project Management Is Transforming Product Development at Toyota and Other Companies.* New York: Free Press, 1998.

Womack, James P., Daniel T. Jones, and Daniel Roos. *The Machine That Changed the World: The Story of Lean Production.* New York: HarperPerennial, 1991.

Chapter 16

Blanchard, Ken, Donald Carew, and Eunice Parisi-Carew. *The One Minute Manager Builds High Performing Teams.* Revised edition. New York: William Morrow, 2000.

Chapter 17

Ahmadjian, Christina L., and James R. Lincoln. "*Keiretsu*, Governance, and Learning: Case Studies in Change from the Japanese Automotive Industry." *Organization Science*, Vol. 12, No. 6, November-December 2001, pp. 683-701.

Dyer, Jeffrey H. *Collaborative Advantage: Winning Through Extended Enterprise Supplier Networks.* New York: Oxford University Press, 2000.

Itazaki, Hideshi. *The Prius That Shook the World: How Toyota Developed the World's First Mass-Production Hybrid Vehicle.* Translated by A. Yamada and M. Ishidawa. Tokyo: The Kikkan Kogyo Shimbun, Ltd., 1999.

Karlin, Jennifer. *Defining the Lean Logistics Learning Enterprise: Examples from Toyota's North American Supply Chain.* Unpublished doctoral dissertation, University of Michigan, Ann Arbor, September 2003.

Chapter 18

Begley, Sharon. "East Versus West: One Sees Big Picture, Other Is Focused." *The Wall Street Journal*, March 28, 2003.

Nisbett, Richard E. *The Geography of Thought: How Asians and Westerners Think Differently ... and Why*. New York: Free Press, 2003.

Chapter 19

Ward, Allen C., Jeffrey K. Liker, John J. Cristiano, and Durward K. Sobek II. "The Second Toyota Paradox: How Delaying Decisions Can Make Better Cars Faster." *Sloan Management Review*, Vol. 36, No. 3, Spring 1995, pp. 43-61.

Chapter 20

Scholtes, Peter R. *The Leader's Handbook*. New York: McGraw-Hill, 1998.

Senge, Peter M. *The Fifth Discipline: The Art and Practice of the Learning Organization*. New York: Doubleday, 1990, p. 1.

Chapter 21

Drogosz, John D. "Applying Lean Above the Factory Floor." *Journal of Ship Production*, Vol. 18, No. 3, August 2002, pp. 159-166.

Morgan, James M. *High Performance Product Development: A Systems Approach to a Lean Product Development Process*. Doctoral Dissertation, University of Michigan, 2002.

Rother, Mike, and John Shook. *Learning to See: Value Stream Mapping to Add Value and Eliminate Muda*. Brookline, MA: Lean Enterprises Institute, Inc., 1999.

Chapter 22

Card, Orson Scott. *Prentice Alvin: The Tales of Alvin Maker, Book Three*. London: Orbit Books, 1989.

Emiliani, Bob, David Stec, Lawrence Grasso, and James Stodder. *Better Thinking, Better Results: Using the Power of Lean as a Total Business Solution*. Kensington, CT: Center for Lean Business Management, 2002.

Goetsch, David L., and Stanley B. Davis, *Quality Management: Introduction to Total Quality Management for Production, Processing, and Services*. Fourth edition. Upper Saddle River, NJ: Prentice Hall, 2003.

Liker, Jeffrey K., and Keith Allman. "The Donnelly Production System: Lean at Grand Haven." Jeffrey K. Liker (Ed.), *Becoming Lean: Inside Stories of U.S. Manufacturers*. Portland, OR: Productivity Press, 1998, pp. 201-246.

Womack, James P., and Daniel T. Jones. *Lean Thinking: Banish Waste and Create Wealth in Your Corporation*. New York: Simon & Schuster, 1996.

Recommended for Further Reading

Akoa, Yoshi. *Hoshin Kanri: Policy Deployment for Successful TQM*. Productivity press, 1991.

Dyer, Jeffrey H. *Collaborative Advantage: Winning Through Extended Enterprise Supplier Networks*. New York: Oxford University Press, 2000.

Emiliani, Bob, David Stec, Lawrence Grasso, and James Stodder. *Better Thinking, Better Results: Using the Power of Lean as a Total Business Solution*. Kensington, CT: The Center for Lean Business Management, 2002.

Ford, Henry. *Today and Tomorrow*, Reprint Edition. Portland, OR: Productivity Press, 1988.

Fujimoto, T. *The Evolution of a Manufacturing System at Toyota*. NY: Oxford University Press, 1999.

Imai, Masaki. *Gemba Kaizen: A Commonsense, Low-Cost Approach to Management*. New York: McGraw-Hill, 1997.

Kotter, John P. *Leading Change*. Boston, MA: Harvard Business School Press, 1996.

Liker, Jeffrey. (Ed.). *Becoming Lean: Inside Stories of U.S. Manufacturers*. Portland OR: Productivity Press, 1997.

Monden, Yasuhiro. *The Toyota Management System*. Portland, OR: Productivity Press, 1993.

Monden, Yasuhiro. *Toyota Production System: An Integrated Approach to Just-In-Time*, Third Edition. Norcross, GA: Engineering and Management Press, 1998.

Ohno, Taichi., *The Toyota Production System: Beyond Large Scale Production.* Portland, OR: Productivity Press, 1988.

Rother, Michael and John Shook. *Learning to See: Value Stream Mapping to Add Value and Eliminate Muda.* Brookline, MA: Lean Enterprise Institute, 1999.

Womack, James P. and Daniel T. Jones. *Lean Thinking: Banish Waste and Create Wealth in Your Corporation,* Revised and Updated, Second Edition. New York: Simon & Schuster, 2003.

Womack, James P., Daniel T. Jones, and Daniel Roos. *The Machine That Changed The World: The Story of Lean Production.* New York: HarperPerennial, 1991.

Index